Neural Darwinism

NEURAL DARWINISM

The Theory of
Neuronal Group Selection

GERALD M. EDELMAN

Basic Books, Inc., Publishers   New York

Library of Congress Cataloging-in-Publication Data

Edelman, Gerald M.
  Neural Darwinism.

  References: p. 331
  Includes index.
  1. Brain—Evolution.   2. Brain—Growth.   3. Neural
circuitry.   4. Natural selection. I. Title. [DNLM:
1. Neurons—physiology.   2. Perception—physiology.
3. Selection (Genetics).   WL 102.5 E213n]
QP376.E32   1987   612.8′2   87–47744
ISBN 0–465–04934–6

To suppose that the eye with all its inimitable contrivances for adjusting the focus to different distances, for admitting different amounts of light, and for the correction of spherical and chromatic aberration, could have been formed by natural selection, seems, I freely confess, absurd in the highest degree. When it was first said that the sun stood still and the world turned round, the common sense of mankind declared the doctrine false; but the old saying of "Vox populi, vox Dei," as every philosopher knows, cannot be trusted in science.

—CHARLES DARWIN
The Origin of Species, Sixth Edition
Organs of Extreme Perfection and Complication

And in the midst of this wide quietness
A rosy sanctuary will I dress
With the wreath'd trellis of a working brain,
　　With buds, and bells, and stars without a name,
With all the gardener Fancy e'er could feign,
　　Who breeding flowers, will never breed the same

—JOHN KEATS
Ode to Psyche

CONTENTS

PART ONE

SOMATIC SELECTION

PART TWO

EPIGENETIC MECHANISMS

PART THREE

GLOBAL FUNCTIONS

CONCLUSION

Contents

LIST OF ILLUSTRATIONS

LIST OF TABLES

PREFACE

The purpose of this book is to describe a theory of brain function aimed mainly at an understanding of the biological bases of perception. The theory of neuronal group selection addresses this problem by attempting to answer several key questions. How are connections specified in large neuronal populations? What principles determine the organization of representations and maps in the nervous system? What are the bases in neural structure of perceptual categorization and generalization? The theory proposed to answer these questions is cast in terms of a rigorously selectionist view relating brain development and evolution to structure and function. In the theory, population thinking, the central theoretical mode of biology itself, is applied to individual brains functioning in somatic time. The theory insists that an adequate explanation of higher brain functions first requires an explanation of those developmental constraints on evolution that lead to somatic variation in both brain structure and brain function. Selection of functional variants from neural populations that emerge as a result of this variation during an individual's development is held to be the central principle underlying behavior. This approach is not at present accepted, nor does it have strong antecedents in the history of a science replete with speculations in other categories of ideas.

To be scientifically sensible at this stage of our knowledge, certain constraints must be put on any attempt to relate the brain to psychological activity. In undertaking this theoretical task, I have therefore limited myself stringently to what might seem to a cognitive psychologist to be a very restricted set of psychological functions. I hardly touch upon some of the grand themes that run through William James's (1890, republished 1950) magnificent *Principles*. Consideration of a more modern list (Norman 1981) of the "essential twelve issues"—belief systems, consciousness, development, emotion, interaction, language, learning, memory, primary perception, performance, skill, and thought—will illustrate how narrow is my sweep. The key list I shall consider is: development, perception (in particular, perceptual categorization), memory, and learning, and I will take up these subjects in that order. My hope is that once a constrained theory adequate to link these processes is built, it may become possible to construct a more comprehensive description, not just in terms of perceptual categorization but also in terms of perceptual experience.

It appears to me that such restraint is necessary if we are ever to get anywhere in the extraordinarily challenging domain of understanding the biological bases of psychology. At the same time, no such limitation must be placed on subject matter: a net must be cast broadly over many fields in search for evidence that may be pertinent. This is the strategy I have used here, in the belief that a sound theory must be consistent with the central principles of developmental and evolutionary biology. One of the implicit assumptions I have made is that, to be successful, the theory must confront several central unsolved problems of these fields, particularly those concerned with the relationships between developmental genetics, epigenesis, and morphologic evolution. Accordingly, in providing support for the theory, I have ranged from molecular biology to ethology and back again.

Some further words about the order of topics may prove useful to the reader. The first part of the book is devoted to a general description of neuronal group selection in somatic time. The second part considers in a rather rigorous fashion the two main epigenetic mechanisms governing such selection during embryogenesis and behavior. These mechanisms are embedded in the context of salient facts of developmental biology and evolution. Because of the generality of the embryogenetic events considered in chapter 4, it may seem to deviate from the central subject of the nervous system. Nevertheless, that chapter describes the first of the epigenetic mechanisms that account for the origin of anatomical diversity, and I therefore deemed it particularly important to connect the central principles of nonneural development to neural development. The second epigenetic mechanism of the theory (that which results in synaptic selection) must be presented in formal terms to be truly convincing. Those readers who find this tedious upon a first reading of chapter 7 may ignore the mathematics; they will find qualitative descriptions of various changes in synaptic efficacy and their consequences interspersed in the material of that chapter. The third part of the book is devoted to an understanding of the integration of the two epigenetic mechanisms within phenotypes capable of motor action, categorization, and learning. Its main aim is to define the smallest selective unit capable of such global functions.

Many recent subjects of central neurobiological significance have not been accorded major treatment. These include, among others, the detailed analysis of the visual system, the regional mapping of neurotransmitters, the endocrine modulation of neural function, and various features of invertebrate nervous systems. The guideline used in choosing the examples that I have discussed is whether they embody evidence relating directly to critical points of the theory. The result may appear at first glance to be a rather unconventional assembly of examples from various biological disciplines. I can only hope that the reasons for my choice will become evident as the reader gains further comprehension of a theory that is itself unconventional. In any case, I have made efforts wherever possible to provide detailed models of particular ideas or processes, in the expectation that the hazards that this procedure entails are more than compensated for by its heuristic value. I believe this approach to be useful at an early stage of understanding of any subject and in particular when confronting the intricacies of brain function.

Because this is both a complex and an unfamiliar subject, I have also used an unconventional device in an effort to help the reader. At the head of each chapter is a running list of the key subjects, examples, or ideas presented in that chapter; main examples that contradict received ideas or that are particularly salient to the theory are italicized. These lists were designed to be useful in anticipating and reviewing the chapter contents, but they are *not* keyed to the section headings, which are listed in the table of contents proper. A short introduction containing a précis of the theory and a brief history of population thinking in neurobiology have been placed in chapter 1, prior to the evidential arguments and the deeper considerations of central ideas that are presented in subsequent chapters. At best, this terse description can give only a hint of what is to come. After having provided a more thoroughgoing description of the theory of neuronal group selection in the main body of the text, I offer a number of specific predictions at the end of the book in an attempt to define the limits of the theory and to show that it is empirically testable.

This book barely touches upon the psychologically important issue of social transmission, but I have been constantly aware of that process in writing it. The frequent interactions with my colleagues at the Neurosciences Institute (NSI), particularly its research director, Dr. W. Einar Gall, have provided a sustaining force for which I am grateful. I am also grateful to Susan Hassler, editor at the NSI, for her help. It has been a privilege to work at the Institute with Dr. Leif Finkel and Dr. George N. Reeke, Jr., on several models that are important to the theory. The opportunity to share ideas with them within the scholarly atmosphere of the NSI encourages me in the hope that the Institute will continue both to support the development of theoretical work in the neurosciences and to encourage younger scientists in its pursuit.

New York, 1986

PART ONE

SOMATIC SELECTION

1

A Summary and
Historical Introduction

INTRODUCTION

It is difficult to imagine the world as it is presented to a newborn organism of a different species, no less our own. Indeed, the conventions of society, the remembrances of sensory experience, and, particularly, a scientific education make it difficult to accept the notion that the environment presented to such an organism is inherently ambiguous: even to animals eventually capable of speech such as ourselves, the world is initially an unlabeled place. The number of partitions of potential "objects" or "events" in an econiche is enormous if not infinite, and their positive or negative values to an individual animal, even one with a richly structured nervous system, are relative, not absolute.

Whether richly structured or simple, nervous systems evolved to generate individual behavior that is adaptive within a species' econiche in relatively short periods of time. Such behavior in a phenotype requires initial categorization of salient aspects of the environment so that learning can occur on the basis of the resultant categories. A fundamental task of neuroscience is thus to show how, in a particular species, the structure and function of the nervous system permit perceptual categorization to occur as a basis for learning and meaningful adaptive behavior. Ultimately, this comes down to the question: How can we relate perceptual psychology to neural structure and function? Many previous attempts to provide an answer to this question have relied on various theories that are based on the notion of information processing. In this book, I shall suggest instead that a satisfactory answer to this question requires a new theory, one that has widespread consequences for neuroscience as well as for our understanding of our own place in nature. In this introductory chapter, I shall outline this theory and briefly consider its historical antecedents. My hope is that this may ease the reader's later course through the various lines of evidence adduced in its support. At the same time, I recognize that this outline has the deficiencies of being overly abstract and that a fuller comprehension of the main ideas of the theory will require a detailed consideration of that evidence.

A Brief Outline of the Theory

The theory of neuronal group selection was formulated to explain a number of apparent inconsistencies in our knowledge of the development, anatomy, and physiological function of the central nervous system. Above all, it was formulated to explain how perceptual categorization could occur without assuming that the world is prearranged in an informational fashion or that the brain contains a homunculus. The reasons for abandoning information processing as the primary mode of brain function will be presented in detail in the next chapter; my main purpose here is to outline the central ideas of an alternative view.

To account for categorization without assuming information processing or computing, the theory proposes that the key principle governing brain organization is a populational one and that in its operation the brain is a selective system. According to the theory (Edelman 1978, 1981; Edelman and Reeke 1982; Edelman and Finkel 1984), the brain is dynamically organized into cellular populations containing individually variant networks, the structure and function of which are selected by different means during development and behavior. The units of selection are collections of hundreds to thousands of strongly interconnected neurons, called neuronal groups, and accordingly these act as functional units. The theory makes three fundamental claims:

1. Diversification of anatomical connectivity occurs epigenetically during development, leading to the formation by selection of primary repertoires of structurally variant neuronal groups. The diversification is such that no two individual animals are likely to have identical connectivity in corresponding brain regions. This structural diversity results from the developmental action of a variety of selective mechano-chemical events regulated by cell and substrate adhesion molecules (CAMs and SAMs), which act to govern cell division, movement, death, and differentiation.

2. A second selective process occurs during postnatal behavior through epigenetic modifications in the strength of synaptic connections within and between neuronal groups. As a result, combinations of those particular groups whose activities are correlated with various signals arising from adaptive behavior are selected. This selection occurs within the original ensemble of anatomically variant groups (the *primary repertoire*), and it results in the formation of a *secondary repertoire* consisting of functioning groups that are more likely to be used in future behavior. Neurons in neuronal groups are populations, and repertoires form higher-order populations.

3. Coherent temporal correlations of the responses of sensory receptor sheets, motor ensembles, and interacting neuronal groups in different brain regions occur by means of reentrant signaling. Such signaling is based on the existence of reciprocally connected neural maps. These maps link the secondary repertoires that emerge dynamically as a result of the selective developmental events and the synaptic selection mentioned above, and their reentrant interactions maintain spatiotemporal continuity in response to real-world signals.

It is particularly important to establish the relationship of these processes to specific mechanisms of development and evolution. During development, in which primary repertoires of variant neuronal groups are established, the local anatomy of these groups is determined by genetic factors regulating cell shape and by epigenetic events regulating the primary developmental processes of cell division, movement, death, adhesion, and differentiation. Although structures in a particular area of the brain are modally similar among conspecific animals, at the level of fine axonal and dendritic ramifications and connections, there occurs a very large degree of individual variation in shape, extent, and connectivity. This variation provides the diversity upon which somatic selection may act, and it arises from the dynamic regulatory properties of cell and substrate adhesion molecules. At the same time, mutations that alter the developmental constraints on temporal regulation of the expression of these molecules are also considered to provide a major basis for the evolution of specific brain regions. Such regulatory properties permit somatic adaptation of the nervous system to various independent evolutionary alterations in the phenotype such as changes in muscles, bones, and sensory receptors. These ideas, which are concerned with relating epigenesis and heterochrony in neural development to morphologic evolution, are embedded in a main hypothesis of the theory called the regulator hypothesis.

As a result of these epigenetic developmental processes, within the primary repertoire of a given neural region subserving a specific function there exists a significant number of nonidentical variant groups, each of which could respond more or less well to a particular input. The presence in each repertoire of such functionally equivalent but nonisomorphic variants of neural structures is called degeneracy, a concept that is fundamental to the theory. Various degenerate networks of neuronal groups made up of neurons with dendritic trees and axonal arbors that are spread over relatively wide areas with large degrees of overlap are an obligate result of the epigenetic events that occur in development. Such overlapping arborization is not inconsistent, however, with the occurrence of anatomical contacts made only with specific cell types, and such contacts may even be restricted to localized regions of particular neurons.

After establishment of most of the primary repertoire, a second epigenetic selection occurs during postnatal behavior. Input signals are abstracted and filtered by the sensory transducers, feature extractors, and feature correlators (mainly sensorimotor systems) that form elements of a global mapping system. Active neuronal groups within particular repertoires receiving such signals are selected over others in a competitive fashion.

Successful selection consists in altering the synaptic efficacies of those portions of the network corresponding to such groups, so that there is an increased probability of their response to similar or identical signals at some future time. The outcome of this competition depends upon the amount of variation in structure in a primary repertoire, upon the operation of independent pre- and postsynaptic rules determining the interactions of neurons in a group, and upon the frequency and location of similar or identical signals. After repeated presentation of these signals, secondary repertoires consisting of dynamically selected neuronal groups are established. The synaptic rules responsible for the selection of secondary repertoires act on synapses as populations, and, therefore, the operation of these rules is intimately tied to the particular arrangement and density of circuitry in a given primary repertoire. A specific population model for synaptic selection, the dual rules model, is presented as an integral part of the theory.

The regulator hypothesis and the dual rules model provide the two main epigenetic mechanisms for selection required by the theory: the first applies to selection during development to form the primary repertoire, and the second applies to selection during behavioral experience to form the secondary repertoire. Neuronal group selection by these means alone, however, cannot account for relationships that preserve the spatiotemporal continuity required for perceptual categorization. For this, various forms of mapping are necessary, and a specific example of local map formation by neuronal group selection in the cerebral cortex (the confinement-selection-competition model) is chosen for extensive consideration.

The theory proposes that coordination and reinforcement of patterns of neuronal group selection must occur among various locally mapped regions of the brain. This is achieved by means of phasic signaling over reentrant anatomical connections between mapped regions. Such phasic reentry between local maps allows dynamic linkage among the different systems of neuronal groups that are being selected and that operate in parallel in real time. Reentrant anatomical patterns (reciprocal or otherwise) that provide a basis for phasic reentrant signaling are seen in numerous regions; examples include the thalamocortical and corticothalamic radiations, callosal connections, and various interareal connections between primary and secondary sensory (Zeki 1975, 1978a; Van Essen 1985) and motor areas. Reentry among maps obviates the need for explicit exchange of time and place markers of the kind required in parallel computing systems.

A central assumption of the theory is that perceptual categorization must both precede and accompany learning. One of the fundamental tasks of the nervous system is to carry on adaptive perceptual categorization in an "unlabeled" world—one in which the macroscopic order and arrangement of objects and events (and even their definition or discrimination) cannot be prefigured for an organism, despite the fact that such objects and events obey the laws of physics. A necessary condition for such perceptual categorization is assumed to be reentry between separate parallel systems of local maps serving different modalities, each of which is capable of independent disjunctive sampling of a stimulus domain. In general, however, sufficient conditions for perceptual categorizations are provided only when a number of such maps are linked together to form higher-order global mappings that involve both motor and sensory systems. The phasic reentry of these multiple parallel systems of the brain provides a major contribution to its rhythmic activity. The motor behavior of the exploring animal in turn provides a main source of the continual sampling necessary for the neuronal group selection that results in perceptual categorization.

Given these assumptions, it is particularly important to show how neuronal group selection and reentry in mapped systems can operate together in a self-consistent fashion to yield perceptual categorization. The self-consistency of the theory of neuronal group selection in providing a basis for categorization has been demonstrated by constructing a recognition automaton embedding the assumptions of the theory. The performance of this automaton in categorizing two-dimensional figures suggests that phasic reentrant linkages between multiple repertoires of groups arranged in maps can result in the emergence of associative functions not originally present in the component repertoires. As shown in chapter 10, selection upon degenerate repertoires of reentrantly connected neuronal groups in this automaton can result in effective categorization without a preexisting explicit program describing the objects to be categorized. In one sense, all of the hypotheses provided in the chapters preceding the description of this automaton will be shown to mesh well in its physical operation. But the theory of neuronal group selection is a biological theory, not simply a physical one, and to understand its ramifications its biological antecedents deserve a brief review. In particular, we must provide a sound evolutionary basis for its claims.

POPULATION THINKING IN NEUROBIOLOGY

In adapting to the environment without special creation or design, animal species rely upon natural selection acting upon variance in populations. Given the changes in the environment and certain isolating mechanisms, a variety of taxa emerge. An individual animal endowed with a richly structured brain must also adapt without instruction to a complex environment to form perceptual categories or an internal taxonomy governing its further responses to its world. The theory proposed here suggests that such adaptation also occurs by somatic selection upon populations of neuronal groups in that animal. In one sense, therefore, it is no surprise that natural selection may have led to neuronal group selection, for there is a certain similarity between the origin of taxa in phylogeny and the origin of populations of neuronal groups and perceptual categories within individuals. But this analogy must not be strained to the point of simple mimicry. There are enormous differences in detail and mechanism between natural selection, neuronal group selection, and clonal selection in immunity, the other biological process in which population variables provide the central basis for recognition mechanisms in somatic time. Despite these differences, a comparison can be drawn on the basis of three essential features shared by all selection theories: variable repertoires of elements whose sources of variation are causally unrelated to subsequent events of selection or recognition, opportunities for encounter with an independently changing environment permitting the selection of one or more favored variants, and, finally, a means of differential reproduction or amplification with heredity of the selected variants in a population.

Unlike the theory of evolution, the theory of neuronal group selection does not deal with ultimate causes but only with proximate ones. Nonetheless, as is true in the argument for natural selection in evolution, we must consider evidence from many fields to support the theory. A short history of population thinking in neurobiology may help place that evidence in a suitable frame. I hope to show that while the theory of neuronal group selection shares principles with other selective theories in biology, it differs in its detailed mechanisms and its evolutionary effects. It would go beyond the intention of this book, however, to give a general historical account of selectionist ideas or to cover population thinking in relation to behavior. The interested reader may consult the remarkable book of Mayr (1982) for the first and a number of review accounts (Gottlieb 1979; Lythgoe 1979; Gould 1982; Griffin 1982; MacPhail 1982; Terrace 1983) in comparative psychology and ethology for the latter.

Selectionist notions in neurobiology have in the past been directed mainly toward describing evolutionary aspects of behavior or the evolution of the brain and its various centers. With the exception of ethological concerns for the origin in brain structure of certain behavior patterns, most of these accounts are either oblivious to or noncommittal about *somatic* selection, that is, neuronal selection as a major principle to account for the ontogeny and physiological function of the brain in somatic time. Ethological concerns have been focused mainly on the grand loop of natural selection upon behavior that will be discussed in chapter 11 (see figure 11.1) rather than on selection as it operates in the detailed cell biology and physiology of individuals.

Interest in applying population thinking to the origin and function of individual nervous systems is a relatively recent development. As sketched in the remarks of the previous section, one of the tasks of a thoroughgoing somatic theory is nonetheless to relate the evolutionary selection of brain structures to individual phenotypic brain functions as they emerge via somatic selection both during and after development. This task distinguishes the notion of somatic selection of neuronal groups and synaptic populations from selectionist ideas in ethology. A brief historical account may make it easier to discriminate among the different levels at which selectionist thinking has been applied and help us avoid conflating these levels, particularly when we address the detailed evidence that supports ideas of somatic selection.

NATURAL SELECTION AND POPULATION THINKING IN RELATION TO BEHAVIOR

Charles Darwin was the first to propose the notion that natural selection alters behavior and vice versa. He discussed the relationship of selection to animal instincts (Darwin 1859) and also speculated on the evolutionary significance of emotions and affects (Darwin 1872). Darwin's ideas were taken up by his contemporary George John Romanes (1884, 1899), who promulgated the notion that behavior is a species-dependent property and that behavioral continuity is phyletic. C. Lloyd Morgan (1896, 1899, 1930) considered how the complexity of somatic neural organization is related to the complexity of behavior. Although he emphasized that the complexity of the behavior of an animal reflects the complexity of its nervous system and thus that evolutionary changes in anatomy can give rise to new behavior patterns, he failed to clarify the relative contributions of instinct and habit.

C. Wesley Mills (1898) was perhaps the earliest to recognize the importance of development to subsequent behavior. Attempts at this time to define the constraints placed on adult brain function and behavior by brain development tended to be confused by Haeckel's view of recapitulation, a false notion the history of which has been exhaustively analyzed by S. J. Gould (1977). Nonetheless, J. M. Baldwin (1895, 1902) was one of the first to understand the importance of alterations of individuals during ontogeny, and he had the clarity of vision to see the issue in Darwinian terms. He noted that, even though individual conspecific animals undergo different experiences, the modal behavior of all animals in a species is rather constant. The so-called Baldwin effect (see Gottlieb 1979 for an analysis) was perhaps the earliest indication that phenomena occurring during ontogeny could influence morphology and behavior; Baldwin's ideas were directed toward explaining how further experience could facilitate and maintain such changes.

DECLINE AND REINSTATEMENT OF SELECTIONIST IDEAS

These early efforts were followed by a remarkable decline in the application of population thinking in psychology, a decline that accompanied the development of behaviorism in the early part of this century. The occasional use of notions of selection to describe behavior during learning might tempt one to suppose a kinship with Darwinian thinking. There is in fact little to support such a view in an unambiguous fashion, although it has been suggested as an analogy (Dennett 1978) to explain the situation-response, or S-R, paradigm of Thorndike (1911). This paradigm was embodied in the "law of effect," which states that the association between a given stimulus and a given response or action is strengthened according to the amount of reward generated by the action. According to this law, behavior leading to results satisfying to the organism is "stamped in" to its nervous system, while behavior leading to discomfort or pain is stamped out. Thorndike emphasized the role of motor activity in yielding satisfying consequences by altering various internal associations. Although he undoubtedly saw the significance of increased brain size for behavior, no general view stemmed from this insight. There is an obvious line from this work to behaviorism; unfortunately, its less obvious but definite relationship to Darwinian evolution seems to have been ignored.

Together with Pavlov's work (see Mackintosh 1983; Staddon 1983; Jenkins 1984), Thorndike's ideas and experiments marked the beginning of behaviorism in learning theory, an approach in which the behavior of an animal could be studied independently of any consideration of the internal workings of its brain. Along with its considerable increase in experimental precision, this approach introduced an instructionistic flavor into the interpretations of behavior. This was accompanied by a diminished appreciation of the important differences in internal organization of the nervous systems of different individuals and different species. Behaviorists neglected the vast differences in the organization of the nervous systems of different species, probably because, as they interpreted behavior, almost any stimulus could be associated with any response through conditioning paradigms. The general appeal of considering stimuli and responses independently of the detailed order and evolutionary origins of nervous systems in relation to the rest of the phenotype kept psychology from pursuing a population approach.

It thus appears that the very success of Thorndike's methods and of those of Hull (1943, 1952) and others removed considerations of population thinking from psychology. The irony of this situation deserves some comment, for as discussed by Dennett (1978), the Law of Effect superficially resembles natural selection in many ways. Although the Law of Effect can be analogized with natural selection, however, it is *not* homologous to it—it is instructive, environment-driven to a very large degree, and allied to a covert notion of an empty animal driven by categories from the outside. That most radical of modern behaviorists, Skinner (1981), has written an article entitled "Selection by Consequences," which makes this same analogy within a ruthlessly behavioristic and instructionistic setting. In these formulations, there is no trace of the idea that brain structures *themselves* are *populations* upon which selection acts or that such selection is the basis of perceptual categorization.

Much of the contemporaneous work done by neurologists and neurophysiologists did nothing to refute the views of the early behaviorists. Indeed, the studies of Hughlings Jackson (1931; Taylor 1931) on the hierarchical organization of the central nervous system (CNS) and those of Sherrington (1906) on reflexes had an apparently cognate flavor—stimulus in, response out—a kind of message passing. By 1949, when Hebb's book *The Organization of Behavior* appeared, however, it had become clear to at least some behaviorists that a recognition of the role of the internal states of the nervous system was necessary. Hebb's contribution was an attempt to relate major psychological principles to nervous system properties. In particular, he placed the Law of Effect at the synaptic level by proposing a correlation model of synaptic modification similar to that of Hayek (1952). This work was seminal in providing a basis for many subsequent theoretical studies, but it neglected Darwinian interpretations and still represented an instructive view of perception and learning, as we shall discuss at the end of this chapter.

A consideration of the nature of generalization and categorization (see chapters 2 and 9) strongly highlights the instructionistic beliefs of the intellectual descendants of Thorndike as well as of those instructionists who reject behaviorism. As Reed (1981) has pointed out, modern conceptualists (those who state that members of a category fall under the same mental representation) come in two flavors. Some are realists or cognitists who insist that categories are represented by criterial features. Some are nominalists and insist that such mental representations do not exist as such. According to this view, what appear to be mental categories are just the frequencies of S-R association; people who espouse this view are in fact behaviorists. There is no hint in either view, however, that perhaps the problem is one of adaptively matching neural variants in a degenerate repertoire to external situations involving disjunct sets of features or properties, thus allowing generalization to occur through processes similar to those by which taxa are created during evolution.

Only with the appearance of modern ethology (see Gottlieb 1979; Terrace 1983) was the trend toward instructionism in interpreting molar behavior reversed, at least in part. This development and the studies based on it made species-specific behaviors apparent. The complexity and adaptiveness of behavioral repertoires in various species, many of which appeared in a normal course of development without any obvious forced learning, argued strongly for a selectionist component to behavior. Ethological studies showed clearly how evolution could affect behavior and how behavior could in turn affect evolution, and thus the importance of the adaptability of behavior in each individual species was shown in a way that could no longer be ignored. But even in the presence of this brilliant contribution, appropriate weight was not given to the possibility that the developmental or epigenetic aspects of neural organization were at least as important to an understanding of behavior as were the evolutionary causation, the survival value, and the function of that behavior. Indeed, in general, a consideration of developmental constraints on evolution (Edelman 1986b; Alberch 1987) is not a central focus of most ethological theory. In an excellent review of this issue, Gottlieb (1979) has pointed out the importance of adding a developmental point of view of the nervous system to the ethological analysis of later behavior. Such a view is becoming increasingly emphasized in attempts to relate developmental genetics to evolution, not only for the brain but for the entire phenotype (see Bonner 1982; Raff and Kaufman 1983; Edelman 1986b). Indeed, recent studies of the development of song by various species of sparrows have prompted some ethologists (Gould and Marler 1984) to suggest that certain aspects of the process might be explained by some form of neuronal group selection as proposed in this book and elsewhere.

We may summarize this brief (and obviously sketchy) account by suggesting that a thread spun out first by Darwin snapped, was rewoven in part after a hiatus, and is currently just being tied into a larger web in which behavior is viewed both in terms of natural selection and of somatic selection as well as in terms that link the two forms of selection. Some of the major features of this web are described in greater detail in chapter 11, in which we attempt to relate perceptual categorization based on somatic selection to learning by the behaving animal.

IDEAS OF SOMATIC SELECTION

One of the most important components of this web is the emerging selectionist view of the function of individual nervous systems *in somatic time*. Although it seems almost impossible to trace all of the influences prompting this idea, it is likely that the success of selectionist ideas in immunology (admittedly by a noncognitive system) played some role (Edelman 1974). But there were other factors, including certain considerations of memory (Young 1973, 1975) and of rather detailed anatomical and physiological issues related to the development of the innervation of muscles (Changeux and Danchin 1976; see Van Essen 1982). All of these influences led to valuable but incomplete notions of somatic selection; I review them briefly here to emphasize their heuristic value.

One of the most clearly defined early proposals was that of J. Z. Young (1965, 1973, 1975), who, in considering the role of neural networks in the memory of the octopus, suggested the mnemon hypothesis. According to this idea, a particular piece of hardwired synaptically connected neural tissue had a certain number of potentially reinforceable connections. Those that led to no reward were suppressed or eliminated selectively until the remaining functional networks were stabilized in terms of connectivity and of potentially adaptive behavior, thus constituting what Young called a mnemon (figure 1.1). The proposed process is a form of eliminative or stabilizing selection (Schmalhausen 1949; Mayr

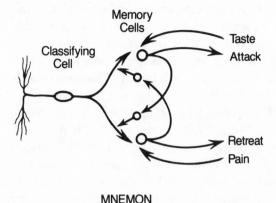

MNEMON

Figure 1.1

A mnemon or single memory unit as proposed by J. Z. Young (1965). The classifying or feature cell responds to the occurrence of a particular type of event (say the presence of an object with a vertical outline). The cell has two outputs allowing for alternative actions. There is a slight bias in favor of one of these, producing, for example, a slow attack on the object. Signals will then arrive indicating the results of the action and will either reinforce what was done or produce the opposite action (retreat). Side branches will then activate the small cells, making them produce an inhibitory transmitter that blocks the unwanted pathway. After these events, this feature detector can produce only one response.

1982). The mnemon concept did not, however, emphasize the populational and statistical nature of neuronal selection. Moreover, it did not consider the influence of development in providing a source of variability, and it omitted an explicit analysis of the relation of selection or memory to the problem of categories. Except for some limited forms of learning, the possibility for adaptive change in the mnemon model is still small, inasmuch as eliminative selective processes generally have lesser constructive adaptive powers than other forms of selection. Despite these limitations, the mnemon hypothesis carried the notion of actual network selection and stabilization in somatic time further than had been previously suggested.

In a curious article clearly influenced by the clonal selection theory (Burnet 1959), Jerne (1967) proposed what appeared to be a selectionist model for brain function. Unfortunately, this model was in fact an essentialist or typological one in disguise—one in which the correspondence between disjunct properties of sets of objects in the outer world and partially adaptive degenerate networks in the brain was not considered. Instead, these issues were skirted, and a form of Platonic vision was reaffirmed for learning and even for such rules and representations as are seen in language. While this was an inadequate theory, it was a selectionist analogy with some heuristic value.

A selectionist proposal that is specifically related to development and epigenesis has been put forth by J.-P. Changeux and coworkers (Changeux and Danchin 1976; Changeux et al. 1984). The argument rested in part on J. Z. Young's proposals (1973), in part on the work of Victor Hamburger (1968, 1975) on neuromuscular development (Van Essen 1982), and in part on a reasoned argument suggesting that the complexity of the genome is insufficient to account straightforwardly for the connectional complexity of the nervous system. It was clearly understood that while genes could affect invariant characters of the nervous system, additional diversity emerges during development. Although the notion of degeneracy was not grasped, much emphasis was placed in this proposal upon redundancy and its removal or alteration during development by the activity of the developing neuronal network. As we mentioned above, the key example of such removal was the decrement with developmental time in the number of synapses at the motor end plate (Van Essen 1982). A model for the selective stabilization of synapses was proposed on the basis of these ideas.

This account, like the previous ones of J. Z. Young, had the virtue of clarifying the internal limits and constraints upon components underlying learning events and of suggesting the importance to learning of epigenetic elements of neural development. It also emphasized eliminative selection, however, and did not consider global functions or those issues of categorization, generalization, reentry, and mapping that seem to be essential features of a robust theory of neuronal selection. Moreover, it considered the unit of selection to be the individual neuron.

In 1975, I made an initial attempt to apply selectionist ideas to the functioning of advanced nervous systems (Edelman 1975) and in 1977 suggested the outlines of a general theory. In the proposal of neuronal group selection (Edelman 1978), the notions of the developmental origin of neuronal diversity, of the neuronal group as the unit of selection, of degeneracy, and of reentry were described. Although this theory had the essential features that are elaborated in this volume, it was a minimal theory and was presented in a highly condensed and abstract form. This was a deliberate decision, the deficiencies of which, it was hoped, would be mitigated by subsequent more concrete and experimentally specific versions (Edelman 1981; Edelman and Finkel 1984). The current work may be considered part of this ongoing effort.

CRITICAL DISTINCTIONS AMONG SELECTIONIST IDEAS

As the preceding brief history suggests, the notion of selection has been variously applied to behaving animals and to their nervous systems. Because population thinking can be applied at various levels of neural and behavioral organization, it is important to tease out and distinguish the different skeins, contexts, and mechanisms of selectionism, so that confusion does not arise in examining evidence from different fields. One way of doing this is to point out generally what all theories of selection have in common, and then to indicate what a satisfactory theory of *somatic* selection in the nervous system must accomplish in particular.

As we have seen, the abstract general requirements on any selection theory are (1) a source of diversification leading to variants, (2) a means for effective encounter with or sampling of an independent environment that is not initially categorized in any absolute or predetermined fashion, and (3) a means of differential amplification over some period of time of those variants in a population that have greater adaptive value. Such amplification may occur in a stochastic manner but must nonetheless eventually increase the ratio in the population of the more adapted. Effective differential amplification implies the existence of some form of heredity or memory, which assures that at least some adaptations are preserved and that they are not completely disrupted by the processes of variation that must also occur.

These requirements obviously are met by evolution, in which mutation, recombination, and gene flow provide major sources of diversity, phenotypic function provides sampling of the environment, and heredity assures that some of the results of natural selection will yield differential reproduction of adapted phenotypes (Mayr 1982). Each of these requirements is also met in the workings of a somatic selective system— the immune system—in which somatic recombination and mutation of antibody variable region gene segments lead to the emergence of a repertoire of different antibody binding sites (Burnet 1959; Edelman 1973). A single different kind of antibody is usually expressed on each lymphocyte, forming a population. Foreign antigens are polled by the complex circulation of lymphocytes, and the binding of an antigen above a certain affinity threshold leads to differential clonal multiplication of those lymphocytes carrying the antibodies capable of binding that antigen more or less well.

The theory of neuronal group selection meets the three general requirements described above by specifying that diversification of fine connectivity occurs in development and that diversification of synaptic efficacies continues later on. Behavior leads to encounter with and parallel sampling of the environment with differential amplification of the synapses of those neuronal groups whose interactions are adaptive. Reentry allows coordinate selection to take place at all levels of the system, and the synaptic mechanism, in allowing for memory, stabilizes some of the selected group variants for future selection events.

While it has a general application and unifies a number of disparate phenomena occurring in complex nervous systems, the theory of neuronal group selection is not simply an analogy to other selectionist theories. Although it shares the basic requirements of a source of diversity, an equivalent of a hereditary mechanism in synaptic change, and of differential amplifications resulting from this mechanism, it is different in both its organization and its mechanisms from the theories of natural selection (Darwin 1859; Mayr 1982) and of clonal selection (Burnet 1959).

A theory is valuable only insofar as it proposes detailed and particular mechanisms to explain a wide variety of phenomena in its domain and insofar as it stimulates new experiments. What new directions or interpretations are afforded by a somatic selection theory of neuronal function? Such a theory emphasizes that the nature of the stimulus is dynamic and polymorphous, that there are two initially independent domains of variation (the world of potential stimuli and collections of neuronal groups), and that the fundamental and prior basis upon which learning rests is perceptual categorization.

The theory of neuronal group selection insists upon the importance of variance in neural populations and upon the developmental origin of diversity within single nervous systems. The emphasis is upon two levels of selection, developmental and experiential. *Ipso facto*, this implies that one cannot construct an adequate theory of brain function without first understanding the developmental processes and constraints that give rise to neuroanatomy and synaptic diversity. During adult experience, selection among populations of synapses becomes a key process; in most cases of postnatal experience, the rules for altering such synaptic populations supersede those for setting up new neuroanatomy (Finkel and Edelman 1985). Reentry and mapping, each continually modified by behavioral processes, become the means by which such a hierarchical system can maintain internal consistency. In realizing the importance of generalization to problem solving and learning, and therefore the need to provide a neural substrate for generalization, the theory emphasizes the fundamental role of degeneracy of neuronal groups in repertoires and of reentrant anatomy and function among the parallel systems and maps constituted by these repertoires.

Theories of neuronal selection have in common a key dogma concerning neural development—"Wiring, while individually diverse, is one-way"—that is, while the pattern of neural circuitry depends upon evolutionary, developmental, and behavioral variables, it is neither established nor rearranged *instructively* in response to external influences and, once established, is in general fixed *as a basis for synaptic selection.* The same holds in regenerating systems—selection theories suggest that, after neural regeneration to form a new network, a new game of synaptic selection is in play. Such theories exclude complete genetic specification of brains and behavior; instead, they consider that the degree of specification depends upon the evolution of each species, ecological requirements, and the time constraints necessary for an individual's somatic adaptive response. This is consistent with the selectionist notion that, in contrast to computers or Turing machines, there is no general-purpose animal—only the adaptive evolution of particular sensory sheets and adaptive motor ensembles and of the somatic selection principle itself evinced by particular mechanisms within the phenotype. The view taken by selectionist theories, in contrast to that of behaviorist models, is thus consistent with ethological constraints and with the unique adaptedness of different species and their nervous systems in particular econiches.

It is important to understand that simple selectionism during development and eliminative selection as a general mechanism are both insufficient to account for adaptive behavior leading to categorization. During the somatic lifetime of neural systems, some diversification must continue under selective constraints, and both positive *and* negative selection must occur. While the original degeneracy of the system is statistically likely to decrease as learning occurs, it remains statistically possible that new variations can occur within interacting neural networks and hierarchies of networks for the lifetime of the organism.

The major experimental tasks set by the theory of neuronal group selection are to discover the developmental origins of variability, the rules governing synaptic populations in degenerate neural networks, and the temporal and physical constraints of reentry, all within the context of the larger evolutionary constraints upon the behavior and form of a given species. This remorseless program of neural Darwinism

(Edelman 1985a) leads to interesting new views on the nature of memory, perception, and learning and suggests a large number of new experiments (see chapter 12).

SELECTION AND INSTRUCTION IN GLOBAL BRAIN THEORIES

In concluding this brief historical and interpretive account, we may usefully draw some distinctions between an earlier very influential global theory of brain function and the neuronal group selection theory, particularly because that fundamental distinction has been blurred or misunderstood. The theory in question is Hebb's cell assembly theory (Hebb 1949, 1980, 1982; Jusczyk and Klein 1980), a powerful expression in instructionist cellular terms of Thorndike's ideas of S-R association and trial-and-error learning. This theory proposed that collections of cells were linked into assemblies according to a particular synaptic rule affecting synaptic strength, neuron to neuron. The linkage was induced through external stimuli; complex series of events led to further linkage of cell assemblies into so-called phase sequences.

A contrast between the Hebb theory and the theory of neuronal group selection is particularly valuable because it allows an appreciation of the difference between a materialistic theory cogently based in instructionism and one remorselessly based on population thinking. Although Hebb's theory by no means shows a slavish acceptance of Thorndike's ideas (Thorndike 1911, 1931), it is at least marginally instructionist in character. The cell assembly theory was not constructed with population thinking in mind. Cell assemblies were not considered in terms of sharp developmental and evolutionary constraints and variance; they were still considered to be "assembled" from individual cells under the drive of specific environmental and neural signals, cell to cell. The theory did not address the problem of embryology or the relationship of evolution and behavior. It was not explicitly concerned with the nature of selection, with the importance of a deeply analyzed notion of categorization in the internal and external environment, or with the need for a precise mechanism of pattern recognition. Although it did explicitly consider the formation of phase sequences of cell assemblies as a result of active testing of the environment, and ultimately of attention and learning, it did not deal clearly with how spatiotemporal continuity could be maintained in a complex parallel network.

nce of the cell assembly theory lies in its vari-
l states, on complex units of response, on the
eption, on perceptual learning and generaliza-
e role of attention in learning. It was the most
time to explain psychology in terms of neuroa-
logy across a very broad front of phenomena,
effort. But without the further constraints of
psychology can be "explained" by cell assem-
es in ways not stringently testable by experi-
ing example, see Bindra 1976).
ssembly theory, the neuronal group selection
ned by structural constancies and population
(1) developmental processes leading to specific
kinds of neuroanatomy (e.g., local group organization, reentrant structures); (2) a population view of neurophysiology (interaction of synaptic
selection rules with the specific anatomy of group structure, and not just
through neuron-to-neuron firing, as in the Hebb rule); and (3) a strict
interdependency between the dynamics of reentrant neural mapping
and perceptual categorization during behavior.

The largest remaining challenge to this population theory is to show
in detail by what routes and mechanisms somatic selection with its
variant populations can lead through evolution to the ability of certain
species to store, transmit, and ultimately process information. We have
seen in this brief historical and critical review that selection upon essentialist categories, eliminative or stabilizing selection, and developmental selection of synapses alone will not in general be satisfactory answers
to this challenge. We must provide a mechanism for the establishment
of variance during ontogeny that is consistent with the evolution of a
particular species in its own niche. We must then show the bases of
experiential selection in the individual brain. These bases must be consistent with the establishment of pattern recognition not only in stable
environments but also in the face of novelty. The mechanism proposed
for this perceptual categorization must provide a basis for conventional
learning.

An adequate theory must account for the emergence of these remarkable properties without homunculi or any arguments from special
design, and it must show how various proposed mechanisms have adaptive value for the organism. As we shall see when we consider the
requirements for neuronal group selection in terms of experimental
data, no single field or descriptive inquiry in neuroscience will provide
sufficient evidence to support these mechanisms. Data from many

fields, ranging from molecular biology through developmental biology to population biology and ecology, will have to be considered as our argument proceeds. In this book, the detailed selection mechanisms proposed in the theory will be examined. Their elucidation should provide a more precise framework within which to evaluate the supporting evidence from these diverse fields. We may begin by illustrating the importance of perceptual categorization and by analyzing the inability of instructionist models to explain its observed properties.

2

Structure, Function, and Perception

INTRODUCTION

In the broad view across taxa, behavior is remarkably diverse and its
relation to neural structure appears to be almost capricious. To wiggle
the tail of a worm may take a network of thousands of neurons (Horridge 1968) but to flick the tail of a fish only one, the Mauthner cell
(Faber and Korn 1978). And if one proceeds upward in complexity from
this homely example and attempts to consider how a nervous system is
organized to give rise to perceptions in primates, the profusion of subject disciplines and even the definition of the task seem so difficult as
to confute serious attempts. In approaching this problem, the custom
has been either to search at the level of anatomy and physiology for
simple unifying principles (e.g., the reflex arc, or the chemical behavior
of the synapse) or to ignore neural structure and mechanisms and to
consider behavior itself under some ruling functional paradigm. A good
functional example current in studies of perception in cognitive psy-

chology (Underwood 1978; Anderson 1981; Norman 1981) is what I shall call the information processing model—one that takes for granted that there are units such as neurons, synapses, and networks, but considers that their particular mechanistic details are less important than the notion that the brain, like a digital computer, processes information by means of programs dictated in part by the environment and in part by neural wiring.

To a neurobiologist who is also a reductionist, the conjugate project, which is to understand neural structure and connect it to function, is obviously much more important, indeed central. Nonetheless, he must admit that the very numbers of neural elements, the intricacy of their connections, and the inability to deduce global function solely from network structure are at the least vexing. For the psychologist concurrently pursuing some form of functionalist interpretation, there is another kind of vexation. Programs, software, and learned routines are for logic machines. Suppose it turns out that despite the existence of programs of the brain (Young 1978), the possession of logic in circuitry is not sufficient for an animal to deal adaptively in its initial interactions with the things of this world.

The position that I will take here is that this is just the case: the environment or niche to which an organism must adapt is not arranged according to logic, nor does it have absolute values assigned to its possible orderings. This position does not deny that the material order in such a niche obeys the laws of quantum physics; rather, it asserts that at the time of an evolved organism's *first* confrontation with its world, most macroscopic things and events do not, in general, come in well-arranged categories. There are, of course, exceptions to this statement; as ethologists have stressed (see Marler 1982; Marler and Terrace 1984), certain arrangements within an animal's niche can be perceived categorically as a result of natural selection. Despite these obvious exceptions, the projects of structure-function analysis by anatomists and physiologists and of global functional description by psychologists must both confront the same critical problem of determining how animals carry out categorization in somatic time. It is my thesis here that the central problem of neurobiology is to understand the neural bases of such perceptual categorization. Curiously enough, one can best understand this problem by first considering rather more developed nervous systems and then reverting to the analysis of simpler ones.

The failure to recognize that, taken separately, the structural and the functional projects mentioned above cannot resolve the problems related to categorization has led to interpretations that evade or obscure a number of critical difficulties, contradictions, and lacunae in neuroscience. But unlike the ultraviolet catastrophe, which could not be ignored in the highly linked structure of physics (see McCormmach 1982), the dispersion of these difficulties across a variety of different neurobiological subdisciplines has masked them and has made it rather inevident that they all reflect the same crisis: the inability to explain how, prior to conventional learning, neural structure and function can result in pattern recognition or perceptual categorization with generalization.

What organizational features of neural networks and their synapses permit an organism to recognize large numbers of different examples of a category after initial confrontation with just a few of them? A biologically satisfactory answer to this question requires a theory of higher brain function formulated mainly in terms of neural structure. The theory proposed here to provide such an answer is radically different both from those that have been proposed before and from those currently accepted, whether tacitly or explicitly. It is therefore important at the outset to describe the origins of this theoretical enterprise as well as its limits.

Darwin (1859) stated that the origin of taxa was natural selection acting upon variants within a population to yield differential reproduction of the most adapted (Mayr 1982). As briefly described in the preceding chapter, the theoretical principle I shall elaborate here is that the origin of categories in higher brain function is somatic selection among huge numbers of variants of neural circuits contained in networks created epigenetically in each individual during its development; this selection results in differential amplification of populations of synapses in the selected variants. In other words, I shall take the view that the brain is a selective system more akin in its workings to evolution than to computation or information processing. The elaboration of this view will be an exercise in population thinking (Mayr 1982), which considers that variance in a population is real and that individuality provides the basis for selection. This exercise in neural Darwinism (Edelman 1985a) must nevertheless be grounded in quite specific mechanisms that require explicit description in terms of our knowledge of the nervous system.

After a general introduction to the problem of perceptual categorization and a further elaboration of the theory, I shall turn to evidence for selectional processes during embryonic development, stressing the molecular origin of connectional diversity. Then I shall consider how selection acting through synaptic rules operates upon repertoires of neurons that have established their connectional diversity during embryonic development to yield regional maps, such as those in the cerebral cortex. Finally, I want to describe how particular reentrant interactions among such regional maps lead to so-called global mappings, providing a potential solution to the central problem of perceptual categorization.

Perceptual Categorization and Generalization

Perception may be provisionally defined as the discrimination of an object or an event through one or more sensory modalities, separating them from the background or from other objects or events. The main reasons for choosing perception as a central focus are that it is close to the interface between physiology and psychology and that, without an understanding of perceptual processes, it is very difficult to study other subjects such as attention, motivation, learning, or memory. Perception involves categorization, a process by which an individual may treat nonidentical objects or events as equivalent. Here I will consider some phenomena related to perceptual categorization in an introductory fashion.

Given our provisional definition of perception, and in the absence of prior immutable categories of things, how in fact do we know what an object is? When we consider the world, there is no given semantic order: an animal must not only identify and classify things but also decide what to do in the absence of prior detailed descriptive programs, with the exception, of course, of certain fixed programs (Marler and Terrace 1984) handed down by evolution. This point deserves emphasis, because it is central to all other considerations: in some sense, the problem of perception is initially a problem of taxonomy in which the individual animal must "classify" the things of its world. Whatever solutions to this problem are adopted by an individual organism, they must be framed within that organism's ecological niche and for its own adaptive advantage. In other words, the internal taxonomy of perception is adaptive but is not necessarily veridical in the sense that it is concordant with the descriptions of physics (Vernon 1970).

From the standpoint of the adapting organism, the categorization of things is relative and depends upon cues, context, and salience (Staddon 1983). Categories are not immutable but depend upon the present state of the organism, which in turn is a function of memory and behavioral "set." At the macroscopic level, such categories are not general in the sense that a quantum description of particles is general. Animals can nonetheless *generalize;* that is, an individual organism can encounter a few instances of a category under learning conditions and then recognize a very great number of related but novel instances (Herrnstein 1982). This ability of individuals in a species to categorize novel objects in classes is a stunning reflection of what might be called the idiosyncratic (i.e., self-adaptive) generalizing power of neural networks.

Before we take up our main task, which is to understand the structural basis of this capability, it may be useful here briefly to explore certain of its phenomenal aspects and limits. First, consider context. In figure 2.1 on this page, you probably see a face, rather cartoon-like. Now consider figure 2.2 on the next page. The same sketch is now accompanied by the title of a Wallace Stevens poem. That contextual matter probably inexorably altered the way in which you perceived the features of this cartoon. The main point is that context, cues, and salience influence how features are seen. For convenience, the example given here used language and obviously crossed into the domain of perceptual experience, but even organisms without language shape features according to certain variables not necessarily intrinsic to the object category. Another example, closer to psychophysics and to the perceptual process, may serve further to show the influence of context and emphasize the difference between the sensory and the physical order.

Figure 2.1
Figure.

FROGS EAT BUTTERFLIES. SNAKES EAT
FROGS. HOGS EAT SNAKES.
MEN EAT HOGS

(WALLACE STEVENS)

Figure 2.2
Context.

This is the Wundt-Hering illusion, given in figure 2.3. If asked about the
lines at the bottom of the figure, most observers would agree that they
are parallel. If asked to prove this in the scientific sense, one would
measure the orthogonal distance at different points, getting the same
number with some variance.

Now, consider the two lines in the Wundt-Hering illusion. In the
middle example the lines appear bowed in, and in the upper example
they appear bowed out. In fact, they are parallel in all three cases. This
rather banal exercise serves to demonstrate that there is only a rough
correspondence between what has been called the sensory order
(Hayek 1952) and the physical order. Furthermore, it bears upon the
point previously made, that the perceptual world is a world of adaptation rather than a world of complete veridicality. Other visual illusions
(Coren and Girgus 1978; Deregowski 1980), the so-called perceptual
constancies (Vernon 1970), and recent experiments on preattentive
vision (Treisman 1979, 1983; Treisman and Gelade 1980; Julesz 1984)
all underline this same point. Less is known about such phenomena in
animals than in humans, but even if we consider data obtained from
studies of humans only, we can draw some forceful conclusions. In
certain contexts, we can extract some features from objects and can
react extravagantly to novelty in the name of safety; in other contexts,
there is a tendency toward stability and coherency in our perceptions
that will overcome even striking changes or differences in the physical
order. In either case, the main conclusion is again that perception is
adaptive rather than strictly veridical. Moreover, extensive data on
perceptual constancies and interrelations and pattern groupings (see
Kubovy and Pomerantz 1981; Dodwell and Caelli 1984) indicate that

diverse cues of a completely different nature can be substituted one for another to yield the same perception, that the attributes of perceived form arise at different levels, and that perceived form can remain unchanged even when different parts of a receptor sheet are stimulated.

An impressive body of evidence can thus be adduced to support the relative and context-driven nature of perceptual categorization. Even more impressive is the evidence showing that creatures without language can also carry out perceptual generalization. Although it is a pride of human beings that their capacity to generalize is vast (largely as a result of language), Cerella (1979), Herrnstein (1982), and others have clearly shown that pigeons are capable of generalization. In figure

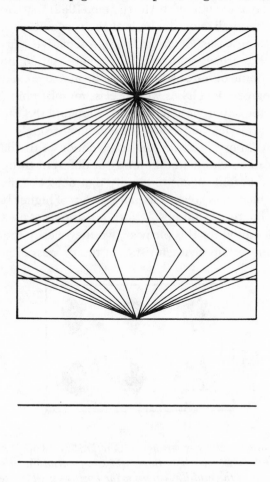

Figure 2.3
The Wundt-Hering illusion.

2.4 are patterns of oak leaves (the modal one from the white oak) that Cerella used as stimuli in an operant conditioning experiment with pigeons. After receiving three or four rewards when faced with an image of a leaf from *Quercus alba,* the pigeon could generalize and distinguish patterns of oak leaves of every genus presented from patterns of all other kinds of leaves. If one is inclined to think that this finding was perhaps the result of some evolutionarily or ethologically determined ability or a hidden cue not obvious to the experimenter, then one must confront Herrnstein's results demonstrating similar generalizing capacities of pigeons that were presented with images of water, of female figures, of trees, and even of fish. If these data are correct, we may conclude with Herrnstein (1982) that animals lacking language can generalize on the basis of the recognition of a few visual patterns. In some cases (Staddon 1983), associative learning may be necessary for the processes that lead to generalization, but it is clearly not sufficient. Some other capability must be invoked to account for the ability to recognize novelty as well as class membership. The context-driven character of perceptual categorization and the capacity to generalize from a few learned examples together strongly challenge any logic-based or "information-driven" explanation of the data. The very same object can be classified differently at different times, and an animal may use different means to classify that object at different times.

One of the major tasks of an adequate theory of higher brain function is to account for these findings. Before pursuing detailed models and hypotheses designed for this purpose, we may clarify the issue by discussing further certain characteristics of the process of generalization

Figure 2.4

Leaf patterns from Cerella's experiments (Cerella 1977). Top: *White oak leaves. The left and right patterns show the extremes of variation in one sample of forty oak leaves, and the middle pattern is the positive used in the experiments.* Bottom: *Non-oak leaves.*

carried out by men and animals. If one considers the problem of categorization from a philosophical point of view, the data suggest that the classical summary description of a class defined by singly necessary and jointly sufficient conditions does not hold. Membership is more like family resemblance: somebody resembles his sister because his chin and eyes are like the father's but his nose and ears are not; the sister's nose and eyes are like the father's but not the chin and ears; and so on. This is one of the major issues considered by Wittgenstein (1953) in his *Philosophical Investigations* (Pitcher 1968). Wittgenstein's considerations led to the idea that categorizations are in fact polymorphous (Ryle 1949) even when language is used to define categories.

The idea of polymorphous sets may be clarified by considering the construction (figure 2.5) of Dennis et al. (1973). The rule for membership in the category labeled *Y* is not at all transparent or evident. But it is obvious when it is stated: "The possession of at least two of the properties black or circular or symmetric defines membership in *Y*." Notice that this kind of definition disjunctively permits *any m* out of *n* possible properties (just as Wittgenstein [1953] did in his discussions of games). A classical realist would have insisted conjunctively upon *n* properties out of *n*, each singly necessary and all jointly sufficient to

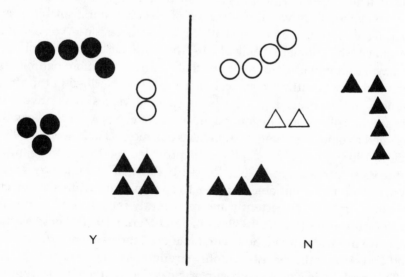

Figure 2.5
Polymorphous rule for set membership, after Dennis et al. (1973). Members of the set (group marked Y, for "yes") have any two of the properties roundness, solid color, or bilateral symmetry. Nonmembers (group marked N, for "no") have only one of these properties.

define a set. A nominalist would have insisted upon the unique disjunction, that is, members of sets have nothing in common except that you may choose to name any one of them in a certain way (one out of n).

From a less abstract point of view, we may briefly consider here some cognate interpretations derived from psychological experiments on the formation of concepts and categories (Smith and Medin 1981). These studies, which are described in greater detail in chapter 9, lead to general conclusions that are more or less consistent with the notion of polymorphous sets: humans do not categorize by closed lists of singly necessary and jointly sufficient conditions with fixed subordinate and superordinate relations among class members. Instead, they employ statistical or disjunctive combinations of attributes or scaled variables, or they use exemplars; in some cases, it is possible that they employ both strategies. Many of the pertinent data, obtained mainly by Rosch and others (see Rosch and Lloyd 1978), relate mainly to *conceptual* issues that are strongly language-bound and, to some extent, culture-bound. Unfortunately, fewer data are available in the arena of perceptual generalization, but the problems and the conclusions seem cognate, as has been suggested by Smith and Medin (1981).

If these observations are taken together with the evidence on generalization in pigeons, a strong case can be made that, in the face of novelty, a closed universal description of objects is not available to an adaptive creature, even to one with concepts; there is no "voice in the burning bush" telling that animal what the world description should be. It may be illuminating to point out that, during evolution, natural objects and events within ecological niches can be described in the same fashion: for the perceiving and behaving animal, values are relative, sets are polymorphous, and in general, no absolute ecological values can be assigned to objects encountered in parts of a niche (see Lewontin 1968; Pantin 1968). The only exceptions are provided by studies on "natural categories" carried out by ethologists: because of evolutionary selection, certain recurrent objects or relatively constant features of objects in a niche may be consistently and recurrently recognized by animals in a given species (Marler 1982; Gould and Marler 1984). These exceptions are not widespread, however, (or at least they are not exhaustive), and by contrast their existence only strengthens the case.

This analysis leaves us with our original question about perceptual categorization, but now it is transformed: What properties of its nervous system allow an animal to deal adaptively with polymorphous sets? Let us turn to the possibility that variance in neural structures is an essential one of these properties.

DIVERSITY AND OVERLAPPING CONNECTIVITY IN NEURAL STRUCTURES

The foregoing argument indicates that there is no evidence for the existence of detailed data structures in the macroscopic world that could provide a program for the nervous system as a hardwired entity in somatic time; moreover, while the laws of physics provide major constraints, they are insufficient to provide such a program at the macroscopic level. The philosophical implications are clear: if this lack of prior categorical structure is the case, we cannot be completely naive realists about psychological matters (see, e.g., Gibson 1979 and compare Ullman 1980); neither can we be radical materialists as extreme as Democritus, whose message was that by convention there is color, by convention sweetness, by convention bitterness, but in reality there are only atoms and the void.

Rather than elaborating upon these philosophical issues, it is more germane to consider some implications of these conclusions for empirical research. So far, the emphasis has been on psychology because it serves so well to pose the problem. Let us change direction and turn briefly to one of our main concerns, the structural diversity of individual nervous systems as one possible basis for solving the problem of categorizing an unlabeled world. My eventual aim is to show the bearing of this diversity upon the problem of generalization and upon phenomena that point up the difference between the sensory and the physical orders (Hayek 1952). To investigate the origin of neural diversity requires inquiries into neuroanatomy, neurophysiology, neuropharmacology, and, above all, developmental neurobiology. We might question the necessity of these inquiries. Could not a precisely wired nervous system carry out generalization even if there is no strict program in the world governing the order of its objects? An adequate answer is not forthcoming, but fortunately we are relieved from considering this question by the facts: at its finest ramifications, the nervous system is highly variant and is not precisely wired in the sense that a computer or electronic device is precisely wired.

A number of sources of variance can be identified at developmental, anatomical, and physiological levels (Edelman and Finkel 1984; see chapter 3 herein, particularly table 3.3). Let us start with development. It has become clear that the basis of neural mapping in development does not rest in prespecified molecular markers or in positional addresses down to the finest level of network connections (Edelman

1984a; Easter et al. 1985). Instead, mapping depends upon complex kinetic constraints on cell motion and neurite extension that are imposed by local surface modulation of particular cell adhesion molecules, or CAMs, which have been characterized mainly in vertebrates. As we shall describe in chapter 4, CAMs operate by constraining or regulating the motion of cell bodies and neurites with ensuing alterations in contingent developmental events. Dynamic control of such epigenetic processes perforce must lead to variability.

That such variability exists even in lower "simple" animals is already evident, although CAMs have not yet been found in these animals. Consider figure 2.6, A. It shows some diagrams taken from Pearson and Goodman's (1979; Goodman et al. 1979) work on the descending contralateral movement detector in the metathoracic ganglion of the migratory locust. This interneuron has about five branches on the average. The important point is that, among the samples from many different animals, these workers could not find a single modal pattern that could be described as general. For example, the dorsal branches which go to the wing muscles are sometimes repeated on one side. The ventral branches, which go to the fast extensor tibiae muscles, sometimes branch and sometimes do not. The variations seen in the locust differ for different neurons, but even in relatively fixed patterns "mistakes" occur (Altman and Tyrer 1977). An analysis of the developmental arborization of sensory neurons in the leech (Kramer and Stent 1985; Kramer et al. 1985) shows similar evidence for variations in branching patterns.

Should it be objected that these examples are from a genetically outbred population, one may turn to the classic experiments of Macagno et al. (1973) on *Daphnia magna,* a creature that in certain situations reproduces as a parthenogenetic female yielding clones. In figure 2.6, *B,* is a picture of the axon of an ommatidial receptor neuron from the optic ganglia on the left and right sides of each individual and

Figure 2.6
Anatomical variability. A: *Four examples of variability in the branching of the descending contralateral movement detector (DCMD) in the metathoracic ganglion of* Locusta migratoria. *(From Pearson and Goodman 1979.)* B: *A schematic representation of the branching sequence of a fiber from an ommatidial receptor neuron of* Daphnia magna. *Neurons on the left* (L) *and right* (R) *of four genetically identical specimens* (I, II, III, *and* IV) *are shown. (From Macagno et al. 1973.)* C: *A longitudinal section of the posterior and lateral columns of the spinal cord to show the arrangement of the posterior roots and the origin of the collaterals. (From Ramón y Cajal 1904.) Note variability in repeated structures.*

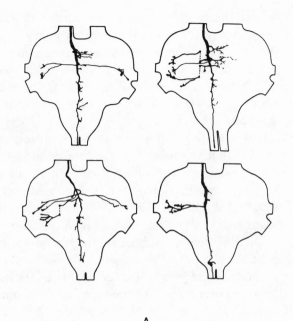

A

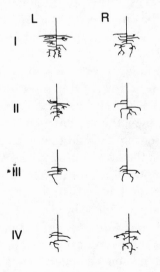

B

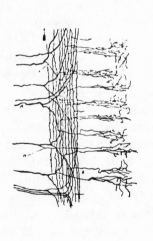

C

also from four genetically identical individuals. Every single case is different. Finally, to pay tribute to that extraordinary neuroscientist Ramón y Cajal, and to consider repetitious structures within one organism, one may view a diagram (figure 2.6, *C*) from his classic studies (Ramón y Cajal 1904) of the medulla of the rabbit; this example indicates the extraordinary diversity of such repeating structures, particularly of their terminal arborizations.

Not only is there variance within repeated structures; there is also increasing evidence that the terminal arbors of dendrites and axons, which emerge from relatively well ordered fascicles arising in different cells, cover relatively large portions of target areas and therefore must overlap extensively (Gilbert and Wiesel 1979; Landry and Deschênes 1981). This means that if significant numbers of synapses occur with cells that lie within the branching domain of these arbors, such synapses cannot be identified in terms of their cell of origin by the cell upon which they terminate. This kind of variance does not necessarily imply, however, that such neural nets or connections are random.

If we consider the functional or physiological implications of such findings, we see additional signs of variance. At any one time, the majority of the anatomical or synaptic connections of a given neuron are not functionally expressed, and over time this majority changes in its membership. Inasmuch as overlapping arbors with multiple synapses occur in the adult organism as well as during development, we conclude that, at many loci, a neuron has no means of uniquely or specifically identifying the origins of signals from input neurons contributing to such arbors.

Perhaps even more striking is the finding in sensory systems that there are extraordinary variations in cerebral cortical maps as determined by neurophysiological methods (Kaas et al. 1983; see Edelman and Finkel 1984). These variations occur even though the map borders are quite sharply defined—much more sharply defined than would be expected from the anatomical structure of the overlapping arbors mentioned above. We shall devote all of chapter 5 to this matter of local maps, for an understanding of their bases and origins is central to the theory of neuronal group selection. Here we may briefly note that different individuals (e.g., owl monkeys) have unique dispositions of map boundaries in areas 3b and 1 of somatosensory cortex, that in area 1 there are major temporal fluctuations in such boundaries, and that intervention—for example, ablation of input by cutting a nerve such as the median nerve—causes major map alterations in adult animals, even in portions of the map onto which the input had not previously been assumed to project (Kaas et al. 1983). Even alterations of available input in adults without surgery, such as the reduction of light touch or repetitious tapping of a single finger, can alter map boundaries.

A number of other observations that cannot be explained solely in terms of classical views of learning or information processing also exist at the borderline between the physiological, psychophysical, and psychological domains. We have already pointed out the surprising case of extensive generalization in the object domain for pigeons, creatures that do not possess language. For our final example (but one that by no means exhausts the list), we may cross into the realm of perceptual experience and risk mentioning subjective impressions. There is a unitary appearance to most human perceivers of perceptual processes that are known to be based upon complex parallel subprocesses and upon multiple connected but quasi-independent neural centers. For example, in vision, as many as thirteen different participating brain areas have been identified in certain species (Zeki 1981; Cowey 1981; Maunsell and Van Essen 1983; Phillips et al. 1984). Recent psychophysical experiments reveal strong differences between unconscious preattentive visual processing of textures and attentive searches (Julesz 1984). Neither the structure of the neural substrate nor such psychophysical analyses of function provide persuasive evidence that perceptual categorization is the unitary or closed process that it appears to be to the perceiver.

CRITICAL CHALLENGES TO INSTRUCTIONIST OR INFORMATION PROCESSING MODELS

This brief consideration of certain structural and functional features of complex nervous systems points up some of the difficulties that must be faced by information processing models of the nervous system, models that to a large extent are based upon analogies to computers (see, e.g., Marr 1982). In describing some of the basic tenets of such models, I shall attempt to show how they fail adequately to account for these features of nervous systems. We shall then be in a position to consider in the ensuing chapter how these same difficulties might be resolved by approaching the problem of perceptual categorization and generalization in terms of population thinking.

According to information processing models, neural signals from the periphery are *encoded* in a variety of ways and are subsequently transformed by various nuclei and way stations; finally, they are retransformed in a variety of ways by increasingly sophisticated relay systems culminating in cortical processing and output. Perforce, this view puts a very strong emphasis on strict rules for the generation of precise wiring during the development of the brain. Such models strongly rely on neural coding (Bullock 1967) and on the transfer of *information* from one particular neuron to another. This view also makes an assumption about the nature of memory which it considers to occur by representation of events through recording or replication of their informational details. The notion of information processing tends to put a strong emphasis on the ability of the central nervous system to *calculate* the relevant invariances of a physical world. This view culminates in discussions of algorithms and computations, on the assumption that the brain computes in an algorithmic manner (Marr 1982). Categories of natural objects in the physical world are implicitly assumed to fall into defined classes or typologies that are accessible to a program. Pushing the notion even further, proponents of certain versions of this model are disposed to consider that the rules and representations (Chomsky 1980) that appear to emerge in the realization of syntactical structures and higher semantic functions of language arise from corresponding structures at the neural level. If statistical variation enters at all into such a view of the brain, it is considered in terms of noise in a signal, which in information processing models is taken to be the main manifestation of variation.

With this admittedly composite description in hand, we are in a position to confront information processing models with a summary list of the difficulties that were mentioned in the preceding section and that will be further documented in succeeding chapters. This list is designed both to sharpen the major issues connecting psychology to neural structure and to expose the inadequacies of various forms of information processing:

1. The facts of developmental biology make it unlikely that there is precise point-to-point wiring (Edelman 1984a, b; 1985a; Easter et al. 1985). They indicate that the mode of action of molecules mediating neural cell adhesion necessarily introduces variability into modally similar portions of the nervous systems of different individuals of a species. Moreover, modern advances in neuroanatomy, which allow definition of the ramifications of individual neurons, confirm the existence of variability with a

vengeance and indicate that precise point-to-point wiring cannot be the basis for neural maps; they also suggest the existence of immense overlap of dendritic and axonal arbors.

2. Data from neuropharmacology confirm the view of local variance by indicating that even repetitive structures can use different neurotransmitters or be chemically heterogeneous in different localizations (Chan-Palay et al. 1981; Ingram et al. 1985).

3. Neurophysiological evidence to support the existence of a variety of neural codes (Bullock 1967) is lacking.

4. Considering higher levels of integration, recent work in neurophysiology indicates that although precise map boundaries can be defined, there are nonetheless immense variations in cortical maps (Kaas et al. 1983). It also indicates the absence of activity of most synapses at any given time. Taken together with the fact of anatomical variability, this means that in general the individual neuron must be "ignorant" of the exact sources of its input (i.e., of sources transmitting the activities of otherwise identifiable single neurons).

5. Certain experiments in psychology reviewed briefly above indicate that the organization of neural networks in the phenotype permits generalization even from a few complex stimuli. This can be dependent on learning, but it cannot in any sense be explained by learning except in the most trivial cases.

6. Psychophysics indicates that the unitary appearance to the perceiver of perceptual processes is based on an organization of plural mechanisms; while not yet precisely traceable to neuroanatomy, these findings are consistent with neuroanatomical data, which show that there are multiple, parallel, and widely dispersed neural areas dedicated to a single sensory function or modality.

7. An analysis of work on the formation of perceptual and conceptual categories indicates that there is no macroscopic theory outside of psychology to account for the physical orders or the shapes of macroscopic objects, that the physical and sensory orders are related but not identical, and that while physical scientific descriptions (with all their skeptical provisions) describe the rules governing properties of the physical universe, they offer no independent means of categorizing the objects of perception for a given species. Furthermore, such scientific descriptions are not simply identical to verbal categories, although sometimes the physical, sensory, and verbal orders do correspond.

This list is by no means complete, but it may be illuminating to consider how it might be interpreted point by point by proponents of various instructionist or information processing models (see table 2.1). We shall see that a crisis is at hand for such models, a crisis particularly evident only when the elements of the list are considered in the aggregate. If precise, prespecified, point-to-point wiring is excluded, the per-

Table 2.1

Some Unresolved Structural and Functional Issues in Neuroscience

Facts	Proffered Explanations
Precise, prespecified, point-to-point wiring is excluded.	"Noise"
Uniquely specific connections cannot exist.	"Derived at higher levels"
Divergent overlapping arbors imply the existence of vast numbers of unidentifiable inputs to a cell.	"Codes"
The majority of anatomic connections are not functionally expressed.	"Silent synapses"
Major temporal fluctuations in maps; unique maps in each individual; variability of maps in adults dependent upon available input.	"Alternative systems"
Extensive generalization in object recognition without the need for language.	"Hidden cues"
Unitary appearance to the perceiver of perceptual processes that are in fact based upon complex parallel subprocesses.	"Algorithms, computations, invariants"

son who insists on the information processing model has to say that anatomical variation must contribute mainly to noise (and thus be overcome by redundancy) or else be overcome by learning. Conversely, to provide both sufficiently precise wiring and reliably coded signals in the face of this noise, he has to assume that during development there is highly specific neuronal recognition: in some sense, this is the equivalent of a little electrician wiring points A to B on different neurons with a green wire, C to D with a red wire, and so on. In fact, theories of this kind have been proposed to account for developmental specificity (see Sperry 1963; Edelman 1984c). If the instructionist modeler becomes convinced that uniquely specific connections cannot exist in general at the microscopic levels of terminal arbors, he may propose that while variation and noise may be present at that level, at one level higher in scale, one cannot fail to be impressed by the enormous precision of neuroanatomy (Brodal 1981). If one points out that there is nonetheless convincing evidence for diverging, overlapping neuronal arbors that go to a variety of neurons in a particular area (e.g., the cerebral cortex), indicating that a given neuron could not uniquely identify those arbors and their source neurons, he could retort that there are neural codes. In other words, certain patterns of firing could constitute a message system identifying a given individual synaptic nexus, distinguishing one neuron from another. Given the enormous complexity of the system, however, he would have to admit that there would have to exist an enormous number of codes with consequent stringent requirements on their reliability in the face of noise.

In turning from these structural issues to the functional data revealed by the methods of physiology and psychology, the proponent of information processing is faced with another problem: the majority of anatomical connections that the microanatomist can pinpoint are not functionally expressed during attempts to elicit behavior. A common reply is to name such connections "silent synapses," which implies that they might function but does not specify how. If it is pointed out further that there are major temporal fluctuations in the maps of the brain, that there may be unique maps in each individual, and that map variability in adults depends upon the kinds of available input occurring within an individual's history (Kaas et al. 1983), an instructionist can always fall back on the enormous complexity at the next-highest level and appeal to the existence of alternative systems within neuroanatomy, the function of which had not heretofore been noticed. For example, a response to account for the data on variable maps in the somatosensory cortex might be that, in addition to the lemniscal system, the anterior funiculus also maps onto the areas in question; after disruption of the major normal input, the appearance of new maps might reflect the recruitment of such a system. As we shall see later, however, the variability and continuity of the resultant new maps are much too great to be accounted for by any such system.

If, in this imaginary dialogue, one were to point out that precisely wired, coded systems would have difficulty in accounting for the fact that extensive generalization can be carried out by pigeons and other animals in rich contexts, an instructionist could retort that there were hidden cues in the experimental design—cues providing information about the invariances possessed by an object, although the sources of such invariances would then remain unexplained. Invariance certainly appears to the observer: in preattentive processes (Julesz 1984), there is a unitary appearance to the perceiver of perceptual processes that we know to be the result of parallel subprocesses occurring in a number of different brain centers. The homunculus, that close cousin of the developmental electrician and the neural decoder, emerges at this point. Although this is not the place to discuss this problem of unitary appearances in relation to consciousness or to perceptual experience, it is probably a safe guess that most neurobiologists would view the homunculus as well as dualist solutions (Popper and Eccles 1981) to the problems of subjective report as being beyond scientific consideration. The problem has not gone unnoticed by those inclined toward information processing models: an intelligent if inadequate promissory note for the removal of homunculi from information processing models has been given by Dennett (1978).

It is surprising to observe that neurobiologists who disbelieve any resort to interpretive homunculi can nonetheless believe that precise algorithms are implemented and that computations and calculations of invariances are taking place inside neural structures. These beliefs persist despite the presence of the enormous structural and functional variances that exist in neural tissue—variances that would doom any equivalent parallel computer to producing meaningless output within short order even with the best of error-correcting codes. The algorithms proposed by these workers to explain brain functions work because they have been designed to work according to ingenious and precise mathematical models thought up by scientists in a culture based on social transmission; they have not been thought up by homunculi, and there is no evidence that they actually occur in brains.

The burden of this chapter has been twofold: to provide arguments to support the view that perceptual categorization is a central problem in neurobiology and to describe evidence from a wide variety of fields that reveals the inadequacy of information processing models as a general means of accounting for brain structure and function. An adequate explanation of this evidence requires an alternative theory of neural network organization. The remaining chapters are devoted to a detailed description of that alternative theory and to the additional evidence that supports it.

3

Neuronal Group Selection

INTRODUCTION

In the preceding chapter, I attempted to show that information processing or instructionist models fail to account satisfactorily for a variety
of anatomical, physiological, and psychological findings. At one stage or
another of such models, one sees evidence of typological thinking or
essentialism—the positing of prior categories either in the environment
or in the brain or in both. The chief difficulty of information processing
models is their inability to remove the homunculus (or his relatives)
from the brain. Who or what decides what is information? How and
where are "programs" constructed capable of context-dependent pattern recognition in situations never before encountered? Processors of
information must have information defined for them *a priori*, just as the
Shannon measure of information (see Pierce 1961) must specify *a priori*
an agreed-upon code as well as a means of estimating the probability
of receiving any given signal under that code. But such information can
be defined only *a posteriori* by an organism (i.e., the categories of
received signals can be defined only after the signals have been re-

ceived, either because of evolutionary selection or as a result of somatic experience). It is this successful adaptive categorization that constitutes biological pattern recognition. In assuming the existence of informational categories in the environment or of computational programs in the brain that can produce a broad range of plastic adaptive behavior, information processing models are forced to take a position similar to the argument of creation from design, which dominated pre-Darwinian thinking about species (Mayr 1982).

The theory of neuronal group selection derives from an alternative view that, while at the root of all biological theory, is somewhat unfamiliar in neurobiology—that of population thinking (Mayr 1982; Edelman and Finkel 1984). According to this view, at the level of its neuronal processes, the brain is a selective system (Edelman 1978). Instead of assuming that the brain works in an algorithmic mode, it puts the emphasis upon the epigenetic development of variation and individuality in the anatomical repertoires that constitute any given brain region and upon the subsequent selection of groups of variant neurons whose activity corresponds to a given signal. Under the influence of genetic constraints, repertoires in a given region are modally similar from individual to individual but are nonetheless significantly and richly variant at the level of neuronal morphology and neural pattern, particularly at the finest dendritic and axonal ramifications. During development, an additional rich variability also occurs at synapses and is expressed in terms of changing biochemical structure and the appearance of increasing numbers of neurotransmitters of different types. The total variability provides a preexisting basis for selection during perceptual experience of those active networks that respond repeatedly and adaptively to a given input. Such selection occurs within populations of synapses according to defined epigenetic rules but is not for individual neurons; rather, it is for those groups of neurons whose connectivity and responses are adaptive.

At first blush, this view (Edelman 1978, 1981; Edelman and Reeke 1982) does not seem to have the attractive simplicity of the information processing model. How could cogent neural and behavioral responses be elicited from such variable structures without preestablished codes? And could not classical and operant learning paradigms along with evolutionarily adapted algorithms (see chapter 11) better account for perceptual as well as other kinds of behavior? What is the advantage of such neural Darwinism over the information processing model?

The answer is that the selection theory, unlike information processing models, does not require the arbitrary positing of labels in either the brain or the world. Because this population theory of brain function requires variance in neural structures, it relies only minimally upon codes and thereby circumvents many of the difficulties described in the preceding chapter. Above all, the selection theory avoids the problem of the homunculus, inasmuch as it assumes that the motor behavior of the organism yielding signals from the environment acts dynamically by selection upon the potential orderings *already* represented by variant neural structures, rather than by requiring these structures to be determined by "information" already present in that environment.

Before considering the actual evidence in support of the idea that selection is the major mechanism of neural function, let us return to the theory outlined in chapter 1 and expand upon some of its key ideas. The three major tenets of this theory are (1) the developmental origin of variability in structure of neural networks as a basis for (2) the selection of neuronal groups within such networks by alterations of synaptic strengths in populations of synapses and (3) the existence of reentrant connections and signals linking hierarchically arranged repertoires of groups in maps in such a way as to provide spatiotemporal continuity in the responses to a stimulus object. For the moment, let us ignore reentry and focus upon the first two tenets.

According to the theory, *primary repertoires* of neuronal groups are established during development, their local anatomy being determined by cell type and the primary processes of development (Cowan 1973, 1978). While anatomical structures in a given area of the brain are modally alike in different individuals of a species and are constrained by genetic programs, enormous epigenetic variation occurs during development at the level of fine axonal and dendritic ramifications and connections. This developmental process leads to the formation of degenerate networks of neuronal groups whose dendritic trees and axonal arbors spread over relatively wide areas (up to millimeters) with a great degree of overlap.

During experience and after the receipt of input signals that are filtered and abstracted by sensory transducers, by feature extraction networks, and by feature correlators in mapped reentrant sensorimotor systems, certain neuronal groups are *selected* over others in a competitive fashion. The selection is based upon the variation in their structures and activities and is mediated through at least two independent synaptic rules (Finkel and Edelman 1985) that act jointly to guide the temporal interactions (and therefore the electrical and biochemical activity) of neurons within a group (see chapter 7). Selection is a competitive process in which a group may actually capture cells from other neighboring groups by differentially altering the efficacy of synapses. This process, in which groups that are more frequently stimulated are more likely to be selected again, leads to the formation of a *secondary repertoire* of selected neuronal groups which is dynamically maintained by synaptic alterations. It should be emphasized that this synaptic selection is upon a dynamic, highly active neuronal substrate and that it is based upon the electrical and biochemical activity of that substrate.

In proposing mechanisms whereby a secondary repertoire is competitively selected from the primary repertoire, the theory of neuronal group selection must explain the expression and adaptive significance of selected parts of the variant anatomical substrate. Structural variability in the primary repertoire must be constituted in such a fashion that significant *functional* variability can occur within the secondary repertoires—a functional variability ultimately manifested in the perception and behavior of the animal. Since the dynamic formation of neuronal groups is considered to be necessary for learning as well as memory and since both of these are evolutionarily adaptive for the individual organism, there is survival value in the maintenance of repertoires of groups whose function leads to increased capacity for adaptive behavior.

With this background, we may now consider and refine the definitions of neuronal groups, degeneracy, variability, and reentry. We may then ask how well the theory accounts for the data that we found so difficult to reconcile with instructionist models.

DEGENERACY AND THE DEFINITION OF A GROUP

Before examining the developmental origin of both variability and constancy, let us consider two rather more abstract issues: (1) how variability is related to the size and diversity of distributed structures in the brain, and (2) whether different variable structures can carry out equivalent functions. This will require an examination of the concept of degeneracy; the argument to be pursued will lead to certain predictions as well as to important restrictions on the mechanisms of recognition of signals by neuronal groups.

First, let us define a neuronal group; we will further refine and qualify this definition later (see chapter 6), after taking account of specific aspects of neuroanatomy. For the present, we may consider a neuronal group to be a collection of cells of similar or variant types, ranging in number from hundreds to thousands, that are closely connected in their intrinsic circuitry and whose mutual dynamic interaction may be further enhanced by increases in synaptic efficacy. The set of cells constituting a group can vary dynamically as a result of changes in input or output requirements or of competition with other groups. Such variations do not occur anatomically but rather are the result of alterations at either excitatory or inhibitory synapses. We may define a primary repertoire as a diverse collection of neuronal groups whose extrinsic connectivities and potential functions in a given brain region are prespecified to some extent during ontogeny and development. Without further qualifications at this point, we shall assume that, if a neuronal group responds with characteristic electrical output and chemical change more or less specifically to an input consisting of a particular spatiotemporal configuration of signals, there is a "match" between that group and the signal configuration.

In order to develop the notion of selection from a repertoire of neuronal groups, it is essential to consider the general requirements placed upon such a repertoire, particularly those concerning its size and the nature of its diversity. A main requirement is that this repertoire be sufficiently large; that is, it must contain enough diverse elements to assure that, given a wide range of different input signals and a response threshold, a finite probability exists that for each signal at least one matching element in the repertoire can be found. Furthermore, for at least some elements of the repertoire, the match with input must be sufficiently specific to allow distinctions among different input signals (i.e., to "recognize" them) with relatively low error. It is essential to understand that in a selective system such "recognition" can *in general never be perfect*—it can be only more or less good above some necessary threshold for recognition. The opposite assumption would either require a reversal of cause and effect in independent domains (world and brain) or necessitate the presence of an instructive mechanism.

What general properties of a large repertoire of neuronal groups might render it capable of both a wide range of recognition and of specificity for individual signals? For any arbitrarily chosen large number of different input signals, there must be a significantly large number of combinations in the repertoire capable of matching these signals (figure 3.1). Let a match be defined in terms of some threshold that gives the system the capacity to distinguish two closely related events within certain limits of error. If there are N elements in the repertoire and there is a probability p of a match between any such element and any signal, we may define a recognition function $r = f(p, N)$ that measures the effectiveness of the system in recognizing a range of possible input signals. Several such functions can be defined (Edelman 1978; Lumsden 1983), depending upon the particular measure of effectiveness chosen.

As shown in figure 3.1, if N is small and if the inputs are not specially chosen, then r will be close to zero. For N above a certain number, r will increase until, at some high value of N, a significant further increase in the efficacy of matching can no longer be achieved by a further increase in the size of the repertoire. In view of our previous statement that at any first encounter, matching above threshold can *in general* never be uniformly great and certainly not perfect, this reasoning sug-

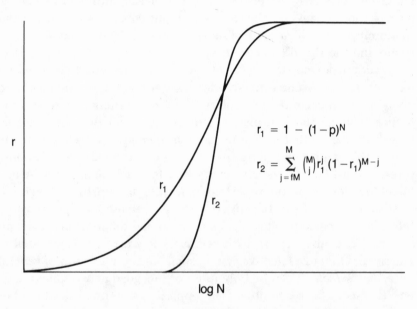

$$r_1 = 1 - (1-p)^N$$

$$r_2 = \sum_{j=fM}^{M} \binom{M}{j} r_1^j (1-r_1)^{M-j}$$

log N

Figure 3.1

Dependency of two forms of recognition function on the number N of elements in a repertoire, calculated according to a simple model. In this model, each element is assigned a constant a priori probability p of recognizing a randomly chosen signal. Here r_1 represents the expected fraction of all possible signals that will be recognized, and r_2 represents the probability that more than a fraction f (in this case 63 percent) of the M possible signals will be recognized. The shape of the curve is not sensitive to the value chosen for M if M is large. Similarly, if p is changed, the entire curve shifts left or right, reflecting the altered specificity of recognition, but the shapes of the curves do not change significantly. A more realistic model would assign different p values to different repertoire elements (Lumsden 1983); this would increase the computational complexity, but the nature of the dependency of r upon N would not be fundamentally altered.

gests that for the central nervous system, N must be large. In general, for simple recognition functions of the kind shown in figure 3.1, the critical value of N will be on the order of $1/p$, but the exact value will depend upon the details of the model; our later considerations of non-linear interactions and reentry will make this simple estimate inappropriate. We may assume for argument here that, in view of the numbers of cells available in any particular region of the human brain, a repertoire consisting of at least 10^6 different cell groups, each comprising 50 to 10,000 cells, would not be unrealistic.

A key consequence of this argument and of the notion of selective matching is that, in order to match any significant number of signals or configurations of signals, the repertoire must be degenerate. Degeneracy means that, given a particular threshold condition, there must in general be more than one way satisfactorily to recognize a given input signal. This implies the presence of multiple neuronal groups *with different structures*, each capable of carrying out the same function more or less well: degeneracy entails that some nonisomorphic groups must be isofunctional.

The need for degeneracy is perhaps most easily seen by assuming two extreme cases of recognition, one without any degeneracy and the other with complete degeneracy (figure 3.2). First, consider a repertoire in which, for any one arbitrarily chosen input signal, there is only one neuronal group capable of recognizing that signal. Under these

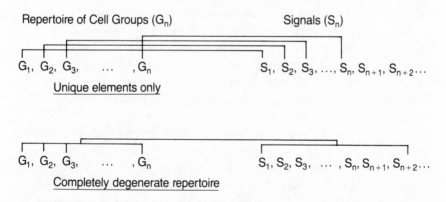

Figure 3.2

Two extreme cases of repertoires having unique (nondegenerate) and completely degenerate elements. In the first case, extension of the range of signals to be recognized (e.g., beyond S_n) leads to a frequent failure of recognition. In the second, there is a loss of specificity and a frequent failure to distinguish different signals inasmuch as each G can respond to all signals.

conditions, in a system capable of recognizing previously unencountered signals, there must ultimately ensue a failure of range—that is, there would have to exist many inputs, beyond the n recognized by N groups, that would go unrecognized. If we insist nevertheless that this very wide range of different previously unencountered signals be recognized and distinguished with high frequency by such a repertoire, then the fundamental requirement that there be no participation of the signal in forming the repertoire would have to be breached and the system would have to be an instructive one. Now consider the other extreme—that *every* element in the repertoire match *any* input signal. In this case, the range requirement would be satisfied, but there would be a total loss of specificity and consequently of the capacity to distinguish between different but closely related signal patterns. We conclude that the composition of the repertoire must be constituted to fall between these extremes so that there are several (and possibly many) different cell groups capable of distinguishing a given input more or less well (i.e., sufficiently above the threshold requirement for recognition).

This analysis indicates that degeneracy is a property fundamental to reconciling specificity of recognition with range of recognition. As we shall see, degeneracy is consistent with a number of other properties of the central nervous systems of man and certain other animal species. Notice that degeneracy is a population property (i.e., it requires variance) and that it must be distinguished from redundancy, which is used here strictly to refer to the existence of repeated units or groups having identical structure and response characteristics. Redundancy alone is insufficient for a wide range of specific recognition because it does not provide the overlapping but nonidentical response characteristics needed to cover a universe of possible stimuli. Degeneracy can, however, act like redundancy to provide reliability in a system composed of unreliable components (von Neumann 1956; Winograd and Cowan 1963).

The burden of the foregoing somewhat abstract and slightly oversimplified argument is that for a selective nervous system to be able to deal adaptively with the rich classificatory challenges inherent in perception of the real world, there must be a great deal of degenerate variation in the primary repertoire. The existence of degeneracy is a *prediction* of the theory, and evidence must be found for it.

It may be thought that degeneracy would ruin the selectivity of the nervous system. As we shall see in later discussions, however, even in the presence of considerable amounts of anatomical degeneracy of various kinds, the physiological effects of certain afferent or efferent connections will be sharply restricted by the behavior of synaptic populations and by reentry so that, within a degenerate primary repertoire, quite sharp selections can be made; only certain neurons may be driven and even these cover only a small fraction of their fields of distribution. These events lead to selection from an anatomically degenerate repertoire, resulting in formation of a much more adapted and less degenerate secondary repertoire.

To give some specific flavor to the notions of repertoire size, amplification, and degeneracy, it may be useful to discuss a minimal computer model for a selective recognition system. Although it is abstract, this model developed by G. N. Reeke, Jr., and myself (Edelman 1981) has the value of being extremely simple; it is most definitely not intended to reflect the workings of the nervous system. Instead, it concerns the similarity of 32-bit binary numbers to other 32-bit numbers, as established by a matching rule. The key idea, which bears some resemblance to those describing the immune response, is to show how any randomly chosen 32-bit binary number ("a stimulus") may be adaptively matched by a selective recognition system consisting of a repertoire of other such numbers (for some examples, the reader may glance at table 3.2, which will be described in detail later).

The model, which we shall call Darwin I, consists of a repertoire generator that produces a repertoire of random bit strings, a stimulus generator that produces input bit strings or "stimuli" to be matched, a matching rule that searches for matches or correspondences between a given randomly selected stimulus and individual elements of the repertoire, and an amplifier that increases the future probability of response by those repertoire elements that have been successfully matched to input stimuli.

Let us consider these characteristics in more detail. No information on the nature of the stimuli is available to the repertoire before the matching between any repertoire element and any stimulus takes place. The repertoire consists of any 10^4 bit patterns randomly chosen from the total of $2^{32} \cong 4.3 \times 10^9$ possible patterns. Stimuli also consist of 32-bit numbers chosen at random from the universe of all possible 32-bit numbers. In any subset of stimuli, half of the bits are fixed by some arbitrary convention (e.g., all ones or all zeros), and the other half is allowed to vary randomly. To match a given stimulus to any repertoire element, a "matching function" can be defined. Let us choose one that simply counts the number of bits that are identical in position and value in the two strings (repertoire element and stimulus) that are being compared. A threshold score can then be set for accepting a match as a "recognition"; to give an example, a score of 27 or more means correspondence between a repertoire element and a stimulus in 27 or more bits in any positions. For any chosen stimulus and score, the entire repertoire is then serially scanned for matches.

A list of matches is made for each stimulus, and the repertoire elements giving the highest match scores are amplified. This amplification is at the heart of the adaptive behavior of the system. In the model, amplification consists of making some predetermined number of copies of a successful repertoire element (one matching above threshold) and depositing these copies in random locations in the repertoire array. The number of copies made may be allowed to depend on the match score or may be fixed. For implementation in a computer, the size of the repertoire is kept constant, and amplified elements simply replace other elements at random. For a repertoire sufficiently large compared to the amplification factor, this procedure gives almost the same behavior as expansion of the repertoire during amplification.

We can now ask several illuminating questions: Does Darwin I obey the recognition function shown in figure 3.1? Is its recognition degenerate? Can cross-recognition or generalization take place given appropriate amplification and thresholding procedures?

As shown in figure 3.3, statistics of actual matches for various threshold scores M and numbers of repertoire elements N are entirely consistent with the theoretical predictions of the recognition function seen in figure 3.1. Moreover, Darwin I incorporates degenerate recognition— many repertoire elements can respond above threshold to any one stimulus and be "amplified" accordingly. In table 3.1 are shown the statistics of amplification as measured by the mean number of matches above threshold, or "hits." Under the conditions used, the response to unrelated control stimuli is virtually unaffected by the amplification procedure, showing that significant capacity remains for recognizing and responding to new stimuli of different classes that may be presented later. The only evident effects on control stimuli are a slight reduction in the percentage recognized as a result of the fixed repertoire size and an increase in the number of matches found for stimuli that are recognized as a result of cross-recognition of the test stimuli.

The possibilities for cross-recognition are illustrated in more detail in table 3.2. In this example, four different stimuli were used: S1 is the test stimulus that was used for amplification; S2 and S3 are "related" stimuli differing from S1 in four and eight bit positions, respectively; and S4 is a "relatively unrelated" stimulus differing in twenty positions from S1. Before amplification, the four stimuli showed similar levels of response,

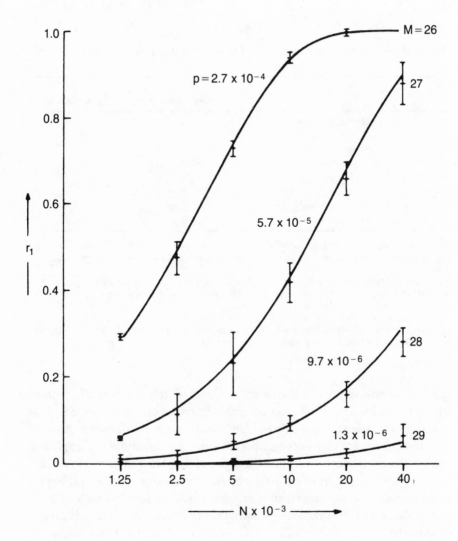

Figure 3.3

Comparison of theoretical and experimental recognition functions r_1 as a function of match threshold and repertoire size in Darwin I. r_1 = fraction of stimuli presented that are expected to be recognized. Solid curves were calculated according to $r_1 = 1 - (1 - p)^N$, where p = probability of recognizing any one stimulus, N = number of elements in repertoire (see figure 3.1). Experimental data are presented as dashes with vertical error bars, representing standard deviations of r_1 for four series of 100 trials each. Each curve is labeled with the match threshold M (number of bits out of 32 that must be identical in the stimulus and repertoire element for a "recognition" to occur) and the corresponding recognition probability p. As expected, the statistical distribution of matches obtained from the model closely approaches the theoretical values.

Table 3.1

Statistics of Selective Recognition in Darwin I, a Minimal Computer Model[a]

	Before Amplification	After Amplification[b]
Test stimuli[c], percentage matched	44	38
Mean hits (all stimuli)[d]	0.57	4.63
Mean hits (matched stimuli)	1.28	12.18
Mean trials to first match	4471	3289
Control stimuli[e], percentage matched	38	36
Mean hits (all stimuli)	0.48	0.46
Mean hits (matched stimuli)	1.28	1.28
Mean trials to first match	4801	4659

[a]Repertoire size was $10,000 \times 32$ bits.
[b]Amplification: for each test stimulus, the best three matches were each replicated five times.
[c]Test stimuli: 400 stimuli were selected at random from one of four classes, each class having 16 bits fixed and 16 bits random. Test stimuli were amplified upon successful matching as described above.
[d]Hits = mean number of matches above threshold.
[e]Control stimuli: 200 stimuli with all bits random were used as controls. No amplification was performed when these stimuli were presented.

averaging two hits each above a threshold match score of 27. One of these hits, element 3579, was common to two stimuli, S1 and S2. This element represents a preexisting, accidental cross-recognition. A more interesting kind of cross-recognition arises if the threshold for amplification is lowered during the presentation of S1. After all repertoire elements matching S1 in *twenty-four or more positions* were amplified by being replicated ten times, an increased response to S2 as well as to S1 was obtained *at the original 27 match-score level.* The elements giving rise to the matches above 27 for S2 were not all derived from element 3579, which matched originally; some were among the poorer (24–26 score) matches of S1 that were also amplified. Thus, elements that respond weakly to a particular stimulus (S1) can be amplified if the threshold is set low enough, strengthening the later response to a related stimulus that has not yet been encountered (S2), even when the stringency of that response is greater than that used for amplification. These results show how cross-recognition arising from overlapping specificities in a degenerate repertoire can give the system an enhanced ability to generalize, that is, to recognize stimuli that are new but similar to some of those already encountered. This ability can be particularly advantageous in the early stages of adaptation, when relatively

Table 3.2

Cross-Recognition of Related Stimuli in Darwin I[a]

	Stimulus		Bit Pattern	Bits Different from S1
1. Stimuli	S1		1111000011111100111100011111110110	0
	S2 (X-R)[b]		0111000011111110111101011011 0110110	4
	S3 (X-R)		1111110111110100111001111111011	8
	S4 (NX-R)[c]		00011110010001101010101001011111	20

	Stimulus	Repertoire Position	Repertoire Element	Total Hits[d]
2. Response before Amplification	S1	3579	11110010111101101111000110110110	2
		6520	11110010011101101111000111110100	
	S2 (X-R)	3579	11110010111101101111000110110110	3
		3147	10100000011111111111010110110110	
		3575	01010100111111011011111110110110	
	S3 (X-R)	2336	11111101111100001011011111010011	2
		8289	11111001101111001111101111101011	
	S4 (NX-R)	1658	00011110001000101010101101010111	1

	Stimulus	Repertoire Position	Repertoire Element	Total Hits[d]
3. Response after Amplification[e]	S1	445	11110010111101101111000110110110	21
		2627	11110010111101101111000110110110	
		7751	11110010111101101111000110110110	
		9636	11110010011101101111000111110100	
			. . . 17 more . . .	
	S2 (X-R)	2627	11110010111101101111000110110110	20
		3147	10100000011111111111010110110110	
		5090	10100000011111111111010110110110	
		8244	10100000011111111111010110110110	
			. . . 16 more . . .	
	S3 (X-R)	2336	11111101111100001011011111010011	2
		8289	11111001101111001111101111101011	
	S4 (NX-R)	1658	00011110001000101010101101010111	1

[a]Repertoire size in this run was 10,000 elements of 32 bits each.
[b]X-R = related stimulus, possibly cross-recognized.
[c]NX-R = relatively unrelated stimulus, not cross-recognized.
[d]Number of matches with 27 or more bits identical in stimulus and repertoire strings.
[e]Repertoire elements with match scores against S1 greater than 24 were each replicated 10 times.

few stimuli have been encountered, but it might later interfere with the highly selective processes needed for distinguishing among similar, familiar stimuli.

These considerations suggest a need for some kind of gating system to vary recognition thresholds at different times and in different sub-

repertoires of a selective system. Such a system allows adjustment of the
degree of precision in matching to correspond with the degree of repertoire specificity already attained.

Darwin I serves a heuristic purpose by exemplifying some of the
requirements placed upon selective systems in general. It incorporates
the ideas we have been elaborating here, but it ignores most of the
features of the nervous system—it lacks early processing of the stimuli,
it has no signaling between elements of its repertoire, and it obviously
lacks any network configurations. A selective recognition automaton
called Darwin II described in chapter 10 has such properties and much
more closely resembles real nervous systems.

We may now summarize the argument related to repertoire size and
degeneracy in a less formal way. In a large repertoire, in which there
is no degeneracy (figure 3.2), a highly unlikely combination of events
may occur such that group 1 matches signal 1, group 2 matches signal
2, all the way on up to group N. But there must come a point above
n signals at which the system will fail absolutely. If we take the opposite
case and assume that every single group will recognize every single
signal (the case of complete degeneracy), then everything will be barely
recognized but nothing will be distinguished. We conclude that, in
addition to the general requirement for the existence of larger repertoires, there is another key requirement to be met by selective systems:
they must be tuned somewhere between the extremes of absolute specificity and complete range. When this occurs, there can be subtle
variations in the resulting behavior of the system, giving the organism
a flexibility and range of choices it would not have with strictly mono-
functional units.

There is, however, an efficiency limit in increasing the size of degenerate systems. We have assumed functionally that, in the construction
of a selective system, there is no information transfer from that which
is to be recognized to that which is doing the recognizing. The neural
circuits that are made during embryogenesis in advanced animals have
little or no information about what they will encounter in the experiential phase (see Hamburger 1963, 1970). Obviously, if the number of
elements in the repertoire is too low, there will be a very low probability of recognizing anything. But, by the very assumptions of a selective
system, recognition can never be perfect (at least for all elements in the
system), and there must be some number above which increasing the
size of the repertoire will lead to no further gain; other mechanisms
must be brought into play to improve performance.

Does *each* group do just one thing at a time and could all groups do just one thing at any time? The assumption of degeneracy implies that there can be isofunctional elements in the repertoire that have completely different structures; that is, one particular structure can carry out more than one function, and one function can be carried out by more than one structure. While a group can carry out a function at a given time, it can carry out another at a different time. Because degeneracy implies many-to-one mapping with more than one choice, this key characteristic of selective systems can be brought to bear in various combinations as dictated by the exigencies of the environment or even by chance. With these ideas as background, we may now turn to a further consideration of variability as an empirical basis for degeneracy in real neural networks.

SITES OF VARIABILITY

What is the detailed evidence that there is a large amount of variation in the nervous system from individual to individual, and at what levels does it occur? Certainly, most neurobiologists would agree that variation in structure and activity is not hard to find, particularly in places like the cerebral cortex or even in highly regular structures such as the cerebellum (Chan-Palay et al. 1981, 1982; Ingram et al. 1985). The problem is to define and categorize this variation, to determine both its quantitative distribution and its significance at various levels of function, and to analyze the mechanisms by which it is generated. In view of the two stages of selection (developmental and experiential) proposed in the theory of neuronal group selection, it is also important to make a clear distinction between local structural variation (microanatomy) and dynamic variations in cellular and synaptic states.

Unfortunately, little has been done to study the populational or numerical aspects of neuroanatomy in well-controlled situations. But as shown in table 3.3 one can at least identify reasonable candidate levels at which variation may be expressed. A population of neurons may vary in structural or functional characteristics. Microanatomically, neurons of a given type may differ in the location, shape, and size of the soma, and in their dendritic and axonal arborization patterns and connections. Biochemically, they may vary in their intracellular structures, axoplasmic flow, transmitter type, and membrane receptors. These may in turn be reflected in variant receptive field characteristics and electrical properties.

At this point, we defer a detailed discussion of any temporal neuronal

Table 3.3

Sites and Levels of Neuronal Variation

A. Variation in genetic traits and developmental primary processes: cell division, migration, adhesion, differentiation, and death (see figure 4.1)
B. Variation in cell morphology
    1. Cell shape and size
    2. Dendritic and axonal arborizations
        a. Spatial distribution
        b. Branching order
        c. Length of branches
        d. Number of spines
C. Variation in connection patterns
    1. Number of inputs and outputs
    2. Connection order with other neurons
    3. Local vs. long-range connections
    4. Degree of overlap of arbors
D. Variation in cytoarchitectonics
    1. Number or density of cells
    2. Thickness of individual cortical layers
    3. Relative thickness of supragranular, infragranular, and granular layers
    4. Position of somata
    5. Variation in columns
    6. Variation in strips or patches of terminations
    7. Variation in anisotropy of fibers
E. Variation in transmitters
    1. Between cells in a population
    2. Between cells at different times
F. Variation in dynamic response
    1. In synaptic chemistry and size of synapse
    2. In electrical properties
    3. In excitatory/inhibitory ratios and locations of these synapses
    4. In short- and long-term synaptic alteration
    5. In metabolic state
G. Variation in neuronal transport
H. Variation in interactions with glia

---

variation in activity (Burns 1968; Bindman and Lippold 1981) or of any variation in types of neurotransmitters. These variations are no doubt important in selection of both the primary and the secondary repertoires and will be considered later. Here, it is useful to note that complex variants of chemical synapses can arise during development and can persist even in highly "regular" tissues such as the cerebellum (Chan-Palay et al. 1981, 1982). Variations related to sexual dimorphism may also play a role, for example, in the formation of callosal connections (de Lacoste-Utamsing and Holloway 1982).

What can be said about the anatomical origin of degeneracy? Examples of anatomical bases for degeneracy can be seen in the surprisingly divergent terminal arborizations of afferents in many different regions of the nervous system. For instance, individual pyramidal motor neuron axons are found to terminate over several spinal segments (Shinoda et al. 1981, 1982, 1986), retinotectal afferents can spread over regions up to one-quarter of the tectum (Schmidt 1982, 1985; Meyer 1980), X-cell axons distribute widely over the lateral geniculate nucleus (Sur and Sherman 1982), and the arbors of individual lateral geniculate nucleus fibers can in turn cover an entire ocular dominance column in area 17 (Gilbert and Wiesel 1979). Moreover, thalamocortical axons in AI of auditory cortex must extend over the entire 2–3 mm wide isofrequency dimension (Middlebrooks and Zook 1983; Merzenich et al. 1984a).

These examples do not represent the only kinds of anatomical degeneracy possible. For example, degeneracy may be reflected anatomically in certain fascicles or nerve trunks as they are compared bilaterally, and it may in this case be without any particular functional consequence. Moreover, by evolutionary selection and other mechanisms, degeneracy may in some species and in some neural areas be reduced to a minimum (Horridge 1968; Faber and Korn 1978).

There is obviously a great need to quantitate experimentally the populational distributions of both the static and dynamic types of neural variation that are qualitatively illustrated in table 3.3. None of this exercise would be of particular value, however, unless variability and degeneracy were related to function. One of the most intriguing problems relating function and microscopic anatomical variability is posed by the existence of variability in cortical maps (Edelman and Finkel 1984; Merzenich et al. 1984a). This issue will be discussed at length in later chapters for the following reasons: (1) it ties anatomical variability to functional variability; (2) it focuses attention on the interaction of populations of neurons; (3) it is intimately concerned with input-output relations and therefore brings out the interplay between the function of neurons evolved to carry out selection during sensory input and those concerned with motor and behavioral acts; and (4) it will bring us to a detailed examination of maps themselves, particularly to the issue of how functioning maps may be established and related to each other in a reasonably orderly manner despite the variation induced during development. This last issue leads us directly to a consideration of reentry.

THE NEED FOR REENTRANT STRUCTURE AND FUNCTION

The notion of reentry, particularly between maps, is central for selective theories of neuronal networks. This idea is essential both because of the nature of the parallel neural processes required for categorization of the physical world and because of the distributed properties of the neutral populations that result in degeneracy. We may particularize the issue in a question: How do the various neuronal groups in a complex chain of linked and mapped structures such as those found in the visual or somatosensory systems coordinate their responses around a given input object?

If different collections of neuronal groups at a variety of levels responding to features of an object are to be related to that same external object *solely* within the brain, then a real-time correlation must occur between the states of these groups. This requirement becomes even more stringent in considering representations of multiple objects in motion that stimulate various sensory modalities. Because of the distributed and parallel nature of the central nervous system, the continuous correlation of temporal sequences of signals from multimodal inputs is a formidable problem. In computers, even a partial ordering of such sequences requires considerable housekeeping—time or date stamps, stacks, and a complex set of informational tags (Lamport 1978). While schemes have been devised to route information in networks to the site of a "request" without specific information on the location of that site, they require precise restrictions on the local directivity of input and output (Sahin 1973). This severe requirement, and the variability, parallel arrangement, and complexity of nervous systems, makes it unlikely that such schemes would be applicable. Moreover, any distributed degenerate system that does not refer back to the stimulus object but only to the neural representations of that object must maintain (1) *multiple* representations, with tags to correlate features in one representation with those in other representations, and (2) a single real-time clock to cross-correlate the inputs from the very recent past. If one adds to these requirements the need to cross-correlate various *degenerate* neural representations of the object (see figure 3.2), the informational burden becomes immense.

One solution to this problem is reentry at a particular place (e.g., onto a map in a primary receiving area) of already processed signals, so that they may be correlated at later times with succeeding input signals (Edelman 1978). A reentered signal could be correlated with the mapped features of the next signal in a temporal sequence. This temporal correlation could then be "read" by neurons in groups at higher levels that are responsive to the paired and interactive reentrant signals (Edelman 1978). This mode of correlation would permit a continuous spatiotemporal representation of the object. In particular, it would obviate the need for elaborate tag systems in object representations and relieve the requirement for a complete temporal ordering of individual signals within the distributed system. Reentry of this type would obviously not work in an information processing system with specific data streams, but it is particularly geared to a selectional system in which mapping and amplification can occur. Reentry not only allows linkage of signals among systems of neuronal groups operating in parallel in real time but, as shown in a computer model, specific linkages of a reentrant type between two sets of groups can lead to the emergence of new associative functions not originally present in either set of groups (Edelman and Reeke 1982; see chapter 10). One of the most powerful consequences of this type of reentry is that it enables representation of categories of external objects by at least two independent sets of properties that relate to different object features or correlations. In addition, reentry is a major means of mediating the linkage of the ensuing neural representations, particularly those in maps.

In accord with the associative properties (Edelman 1978; Reeke and Edelman 1984) of a distributed degenerate system, each cycle of reentry between any two levels or maps would call upon a very large number of associable neuronal groups. In the nervous system, the associations would continually shift in response to small variations in the sensory input, to altered motor states, or to changes in the arousal system. Whatever other functions the arousal system carries out in the nervous system, the theory postulates (Edelman 1978) that it helps to coordinate the temporal simultaneities of cellular response required both for reentry and for resolution of redundancies of potential command.

If dynamic categorizations are to be carried out disjunctively in an uninstructed system, then at least two different and independent abstractions must be made of a stimulus object or category. This means that a minimum of two independent abstracting networks must work simultaneously (and disjunctively) in response to a stimulus and then interact by reentry to provide some abstract higher-order linkage of their representations. To illustrate these ideas, we choose one form of anatomical and dynamic reentry. Two independent networks are used in this example, but we must remember that more than two networks working simultaneously are not only possible but also likely in real nervous systems. The illustrative case, named a classification couple, is shown in figure 3.4. A classification couple consists of (1) one set of sensory feature detectors (obviously not necessarily alike in different animal species); (2) another set of feature detectors working simultaneously in a different modality or, alternatively, a sensorimotor system that independently *correlates* connected features of a stimulus category or object by means of motion; (3) independent networks or repertoires of degenerate groups to which these two sets separately connect, usually in mapped fashion; and (4) a preexistent reciprocal mapping or connection of these higher-order networks to each other at the anatomic level and a synaptic means of controlling or correlating the direction and reentrant flow (usually two-way) of signal traffic between them.

If certain groups in a mapped network show simultaneous activity in real time with certain groups in another mapped network, then the possibility of linking the independently activated groups in each separate network arises (e.g., by strengthening of their mutual connectivity

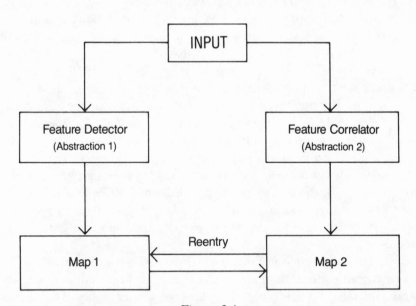

Figure 3.4

A classification couple operating through reentry in real time. The input is independently sampled by two different networks, one of which carries out feature detection and the other, feature correlation. Selected mapped responses at higher levels are related through reentry by reciprocally arranged connections between mapped areas. See text for details; an explicit example is discussed at length in chapter 10.

via synaptic alterations in reentrant fibers that happen to connect those groups; see figure 3.4). If such synaptic alterations were maintained, this linkage could serve to correlate certain simultaneously occurring features of the object or stimulus. It is important to note that such a correlation or categorization by disjunctive sampling on a polymorphous set (see figure 2.5) could not occur via any single network in any but the most trivial way. Because of the reentrant cross-connections in the two networks, a new network function can arise between them. Obviously, the efficacy of this kind of system depends upon the actual anatomical distribution of reentrant fibers and upon the phasic or time-correlated control of the direction of signal flow. A detailed example of the simulation and operation of a classification couple will be given in chapter 10.

Reentry within sensory systems only is not in itself sufficient for adequate functioning of a group selective system. The brain functions for action, and output to motor systems is required for two essential tasks. The first task is to aid in selecting appropriate inputs by altering the relationship of sensory systems to the surroundings by spontaneous or learned movement. This further focuses or reinforces the selective features of the system, and it makes feature correlation possible. A second task of motor systems is to verify and corroborate through action the instantaneous and dynamic responses as well as the enhanced connectivities that result from the action of groups in both primary and secondary repertoires. Both of these tasks serve to update (MacKay 1970) responses in these repertoires. While the process of reentry is itself one of updating in a continuous fashion, this process is highly reinforced by motor activity related to a particular sensory task, and by this means a number of errors of correlation that might arise may be canceled by motor responses.

As we shall see in chapter 8, such activity requires the existence of a composite structure called a global mapping. According to this view, motor activity serves continually to verify or check for internal consistency in the workings of a reentrant system. A further reduction in the possibility of errors arises from the fact already mentioned, that degeneracy can serve in the same manner as redundancy to reduce unreliability in a distributed system. Finally, motor activity provides the main basis (called "topological" by Bernstein 1967) for establishing the continuity properties and global correlations of sets of features.

The reason for discussing reentry at such length is that one of the most important functions of an advanced nervous system is the ability to link various parallel modes of a four-dimensional input initially to various two-dimensional sensory sheets representing different mapped sensory modalities as well as to various motor responses, resulting in a multidimensional correlation. This requires transformation of object stimuli into responses in reentrant maps in order to assure spatiotemporal correlations among various internal representations at different loci in the brain. Moreover, reentrant anatomical arrangements are necessary to allow interactions between different brain nuclei and regions (each with different evolved functions) in order to guarantee the generation of new somatic functions as well as to correlate multiple regions in one sensory modality.

In summary, reentry assures spatiotemporal correlation of the properties of external objects, similar correlation of internal categories in memory, and the possibility of generating new functions in a parallel system. As we mentioned previously, it also removes the requirement (which is absolute in an effective information processing model) for time and place markers on signals in cross-connected parallel networks operating together in real time. Because of these properties, reentrant networks obviate the necessity for *a priori* or instructive object definitions. Reentrant networks are necessary for internal correlation in selective systems: in their absence, different degenerate repertoires subserving different neural functions could not operate together to relate independent features of dynamic categories to each other. It is relevant that a large majority of neuronal networks in the vertebrate brain are anatomically reentrant, either locally or at long distances, or both (Brodal 1981). No physiological *proof* of the phasic nature of reentry exists so far. Nonetheless, because of the distributed and degenerate nature of the nervous system, the requirement for phasic reentry is a strong one—if such reentry can be shown not to occur, the neuronal group selection theory is likely to be invalid.

EXPLANATORY POWER OF THE THEORY

We may now restate the premises of the theory in order to show how they can account for the difficulties discussed in chapter 2. The premises are:

1. The existence of primary repertoires of neuronal groups created by developmental mechanisms that introduce variation into regions containing multiple identifiable neural structures. This generation of diversity is constrained by the balance between evolutionary selection for

particular kinds of neurons and by epigenetic variation in connectivity out of which primary repertoires of groups are constructed. We may call this the period of developmental selection.

2. The subsequent selection, during an animal's sojourn in its ecological niche, of a secondary repertoire from the groups of the primary repertoire. Such selection occurs among populations of synapses by amplification of some synaptic strengths and diminution of others, a process that leads to formation of a secondary repertoire. We may call this the period of experiential selection. Synaptic alteration may be seen as a continuing process of development by a process of selection that differs at the mechanistic and behavioral level from the selective processes used to construct the primary repertoire. Moreover, the adaptive value of experiential selection differs from that of selection in the early developmental period (see below). In both periods of selection, variations occurring in the external or physical order and those occurring in the neural order are (and must be) distinct in causation, at least in the initial or early encounters of an animal with the environment.

3. The existence of a dynamic, time-dependent process of reentry at all levels of connection (both local and long-range) within the distributed (Mountcastle 1978) neural system. This has its basis in reentrant anatomy, both in register (e.g., corticothalamic and thalamocortical radiations) and in more complex arrangements, as seen in connections among cortex, cerebellum, and basal ganglia. One of the most striking examples of reentrant connectivity is provided by the visual system. In certain species of monkey, there may be as many as fifteen visual areas carrying out different functions. The functional organization of projections (Zeki 1975, 1978a) is consistent with reentrant connectivity. Indeed, reciprocal connections that would sustain reentry are found between all visual areas tested so far (Van Essen 1985). Reentry is necessary to assure that selection of neuronal groups at various levels in the highly parallel nervous system is correlated with the existence of coherent signals from objects or other neuronal groups. This mechanism is required *a fortiori* because the theory abandons any general notions of fixed categories of information in the macroscopic physical order and also because it relinquishes any form of specifically coded place or time tags for coordinating events within parallel connected neural nets. The idea of reentry is a minimal assumption necessary to account for neural representations of spatiotemporal continuity.

After this summary, it is illuminating to subject the neuronal group selection theory to the same critical confrontation with the problems considered in the preceding chapter. It will come as no surprise that many of the elements contributing to difficulties for instructionism and information processing models are turned about and actually become requirements for neuronal group selection (see table 2.1, the order of which is followed here).

In a selective system, there must be mechanisms in development that guarantee not only common structures but also variation. As we shall see in later discussions of development (chapter 4), there is a molecular basis for such mechanisms. Prespecified point-to-point wiring, while not incompatible with particular versions of the theory, is generally not required, nor are highly specific connections at certain points of dendrites. Overlapping dendritic and axonal arbors actually enhance the possibility of combinatorial variance and degeneracy in the primary repertoire. Moreover, inasmuch as the theory assumes that the neuron is "ignorant" and that no prior coded information goes to it in any uniquely necessary way, unidentifiable inputs to a cell are no embarrassment.

One need not invoke "silent synapses" to account for the fact that the majority of anatomic connections are not functionally expressed; at any one time in a selective system, the majority of variants are not selected. The adaptive selection of neuronal groups by synaptic rules acting upon populations of synapses (as shown in chapters 6 and 7) can easily account for temporal fluctuations in map borders as well as for their individuality and for the dependence of their disposition upon available input. This subject of mapping is so important to matters of correlating input and output and to the problem of categorization that it will receive extensive treatment in several chapters.

The central problems of categorization and generalization are the major stumbling blocks for information processing models. While it would be an overstatement to suggest that the selection theory has solved these problems completely, a model of the theory has been embedded in an automaton that can perform limited categorization and generalization (Edelman and Reeke 1982; Reeke and Edelman 1984). The automaton carries out these tasks without an explicit program and without explicit prior knowledge of the categories that it develops procedures to represent. At this point, the reader will have to take these assertions on faith; they are documented in chapter 10.

As embodied in such a model, the neuronal group selection theory deals with adaptation to a relative, changing, polymorphous world in the same fashion as Darwinian natural selection: from the bottom up (Mayr 1982). Typological, essentialist (or top-down) assumptions are avoided. By having the environment act dynamically on potential orderings already present in the organism, selection theories of brain function avoid the problem of the homunculus, just as evolution avoids the argument from design. Such orderings are already implicit and result from the existence of variant neural structures that display degeneracy; to be ordered, such structures are not required to react solely to categories defined from without that are then interpreted by little green men within. Moreover, as we shall see in chapter 10, homunculi can be avoided and categorization may still take place.

In considering how the neuronal group selection theory confronts the various crises shown in table 2.1, there is one area of explanation that, because of our deliberate avoidance of any extended consideration of perceptual experience, at best is incomplete and at worst remains unresolved. This concerns the apparent phenomenal unity of the sensory order to a conscious individual despite the plurality of neural mechanisms present even in a single sensory modality. Here, it suffices to point out that the neuronal group selection theory with its notions of degeneracy and reentry at various hierarchical levels is entirely consistent with the existence of multiple representations and nuclei in complex neural systems functioning as a unit. The concept of reentry provides a suitable mechanism for synchronizing neuronal activities at these various levels. In part 3, we shall take up the question of how to generate higher-order functions and global mappings from such mechanisms. At this point, it may be useful briefly to consider in a general fashion how enhancement of the capabilities of neuronal group selection during evolution increases the likelihood of adaptive behavior and learning. The connection of these adaptive capabilities to the evolutionary emergence of actual information processing is discussed at the end of chapter 11.

THE ADAPTIVE SIGNIFICANCE OF NEURONAL GROUP SELECTION

Neuronal group selection comprises a series of somatic events that are historical and unique in each organism. With the exception of certain epigenetic events in development, individual selective events cannot have been *directly* influenced by evolution, inasmuch as they are all based on somatic generation of diversity. Such diversity arises evolutionarily because of the necessity in somatic time for categorization by degenerate networks under environmentally fluctuating conditions. This focuses attention on the question of the adaptive value of the mechanisms of group selection. The answer to this question is important to an understanding both of evolutionary events that lead to the emergence of primary repertoires and of epigenetic mechanisms of somatic selection.

Because no instruction takes place at the level of neurons (the doctrine of neuronal ignorance) and because group selection leading to perceptual categorization is *required* for versatile learning (see chapter 11), it is clear that during evolution there would be a selective advantage in increasing the size and variance of certain neuronal repertoires while decreasing these parameters in others, thereby altering their sensitivity to synaptic modification rules. New kinds of learning and the increased versatility of learning provided by such changing arrangements can affect perception and allow certain phenotypes with particular sets of repertoires to be selected by evolution. As we shall see in chapters 4 and 6, evolutionary selection for particular repertoires and maps is largely upon developmental variants created by epigenetic alterations that result from the altered action of regulatory genes.

The main pattern of neural circuits eventually becomes fixed in an individual, and the versatility of learning must then depend upon secondary repertoires and synaptic modification. Presumably, this mechanism evolved because of temporal constraints on cellular systems—only by differential amplification rather than by differential reproduction can a neurally based somatic selective system respond to motion quickly enough to result in learning behavior that leads to survival.

It is at this point that (everything else being equal) an organism with particularly rich primary repertoires and with powerful transmitter logic (see chapter 7) can have a greater opportunity to adapt quickly to local threat and to local needs in a rapidly changing econiche. The grand loop of evolution (shown in figure 11.1)—natural selection → somatic selection based on ontogeny → adaptive behavior → further natural selection within a species—has as a critical component the evolution of somatic selective systems for perceptual categorization that are coupled to adaptive behavior and more efficient learning. Given the evolution of such systems, the stage is set for the development of social transmission (Boyd and Richerson 1985) in certain species and for further evolutionary achievements related to higher brain functions.

Because it is based on selection from diversity, the neuronal group selection theory meets the classic requirements of population thinking. It relates individual variance in neural structure to behavior and to evolution. By proceeding through perceptual categorization to learning (chapter 11), it shows how the fixation of information processing within a species can occur by mechanisms of categorization that are nonetheless remorselessly bottom-up within each individual. As we shall see later, information processing descriptions can be useful in analyzing certain aspects of learning, but when applied to brain structure and to the evolution of mechanisms of perceptual categorization, they are inexorably trapped by circular reasoning. In contrast, the theory of neuronal group selection can account for the transition from the stochastic somatic selection processes occurring in individuals, in which information cannot be sensibly defined, to descriptions in which information can be defined and stabilized by communicated learning and by memory within multiple individual nervous systems in a species.

PART TWO

EPIGENETIC

MECHANISMS

4

Developmental Bases
of Diversity:
The Primary Repertoire

INTRODUCTION

A central feature of the theory of neuronal group selection is that the mechanisms leading to the formation of both the primary and the secondary repertoires are epigenetic: while bounded by genetic constraints, events occurring at both developmental and experiential stages of selection lead to increases with time in both heterogeneity and spatial diversity of cells and cellular structures. Such events depend upon the prior occurrence of other events in time courses that are long compared with those of intracellular events, and the cells involved exhibit interactive and cooperative spatial orderings that could not have been stored directly in the genetic code.

The main task of this chapter is to provide evidence supporting the first of the major claims of the theory of neuronal group selection: that the epigenetic molecular mechanisms by which neurons and glia interact in development provide an inevitable source of anatomical variation and thus of individual diversity in primary repertoires.

How does diversity in the anatomy of individual nervous systems arise across a pattern of constancy characteristic of a species? This problem, which focuses attention on the molecular origin of neuronal pattern, is the most exquisitely complex of all problems of morphogenesis. Although it is likely to be based in part on mechanisms specialized for the nervous system only, it also shares fundamental cell biological properties and mechanisms with other histogenetic systems. It is therefore useful to set neural development in a large frame in preparation for a reexamination of the picture of neurogenesis drawn by more classical studies (Spemann 1924, 1938; Ramón y Cajal 1929; Harrison 1935; Weiss 1939, 1955; Sperry 1965; Hamburger 1980).

Recent studies suggest a central role for adhesion molecules in mediating the developmental mechanisms producing variation in the primary repertoire. The control of expression of these molecules also bears upon evolutionary events that lead to constancy of neural patterns. We will first consider some properties of these molecules as well as their distribution in the nervous system. We will then propose a general hypothesis relating the developmental genetic and mechanochemical bases of neural pattern to the fundamental problem of morphologic evolution. This proposal, called the regulator hypothesis, will be framed here in terms of morphogenesis and pattern formation; its evolutionary implications for the nervous system will be discussed in chapter 6. To realize our aims will require an excursion into molecular and cell biology. The reward for taking this excursion will be the provision of a cogent mechanism for the origin of connectional diversity in the nervous system.

CAMs and Cell Surface Modulation in Morphogenesis

According to the theory, although the genome itself cannot contain specific information about the exact position of the participating cells in time and space, both neural and nonneural morphogenesis are under genetic control. To help resolve the apparent paradox, we may pose the basic problem of morphogenesis in the form of two general questions:

1. How does a one-dimensional genetic code specify a three-dimensional animal?

2. How is the answer to this question consistent with the possibility of relatively rapid morphological change in relatively short periods of evolutionary time?

The answers to both questions must be cast largely in terms of developmental genetic and epigenetic events (Raff and Kaufman 1983). Such answers require the identification of gene products whose expression could mechanochemically regulate the primary processes of development that act as driving forces such as mitosis and form-producing movements (figure 4.1), creating conditions for a succession of signals regulating further gene expression. Recent studies on the molecular mechanisms of cell adhesion in animals undergoing regulative develop-

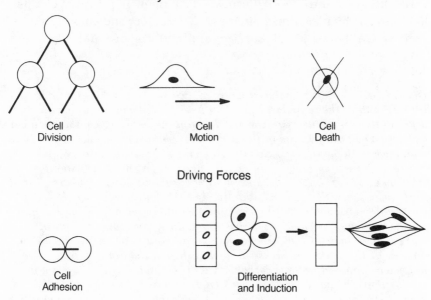

Primary Process of Development

Cell
Division

Cell
Motion

Cell
Death

Driving Forces

Cell
Adhesion

Differentiation
and Induction

Regulatory Processes

Figure 4.1
Cartoons of primary processes. The "driving force" processes—cell division, cell motion, and cell death—are regulated by adhesion and differentiation events. The key event is milieu-dependent differentiation or embryonic induction, which occurs not between single cells but between different cell collectives.

ment have led to the identification of molecules that appear to be appropriate candidates for this role. These are the so-called cell adhesion molecules (CAMs) and substrate adhesion molecules (SAMs) (for reviews, see Edelman 1983, 1985b, 1985d, 1985e, 1985f, 1986a; Damsky et al. 1984; Edelman and Thiery 1985; Obrink 1986). A discussion here of their properties and of their modulation at the cell surface should help clarify how they affect neural patterns.

The key idea may be summarized roughly as follows. These molecules link cells into collectives whose borders are defined by CAMs of different specificity. The binding properties of cells linked by the CAMs are dynamically controlled by the cells themselves as a result of signals exchanged between collectives. Cell binding in turn regulates cell motion and further signaling, and thus the ensuing forms. Control of the expression of CAM genes by the specific biochemistry affecting CAM regulatory genes at particular morphologic sites assures constancy of form in a species. But because the main function of CAMs is to regulate dynamic cellular processes and not to specify cell addresses exactly, variability is also introduced during development. To provide a compelling case for this idea, I shall discuss CAM structure and binding, alterations of CAMs at the cell surface, and patterns of CAM expression

Figure 4.2

Diagram of the linear chain structure of two primary CAMs (N-CAM and L-CAM) and of the secondary Ng-CAM. N-CAM is shown as two chains that differ in the size of their cytoplasmic domains. As indicated by the open bar at the COOH terminus, the ld (large domain) polypeptide contains 261 more amino acid residues in this region than does the sd (small domain) polypeptide. The ld chain is seen only in the central nervous system at very specific sites (Murray et al. 1986b). A third and smallest (ssd) polypeptide, which is linked to the membrane by a phosphatidylinositol intermediate, is not shown. The thick vertical bar *indicates the membrane-spanning region. Below the chains are the fragments Fr1 and Fr2 derived by limited proteolysis. As indicated by* vertical lines, *most of the carbohydrate is covalently attached in the middle domain at three sites and it is sulfated, although the exact sulfation site is unknown. Attached to these carbohydrates is polysialic acid. There are phosphorylation (P) sites as well in the COOH terminal domains. The* diagonal staircases *refer to covalent attachment of palmitate. L-CAM yields one major proteolytic fragment (Ft1), and has four attachment sites for carbohydrate* (vertical lines) *but lacks polysialic acid. It is also phosphorylated in the COOH terminal region. Ng-CAM is shown as a major 200-kD chain. There are two components (135 and 80 kD) that are probably derived from a posttranslationally cleaved precursor. Each is related to the major 200-kD chain (which may be this precursor), and the smaller is arranged as shown on the basis of a known phosphorylation site.*

during development. This should provide the background for a discussion of data indicating that alteration of CAM binding alters morphology and that alteration of morphology alters CAM expression.

So far, three CAMs of different specificity and structure have been isolated and extensively characterized (figure 4.2); several more have been identified but have not been chemically defined. The calcium-dependent L-CAM (liver cell adhesion molecule; Cunningham et al.

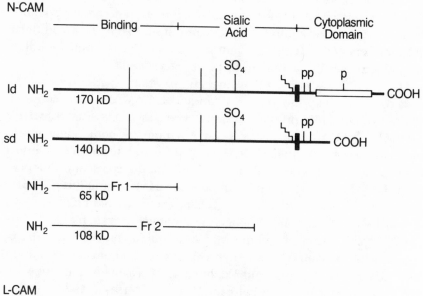

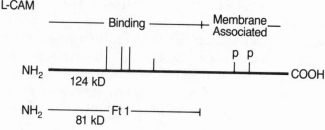

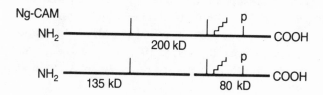

1984) and calcium-independent N-CAM (neural cell adhesion molecule; Edelman 1983) are called primary CAMs and appear early in embryogenesis upon derivatives of all germ layers. Ng-CAM (neuron-glia CAM) is a secondary CAM that is not seen in early embryogenesis and that appears only on neuroectodermal derivatives, specifically on postmitotic neurons (Grumet and Edelman 1984; Grumet et al. 1984). A fourth adhesion molecule, cytotactin (Grumet et al. 1985; Crossin et al. 1986), appears on glial cells somewhat later in development and is involved in the movement of neurons on glia; it appears to be an extracellular matrix protein or SAM (substrate adhesion molecule) that is also found in a variety of extraneural sites (Crossin et al. 1986). Two additional calcium-dependent CAMs (N and P cadherin) have been identified (Hatta et al. 1985) but remain to be characterized.

All of the well-studied CAMs are glycoproteins synthesized by the cells on which they function. N-CAM and L-CAM are intrinsic membrane proteins; this property has not been as firmly established for Ng-CAM. N-CAM and probably L-CAM bind by homophilic mechanisms (figure 4.3, A), that is, CAM on one cell binds to another identical CAM on an apposing cell. While N-CAM binding is calcium independent, L-CAM depends on this ion both for its structural integrity and its binding; these two primary CAMs show no binding or cross-specificity for each other. Although this is not yet proven, the secondary Ng-CAM on neurons may bind by a heterophilic mechanism, that is, Ng-CAM on a neuron to another CAM or to a chemically different receptor on glia (Grumet and Edelman 1984; Grumet et al. 1984).

A fundamental notion (Edelman, 1976, 1983, 1984a, 1984b) is that the cell controls its own binding dynamically and that CAMs act to regulate this binding via a series of cell surface modulation mechanisms, including changes in the prevalence of CAMs at the cell surface, in their cellular position or polarity, and in their chemical structure as it affects binding (figure 4.3, B). All of these mechanisms have been shown to occur for one CAM or another at different developmental times (Edelman 1984a).

The known case of chemical modulation is related to the presence (Hoffman et al. 1982; Rothbard et al. 1982) on N-CAM of α-2-8-linked polysialic acid at three sites present in the middle domain of the molecule. In the electrophoretically microheterogeneous embryonic (E) form of N-CAM, there are 30 grams per 100 grams of polypeptide, and in the discrete adult (A) forms this is reduced to 10 grams per 100 grams polypeptide; during development, E forms are replaced by A forms at different rates in different parts of the brain. *In vitro* studies suggest that N-CAM turns over at the cell surface and that the E form is replaced by newly synthesized A forms containing less polysialic acid. Although the carbohydrate is not directly involved in binding, kinetic analyses (Hoffman and Edelman 1983) of the binding of membrane vesicles containing N-CAM suggest that E-to-A conversion during development can result in a fourfold increase in binding rates. It seems

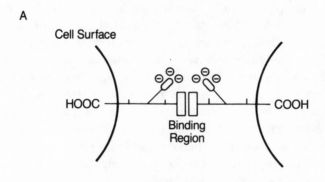

Figure 4.3
CAM binding mode and cell surface modulation. A: N-CAM binding is homophilic, i.e., to the binding domain of N-CAM present on an apposing cell. B: Schematic representation of some forms of local cell surface modulation. The various elements represent a specific glycoprotein (e.g., N-CAM) on the cell surface. The upper sequence shows modulation by alteration of both the prevalence of a particular molecule and its distribution on the cell surface. The lower sequence shows modulation by chemical modification resulting in the appearance of new or related forms (triangles) of the molecule with altered activities. Local modulation is distinct from global modulation, which refers to alterations in the whole membrane that affect a variety of different receptors independent of their specificity.

likely that the negatively charged polysialic acid either modulates the conformation of the neighboring CAM binding region or directly competes with homophilic binding (figure 4.3) from cell to cell by charge repulsion (Edelman 1983). Inasmuch as E-to-A conversion involves regulation of enzymes specified by genes other than the N-CAM gene, and because this change involves turnover at the cell membrane, its influence on cell binding is perforce an epigenetic one.

Even more striking than the effects of E-to-A conversion is the dependency of homophilic binding on changes in N-CAM prevalence or surface density: a twofold increase in E forms at the membrane leads to a more than thirtyfold increase in binding rates (Hoffman and Edelman 1983). This is likely to result from an increase in valence by *cis* association at the cell surface of two or more CAM polypeptides. Similar rate studies across a variety of vertebrate species (Hoffman et al. 1984) suggest that the N-CAM binding mechanism has been conserved during evolution. The nonlinear binding effects resulting from chemical and prevalence modulation make possible an efficient local switching of cellular binding states, a mechanism compatible with the idea that CAMs act as sensitive dynamic regulators of cell aggregation and cell motion.

Recent evidence indicates that another form of modulation of N-CAM may also occur by utilizing alternatively spliced RNAs specified by a single gene. The modulation hypothesis puts an emphasis on the regulation of a small number of genes for CAM expression, not on the existence of large gene families specifying variant versions of each of these proteins. Analysis of the cDNA clones of the known CAMs so far is in accord with this idea. The data (Murray et al. 1984) suggest that the single gene for N-CAM is located in the mouse on chromosome 9 (D'Eustachio et al. 1985) and on human chromosome 11 (Nguyen et al. 1986). There are at most three genes (and possibly fewer) for L-CAM (Gallin et al. 1985). Given the evidence that there is only one gene coding for N-CAM, it is likely that the different polypeptide forms of N-CAM derive from alternative RNA splicing events. Information on the base sequence indicates that the two larger polypeptide forms of N-CAM (ld and sd chains) differ in the size of their cytoplasmic domains but are otherwise similar or identical (Hemperly et al. 1986b); more recent data (Hemperly et al. 1986a) indicate that a third chain (the ssd or small surface domain polypeptide) also arises by RNA splicing. This ssd chain lacks cytoplasmic domains and is linked to the cell surface by phosphatidylinositol intermediates.

In view of the fact that the large domain (ld) polypeptide (see figure 4.2) is nervous system specific (Murray et al. 1986b) and is expressed in neural locations different from those of the small domain (sd) polypeptide, the intriguing possibility emerges that a particular form of cell surface modulation can be effected in the nervous system by signals leading to different RNA splicing events that in turn alter the amounts of ld and sd chains on cells in particular neural locations. Recent studies (Murray et al. 1986a, 1986b) have strongly supported such an interpretation: although the binding properties of neurons with different N-CAM chains have not been tested, one would expect these properties to be influenced by the different cytoplasmic interactions of the different domains in the two types of polypeptide chain, which otherwise have identical binding specificities. Such interactions, particularly with the cytoskeleton, could, for example, alter the clustering or valence states of the chains at the cell surface with consequential changes in cell binding or movement.

It appears that initial control of CAM expression rests in early steps of regulation of the respective structural genes, in splicing events, and possibly in control of the rate of mRNA turnover. Recently, a perturbation system using temperature-sensitive Rous sarcoma virus mutants to transform rat cerebellar cell lines (Greenberg et al. 1984) has been used to analyze the level of the control of expression of N-CAM. The results (R. Brackenbury and G. M. Edelman, unpublished observations) are consistent with the notion that most of the control occurs at the transcriptional level.

All of the facts on cell surface modulation of CAMs are summarized in table 4.1 as well as in a diagram (figure 4.3, B) embodying the idea of local cell surface modulation (Edelman 1976, 1983, 1984a). The basic notion is that, during development, CAMs can undergo changes in the number of molecules per cell, in types of cytoplasmic domains or membrane attachment sites, in distribution on parts of the cell, or alternatively, they can undergo posttranslational chemical changes in structure; each of these modulations by the cell can lead to changes in binding behavior. Modulation of CAM binding in response to local signals could alter the dynamics and interactions of those primary processes of development that act as driving forces, with resultant changes in form. Such modulation mechanisms are compatible with theories of morphogenesis based on epigenetic events (Edelman 1984a, 1984b, 1985b) rather than on the existence of cell-specific positional markers that have been suggested as the basis for neural specificity (Sperry 1963,

1965; see Easter et al. 1985). It is important to stress, however, that the occurrence of modulation does not exclude the existence of a variety of CAM binding specificities necessary for the formation of borders in adjoining cell collectives.

Table 4.1

CAM Modulation Mechanisms

Mechanism	Effect	Examples	Reference
Prevalence (Change in synthesis or expression on cell surface)	Increase or decrease in binding rate	N-CAM homophilic binding twofold increase → thirtyfold rate increase	Edelman et al. 1983 Hoffman and Edelman 1983
Differential prevalence (Change in relative expression of CAMs of different specificity on same cell)	Border formation for cell collectives	CAM expression rules N-CAM/Ng-CAM	Chuong and Edelman 1985a, 1985b Daniloff et al. 1986a
Cytoplasmic domain switch (Alteration in size and structure of cytoplasmic domain by RNA splicing)	Selective expression of ld or sd polypeptides; altered cytoskeletal interaction (?)	Selective expression of N-CAM ld chain in cerebellar layers	Murray et al. 1986b
Polarity (Change in location on selected cell regions)	Localization of binding on cell	Motor end plate (N-CAM) neurite extension and leading edge migrating cells (Ng-CAM) exocrine pancreatic cells	Rieger et al. 1985 Daniloff et al. 1986a
Chemical (Posttranslational change in structure)	Altered binding rates; abrogation of binding (?)	E-to-A conversion of N-CAM: loss of 2/3 polysialic acid → fourfold increase in binding	Chuong and Edelman 1984; Hoffman et al. 1982

CAM EXPRESSION SEQUENCES IN EMBRYOGENESIS AND NEUROGENESIS

If cell surface modulation of CAMs helps govern morphogenesis, one would expect to see defined patterns of CAM expression during development. Although extensive data on CAM gene transcription at different embryonic sites as a function of time are not yet available, correlations of the time and place of cell surface expression of the CAMs with sites of embryonic induction and with key events of histogenesis have been obtained by means of immunocytochemistry. I shall first describe the major expression sequence for the whole embryo (see figure 4.4) and then consider some more detailed examples of histogenetic sequences occurring in the nervous system.

The appearance of CAMs has not been documented in the chick at

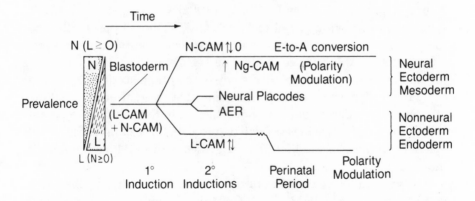

Figure 4.4

Major CAM expression sequence. Schematic diagram showing the temporal sequence of expression of some important CAMs during chick embryogenesis. Vertical wedges at the left refer roughly to relative amounts of each CAM in the different parts of the embryo—for example, the line referring to blastoderm has both N-CAM and L-CAM but that referring to neuroectoderm has relatively large amounts of N-CAM but little or no L-CAM. After a primary induction, N-CAM and L-CAM diverge in cellular distribution and are then modulated in prevalence within various regions of secondary induction (↑ ↓) or actually decrease greatly (O) when mesenchyme appears or cell migration occurs. Note that placodes which have both CAMs echo the events seen for neural induction. Just before the appearance of glia, a secondary CAM (Ng-CAM) emerges. In the perinatal period, a series of epigenetic modulations occurs: E-to-A conversion for N-CAM and polar redistribution for L-CAM.

very early times, but L-CAM appears at the two-cell stage in the mouse (Shirayoshi et al. 1983) and N-CAM appears at later times, preceding neural induction. Both N-CAM and L-CAM are present at low levels on the chick blastoderm before gastrulation. As gastrulation occurs in the chick and cells ingress through the primitive streak, the amount of each of the CAMs detectable on the migrating cells decreases (Thiery et al. 1982; Edelman et al. 1983; Edelman 1984a; Crossin et al. 1985), presumably reflecting the fact that they have been down-regulated or masked. This phenomenon is clearly seen in mesoblast cells that will ultimately give rise to the mesoderm.

Following gastrulation and coincident with neural induction, there is a marked change in the distribution of the two primary CAMs. An increase in immunofluorescent N-CAM staining appears in the region of the neural plate and groove as L-CAM staining disappears. In conjugate fashion, L-CAM staining is enhanced in the surrounding somatic ectoderm as N-CAM staining slowly diminishes (figures 4.4 and 4.5). Neural crest cell migration (Le Douarin 1982) is accompanied by down-regulation or masking of cell surface N-CAM (Thiery et al. 1982). The so-called placodes that will give rise to specialized neural structures first express both CAMs but eventually lose L-CAM in specific differentiating neural regions (for a detailed study of the otic placode, see Crossin et al. 1987; Richardson et al. 1987). Somewhat later, after neurulation, all sites of secondary induction show changes in the cell surface prevalence of N-CAM or L-CAM or both (figure 4.4). For example, the apical ectodermal ridge of the limb bud expresses both CAMs as the limb is induced.

When neural crest cells migrate as an ectomesenchyme, they lack detectable surface N-CAM. The N-CAM then reappears or is unmasked at sites where these cells form ganglia (Thiery et al. 1982). Similarly, migrating secondary mesenchymal cells—for example, those that are destined to induce feather placodes—lose N-CAM but regain it in the vicinity of the L-CAM-positive ectoderm as dermal condensations are formed (Chuong and Edelman 1985a, 1985b).

At certain times, one cell can express two CAMs, as is seen for the primary CAMs in chick blastoderm and for Ng-CAM and N-CAM on neurons. In feather formation and in the induction of pharyngeal and gut appendages, cells from ectoderm or endoderm can also express both L-CAM and N-CAM simultaneously; this is also true of kidney mesoderm (Crossin et al. 1985). In general, the CAM expressions are dynamic and change so that one or the other CAM usually disappears during maturation of such tissues to the adult state.

We can now relate this new molecular embryological information in greater detail to the development of pattern and variation in the nervous system. Within the overall expression sequence previously described, a set of microsequences (table 4.2) can be discerned in the nervous system, particularly as histogenetic events characterized by cellular differentiation occur. Following neural induction and neurulation (figure 4.5), N-CAM is found distributed throughout the nervous system. At E 3.5 in the chick, the secondary Ng-CAM (Grumet et al. 1984) appears on neurons already displaying N-CAM (Thiery et al. 1985; Daniloff et al. 1986a). Although this molecule, which binds neurons to neurons and neurons to glia in *in vitro* assays, is seen only on postmitotic neurons, it can be present on the same neuronal surfaces as N-CAM (Grumet et al. 1984). In the CNS, Ng-CAM is found mainly on extending neurites and is seen only faintly or not at all on cell bodies. This polarity modulation (table 4.1) is also seen on cells known to be undergoing migration along guide glia, as observed in the cerebellum or spinal cord. A contrasting picture is seen in the peripheral nervous system: after its appearance, Ng-CAM is found at all times on neurites and cell bodies (Thiery et al. 1985; Daniloff et al. 1986a).

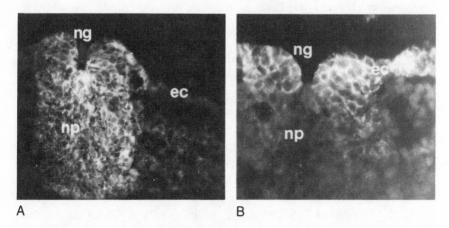

A   B

Figure 4.5
Change in the distribution of N-CAM and L-CAM during formation of the neural plate (neural induction) and groove (neurulation). A: Cross section of the neural plate (np) as the neural groove (ng) forms. N-CAM is present in large amounts in the chordamesoderm and neural ectoderm and in small amounts in ectoderm (ec) and adjoining mesoderm. B: L-CAM staining disappears from the neural ectoderm in the neural groove and becomes restricted to the nonneural ectoderm (ec). Just before these events, N-CAM and L-CAM were present in all regions of the blastoderm that give rise to these structures.

These observations indicate that a consistent microsequence of appearances of Ng-CAM accompanies known developmental sequences of neurite extension and cell migration (Thiery et al. 1985; Daniloff et al. 1986a). The order of appearance shown in table 4.2 is reproducible from animal to animal. This orderly sequence suggests that local signals related to cellular maturation and possibly to growth factors produced by glial precursors are responsible for both the appearance and the remarkable prevalence modulation of Ng-CAM at the cell surface. Indeed, recent studies (Friedlander et al. 1986) have shown that Ng-CAM, which mediates neurite fasciculation as well as neuron-glia interaction, is present in the neural cell line PC12 and that nerve growth factor (NGF) enhances its expression in such cells. This is consistent with the demonstration in the same study that Ng-CAM is identical to the so-called NILE glycoprotein, previously known to be inducible by NGF.

Over the considerable period of developmental time that these Ng-CAM appearances occur, alterations of a lesser degree and with longer time courses can be seen in the prevalence of N-CAM on different cell surfaces. Moreover, the ld chain is seen to appear only at particular sites, such as the molecular layer of the developing cerebellum (Murray et al. 1986b). At a later time in the microsequence (table 4.2), when many neural tracts have been established and myelination is about to begin, Ng-CAM as detected by immunohistochemical methods is down-regulated at the cell surface in those CNS tracts that are to become white matter. No such down-regulation is seen in the peripheral nervous system. At roughly similar times, N-CAM undergoes E-to-A conversion (Chuong and Edelman 1984; Daniloff et al. 1986a), a posttranslational chemical modulation that we have already indicated leads to increases in binding rates *in vitro* and that presumably affects CAM function similarly *in vivo*.

The net result of the various types of cell surface modulation (table 4.1) occurring developmentally for the two well-studied neuronal CAMs is a striking change in their relative distributions in most areas of the CNS (table 4.2). In contrast, in areas of the CNS that are still capable of forming new connections into adult life (such as the olfactory bulb) as well as in the peripheral nervous system, the relative distribution of the two CAMs does not change. A set of maps has been constructed (Daniloff et al. 1986a) that display the changes and constancies for many brain areas in the chick.

Recent evidence suggests that extracellular matrix proteins (or substrate adhesion molecules, SAMs) can also be expressed at particular times on particular tissues and thus alter morphology by means of

Table 4.2

Distributions of Primary and Secondary CAMs with Age during Neural Morphogenesis

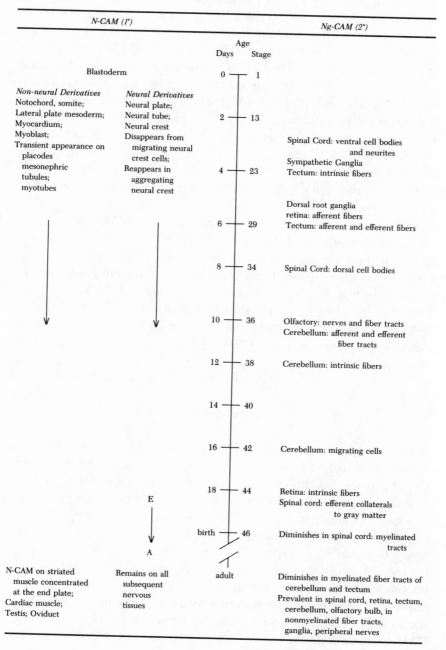

N-CAM (1°)			Ng-CAM (2°)

Age
Days   Stage

Blastoderm — 0 — 1

Non-neural Derivatives
Notochord, somite;
Lateral plate mesoderm;
Myocardium;
Myoblast;
Transient appearance on
  placodes
  mesonephric
  tubules;
  myotubes

Neural Derivatives
Neural plate;
Neural tube;
Neural crest
Disappears from
  migrating neural
  crest cells;
Reappears in
  aggregating
  neural crest

2 — 13

4 — 23   Spinal Cord: ventral cell bodies
                          and neurites
          Sympathetic Ganglia
          Tectum: intrinsic fibers

          Dorsal root ganglia
          retina: afferent fibers
6 — 29   Tectum: afferent and efferent fibers

8 — 34   Spinal Cord: dorsal cell bodies

10 — 36   Olfactory: nerves and fiber tracts
          Cerebellum: afferent and efferent
                          fiber tracts

12 — 38   Cerebellum: intrinsic fibers

14 — 40

16 — 42   Cerebellum: migrating cells

18 — 44   Retina: intrinsic fibers
          Spinal cord: efferent collaterals
                          to gray matter

E

birth — 46   Diminishes in spinal cord: myelinated
                          tracts
A

adult   Diminishes in myelinated fiber tracts of
          cerebellum and tectum
N-CAM on striated   Remains on all   Prevalent in spinal cord, retina, tectum,
  muscle concentrated   subsequent   cerebellum, olfactory bulb, in
  at the end plate;   nervous   nonmyelinated fiber tracts,
Cardiac muscle;   tissues   ganglia, peripheral nerves
Testis; Oviduct

modulation mechanisms. For example, the glycoprotein cytotactin appears in basal laminae of the early embryo, in smooth muscle, and in the CNS (Grumet et al. 1985; Crossin et al. 1986). This molecule, which is clearly an extrinsic protein and thus differs from CAMs, is expressed at about nine days on glia in chick brain. Cytotactin mediates neuron-glia adhesion *in vitro*, and antibodies to the molecule block or delay migration of external granule cells on Bergmann glia in cerebellar tissue slices (Chuong et al. 1987). This matrix protein may thus be a SAM involved in neuronal migration on radial glia *in vivo*. As we shall discuss, Ng-CAM does not bind to this glial protein, but it also seems to play a necessary (and possibly a selective) role in this migration of external granule cells on cerebellar radial glia. The combined results are consistent with the proposal that regulation of the expression of surface molecules (such as CAMs and SAMs) that mediate adhesion and promote or control migration is a key factor in determining constancy and variation in neural patterning.

The data on microsequences in the nervous system show that surface modulation events and CAM and SAM expressions can occur in relatively small cell populations in a defined order. This conclusion is reinforced by additional results obtained on microsequences of primary CAM expression in feather histogenesis (Chuong and Edelman, 1985a, 1985b; see also figure 4.7) and on nerve-muscle interactions mediated by N-CAM (Rieger et al. 1985; see also figure 4.6), which also suggest that the successive signals for CAM expression are sharply localized in time and space.

CAUSAL SIGNIFICANCE OF CAM FUNCTION

While expression sequences reveal correlations among times of CAM appearances, surface modulations, and key morphogenetic events, they do not provide any direct indication of the causal role of the CAMs in neural morphogenesis. Considered *a priori*, CAM expression could be a cause or an effect; indeed, if CAM expression occurs in cycles and in parallel with other processes, it could be both cause and effect. By means of perturbation experiments and by identifying and characterizing the regulators of CAM genes, one may provide the bases to search for the appropriate initiating signals and thus analyze the causal sequences of cellular controls affecting neural pattern. In the remaining sections of this chapter, I will summarize some relevant observations on CAM perturbation that bear on the causal roles of CAMs, and outline a theoretical model of CAM regulation that can be tested in systems of embryonic induction. This model, embodied in the regulator hypothesis, is a major component of the theory of neuronal group selection inasmuch as it provides a basis for constancy and variability of pattern.

Experiments on perturbation of CAM function or alterations of CAM expression have been carried out in a number of systems (Edelman 1983, 1984a, 1985b). Addition of anti-L-CAM antibodies leads to failure of histotypic aggregate formation by liver cells (Bertolotti et al. 1980). Anti-Ng-CAM antibodies disrupt neural fasciculation *in vitro* (Hoffman et al. 1986), and anti-N-CAM greatly disrupts layer formation in the chick retina during organ culture (Buskirk et al. 1980). Implanted anti-N-CAM antibodies disrupt retinotectal map formation *in vitro* in the frog (Fraser et al. 1984). When applied to cerebellar tissue slices *in vivo*, anti-Ng-CAM antibodies inhibit the normal movement of external granule cells along radial glia to the internal granule cell layer (Hoffman et al. 1986); these antibodies appear to prevent entry of cells into the molecular layer. In kinetic analyses, it has been shown that anticytotactin (and to some degree anti-Ng-CAM) slow migration of granule cells that are already in the molecular layer (Chuong et al. 1987). These observations indicate that both CAM and SAM expression by neurons and glia, respectively, play a role in form-shaping movements. When neural cells, including cerebellar cell lines, were transformed by a temperature-sensitive mutant of Rous sarcoma virus (Greenberg et al. 1984), they retained normal morphology, adult N-CAM levels, and normal aggregation behavior at the nonpermissive temperature. At the permissive temperature, however, the cells transformed and, within hours, down-regulated their surface N-CAM and became more mobile. A pattern of aggregation similar to that of cells in the original culture could be obtained by shifting cells from the nonpermissive to the permissive temperature.

All of these studies show that disruption of CAM and SAM function can disrupt morphology. If the notion that modulation underlies tissue pattern is correct, however, it also follows that regulation of the levels and sites of CAM *expression* must in turn depend upon morphology, that is, upon tissue integrity and collective cell interactions involving mutual signaling. In accord with this idea, it has been found that perturbation of normal cell-cell interactions and connectivity of tissues *in vivo* results in alteration of CAM expression and distribution. For example, N-CAM is present at the end plate of striated muscles (Rieger et al. 1985) but is absent from the rest of the surface of the myofibril. After the sciatic nerve is cut, the N-CAM diminishes in amount at the end

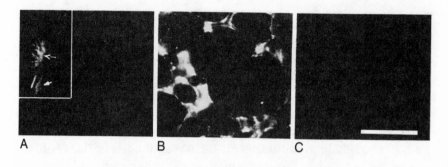

A   B   C

Figure 4.6

N-CAM at the motor end plate and changes in prevalence in muscle after denervation (Rieger et al. 1985; Daniloff et al. 1986b). Cross sections of chick gastrocnemius muscles stained with polyclonal anti-N-CAM (A–C) showed that the surfaces of muscle fibers were faintly labeled in normal chicken muscles (A). The inset shows a whole-mount preparation of normal adult chicken muscle fibers (×7). The muscle surface was faintly labeled with anti-N-CAM; a motor end plate (open arrow) and several mononucleated cells that are probably satellite cells (filled arrow) were intensely labeled. Ten days after the sciatic nerve was cut, a dramatic increase occurred in the intensity of N-CAM (B); a normal pattern was restored after 150 days (C). Calibration bar = 50 μm. (From Daniloff et al. 1986b.)

Figure 4.7

Causal roles of CAMs in modifying embryonic induction and border formation. A and B: Perturbation of pattern of feather induction in N-CAM linked mesoderm by anti-L-CAM acting on L-CAM linked ectoderm. Whole mounts of chick skin explants in culture were maintained, fixed, stained, and viewed with transmitted illumination. As induction of feather germs takes place, N-CAM positive dermal condensations induce L-CAM positive ectoderm. A: Seven-day embryo skin cultured for three days with 1 mg/ml nonimmune rabbit Fab'. B: Seven-day embryo skin cultured for three days with medium containing anti-L-CAM Fab', 1 mg/ml. C: Tracing of the pattern of condensations in panel A. D: Tracing of the pattern of condensations in panel B. Note the change of pattern from a sixfold arrangement of circular condensates to stripes following the perturbation; this shows a causal role for CAMs in response to induction. E and F: Transverse sections of later-developing feather follicles from a newly hatched chick wing, showing alternating sequence of expression of L-CAM (E) and N-CAM (F) during adult feather histogenesis. The same sections were doubly stained with fluorescent antibodies to each CAM. Formation of the barb ridges (br) starts from the dorsal side (the side with the rachis) and progresses bilaterally toward the ventral side, making a dorsoventral maturation gradient. Positions of the last-formed ridges are marked by curved arrows. Anti-L-CAM (E) stains all of the cells of the barb ridge epithelium. Bright anti-N-CAM staining starts to appear (F) in the valleys between pairs of the barb ridges. N-CAM appearance starts about eight ridges away from the last formed ridge and increases in staining intensity and distribution dorsally until it reaches the rachis (rc). Ultimately, all L-CAM bearing cellular areas will become keratinized, and all N-CAM bearing cellular areas will die.

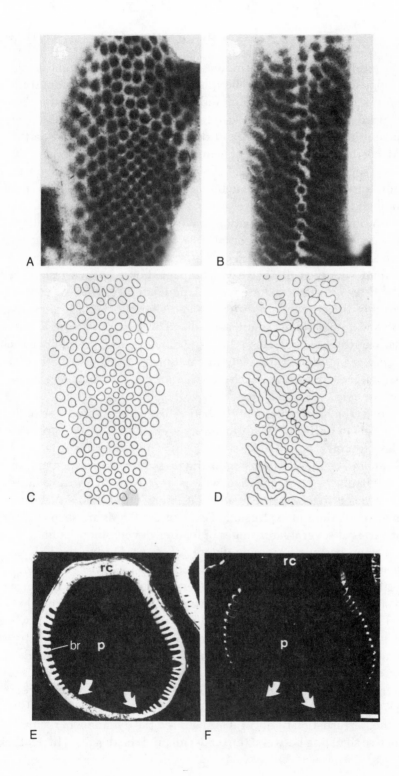

plate, anti-N-CAM staining is increased in the cytoplasm, and the molecule appears diffusely at the cell surface (figure 4.6). More recent studies of peripheral nerve generation and regeneration indicate that large changes also occur in Schwann cell expression of N-CAM, Ng-CAM, and cytotactin at the site of a cut and that alterations in N-CAM and Ng-CAM occur in the dorsal root ganglia and the ventral horn in the affected segment (Daniloff et al. 1986b). All of these findings show that perturbation of morphology can be accompanied by altered CAM modulation and expression.

Alterations in CAM modulations have also been seen in genetic defects affecting neural connectivity. In the mouse mutant *staggerer*, which shows connectional defects in the cerebellum between parallel fibers and Purkinje cells that are accompanied by extensive granule cell death, E-to-A conversion (or chemical modulation) of N-CAM is greatly delayed in the cerebellum (Edelman and Chuong 1982). N-CAM, Ng-CAM, and cytotactin are found colocalized in specific patterns at nodes of Ranvier (Rieger et al. 1986). In dysmyelinating mutants of mice such as *trembler* and motor end plate disease *(med)*, these distributions are grossly altered, reflecting the altered relationship between neurons and Schwann cells.

Perhaps the most striking perturbation experiments are those (figure 4.7) in which anti-L-CAM antibodies were used on tissue explants of six-day-old chick skin (Gallin et al. 1986). The epidermis is linked by L-CAM, and condensations of inducing mesodermal mesenchyme that are originally N-CAM negative will express N-CAM as they induce feather germs in a hexagonal pattern (Chuong and Edelman 1985a, b). Similar regulations of expression of each of the CAMs are seen at tissue boundaries at several later stages of feather development culminating in barb and barbule formation (figure 4.7, *A–F*). During the last stage of feather induction in culture, antibodies to L-CAM (which cannot directly affect the mesoderm) have been observed to lead to the formation of mesodermal stripes of condensations, breaking the normal hexagonal pattern (figure 4.7, *A–D*). When unperturbed cultures were grown for ten days, they developed regular filamentous structures resembling feather precursors. In contrast, the antibody-perturbed cultures developed plaques that resembled scales. Because L-CAM is absent from mesoderm and there is no evidence that L-CAM acts directly as a signal to the mesoderm, it has been concluded (Gallin et al. 1986) that the perturbation by anti-L-CAM altered the dynamics of reciprocal inductive signaling between the epidermis and the dermis. This feather perturbation experiment allows us to conclude that, in addition to their role in border formation, CAMs may play a causal role in embryonic induction.

The data we have reviewed indicate that perturbations in CAM binding can lead to altered morphogenesis and that altered morphogenesis can lead to changes in CAM expression and modulation patterns. These conclusions set the stage for understanding how such modulations regulate form and at the same time lead to individual variation.

THE REGULATOR HYPOTHESIS

The observations reviewed above suggest that, rather than acting just as markers for differentiated cells, CAMs act to link cells into collectives and to provide a series of borders between collectives. Such borders are formed between epithelia and mesenchyme and are possible sites for the exchange of signals related to embryonic induction and the regulative aspect of development. In regulative development (Weiss 1939; Slack 1983; Nieuwkoop et al. 1985), cells with different histories are brought together by morphogenetic movements, resulting in embryonic induction or milieu-dependent differentiation. Embryonic induction depends upon position (which in turn depends upon previous movement and history) and acts upon linked collectives of pluripotential cells whose competence changes with history and time of development (Jacobson 1966).

If CAM modulation is related to the formation of borders between these collectives, one should see not only a causal role in pattern as found in feather induction but also a regularity in the patterns of expression of CAMs across a variety of tissues. Just such a regularity has been found for two of the primary CAMs. Mesenchymal tissues undergoing conversion from epithelia and stable epithelia show two different rules or modes (Crossin et al. 1985) of modulation of CAM expression (table 4.3). At sites of induction, cells in collectives that have obeyed rule I ($N \rightarrow O \rightarrow N$), which is related to mesenchymal conversion, are found bordering cells in epithelial collectives that have obeyed rule II ($NL \rightarrow N$ or $NL \rightarrow L$).

These observations are related to a larger overall pattern. Mapping onto the chick blastoderm of CAM distributions at early times along with a classical map of tissue fates on the blastoderm shows a less

Table 4.3

Sites Showing Epigenetic Rules for CAM Expression during Chicken Embryogenesis

Rule I: Mesenchymal conversion[a]	Rule II: Epithelia[b]
Ectodermal	*Ectodermal*
$N \rightarrow 0 \rightarrow N$	$NL \rightarrow N$
Neural crest	Neural tube
—Peripheral nerve	Placode-derived ganglia
—Ganglia	$NL \rightarrow L$
	Somatic ectoderm
Mesodermal	Stratum germinativum
$N \rightarrow 0 \rightarrow N$	Apical epidermal ridge
Somite	Branchial ectoderm
—Skeletal muscle (end plate only)	$NL \rightarrow N \rightarrow *$
—Dermal papilla (feather)	Lens
Nephrotome	Marginal and axial plate
—Germinal epithelium of gonad	of feather
—Gonadal stroma	$NL \rightarrow L \rightarrow *$
Splanchnopleure	Stratum corneum
—Spleen stroma	Feather barbule, rachis
—Lamina propria of gut	
—Some mesenteries	*Mesodermal*
$N \rightarrow 0 \rightarrow N \rightarrow *$	$N \rightarrow NL \rightarrow L$
Somite	Wolffian duct
—Chondrocytes	Mesonephric tubules
Lateral plate	Müllerian duct
—Smooth muscle	
	Endodermal
	$NL \rightarrow L$
	Epithelium of:
	Trachea
	Gastrointestinal tract
	Hepatic duct
	Gall bladder
	Thyroid
	Pharyngeal derivatives
	NL
	Parabronchi (lung epithelia)

[a]Rule I shows cyclic changes in, or disappearance of, N-CAM. Some of these transitions occur with movement; 0 represents low levels of CAM. The original tissues are listed at the left margin. Tissues containing high levels of N-CAM are preceded by a dash. Where * appears, the CAM can be replaced by a differentiation product.
[b]Rule II shows replacement of one CAM by another or the disappearance of the CAM. * represents differentiation products (e.g., keratin, crystallin) with disappearance of the CAM.

detailed but congruent CAM map (figure 4.8) with overlapping N-CAM and L-CAM distributions at the tissue fate borders. The overlap of the two CAMs disappears in most tissues (Crossin et al. 1985) as the adult state is achieved and as mode II modulation occurs. Nonetheless, it is an important observation that the map of these primary CAMs clearly shows that the distribution of each CAM crosses different tissue boundaries; taken together with the expression sequence (figure 4.5) this implies that CAMs have a general role in setting up early borders during histogenesis prior to many cytodifferentiation events.

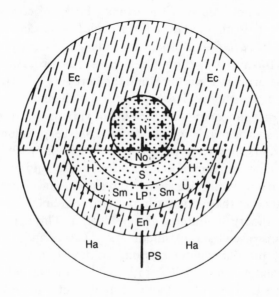

Figure 4.8

Composite CAM fate map in the chick. The distribution of N-CAM (stippled), L-CAM (slashed), and Ng-CAM (crossed) on tissues of five- to fourteen-day-old embryos is mapped back onto the tissue precursor cells in the blastoderm. Additional regions of transient N-CAM staining in the early embryo (five days) are shown (larger dots). In the early embryo, the borders of CAM expression overlap the borders of the germ layers; that is, derivatives of all three germ layers express both CAMs. At later times, overlap is more restricted: N-CAM disappears from somatic ectoderm and from endoderm, except for a population of cells in the chick lung. L-CAM is expressed on all ectodermal epithelia but remains restricted in the mesoderm to epithelial derivatives of the urogenital system. The vertical bar *represents the primitive streak* (PS); Ec, *intraembryonic and extraembryonic ectoderm;* En, *endoderm;* N, *nervous system;* No, *prechordal and chordamesoderm;* S, *somite;* Sm, *smooth muscle;* Ha, *hemangioblastic area.*

The observation of rules for expression of the primary CAMs in bordering collectives of cells at various sites of embryonic induction provides a striking generalization that is consistent with the conclusion that CAMs play a key role in forming morphogenetic borders and structures prior to histodifferentiation. The successive application of these rules in differentiating cell populations has been observed to accompany both morphological transformation and tissue transformation at many sites (Chuong and Edelman 1985a, 1985b; Crossin et al. 1985; see table 4.3 and figure 4.7 for an example).

We now reach a key conclusion. In view of the kinetic (and, at certain sites, the stochastic) nature of the driving forces of cell motion, cell division, and cell death, such *transformational* processes are obligately accompanied by *variational* processes leading to microscopic diversity of pattern. In the nervous system, these variational processes are critical in forming the primary repertoire, and they provide the origin of diversity required by the theory. This picture of the mechanochemical regulation of the morphogenetic movements of various tissue sheets, cells, and cell processes by regulation of CAM and SAM expression and signaling across borders allows a connection to be made between the primary processes of adhesion, movement, division, death, and induction.

A unifying framework relating such developmental changes to evolution is embodied in the regulator hypothesis (Edelman 1984c), an idea central to the theory of neuronal group selection. This hypothesis states that, by means of cell surface modulation, CAMs and SAMs are key regulators of morphogenetic motion, epithelial integrity, and mesenchymal condensation leading to border formation among various cell collectives exchanging inductive signals, not only in the nervous system but in all tissues. We will defer the evolutionary implications of the regulator hypothesis to chapter 6 and consider here mainly its implications for embryogenesis and neural histogenesis.

Inasmuch as CAM expression in most induced areas initially precedes the expression of most cytodifferentiation products, the hypothesis suggests that the genes affecting CAM and SAM expression (morphoregulatory genes) act independently of and prior to genes controlling tissue specific differentiation (historegulatory genes). This is consistent with the observation that the expression of CAM types in tissues (figure 4.8) overlaps the classical fate map borders that indicate the fates of different tissue types.

At the level of a given kind of cell in a collective and the descendants of that cell, CAM expression may be viewed as occurring in a cycle (figure 4.9). Traversals of the outer loop of this cycle lead to either the switching on or the switching off of one or another of the CAM genes. Following the modal rules (table 4.3; Crossin et al. 1985), the switching on and off of the same CAM genes (rule I) is suggested in the case of mesenchymal cells contributing to secondary induction sites as well as in the case of neural crest cells. Switching to a different CAM gene (rule II) is suggested in epithelia. The subsequent action of historegulatory genes (*inner loop*, figure 4.9) is pictured to be the result of signals arising in the new milieux that occur through previous CAM-dependent cell aggregation, motion, border formation, and tissue folding. It is important to notice that, within the framework of the cycle, interactions of the different historegulatory gene activations at the cellular level can also lead to changes in form. If, for example, the expression of historegulatory genes led to altered cell motion or shape or to altered posttranslational events affecting CAMs, this would alter the effects on morphogenesis of subsequent traversals of the outer loop. A known case that directly affects cells containing N-CAM concerns the historegulatory genes specifying the enzyme or enzymes responsible for E-to-A conversion.

Combination of the outer and inner loops of the cycle and the linkage of two such cycles to form "CAM couples" obeying the modal rules of expression in cell collectives at bordering sites of induction could lead to a rich set of effects that would alter the path of morphogenesis. This clearly happens in the feather [the initial induction of which is altered to yield a new pattern after perturbation by antibodies to L-CAM (figure 4.7, *A–D*)]. The later stages of feather formation show evidence of successive CAM cycles and successive application of the rules (figure 4.7, *E, F*).

In considering how two cycles (each related to a different CAM) might interact via the CAM rules, we are brought back to a major unsolved problem: the nature of the signals during induction that activate morphoregulatory and historegulatory genes. It remains unknown whether these signals are morphogens released by cells linked by a particular CAM (figure 4.9, *left large arrow*) or whether they are derived from mechanical alterations of the cell surface or cytoskeleton (figure 4.9, *right large arrow*) through global cell surface modulation (Edelman 1976). It is possible that both kinds of signals are simultaneously required. The experiments indicating that nerve growth factor can alter Ng-CAM expression (Friedlander et al. 1986) provide the first hint regarding the nature of some of these signals.

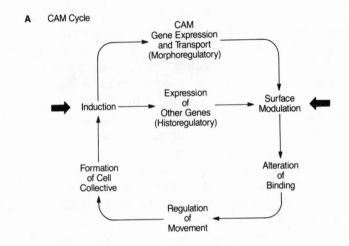

A   CAM Cycle

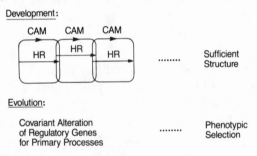

B   Epigenetic Sequences

Figure 4.9

The regulator hypothesis as exemplified in a CAM regulatory cycle and in epigenetic sequences. A: Early induction signals (heavy arrow at left) lead to CAM gene expression. Surface modulation (by prevalence changes, polar redistribution on the cell, or chemical changes such as E-to-A conversion) alters the binding rates of cells. This regulates morphogenetic movements, which in turn affect embryonic induction or milieu-dependent differentiation. The inductive changes can again affect CAM gene expression as well as the expression of other genes for specific tissues. The heavy arrows left and right refer to candidate signals for initiation of induction that are still unknown. These signals could result from global surface modulation as a result of CAM binding (right) or from release of morphogens affecting induction (left) or from both; in any case, a mechanochemical link between gene expression and morphogenesis is provided by the cycle. B: Epigenetic sequences based on successive CAM cycles with evolutionary change based on mutations in morphoregulatory and historegulatory genes. Such change occurs under morphological constraints set by such cycles. In an embryo, more than one cycle can occur simultaneously and thus the arrangement of cycles is series-parallel.

The regulation of expression of morphologically significant gene products would very likely involve cascade control by various types of genes affecting transcriptional events. Although the diagram in figure 4.9 does not indicate such genes, they are likely to be an important part of the pathway initiated by various morphogens or by surface modulation *(two large arrows on right and left)*. Reasonably convincing evidence for such control cascades has emerged in analyses of gene expression in *Drosophila* embryogenesis (Scott and O'Farrell 1986). The analysis of such gene action in vertebrates and the extension of the molecular analysis of cell interaction as seen in vertebrates to *Drosophila* should provide a more detailed and realistic picture of the signal path from gene expression to the actual establishment of cellular pattern.

The dynamic picture of regulation of morphogenesis provided by the regulator hypothesis implies that these signals must operate at several levels. The hypothesis assumes that the cell is the unit of control, that the cell surface is the nexus of control events, that cell adhesion and differentiation order the driving forces of the processes of cell movement and cell division, and that adhesion acts by generating collectives; these release local signals that in turn epigenetically affect bordering collectives in CAM couples (for an example, see figure 4.7). Although the cell is considered to be the unit of control, the unit of induction (producing the appropriate signals) is considered to be a cell collective of sufficient size linked by a particular primary CAM or combination of CAMs. Border formation relating structure to exchange of signals is assured by the different specificities of CAMs in each collective.

According to the regulator hypothesis, CAMs (and SAMs) are molecules that provide the linkage between the genes and the mechanochemical requirements of epigenetic sequences. Linked CAM cycles occurring in various contexts provide a potential solution to the problem of mechanochemical control of pattern ranging over the various levels from gene through organ and back to gene during regulative development. This is *a fortiori* true in the nervous system, although its complexity and synaptic organization may require a more refined and complex system of signals than is found at any of the other morphogenetic loci. Experimental tests of this proposal are now feasible, particularly those that involve perturbation of *in vitro* induction systems and neuronal cultures by antibodies to CAMs combined with analyses of gene expression using appropriate cDNA probes. The experiments on perturbation of feather induction systems *in vitro* with anti-L-CAM antibodies have already demonstrated an early breakage of the symmetry of feather fields from hexagonally arranged spots to stripes with a subsequent alteration in morphology to flat structures more analogous to scales (Gallin et al. 1986). These experiments definitely place CAMs in the complex causal chain of embryonic induction and in view of the generality of CAM action, it would not be surprising if the development of blobs and stripes in neural structures (Hubel and Wiesel 1970) showed similar bases.

VARIABILITY AND CONSTANCY OF PATTERN IN NEURAL STRUCTURE

We are now in a position to tie together some known features of neuronal patterning and certain aspects of the regulator hypothesis in a generalization that provides a basis for variation in the primary repertoire and that is therefore central to the neuronal group selection theory. The aim is to correlate structural variation in the nervous system (see table 3.3) with molecular variation and modulation of CAMs in ontogeny and to show that the number of molecular specificities can be much smaller than the number of patterns achievable by modulation mechanisms.

It is not known how many CAMs with different specificities are present during morphogenesis, but the data summarized so far suggest that, in view of the existence of different modulation mechanisms, a relatively small number of molecules of different specificity (perhaps dozens but not hundreds) undergoing dynamic changes could account for the establishment of patterns both in the nervous system and elsewhere. Although the facts do not allow us to estimate the number of different specificities that are required in neural patterning, they do indicate that dynamic regulation of the known CAMs takes place in a precise order.

These interpretations may be highlighted by contrasting two types of morphogenetic theories: (1) structural or strict chemospecificity theories (Sperry 1963; see Cowan and Hunt 1985; Easter et al. 1985) in which neural pattern arises from the complementary recognition of mutually specific cell surface markers making up a very large repertoire; and (2) regulatory theories proposing dynamic modulation mechanisms (Edelman 1984b, 1985b). In such regulatory theories, which propose that patterns arise selectively and dynamically by far-from-equilibrium processes, patterned transitions from one state of cellular assembly to another result from modulation of the chemical structure or the distribution of CAMs or SAMs, which in turn regulate driving forces such as cell movement and cell division.

The existence of dynamics in itself cannot disprove either kind of theory. Nonetheless, the occurrence of surface modulation in neural induction and the subsequent correlation of CAM appearances with secondary induction are more in accord with regulatory theories of morphogenesis. It is necessary and sufficient, for example, to block only N-CAM or Ng-CAM binding to disrupt neural patterns in a variety of tissues. Neuronal CAMs change binding efficacy by modulation, that is, under cellular control; they do not make up a very large family of different molecular specificities and are not specified by a large gene family. Indeed, the same N-CAM sd chain that plays a key role in early neural induction is ubiquitous on differentiated neurons and also plays a key role in later histogenesis.

Neural patterning depends critically upon neuron-glia interactions as well as upon neuron-neuron interactions (Sidman 1974; Rakic 1981a), and in their expression Ng-CAM and cytotactin also show modulation rather than a host of different specificities. Moreover, various primary processes of development contribute to neural pattern in a dynamic fashion that itself is responsive to CAM expression. A striking example is the modulation of N-CAM on the surface of neural crest cells in which both cell movement and CAM expression are temporally correlated. Another example is the appearance of cytotactin on glia at sites where movement of neurons is to occur. A reasonable hypothesis is that the basis of pattern in tissues formed by these cells is an alteration in the differential selectivity of a relatively small number of CAM and SAM specificities expressed differentially and interacting by several mechanisms at different times to influence differentiation and movement (Hoffman et al. 1986; Chuong et al. 1987). Such dynamic changes in selectivity would result from changes with time in cellular expression of these molecules in response to local signals at the tissue level. That modulation of a CAM can occur in response to a signal such as NGF has already been shown *in vitro* (Friedlander et al. 1986).

This dynamic picture and the data on CAM expression sequences (figure 4.4, table 4.3) are difficult to reconcile with the idea that very large numbers of specific molecules define precise positions, addresses, and connections of neural cells. If such addresses existed, the sequences of movements would require extraordinary coordination of the local expression of each molecule at the level of individual cells, because the existence of sequences of primary processes rules out the possibility of thorough mixing and of the polling of each cell by every other cell.

When such encounters do occur, as in sorting-out experiments on histo-typic aggregation *in vitro* (Holtfreter 1939, 1948), the experiments yield pseudo-tissues but no form and no global organization. Genes cannot contain prior information about the spatial distribution of cells in the neural network, and local information hardly seems sufficient to control the coordinate expression and suppression at the individual cell level of very large numbers of markers. We conclude that the "electrician" (the developmental second cousin of the homunculus) does not exist. Consistent with the dynamics of CAM modulation, neither does precise wiring in complex nervous systems at the level of their finest ramifications.

A summary comparison of the two opposed views of neural pattern-ing in terms of their different requirements as well as of the accrued evidence (table 4.4) clearly favors modulation over strict chemospecifi-city. This evidence is consistent with the existence of as many as several dozen CAMs under dynamic regulation but not with thousands and millions. It is nonetheless conceivable that individual neurons might produce molecules that are not directly involved in cell adhesion but that interact on the same cell with neuronal CAMs to further modulate their interactions. Notice, however, that the effect of such molecules would not be to change the specificity of binding but only to alter its selectivity, consistent with a dynamic picture of border formulation and patterning by modulation.

According to the regulator hypothesis, an extraordinarily large num-ber of neural patterns can result from the functions of a relatively small number of CAMs of different specificities under the influence of five or six surface modulation mechanisms. The early regulation of CAM genes with subsequent and relatively independent expression of cell differen-tiation under control of historegulatory genes, as is seen in the CAM cycle, could lead to a virtually unlimited set of patterns. Diversity in these patterns would originate from the obligate local fluctuations in modulation mechanisms.

Although the regulator hypothesis provides a mechanism for the origin of somatic diversity in the primary repertoire, it is important to note that the hypothesis is also consistent with an evolutionary basis for constancy of regional neural pattern within a particular species (Edel-man 1985c, 1986b). Such constancy would arise from the temporal control of the relatively small number of morphoregulatory genes for CAMs and SAMs (see chapter 6). At the same time, modally similar structures in particular regions of the brain would arise from the evolu-tionary selection of specific patterns of CAM gene expression (table 4.3)

Table 4.4

Comparison of Modulation and Strict Chemoaffinity

	Modulation	*Chemoaffinity*
Number of different molecules	Tens	Up to millions
Specificity	Each CAM specific for binding partner Homophilic: N-CAM to N-CAM Heterophilic: Ng-CAM Two major ion dependencies: Ca^{++} for L-CAM, none for N-CAM	Highly refined; sufficient to distinguish each marker pair
Affinity changes	Very great; dynamic	Not explicitly considered but presumably reflected in different specificities
Same molecules in early and late development?	Yes, with several new additions	Possibly, but with *many* new additions
Same molecules in different species?	Yes, with expected levels of genetic polymorphism; possible use of different molecules in widely separated taxa	Many differences required to generate the detailed structural differences between species
Method of form generation	Selective constraints upon interactions of primary processes	Recognition of appropriate complementary cell markers
Evolutionary basis of altered neural form	Altered regulatory gene pattern for CAMs and primary processes; modulatory CAM cycle (see figure 4.9)	Changes in number or in type of markers by mutation and gene expression

in coordination with the expression of particular historegulatory genes. Because of genetic influences on the dynamics of regulation, neural patterning may be modally alike in different individuals, but it must also be variant at the level of individual neurons and their processes. Within the modal three-dimensional anatomical structure characteristic of a species, the local variability in connectivity could be immense.

According to this view, somatic variance in the primary repertoire arises from the regulation, interaction, and feedback (positive and negative) of cell adhesion with the other primary processes of development. Obviously, CAMs and SAMs and their modulations are a necessary but not sufficient condition for diversification of neural structure. As we shall see in the next chapter, additional mechanisms of synaptic activity and alteration are required to account for the increasingly microscopic details of later neural histogenesis.

The main conclusion of the argument pursued here is that molecular mechanisms of cell adhesion during development of the nervous system are completely consistent with the modal constancy of mapped structures as well as with the individual variation in microscopic neural networks that is required by selective theories. The establishment of this latter point on the molecular origins of diversity has been the central concern of the present chapter. The regulator hypothesis provides an epigenetic mechanism at the molecular level to account for the origin of variability in neuronal groups. It does not, however, provide a complete solution to the problem of how specific neuroanatomical and functional maps are made in the nervous system. In the next chapter we will consider this problem in more detail and show that, although the mapping problem is not yet fully solved, variance introduced by primary processes and the control of cell adhesion both contribute to the mechanism of mapping.

5

Cellular Dynamics
of Neural Maps

INTRODUCTION

In previous chapters, evidence has been presented stressing the bases of variability in neuronal structure, function, and development. However, even the compelling molecular and cellular evidence reviewed in chapter 4 does not fully address a body of facts pointing to the constancy of neuroanatomy—facts that might tempt us to reach conclusions contrary to those of the molecular evidence. From the standpoint of neuroanatomy, at least at one scale of magnification, the striking feature of brains is order and specificity (Brodal 1981), not variability. How, for example, can we reconcile the existence of anatomical and functional maps in a structure like the cerebral cortex, which shows elaborate cytoarchitectonics (see Schmitt et al. 1981; Edelman et al. 1984), with the existence of variability at the molecular, developmental, and individual neuronal levels?

To develop a deeper understanding of the epigenetic basis of neural pattern and a proper context in which to confront this apparent paradox, we deferred detailed considerations of major cellular and anatomical issues of developmental neurobiology to the present chapter. Because of the central importance of neural maps to the theory, we shall pick them here as main examples within which to relate molecular regulation to developmental neuroanatomy and function. Mapping is a key aspect of group selective networks with reentrant circuits, and it plays a major role in the matching of changes in the environment with dynamic structures that are established in the brain. As we shall see later, the theory considers that the evolution of orderly mechanisms of mapping is essential in order for the organism to deal with the ethological and behaviorally adaptive aspects of perceptual categorization. Work on the evolutionary, developmental, and functional aspects of maps represents one of the most active arenas of neurobiological research (see Edelman et al. 1984). The purpose of this chapter is not to review all of this work in detail but rather to extract from it evidence for and against the neuronal group selection theory. We shall see that mapping involves two kinds of selective events, anatomical to form primary repertoires and synaptic to form secondary repertoires; at certain stages of development, these two kinds of events interact to form or fix particular kinds of maps.

To provide a background for this evidence, we shall first consider the interpretation of mapping given by the theory. We shall then briefly survey general principles (Cowan 1978; Edelman et al. 1985; Purves and Lichtman 1985) governing the development of neural projections and thus constraining map formation. This will entail a short review of cellular behavior in embryonic development. In order to connect the mapping of fiber tracts during embryogenesis to the CAM modulation mechanisms described in the preceding chapter and to emphasize some of the variables responsible for the anatomy underlying maps, we shall then consider the development of the retinotectal projection (Easter et al. 1985; for recent reviews, see Edelman et al. 1985). Finally, we shall address the evidence for variability within functional maps that are already established as secondary repertoires in anatomically fixed structures by reviewing the relationship between anatomy and neural function in adult maps that obey cytoarchitectonic rules. This functional variability in adult maps which is reflected in secondary repertoires (Merzenich et al. 1983a) provides some of the strongest evidence in support of neuronal group selection.

At the outset, it is important to note that the definition of a map can be extremely flexible—even in species that have few neurons and limited repertoires of behavior, one might be tempted to speak of any connectional order as a mapping. Here, we shall restrict the term to the ordered arrangement and activity of groups of neurons and large fiber tracts projecting onto laminae and nuclei with defined delimitations of function that are found in organisms with brains having a large variety of functions (Palmer et al. 1978; Tusa et al. 1981). The map order to which we shall refer relates "point to area" or "area to area" in a more or less continuous fashion. The reason for making this restriction is to avoid the confusion that might arise if single neural connections were considered at the same time as those ensembles of connections in large areas that have arisen during evolution to carry out particular functions, either motor or sensory. This restriction also serves to emphasize that the neuronal group selection theory avoids notions of equipotentiality (Lashley 1950) and that it is not designed around individual neurons or around randomly connected ensembles of neurons.

REPRESENTATION AND MAPPING

It is useful to consider some general functional aspects of maps before attempting to review the developmental and physiological variables that lead to their formation. According to the theory, it is necessary that most neural circuitry be arranged in an overlapping and degenerate fashion (Edelman 1981). This implies the following: (1) within the primary repertoire there are variant groups of cells that can carry out the same group functions more or less well; (2) this degeneracy can serve in a similar fashion as redundancy to offset the problem of unreliability in a distributed system, but, in addition, it goes beyond redundancy in dealing with the "unreliability" engendered by novel situations; (3) even after the group selection that occurs during the experience of the animal, the primary repertoire may still contain cell groups that are functionally equivalent to or even potentially more effective than those functioning in the secondary repertoire; and (4) during the selection of this secondary repertoire, neuronal groups may be subject to competitive exclusion.

These properties, and others to be discussed later, imply that the brain constitutes a distributed system (Mountcastle 1978) in which a

function may be carried out at many different levels. Because repertoires of neuronal groups constitute a degenerate distributed system,
differences in the timing of signals, in signal correlation and representation, as well as in associative storage and recollection, all become critical
issues. At this point, we confront a central problem related to the nature
of representation necessary for perception: whatever means is used for
this purpose, it must allow continuous and coherent correlation of various temporal and spatial aspects of a neural construct with at least some
features of a real-world object.

To face this issue of representation, particularly in relation to the
problem of categorization, we may ask a number of questions. Is there
a need at all in the brain for topological and topographic representations or isomorphic maps of the geometrical or physical properties of
real-world objects? If so, is the brain so constructed that it makes a series
of maps—for example, maps of maps? If motion occurs in the environment, how, in the neural representation that is critical to perception,
are features "saved" in time or correlated with a second presentation
of the same scene? In addressing these questions, we shall use the
cerebral cortex (Schmitt et al. 1981; Edelman et al. 1984) as an example;
the principles derived are likely to apply to other mapped regions with
only minor variations.

It seems necessary that there be in the brain at least one level of
representation of sensory input that has the features of a topographic
or spatial map corresponding to at least parts of real-world objects in
space (Edelman and Finkel 1984). If there were no topographic invariance at some early stage of neural processing, it would be difficult to
establish or maintain correspondences to the spatiotemporal locus or
continuity of an object (or its parts) in any subsequent neural representation. It is sufficient, however, that such an early map maintain only
certain basic features relating to the spatiotemporal continuity of an
object; a complete point-to-point mapping in the mathematical sense is
not required. No point-to-point map has so far been shown to exist in
the nervous system; instead, all local mappings studied have been point-
to-area and area-to-area, consistent with the presence of degeneracy.
Indeed, the partially shifted overlap that has been observed in primary
sensory cortex (Mountcastle 1978) appears to represent a special case
of degeneracy, and it can be taken as an indication that degeneracy
exists at the level of function. The point-to-area relationship of afferent
input to initial cerebral representation in such regions is sharpened
both by lateral inhibition and by a number of dynamic properties of the
system. An obvious example of the latter is the movement of the recep-

tor sheet over the external scene. Even in audition, where this is not strictly true, head movements greatly sharpen the capacity to localize sound (see Edelman et al. 1987b).

The arrangement of the cerebral cortex into vertically organized assemblies not only serves to map multidimensional properties of a given modality onto a two-dimensional sheet (Mountcastle 1978) but also helps "translate" certain physical properties of the real-world object (such as orientation, pitch, etc.) into neural properties at defined locations. Viewed in this way, a primary cerebral map may be considered to be a translation that makes it possible to sample and preserve selected coherent portions of the gross topographic order of the external scene in time and space. This appears to be a major function of cerebral columns in primary receiving areas (Hubel and Wiesel 1977). Such an arrangement need not map all features densely, and apparently it does not (Mountcastle 1978). By the same token, however, such a local map does not appear to be sufficient for perception (Uttal 1978, 1981), and further reentrant mapping with multidimensional characteristics seems to be required (Zeki 1981).

This first-order translation and lower-level abstraction in a local map is of particular importance in a selective distributed system, because it allows higher-order neuronal groups present in a global mapping (see chapter 8) to refer without ambiguity in a reentrant fashion to specific lower-level groups that already can respond to particular features and properties of an object. From these considerations, we infer that such early local maps must maintain some degree of continuity corresponding to the characteristics of primary sensory inputs, for they serve as an inner representation during early sensory processing to which later, higher-order processing can be referred by reentry.

According to this view, the existence of local maps has the following functional significance. (1) A first representation is generated in the cortex that maps multidimensional properties of an object onto the two-dimensional cortical sheet. This translates some physical properties of real-world objects into neural properties in certain regions. Although this early map has the property of local continuity, it does not need to be isomorphic with the entire collection of object features. (2) The cortical region or domain of a map is not uniquely defined (although the *limits* of its boundaries are determined ultimately by input or output projections). Instead, the actual extent and position of regions of the map must reflect the outcome of functional competition during neuronal group selection. We will provide evidence for this statement both in the later portions of this chapter and in the next chapter. (3) The main function of such a map is to provide a reference for higher-order input-output relationships and successive mappings in a reentrant system. Inasmuch as other regions of the nervous system (and of the cortex in particular) must carry out routines involving multimodal input, abstractions, and map-free routines, a place must be maintained for continual reference to continuity properties. This place is the local map and its constituent domains within the primary receiving areas. But this also strongly implies that, in the reentrant degenerate system assumed by the theory, *all* map-to-map interactions must be dynamically maintained and rearranged upon perturbation.

Before further examining the evidence for these assertions, we must confront the paradox mentioned at the beginning of the chapter—the apparent inconsistency between the variability introduced by the molecular mechanisms of development and the emergence of ordered anatomical and functional maps during ontogeny. To do so, we must relate conclusions derived from neuroanatomical studies on the development of projections to the molecular evidence discussed in the preceding chapter. Although a complete explanation of the principles of developmental mapping has not emerged from any experimental system, the evidence from a variety of systems studied at the cellular level points to a set of quite definite conclusions that are in complete agreement with the requirements of the neuronal group selection theory. It is in this arena that the developmental requirements of the theory come into direct confrontation with strict chemoaffinity models (Sperry 1963, 1965) of neural patterning. In our discussion of this issue, the basic conclusions and general principles will be extracted from a very large body of cellular studies (for overviews, see Cowan 1978; Purves and Lichtman 1985; Edelman et al. 1985).

DEVELOPMENTAL CONSTRAINTS ON MAP FORMATION

How can we reconcile the obligate variability of dynamic molecular regulation during development with the evidence that fiber tracts actually form an ordered map? Consideration of the general anatomical principles of neuronal development supports the view that neural structures (including maps) arise as a result of a complex mix of primary developmental processes, cellular competition, and neuronal activity. Here we follow the superb analysis of Cowan (1978). In analyzing the formation of connections, he has pointed out three major issues: (1) how neurons acquire the capability of forming topographically ordered structures, (2) how neuronal processes find their way, and (3) how specific types of cells are contacted by these processes, sometimes in quite specific positions on cell specializations.

Although the term "neural specificity" has been used to refer to apparently stereotypic anatomical patterns in the nervous system, at the level of molecular mechanisms a clear distinction must be maintained between the consequences of dynamic selectivity and those of molecular specificity (see table 4.4). To emphasize that selectivity plays an important role in patterning, we turn to a series of generalizations derived from studies of the detailed cellular processes of development. Cowan (1978) points out that a number of sequential events (table 5.1) are recognizable in the patterning of neural populations in the CNS. These include proliferation, migration, aggregation, cytodifferentiation, death, formation of connections, and center-periphery adjustment. We will take up each of these events in order, beginning in each case with a generalization or conclusion of particular significance for the theory and following with some supporting evidence; detailed references may be found in Cowan's (1978) review. Considered collectively, these conclusions are consistent with the regulator hypothesis (Edelman 1984b) presented in the preceding chapter. They indicate strongly that certain primary processes of neural development can act independently, and they also highlight the statistical, selective, and populational nature of such primary processes as they act during the epigenetic emergence of the nervous system.

1. Cell Proliferation. *Cell proliferation to form populations that constitute maps in the CNS is autonomous and is independent of the mapped input.* Various experiments indicate that neural subpopula-

Table 5.1

Phases of Neurogenesis (Cowan 1978)

Cell proliferation
Cell migration
Selective cell aggregation
Neuronal cytodifferentiation
Cell death during neural development
Formation of connections:
    Acquisition of positional information
    Axonal outgrowth and pathfinding
    Target locus identification
Center-periphery adjustment and interrelations

---

tions are generated in limited periods of time and in specific sequences. These sequences can be from the inside out (e.g., cerebral cortex—layer VI first, layer I last), from the outside in (retinal ganglion cells first, receptors last), or mixed (chick tectum—internal superficial layer first, deep layers last). Neuronal proliferation in the CNS appears not to depend upon connectivity to afferents or efferents. Larger neurons are generated earlier than smaller neurons; a rostrocaudal gradient of cell proliferation is seen in both the brain stem and the cord, with rostral development preceding caudal. In most regions, glial formation can be delayed in onset, but at later times glial proliferation (and the capacity to induce it in later life) far outlasts neuronal proliferation. By late embryonic life, cell cycle times are already very long, and by adult life CNS neurons no longer proliferate. In the peripheral nervous system, by sharp contrast, proliferation is postmigratory and growth is under the control of the innervation field, as we will see later in considering center-periphery adjustment (Purves 1983; Purves and Lichtman 1983).

2. Cell Migration. *Factors determining neuronal migration differ from those determining axon outgrowth.* All neurons in the CNS are gypsies for some part of their career—migration appears to occur after the withdrawal from the cell cycle. There is a considerable body of evidence (Rakic 1971b, 1981a) indicating that radial glia provide many (but not all) of the pathways governing neural migration (figure 5.1).

The fundamental significance of these observations for our purposes is that, in many cases, two *different* kinds of cells interact in a distinct sequence to allow cell positioning. It is difficult to imagine radial glial guidance occurring except in terms of selective dynamic interactions between neurons and glia mediated by CAM expression, migration on matrix materials such as cytotactin, and subsequent interactive morphological shapings of two different families of cells adhering by heterotypic and heterophilic mechanisms. The work of Rakic (1971a, 1971b, 1972a, 1972b, 1978, 1981a) is entirely consistent with the observations that a blockade of these molecules with appropriate antibodies prevents proper migration of external granule cells in cerebellar slices in culture (Lindner et al. 1983; Hoffman et al. 1986; Chuong et al. 1987). Such migration mechanisms, while not yet shown for retinotectal systems, play a major role in forming the cerebral and cerebellar cortex. Consistent with the observations on polarity modulation of Ng-CAM, neurite extension is separate from cell migration. Cowan (1978) points out, for example, that ectopic cells in the tectal system (e.g., a small

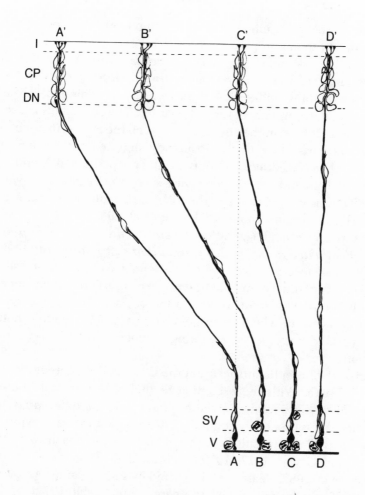

Figure 5.1

Schematic drawing of four radial glial cells and cohorts of associated migrating neurons as depicted by Rakic (1981a). Cells located between the illustrated columns have been deleted in order to simplify the diagram and to emphasize the point that all neurons produced in the ventricular (V) and subventricular (SV) zones at the same site (proliferative units A–D) migrate in succession along the same fiber fascicle to the developing cortical plate (CP) and establish ontogenetic radial columns (A–D). Within each column, the newly arrived neurons bypass more deeply situated neurons (DN) that were generated earlier and come to occupy the most superficial position at the borderline between the developing cortical plate and the cortical layer (1). Radial glial grids preserve the topographic relationships between generation of neurons produced in proliferative units at their final positions and prevent mismatching that could occur, for example, between unit A and column C' if the cells were to take a direct, straight route (dotted line).

percentage that miss migrating to the isthmo-optic nucleus) can still send axons to the appropriate contralateral eye.

3. Selective Cell Aggregation. *The evidence is compatible with competitive epigenetic mechanisms consisting of local signals inducing regulation or CAM modulation at the cell surface.* This generalization was discussed extensively in the last chapter. The only additional point to make here is that, in the cerebral cortex, all the late-formed neurons must migrate past those that have already migrated, that have formed collections in early periods and thus are already positioned. Modulation of N-CAM, Ng-CAM, or glial molecules such as cytotactin by a variety of mechanisms is implicated in the differential adhesivity and regulation of this *en passant* motion (Chuong et al. 1987).

4. Neuronal Cytodifferentiation. *Overall neuronal shape appears to be genetically determined; in contrast, arbor distribution and branching is not and depends upon input.* The defined course of neural shapes and the extraordinary epigenetic variance of arbors which depends finally upon input suggest the operation of a complex, dynamic, and selective system in which some population variables (such as neuron type) are fixed but others are contingent upon statistical events of interaction.

Neuronal differentiation occurs at the same time as afferent ingrowth and cell death. With the exception of their fine terminal branches, which reveal considerable variation, most neurons differentiate to a characteristic morphology independent of milieu for each type. This can be shown in tissue culture (Scott et al. 1969; Fischbach 1970, 1972; Banker and Cowan 1977, 1979; Dichter 1978; Peacock et al. 1979; Moonen et al. 1982; Neale et al. 1982) and in isogenic animals (Macagno et al. 1973). In tissues such as the cerebellum (Rakic 1972b), arborization is under the influence of the particular set of afferents in the vicinity. Thus, the final branching pattern but not the overall morphology of most neurons is affected by variation in particular connectivities set up by connections with fiber inputs. In the cerebral cortex, there is a very large difference in branching patterns and dendritic lengths (see table 3.3). Spine formation on dendrites appears to be an autonomous process in the sense that it occurs in the absence of input, but it too shows considerable variation.

As we shall see in our discussion of the retinotectal projection, a large number of molecular processes enter into the final phenotypic expression of a functioning neuron. Functional aspects of neural differentiation are influenced by the timing of the onset of activity, the types of ion channels present, the mode of synaptic transmission, and the kind of transmitter chosen if transmission is chemical. Although definitive studies on central neurons are lacking, analysis of ganglion cells suggests that one precursor cell can first synthesize norepinephrine and then produce acetylcholine (Patterson and Chun 1974; Johnson et al. 1976). Such choices can be determined by local spatial variables. It has been shown, for example, that the particular position of neural crest cells is the decisive factor in whether they become adrenergic or cholinergic (Le Douarin 1982). All of these considerations emphasize the possible importance of function in shaping neural maps; this will be seen clearly in our review of the retinotectal projection.

5. Cell Death. *Death occurs during patterning, can be stochastic, can involve large numbers of cells in a population, and is generally not preprogrammed* (Cowan and Wenger 1967; Prestige 1970; Cowan 1973; Hamburger 1975; Berg 1982). Whether death occurs spontaneously or not depends upon the establishment of connections in a projection field at an appropriate time, and this provides further evidence for selective and competitive models of neural patterning. No stronger case can be made for selection in neural patterning than that which derives from a consideration of the evidence on cell death. Up to 70 percent of cells die in certain areas during development, and the death can occur in a very short period of time. Most of this death is not preprogrammed but depends upon the neuron connecting to the appropriate innervation field. This must occur largely epigenetically and to some extent stochastically: even in the so-called granuloprival mutants of mice (particularly *staggerer*), the large granule cell loss is not preprogrammed; rather, it depends upon the failure of contingent events (Rakic and Sidman 1973; Messer and Smith 1977; Messer 1980). Thus, in two different individuals, while the same percentage of cells may die in a region, different cells die within each comparable population.

6. Formation of Connections. *The outcome of neural process outgrowth to form and stabilize connections depends upon a complex set of cooperative and competitive mechanisms that are dynamic* (Cowan 1978; Purves 1980; Purves and Lichtman 1983, 1985; Easter et al. 1985) and *also to some extent stochastic in their actions.* We mentioned this important issue earlier, in connection with neuromuscular synapses. It is closely related to the issue of center-periphery adjustment, which we shall consider next, and it will be particularly pertinent when we discuss the formation of the retinotectal projection. Consistent with the idea that dynamic mechanisms are at work in axonal outgrowth, N-CAM and Ng-CAM are present on growth cones and mediate fasciculation (Hoff-

man et al. 1986). The work on muscle regeneration reviewed in the preceding chapter shows that there is a reciprocal control loop between CAM regulation and synapse integrity. It is likely that similar loops exist in the CNS.

7. Center-Periphery Adjustment. *Synaptic connections can be reduced across normal population boundaries, and there is quantitative regulation of pre- and postsynaptic distributions.*

These issues may be exemplified by two cases (Purves 1983; Purves and Lichtman 1983) that relate to innervation in the periphery: analysis of the spinal cord, in which there is innervation of individual motor neurons by stretch-sensitive afferents from muscle spindles, and elegant studies of the peripheral autonomic nervous system. In the spinal cord, individual motor neurons can send processes over several segments (Shinoda et al. 1981, 1982, 1986), and motor neuron pools innervate particular muscle groups corresponding to given positions both rostrocaudally and in the transverse plane. Location is not absolutely strict, however, and different pools can overlap in a pattern suggesting degeneracy. Nonetheless, afferents generally grow into the cord and innervate the motor neurons supplying the appropriate muscle. This occurs even though the target neurons are surrounded by irrelevant neurons. While this experimental model does not allow direct reinnervation studies, it is striking that removal of a dorsal root ganglion supplying the forearm of a tadpole results in the extension of processes from an adjacent ganglion to send new processes to the forearm (Purves and Lichtman 1983). These new afferents to a given muscle are found to innervate the motor neurons to that muscle more extensively than irrelevant motor neurons. Thus, while it is selective, mapping is not specifically predetermined in terms of a rigid set of markers.

Studies of the superior cervical ganglion (Purves 1983) indicate that while the ganglion receives input from preganglionic neurons that are found in as many as eight segments of the spinal cord, individual ganglion cells at a particular level receive axons from a particular contiguous subset of the input. Cells that send postganglionic fibers to different levels in the periphery receive preganglionic inputs from axons at different rostrocaudal positions in the cord. In view of the *absence* of a topographic map, the explanation of these findings seems to lie in a *competitive* balance among different classes of preganglionic fibers. This is Purves's (1980) main conclusion, one that is highly significant for selective theories in which competition plays a major role.

On the basis of these and other studies, Purves and Lichtman (1983) point out three criteria that must be met to explain specific neural patterning. (1) One must account for normally limited pre- and post-synaptic connectivity and also for the capacity during development to reduce previously made synaptic connections across normal population boundaries. (2) One must account for the fact that normal "recognition" is relative, not absolute, reflecting a "bias." While position may be involved, it does not necessarily reflect exact anatomical position (this is clearly the case in ganglia, which are not topographic in their organization). (3) As in neuromuscular junctions, the *quantitative* regulation of the pre- and postsynaptic distributions of neurons must be accounted for, possibly in terms of trophic substances and feedback.

All of these criteria suggest that there is a mismatch between the notion of neural specificity and the idea that there is molecular specificity at the level of recognition of single neurons. Consistent with our conclusions in chapter 4, neural specificity appears to be related to selectivity, occurring as a result of competition among dynamic systems rather than to preexistent markers for recognition. The themes of competition and of locally contingent epigenetic events rather than preprogrammed events emerge at many stages of neuronal interaction. The addition of genetically controlled neuronal differentiation to this picture further increases the level of refinement at which selective epigenetic events can balance constancy against variation, but it does not change the basic interpretation.

Cellular Primary Processes and Selection

The generalizations mentioned in this brief survey of primary processes may now be incorporated into our argument for a dynamic selective theory of neural patterning during development. The facts are consistent with the notion that, as neuronal division, migration, and process extension proceed, an epigenetic series of contingent selections occur that are constrained to a certain extent by the genetic determination of neuronal shape. This set of selective events alters neural patterning and at each stage depends upon a fairly large number of key processes. These include the extraordinary variability of terminal arbors, their overlap and competition, the contingent and locally statistical dependence of their final shape upon afferent connectivity and actual neural function, the competitive interactions of neuronal fibers extending into occupied and unoccupied territories, the dependence of patterning in the CNS upon selective and sequential interactions between the two great cell systems, neurons and glia (particularly in the case of migration), the extraordinary and widespread occurrence of cell death, the selective processes of synapse elimination and stabilization, and the quantitative matching of neural populations to the requirements of the periphery.

In each of these processes, we can see the elaboration and extension of the selective and regulative principles reviewed in the preceding chapter. All of the phenomena cited here are consistent with modulation mechanisms of cell adhesion as well as with the interplay between CAMs of different specificity. The evidence obtained from studies at the cellular level is inconsistent with the idea of strict recognition by a huge number of local cell markers, and it is totally consistent with the presence of enormous degrees of local microscopic variation of terminal arbors. Despite this variation, particular neurites guided by growth cones can adopt particular paths during neurogenesis, especially in tract formation.

To focus the picture that emerges from these conclusions in terms of the opposition between specificity and variance mentioned in the introduction to this chapter, we may profitably discuss how cell surface modulation in a CAM or SAM cycle (see figure 4.9) might lead to specific patterns. Consider a pioneer neuron extending a neurite along a substrate such as cytotactin and reaching a choice point at which the growth cone meets other neurons and tracts. At this point, the neurite must make a definite choice so that it grows in a particular direction and path. How can this kind of event occur in the nervous system in the absence of myriad markers and addresses? The first point to notice is that such a pioneer neurite in general must make its decision in a very small domain—of the order of microns in radius. Second, under these spatial constraints and at this early time, the number of alternative pathways is usually less than ten. Given a small number of CAMs and SAMs (of the order of a dozen), and half a dozen modulation mechanisms, a sufficient basis for choice of path exists.

Suppose the neurite has one or two CAMs on its surface at the time it must make the choice. Neurons around the target or branch point have developed independently and may or may not possess the same CAMs on their surface at this time. Consider the case in which they do not. If an inductive signal (morphogen or growth factor) is produced at this site by target neurons, the growth cone of the pioneer neuron may take it up and either down-regulate the CAMs on that neuron or switch the neuron to expression of a new CAM. All that is necessary for a choice is that the target neurons have more of the ligand for this CAM (or possess it exclusively) among the *small* number of neurons in the neighborhood. Under these conditions, the pioneer neuron can now move onto the target. The requirements of this selection model based on the CAM cycle is that the target neuron release an inductive signal and that it have the appropriate CAM conjunctively, that is, within some reasonably small time interval after release of the signal. Obvious variants of this model involve differential CAM modulation, strong facultative increases of a CAM already present, and the like. The model is similar to that proposed by Bastiani et al. (1985) for growth cone guidance in grasshoppers, a proposal that is also based on cell surface modulation. In the present instance, more emphasis is placed on the combinatorial aspects of CAM specificity and diversity of modulation mechanisms and less on "cell recognition" *per se.*

This type of model for neural guidance depends upon exploration of a small region by the growth cone, permissive signaling for motion (which will not continue unless the correct combination of signal and CAM is found in the perimeter), and uptake of an inductive factor by the cone. Once the choice has been made, these conditions do not in general need to be repeated for every fiber that follows this path. Nonetheless, fibers in a fascicle could carry out a modulatory response similar to that for a pioneering fiber by virtue of their amplification of the original response resulting from their enhanced straight motion in the direction of the inductive signal.

The modulatory control of neural patterns by means of a CAM cycle is in principle similar in its ingredients to that seen in the induction of feather patterns (see figure 4.9). What differs is the active searching of growth cones in neurites, the scale of events, and the invocation of somewhat larger numbers of modulation mechanisms and CAMs (perhaps up to dozens, see table 4.4). As a result of such elaborated "mini-induction" events, definite neural patterns could emerge. Notice, however, that although this applies to definite branchings, it need not always apply: at the next scale smaller, that of dendritic branching and more rarely axonal branching, considerable variance can and will occur. Moreover, once a series of basic decisions for branching occurs (as governed by the sequence of epigenetic events and ultimately by evolution), cell death and successive neurite ingrowth can vary the resulting pattern yet again.

Our main conclusion is that a modulatory cycle involving a relatively small number of CAMs and SAMs that is epigenetically repeated and that interacts with the cellular primary processes can lead by selection both to defined patterns and to individual variation. Cowan (1978) has quoted a prescient remark by Ramón y Cajal:

> I was attracted by the question how a pyriform neuroblast, devoid of processes, is converted into the prodigious tree . . . of the Purkinje cell. . . . I noticed that every ramification, dendritic or axonic, in the course of formation, passes through a chaotic period, so to speak, a period of trials during which there are sent out at random experimental conductors, most of which are destined to disappear. . . . Later, when the afferent nerve fibers have arrived, or when the neurons mold themselves and attain in due time functional solidarity, the useful expansions remain and become fixed and the useless or exploratory ones are reabsorbed. (Ramón y Cajal 1937)

The evidence that has accrued supports this view: the anatomy underlying mapping is likely to be the result of a series of quite complex local events with feedback, not of a preestablished detailed pattern.

Anatomical events of this kind obviously lead to variability. Nonetheless, it is important to stress that, with certain exceptions, once anatomical development is complete, the burden of mapping is taken up by synaptic variation under generally different selective conditions. This is the main dogma (see chapter 3) of the neuronal group selection theory: development of degenerate circuitry proceeds *in one direction* to provide a primary repertoire; all subsequent selection for secondary repertoire occurs at synapses. The one-way dogma implies, for example, that sprouting in the adult, as seen in the regeneration of connections in the olfactory bulb (Graziadei and Monti Graziadei 1978, 1979a, 1979b) or in the song center of birds (Nottebohm 1980, 1981a, 1981b), is a specialized variant providing a new chance for synaptic selection. According to this view, sprouting alone cannot and does not yield anatomical and synaptic patterns identical to the circuits that existed prior to the sprouting events, although they might be functionally equivalent. Of course, the establishment of final connections in the CNS is not necessarily coincident with birth or hatching, and, depending upon the species, it can overlap with the beginnings of adult behavior and be influenced by that behavior in the external environment (Marler 1984); this subject is discussed in detail later in this chapter and in chapter 11. It is no contradiction to the view taken here that certain patterns of regeneration may proceed according to residues of patterns laid down during earlier development.

MAP ORDERING IN DEVELOPMENT

Against this background of the molecular and cellular developmental constraints on map formation, we may now consider the evidence on the establishment of order in actual maps. We will first take up a well-studied system of mapping during embryonic development, the retino-tectal projection; we will then contrast this example with the organization and plasticity of adult maps formed in the somatosensory system. The exact mechanisms of mapping have not been fully established in either example, but taken together they provide strong evidence for a developmental continuum in which selection for circuitry by regulatory mechanisms on primary processes gradually gives way to selection of circuitry by synaptically driven mechanisms.

The retinotectal projection may be considered the classic case of a continuous map constructed in development (figure 5.2). If, while recording from the surface of the tectum of a frog, the retina is illuminated in successive positions with a fine spot of light, the electrical response (which is that of the presynaptic fibers) is revealed as a map roughly reflecting the geometric optics of the visual field, the retinal order, and an orderly relation between retina and tectum. It was the work of Sperry on the newt (1943a, 1943b) that provided the investigation of this system with a major impetus and that also gave rise to the notion of strict chemoaffinity (Attardi and Sperry 1963; Sperry 1963, 1965). While extremely significant work has been done in other systems (see Schmitt et al. 1981; Edelman et al. 1985), the retinotectal system remains a key paradigm: it is a reasonable surmise that a complete description and explanation of this mapping will probably reveal the major principles guiding all other mappings in complex vertebrate brains.

A number of experiments have been carried out on the regenerating tectal system after optic nerve section. In the classic experiment, the eye was rotated 180 degrees after the nerve section; newts with regenerated systems responded to stimuli in such a way as to suggest that the visual fields were inverted and that the original left and right sides were interchanged. A variety of experiments (for a review, see Cowan and Hunt 1985) suggested that given retinal regions were remapped to contact the part of the tectum that had been their original target. Other investigators (Straznicky et al. 1981) carried out more sophisticated variations on this theme and the results suggested that cell recognition

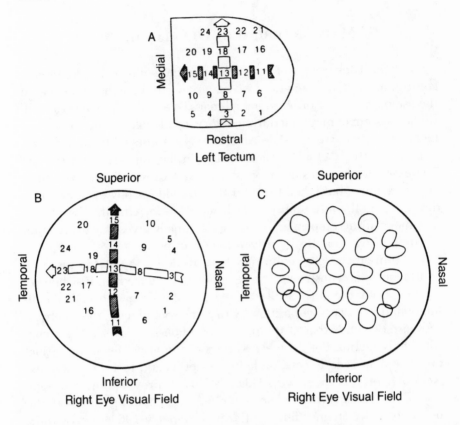

Figure 5.2

Retinotectal map in Xenopus *(Fraser 1985). An electrode was inserted in the tectal neuropil at each of the numbered electrode positions (A), and the region of visual field that elicits activity at each electrode position number was determined (B). The entire visual field region (shown in C) that elicits activity at the electrode tip, which is the sum of signals from many optic nerve fiber terminals, is termed a multiunit receptive field.*

by specific markers, as detailed in the chemoaffinity hypothesis, was the most reasonable explanation.

Experimental data obtained subsequently make it difficult, however, to account for the projection on this basis. Size disparities created experimentally between retina and tectum introduced by ablating portions of either or both showed, for example, that it was possible to map an entire retina (Gaze and Sharma 1970) onto half a tectum. Moreover, partial retinae could project onto the entire contralateral tectum. If they are to be explained adequately, these "compressions" and "expansions" of the map (Schmidt et al. 1978) require major and complex alterations of the strict chemoaffinity theory.

Attempts to show that the map can be accounted for by a "propagated order" already achieved by the temporal development of nerve fibers are unconvincing, even in cases where such orderly arrangements (Scholes 1979) can be seen in the optic nerve (Purves and Lichtman 1985). Indeed, in some animals, such as the cat, there is a rather confused distribution in the nerve and, in other animals, optic nerve axons rearrange when they reach the tectum.

The most striking argument against any single set of predetermined markers comes from studies originally done by Gaze and coworkers (Gaze and Sharma 1970) and confirmed recently by other researchers. This has been elegantly reviewed by Easter et al. (1985). The main conclusion is that while initially entering fibers form a retinotopically ordered map upon the rostral pole of the tectum in *Xenopus*, this projection is modified regularly as the tectum grows by cell division. This phenomenon prompted the sliding-connection hypothesis—that mapped synapses are formed, broken, and re-formed in a continually shifting fashion until the tectum ceases to grow. Easter (1985) has shown, moreover, that because of the different geometry of growth manifested by goldfish retinae and tecta, there is a topologic dissimilarity between the two growth zones. Nevertheless, in small fish (before the dissimilarity) and in large fish, the maps are not only orderly, but also similar (Easter 1983; Easter and Stuermer 1984). In this case, too, late-entering fibers must form connections that displace old connections and yet allow displaced fibers to form appropriate new connections.

In certain experiments bearing upon the chemoaffinity hypothesis, conclusions were reached using data on regenerating systems; in other experiments, the data were obtained from developmental systems. It is clear from the discussion in the preceding chapter that these systems cannot be strictly identical. Moreover, the classical experiments did not distinguish among the separate cellular developmental mechanisms of synapse formation, target recognition, and axon guidance described earlier in this chapter. These deficiencies and the contradictions mentioned above all suggest that an alternative *set* of mechanisms that do not invoke strict chemoaffinity is needed to account for the retinotectal map; moreover, it is likely that different mechanisms in such a set must be somewhat differently emphasized during the development of maps in different species.

Although the evidence is not complete, three or four observations suggest that retinotectal mapping is based on mechanisms consistent with the principles of the neuronal group selection theory. The first (Schmidt 1985) is that individual fibers extend arbors over a considerable part of the tectal surface. (It must be remembered that individual growth cones can have very extensive dimensions.) The second observation is that, while the original early map is more or less orderly, it is coarse and that individual optic nerve fibers have very wide receptive fields. This coarse map is refined as a result of activity: treatment of the retina with tetrodotoxin leads to elimination of refinement of the map (Schmidt 1982, 1985). Moreover, blockade of areas of fish and frog tecta with α-bungarotoxin leads to elimination of neurites and synapses from the affected area. Thus, refinement of the map depends upon neural function and activity and presumably upon selective retraction of those terminals of overlapping arbors that do not correspond to the appropriate coactivation of synapses in the input. This suggests that a competitive situation exists, the resolution of which depends upon function. This interpretation is entirely consistent with the observations on sliding synapses and has in fact been modeled as such by Fraser (1985). Most aspects of this model are consistent with the conclusions of the preceding chapter, except for the assumption of differential adhesion as an equilibrium situation. It is likely, however, that with kinetic assumptions based on CAM modulation, a similar model can be constructed and will yield similar mapping.

A more recent observation is directly related to the work on CAMs and formally connects the experimental situation of mapping to the issues of CAM function (Fraser et al. 1984; figure 5.3). Spikes of agarose containing anti-N-CAM antibodies placed *in vivo* in specific positions of one side of a *Xenopus* tectum after nerve transection yielded a distorted and extraordinarily coarse and overlapping map on the side of the implant. The map showed very large receptive fields (larger than those found for tetrodotoxin-treated animals); these fields were highly overlapping, and the termini of retinal axons were spread over much larger distances than normal. Depletion of the antibody over time resulted in reconstitution of a reasonably normal map. Given these experimental results on the target, and given that N-CAM is likely to be responsible in part for interactions between retinal fibers and the tectum, it is difficult to conceive of an explanation of mapping based on fixed markers. Instead, it seems reasonable to assume that the maps are the result of the interaction of complex dynamic variables. These include overlapping degenerate arbors, competition, and alteration of N-CAM, Ng-CAM, and cytotactin binding by local feedback mechanisms that eventually become dependent upon coactivation of input fibers. While a complete study of such mechanisms remains to be done, the currently available data suggest that the formation of an ordered map depends upon modulation mechanisms and upon selection with competition.

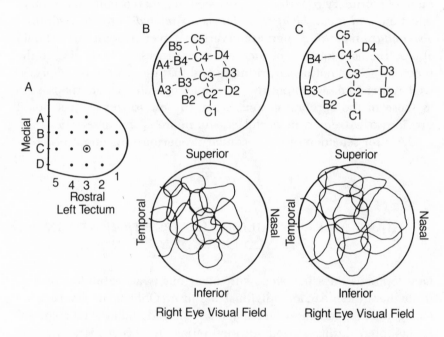

Figure 5.3

Effects of CAM antibodies upon the order of retinotectal maps. The metal microelectrode was lowered in the tectum at each of the positions indicated by dots on the representative tectum (A); the anti-N-CAM implant consisting of antibodies in an agarose spike was made at the circled position near the center of the tectum. Large circles in the other diagrams represent a 200-degree range of the field of view of the right eye, the center of which represents the fixation point of the eye. The center of the responsive region of the frog's visual field for each electrode position is marked in the upper row of circles by the code of the electrode positions shown in A. Below each of these diagrams are shown the diagrams of corresponding multiunit receptive fields. Class 1 patterns (B, upper) *obtained with nonimmune antibodies show the same rectilinear ar-rangement of receptive fields for the rectilinear set of electrode positions that is seen in normal animals. The size of the receptive fields* (B, lower) *in the projection shown here was among the largest of those seen in animals with class 1 projection patterns.* C: *Class 2 patterns obtained with anti-N-CAM show a distortion of the projection* (upper) *and an enlargement of the receptive fields* (lower). *This distortion is readily seen by comparing the positions of the corre-sponding receptive fields B3, C3, and D3 in* B *and* C.

Our previous brief survey of the cellular processes contributing to neural pattern during development also seems consistent with the idea that primary repertoires arranged into maps are formed by a *combination* of selective structural and functional events at different levels rather than by preassigned addressing. In other words, the achievement of a primary repertoire as it is seen in a map occurs as a result of selection, *and it can be affected by events related to the formation of a secondary repertoire.* Significant variation even in adult maps should also be the consequence of such selective processes. According to the theory, it would not be surprising to find that these same principles as well as certain new competitive principles operate in adult maps, such as those of the cerebral cortex. We turn now to this subject, for it provides an extremely powerful case for neuronal group selection, particularly for selection of the secondary repertoire by alteration of synapses.

ADULT MAPS: STABILIZED COMPETITION WITHIN FIXED CIRCUITRY

Development does not stop with birth but is a continuing process throughout the life of an individual organism. Only its mechanisms are changed: old mechanisms are shaped or altered and new mechanisms are adopted during periods of maturation. In this section, we shall consider evidence that, despite the relatively fixed cytoarchitectonics and anatomy established by developmental processes in the cerebral cortex, a considerable degree of individuality and plasticity affecting map boundaries remains in certain areas. This plasticity, which was commented upon early by Leyton and Sherrington (1917; see also Walshe 1948, esp. p. 161) provides an important clue to synaptic mechanisms as they bear upon mapping. Even within the confines of relatively static neuroanatomy, there is evidence for the existence of extraordinary potential variability based on competition and on interactions between structure and synaptic function. We therefore shift here from our previous emphasis on developmental neurobiology to neurophysiology.

Before doing so, we must stress that the data to be reviewed do not imply that cortical cytoarchitectonics are unimportant or do not exist. Indeed, Rose and Woolsey's definition (1949) of a cortical field as an area that has distinctive cytoarchitecture, has a unique relationship to a specific thalamic nucleus, and is coextensive with a physiologically definable area still holds. It is the last part of this definition that deserves scrutiny in the light of the work to be discussed here, however, for within certain bounds this part of the definition must be relaxed or at least reinterpreted.

Variability in Functional Maps and Map Reorganization

Recent experiments by Merzenich and his collaborators (Sur et al. 1980; Kaas et al. 1983; Merzenich et al. 1983a, 1983b, 1984a) support this view. Their studies represent a detailed analysis of densely mapped regions (every 100–150 μm) of areas 3b and 1 in the somatosensory cortex of adult owls and squirrel monkeys (figure 5.4). These investigators made extremely careful maps of individual normal monkeys for comparison and then remapped the same cortical areas at subsequent times after one or more of the following procedures had been performed: (1) transection of peripheral nerves such as the median nerve, either allowing or preventing conditions for regeneration; that is, the nerve was transected and tied to prevent regeneration, or transected and reconnected to promote regeneration; (2) amputation of single or adjacent digits (usually digit 2 or 3); (3) functional alteration without transection by appropriate bandaging, casts, or finger-tapping protocols; (4) local cortical ablations. The results of these studies compel a reassessment of cortical mapping in terms of neuronal group selection. The key observation is that cortical maps rapidly reorganize following nerve transection or digit amputation in adult monkeys.

Immediately after transection of the median nerve, an incomplete new representation arises within a part (but not all) of the cortical area that formerly represented the median nerve field (Merzenich et al. 1983a; figure 5.5). Over the next several months, this new representation gradually changes so that the skin site represented at any cortical location changes with time after the nerve transection (Merzenich et al. 1983b). The receptive field recorded at any cortical site is but one of the many possible receptive fields that, under different conditions, could be expressed at that cortical site. In the new maps, receptive fields originally located at a particular cortical site may occasionally be represented at various distances up to millimeters away from that site; thus, the same receptive field can be expressed anywhere over a relatively wide area of cortex. As the maps are restructured, basic topography is always maintained, so that continuity and global somatotopy are preserved at all times. Although there is movement of borders (such as

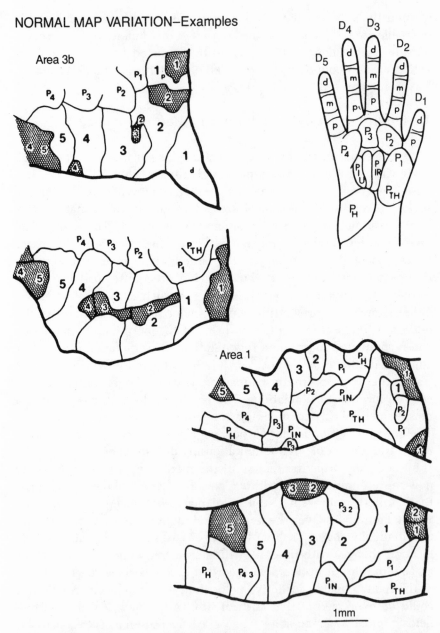

NORMAL MAP VARIATION–Examples

Area 3b

Area 1

1mm

Figure 5.4

Normal somatosensory map variations (Merzenich et al. 1984a). On the owl monkey hand (upper right), D_1–D_5 refer to digits; d, m, and p refer to distal, medial, and proximal phalanges; P_1–P_4 are the palmar pads; P_H is the hypothenar pad; and P_{TH} is the thenar pad. The two maps at the upper left show the internal topography of area 3b in two different adult owl monkeys, and the those between representations of glabrous and dorsal skin, and even those between hand and face areas), throughout this process the borders are always sharp. For example, cells on one side of a border might respond exclusively to glabrous inputs, while those on the other side might respond exclusively to stimulation of skin on the dorsum of the hand.

In normal maps of the hand in area 3b, glabrous regions are centrally represented (figure 5.4), with dorsal representations principally represented in zones along the medial and lateral margins of the hand representation (Merzenich et al. 1983a, 1983b). However, the normal map usually also contains small islands of dorsal representation scattered within the sea of digital representations of the glabrous surface. After median nerve transection, a larger dorsal representation immediately arises within the former median glabrous field, predominantly arranged around and in topographic continuity with the normal dorsal islands (Merzenich et al. 1983b). This supports the notion that the anatomical basis for this larger representation was always present but was effectively suppressed. Note that the novel dorsal map arises immediately only in the original territory of representation of the glabrous digits, not in the former region of representation of the palm, in which the normal representation does not manifest islands of "dorsal within glabrous" mapping.

After median nerve transection, large silent areas in which cells cannot be activated by any peripheral stimulation are also seen in the former representational area of the nerve. However, adjacent to these areas are cortical sites activated by new receptive fields. The location of the silent areas shifts with time (figure 5.5); they generally shrink but occasionally shift to a region that was previously active after transection

---

two maps at the lower right show that of area 1 in two different adult squirrel monkeys. The variability in the internal organization of area 1 is greater than that recorded in area 3b, but is very significant in both fields. In these examples, note (1) the large differences in the areas of representation of digits in the two area 1 maps; (2) the separation of the representation of digits 1 and 2 in one area 1 map (top) and their contiguous placement in the other; (3) the double and reversed representation of the first palmar pad and the thenar eminence recorded in area 1 in one monkey (top) and the more normal arrangement recorded in the other (many other differences are apparent on close examination of these maps); (4) the split representation of digit 1 in area 3b in one monkey (top), not seen in the other; (5) the significant difference in territory of representation of digit 1 in area 3b between the two monkeys; and (6) the differences in representation of dorsal digital surfaces in area 3b.

Time Sequence Postsection Maps

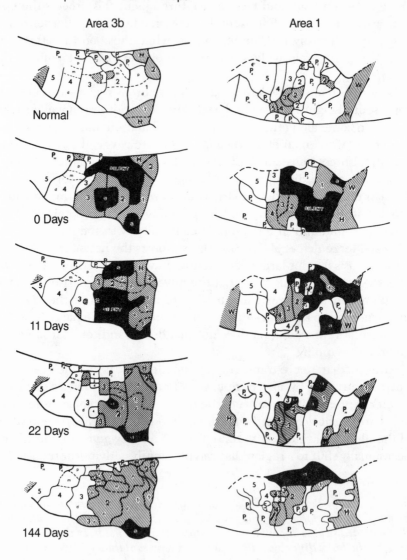

Figure 5.5

Temporal changes in somatosensory maps after lesions (Merzenich et al. 1983b). Cortical maps of the hand in area 3b (left) and area 1 (right) of a single squirrel monkey studied before, immediately after, and 11, 22, and 144 days after median nerve cut. Regions not derivable by cutaneous stimulation are shaded black; the representations of the dorsum are hatched; 1–5 refer to digits; H, hand; W, wrist; P, various palmar pads; other abbreviations as in figure 5.4.

(Merzenich et al. 1983b). After multiple amputations of adjacent digits, some silent areas remain and never completely fill in (Merzenich et al. 1984a). This indicates that the range of the anatomical basis for potential alternative maps is limited, being restricted to representations of body sites reasonably close to the original representation.

During reorganization, the representations of different hand surfaces (e.g., hypothenar pad, insular pad, dorsal digits) innervated by other nerves having bordering skin fields expand and contract in different sequences (Merzenich et al. 1983b, 1984a). In time (usually weeks), the radial nerve captures more of the previous median nerve territory in area 3b than does the ulnar nerve, but in area 1 the ulnar nerve captures more territory than the radial. By two to three weeks, reoccupation of the median field is complete, yet the map continues to reorganize internally for months (Merzenich et al. 1984a). If allowed to regenerate after resuturing, the median nerve initially forms a fragmented, disorganized, multiple representation. In time, the representation congeals and organizes to regain limited somatotopy (Merzenich et al. 1983b) and reoccupies an area quite similar but not identical to that before transection.

Several semiquantitative measurements were made of both receptive field representation and overlap and of distance limits during reorganization (figure 5.6). The larger the area of cortex devoted to a body part (the greater the magnification factor of the representation), the smaller the receptive fields on that body part. Conversely, smaller cortical representations yielded larger receptive fields. Thus, two-point discrimination, which improves with smaller receptive field size, may be attributable to the size of the cortical representation (Laskin and Spencer 1979; Merzenich et al. 1984a).

Particularly significant is the fact that the percentage overlap of the areas of the receptive fields of two cortical cells is a monotonically decreasing function of cortical separation of the cells (figure 5.6). There is reason to believe that the function decreases stepwise (Merzenich et al. 1983b), reaching zero overlap at critical separations of approximately 600 μm in normal animals (Sur et al. 1980). It is especially relevant to competition models of neuronal group selection that, for the first eleven days after nerve transection, receptive field overlap is greatly increased, the slope of the decreasing function is several times shallower than normal, and neurons 2 mm or farther away can have overlapping receptive fields.

Finally, there appears to be a distance limit of approximately 600 μm over which expansion of a representation can take place. After adjacent

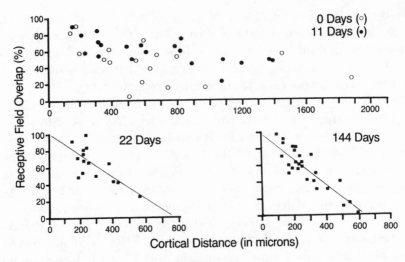

Figure 5.6

Receptive field changes in somatosensory cortex after a peripheral lesion (Mer-zenich et al. 1983b). Percentage overlap of receptive fields versus distance between cortical recording sites immediately after median nerve cut and 11, 22, and 144 days later. Receptive fields were on the backs of the middle and proximal phalanges of digits 1–3, and recording was in the area of former median nerve cortical representation. Note that the slope of the graph becomes less steep after transection, but that by day 144 the normal 600-μm limit is restored.

digit amputation, a silent area that extends over more than 600 μm in radius can never be completely reoccupied. Inasmuch as the sites of representations can effectively move distances of up to a millimeter, this is another indication that the anatomical basis for these translocated representations must have preexisted in a suppressed form in the vicinity. Any detailed model must specifically explain the similar 600-μm limit for expansion and for overlap of receptive fields.

There was no evidence that any sprouting takes place either peripherally or centrally after nerve transection and ligature. Changes in the map occur immediately after transection and continue to reorganize for months, whereas sprouting would follow a different time course. Even if sprouting did occur, it could not account for the observations on early or immediate changes. Moreover, different types of changes occur in area 3b versus area 1, although the two areas receive similar inputs. After noninvasive procedures such as finger tapping, related map changes are normally seen in area 1 and in area 3b, and it is difficult to postulate sprouting as an explanation for this correlation.

Finally, similar experiments by Wall et al. (Wall and Eggers 1971; Wall 1975; Devor and Wall 1981) on remapping in dorsal column nuclei indicate that remapping can occur in short times after blockade of the activity of lumbar spinal roots by low temperature. Moreover, this suggests that map reorganization is extensive in reentrantly connected areas at different levels.

A central conclusion (Edelman and Finkel 1984) directly supportive of the theory of neuronal group selection is compelled by these facts: from the degenerate anatomical substrate (or primary repertoire), a dynamic process must *select* particular neuronal groups in a secondary repertoire to form the functional map (Merzenich et al. 1983a, 1983b). The dynamic characteristic of this selection is indicated by the movements of representations and by the reestablishment of receptive field structure after transection. Indeed, evidence has been reviewed (Kaas et al. 1983; Merzenich et al. 1983a, 1983b) to indicate that normal (unlesioned) map structure is also dynamically maintained in adult primates. The results are consistent with the idea that maps are reorganized by selection over a degenerate network, and they suggest that the preexisting cortical anatomy provides the basis for limited territorial competition. In other words, following development, there exists a degenerate anatomical substrate upon which selection operates competitively at the synaptic level to create a functional map from a manifold of possible maps.

The major determinant of the competitive selection process during adult life appears to be significant neuronal activity resulting from temporal correlation of the inputs from overlapping afferents (Merzenich et al. 1983a, 1983b). We will provide a detailed model (see Edelman and Finkel 1984) of this entire process consistent with group selection theory in the next chapter, after discussing some evolutionary constraints on the formation of anatomical specializations. Before describing this model, however, we must mention some neuroanatomical data supporting the existence of extensive overlapping arbors in the primary repertoire. We must also consider some apparently contradictory intermediate cases in which map plasticity is definitely confined to short critical periods of developmental time and is not seen in adult life.

Arborization and Overlap

In order to account for map changes by selection upon a preexisting repertoire to create a secondary repertoire, it is necessary to show the prior existence of arbor extension, variability, and overlap. Horseradish peroxidase fillings of thalamic afferents to somatosensory cortex in the cat by Landry and Deschênes (1981; Landry et al. 1982) reveal axonal arborizations (figure 5.7) quite similar to those observed in visual cortex (Gilbert and Wiesel 1979, 1981). Single afferents usually give off collaterals before reaching the cortex, each of which ramifies in a bushy termination of approximately 400 μm diameter. Often, two bushy regions from the same collateral are aligned mediolaterally and are separated by a less dense region constituting a gap of about equal size (Landry et al. 1982). Other collaterals may end in bushes some distance away, usually in the anteroposterior directions, occasionally in another cytoarchitectonic area. Thus, in this species, terminals from a single afferent in area 3b are spread densely over about 0.5 mm^2 to 1.0 mm^2 of cortex, with other regions of collateral innervation some distance away. There may be significant anatomical differences between cat and monkey. For example, Pons and colleagues (1982), working in area 3b of the owl monkey, have found that, in general, there are somewhat smaller arbors without distant collateral branches. The basic argument remains unaffected by these differences.

In contrast to these known distance measurements, the precise degree of anatomic overlap between separate afferent arbors has been difficult to ascertain, particularly because there is currently no quantitative information regarding the density of cortical innervation. Degeneration studies shed some light on the matter. Small thalamic lesions in the cat (Kosar and Hand 1981) lead to anteroposteriorly oriented strips of degeneration 80–120 μm wide and 2500–3000 μm long. In the monkey (see Jones 1981), strips of different dimensions have been found by means of different techniques. Nonetheless, the relative dimensions indicate a marked anteroposterior anisotropy in the afferent terminations. In several different monkey genera, strips of degeneration seen after transection of commissural or interareal association fibers are in both cases 500–1000 μm wide and of varying lengths (Jones 1975; Jones et al. 1975).

Another source of information for estimating overlap, albeit in a specialized region, is provided by the mouse whisker barrel fields. Barrel C-1 has an average area of 57,000 μm^2 (Pasternak and Woolsey 1975) and receives input from the 162 peripheral fibers innervating vibrissa C-1 (Lee and Woolsey 1975). Assuming that convergence and divergence through the intervening synaptic relays keep the number of innervating fibers to within the same order of magnitude, we can calculate that there is a spacing of approximately 20 μm between adjacent afferents. This calculation assumes that the afferents are regularly spaced, and so does not apply strictly to the barrel fields themselves, but

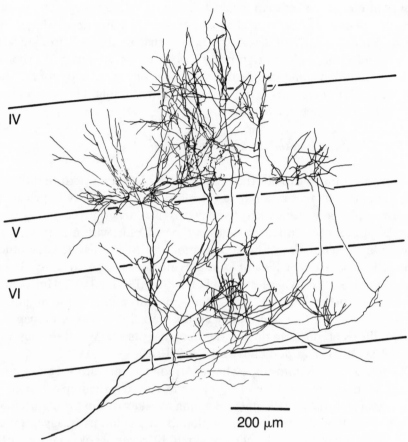

Figure 5.7
A thalamic afferent to area 3b in the cat as revealed by horseradish peroxidase injection (Landry and Deschênes 1981). The receptive field was on digit 5. The arbor extends over an area of approximately 1 mm of cortex in this section. Roman numbers refer to cortical layers.

it suggests roughly what the innervation density might be in other cortical regions.

Although these examples come from different species, and interspecies differences must ultimately be taken into account, two major conclusions of great significance for neuronal group selection and for the idea of the degeneracy emerge from this anatomy: (1) there is significant overlap between afferent axonal arborizations, perhaps greater in some directions than others; and (2) every cortical cell receives synapses from a large number of afferents, especially considering the possible interactions of widespread axonal arbors with large dendritic trees. To

explain how a precise map is selected on the background of this extensively degenerate anatomical substrate, we must analyze in detail the
distribution of activity across the cortex that might lead to neuronal
group selection. Before attempting this in the next chapter, we should
briefly mention some contrasting examples of *confined* plasticity that
actually occur only during development and that might appear on first
view to contradict our hypothesis.

Map Changes Linked to Critical Periods

Any attempt to explain the adult changes based on peripheral tran-
sections, on changes in input to receptors, and on sensory deprivation
must also be consistent with observations that, in certain cortical subre-
gions, apparently similar changes can occur only within narrow win-
dows of developmental time. Operations on such areas at later times
have little or no effect. Salient examples include changes in the developing visual cortex (Wiesel and Hubel 1963a, 1963b, 1965; Hubel and
Wiesel 1970; Stryker and Harris 1986) and alterations in the organization of the rodent somatosensory cortex (barrel fields) after damage to
the follicles of vibrissae during the neonatal period (Van der Loos and
Woolsey 1973; Van der Loos and Dörfl 1978).

There is a large and somewhat contradictory literature concerning
the effects of unilateral eye closure, removal, or deprivation on detailed
map features in the neonatal and young monkey or the cat (figure 5.8).
It is clear that distinctive ocular dominance columns in layer IV of
monkey visual cortex do not appear until three weeks before birth
(Rakic 1977, 1978, 1981b). At earlier stages, geniculocortical fibers overlap. The truly sharp segregation of such columns occurs at about six
weeks. If there is early closure of one eye by suture, then the columns
corresponding to the deprived eye are narrowed and those of the functioning eye are enlarged. The data suggest that fibers of the functioning
eye do not retract and that this is another example of competitive
balance in developing fiber tracts. After a critical period, however, such
procedures have no effect.

In the case of damage to vibrissal follicles and subsequent alterations
of rodent barrel fields, a similar dependence upon a critical period is
also observed. Anatomical changes, which consist of enlargement and
fusions of barrels to form fused bands in layer IV of rat somatosensory
cortex, only occur if the peripheral damage is inflicted within the first
neonatal week (Van der Loos and Woolsey 1973; Woolsey and Wann
1976; Van der Loos and Dörfl 1978; Woolsey et al. 1981).

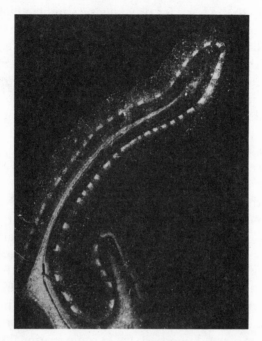

Figure 5.8
Ocular dominance columns (Hubel and Wiesel 1977). Dark-field autoradio-graph of striate cortex in an adult macaque in which the ipsilateral eye had been injected with tritiated proline-fucose two weeks earlier. Labeled areas show as white. Section passes for the most part in a plane perpendicular to the surface. Part of the exposed surface of the striate cortex and the buried part immediately beneath. In all, some fifty-six columns can be counted in layer IVc.

The key question posed by these findings is whether they correspond to the persistent plasticity seen in areas 3b and 1 after manipulation of the afferents from the hand. A clear-cut answer has so far not been forthcoming—but it should be noted that, in these two cases of the visual cortex and the barrel fields, large competitive anatomical changes are induced *while* connections are still being made during development in *relatively small* cortical areas (columns or barrels) that will eventually function for fine spatial discrimination. The changes in anatomy are otherwise consistent with the competitive interactions reviewed earlier. However, unlike the somatosensory case, these two cases involve functional target units that may be small enough to be within the same range of size as the spread of individual thalamocortical afferents, and this mapping of ranges obviously occurs while the anatomy is still being formed. This may have occurred for evolutionary reasons related to the need for precise visual and tactile function dealing with resolution in small regions of space. After fixation of the neuroanatomy following the critical period, one might not expect to see as large a set of shifts as those seen in areas 3b and 1, where the mapped representations and boundaries cover a large number of overlapping afferents. Put in another way, in both the dominance columns and the barrel fields, there may be a correspondence between the border of the *functional* mapping unit and that of the *anatomical* unit as determined by the axonal arbors of the afferents from the thalamus. The competitive interactions seen in these systems, unlike those of the adult somatosensory cortex but like those of later periods of retinotectal map formation, involve the formation of anatomy as well as synaptic competition. As we indicated above, this may be a natural evolutionary consequence of the very early behavioral need for a high degree of spatial refinement in these two systems. This conclusion may or may not be consonant with the observation of the necessity for activity (Schmidt 1985) in the formation of refined retinotectal maps, but an interesting experiment involving pharmacologic blockade in the critical period suggests itself.

Despite the exceptions detailed here, the existence of adult synaptic plasticity seems beyond question: while some neuronal sprouting may occur after early development in such systems, it is likely that the major competitive forces are a result of synaptic changes. We will take this into account in the next chapter, in which we will first review the evolutionary origin and overall connectivity of primary cortical areas and then model the results described here on plasticity of mapping in terms of neuronal group selection. The reason for delaying consideration of this model until some evolutionary issues have been described has to do not only with the need to account for the evolutionary emergence of mapped areas that are structurally and functionally different but also with the fact that natural selection will act differently on the variant phenotypic functions of such areas in behaving animals of a species.

CONCLUSIONS

We may now summarize our views on map development. The preceding chapter presented evidence for mechanochemical mechanisms tying genetics to epigenetics by molecular means and leading both to structural variability and constancy in anatomy as postulated in the regulator hypothesis. In the present chapter, a series of dynamic and more or less independent primary cellular processes consistent with these mechanisms were reviewed to provide a background for understanding how maps are formed. While many types of neurons show what appear to be preprogrammed cytodifferentiation for cell shape, it has been found that connections could shift after forming initial maps, that competitive interactions can occur among neurons for target innervation, and that axonal and dendritic arbors can extend over considerable distances in an overlapping fashion and be remodeled by the activity of contingent connections. The considerable amount of cell death accompanying some of these transactions in development does not appear to be rigidly preprogrammed; instead, it seems to be related to selective interactions among competing neurons for appropriate connectivity, and it can be stochastic. Moreover, in several cases, appropriate establishment of stabilized populations of neurons has been shown to depend, even during development, upon the onset of synaptic function and upon chemical factors so far not clearly defined.

The striking generalization is that the theme of competitive interaction is repeated in a variety of contexts: in retinotectal mapping, in critical-period processes during the perinatal period in certain refined sensory systems, and in adult states for alterations in other sensory systems having much larger receptive fields. The bulk of the evidence suggests a dynamic origin even of highly refined and stereotyped neuroanatomical circuitry; *ipso facto,* this dynamism implies variability and selection. In some instances, the emphasis appears to be on selection in development by mechanochemical means at the cell surface; in others, selection occurs via synaptic function and is particularly sensitive to the nature of the afferent stimulation and input. In yet other instances, such as in the retinotectal system, one form of selection follows upon the other. Clearly, the mix of mechanisms depends upon the phenotypic function of the brain region in question. Before we can provide a detailed theoretical model of how these factors interact in the adult organism to yield reentrant maps, we must therefore turn to the evolutionary origins of neural structures such as nuclei and laminae with diverse phenotypic functions. This consideration of evolutionary origins of different regions is particularly important in documenting the point (see chapter 8) that simple maps are in general insufficient for perceptual categorization. Instead, as further analysis will show, the interactions of complex multiple reentrant maps involving various modalities and continuous activity of the motor system are required.

6

Evolution and Function
of Distributed Systems

INTRODUCTION

So far, we have considered the evidence for the origins of constancy and variability of neural structures within a species, particularly within the individual during development. Although this provides a basis for understanding certain aspects of neuronal group selection in the formation of local maps, it does not account for the evolutionary origins of larger neural structures such as particular nuclei and laminae, for the regionally defined neuroanatomical characteristics of particular maps, or for map-to-map interaction in a reentrant fashion. No brain theory can be considered complete without relating its premises to the evolutionary origins of these structures, especially to the distributed nature of such systems in complex brains (Mountcastle 1978). For this, we must turn to comparative neuroanatomy, relating it to possible function and specifically to evolutionary explanations of interspecies variability. Our goal will be to develop a satisfactory account of the hierarchical, distributed, and yet mapped organization of the nervous systems of late-emerging species having highly developed telencephalic structures. We will therefore restrict the discussion to chordates.

It is a major premise of the theory that the capacity to carry out categorization requires special parallel arrangements of different modalities arranged in a distributed fashion, and an account of the evolutionary emergence of these arrangements is therefore required. Because the theory would not be adequate if it did not show how its developmental premises were consistent with the evolutionary facts, we also wish to determine whether there are evolutionary explanations for the persistence of degeneracy in even the most complex and specific neural structures. Such explanations, if satisfactory, would further reconcile the common macroscopic structure of defined brain regions in a species with the existence of microscopic variability.

In attempting to understand the evolution of these features of complex brains, we confront one of the major conceptual crises of modern neuroscience—the issue of localization of function. Within the context of morphologic evolution, this means that we must relate function to structure during the natural selection of different phenotypes, paying due attention to developmental constraints (Alberch 1979, 1980, 1982a, 1982b, 1987; Bonner 1982; Raff and Kaufman 1983; Arthur 1984; Edelman 1986b). It is a formidable problem to try to account for the evolution of any complex organ, but in the case of the brain it is particularly daunting. As Ulinski (1980) has pointed out, the problem cannot be resolved by simple correlations between environmental properties and the regional activity of a neural system, by prediction of neural circuit properties, or by categorical assignments of functions to given neural components. It is, in fact, usually not possible to assign a particular function to a given neural structure such as a nucleus or a lamina with any assurance that the function is uniquely accounted for or that the structure is not carrying out some other function (Mountcastle 1978). However, given the remarkable specificity of certain sensory systems, it is not reasonable to argue alternatively, as Lashley did (Lashley 1950; see Orbach 1982), that global functions are diffusely and equipotentially represented.

The position taken here (and the only one consistent with neuronal group selection theory) is that the real basis for overall functional responses is the dynamic interaction of specific individual components arranged in repertoires of neuronal groups or populations within different mapped reentrant structures rather than the fixed assignment of function to anatomically distinct regions. Although constrained by input and output, particular cells or groups in a repertoire are not necessarily constantly related to a given function; nonetheless, different primary repertoires will differ in function in globally different brain areas. The function of such entities may be time-dependent and determined by the competitive dynamics of neuronal groups: the same component may function differently in different contexts. Still, as the facts of physiology indicate, a partitioning of global function *does* occur in larger systems: there is, for example, no doubt about the modalities to which particular primary receiving areas are dedicated. As we shall argue in the next chapter, however, even in some of these cytoarchitectonically distinguishable areas, too sharp a distinction between sensory and motor function can be misleading.

Determining the relationship between phenotypic function and neural structure is an exceedingly complex problem for evolutionary theory. Not only are the neural variables themselves determined by nonlinear networks; there is, in addition, a set of nonlinear relationships between the categorization of environmental variables and particular behavioral responses. Despite these difficulties, one may delineate certain interrelated problems of a smaller scale that must be solved before these larger issues can be analyzed satisfactorily, even from a theoretical point of view.

These problems will be considered in sequence in the present chapter. They concern (1) the general features exhibited by neural networks, groups, and cells across various taxa as a result of evolutionary change; (2) the bases for interspecies variability and for the general increase in complexity and specificity of neural systems over evolutionary time; (3) the relation of such evolutionary change to developmental genetics and the nature of the developmental constraints on evolutionary change as proposed in the regulator hypothesis; and (4) some functional bases through which natural selection may act on the phenotype. These problems will be clarified by an analysis of the dynamic properties of somatosensory maps in adult animals (see chapter 5), particularly in their relation to distributed systems (Mountcastle 1978). The analysis will take into account the evolutionary, morphogenetic, and physiological principles covered in previous discussions and will result in a more refined definition of a neuronal group.

Each of these problems is exceptionally challenging, each is linked to the others, and each requires examination of a large body of data that obviously cannot be reviewed here in detail. We will attempt instead to trace the interrelations among these problems. The first problem will be approached in terms of some descriptive generalizations derived from comparative neuroanatomy. For the remaining three problems, we will invoke organizing principles based on the theory of neuronal group selection, relating morphologic evolution to the developmental constraints imposed by the regulator hypothesis, described in chapter 4. This will lay the groundwork for a theoretical proposal to account both for interspecies variability and for the origin of new and more complex brain structures. We will then be in a position to synthesize both the anatomical findings and the functional results in a model for one evolved region, the somatosensory cortex. Our model will provide some bases for understanding the modes by which natural selection might act on the phenotype to select variants of a functioning brain region.

EVOLUTIONARY CHANGE IN NEURAL NETWORKS

During phylogeny, the brain is the most variable of all complex organ systems and the telencephalon is the most variable of brain regions. Given the general tendency of evolutionary systems toward greater complexity (Stebbins 1968) and the known behavioral complexities of phenotypes with large brains, this is perhaps not surprising. As a brief review of chordate and vertebrate neural evolution (Masterton et al. 1976a; Sarnat and Netsky 1981) will show, despite this variability, one can still discern some specific trends that bear upon the common origin of constant features of nervous systems in different species. Ebbesson (1980) has pointed out, for example, that the lower brain stem has a great number of common features in most vertebrate species; in contrast, tectal, thalamic, and telencephalic regions show a high degree of diversity. Inasmuch as the functions of a given component of the brain are not necessarily locally defined, such evolutionary deductions from comparative neuroanatomy (Dullemeijer 1974) must be based mainly on morphological and structural criteria; that is, homology can be inferred only for anatomic *structures* and not for function (but see Masterton et al. 1976a; Bullock 1984).

Within the emerging constraints of different extrinsic connections and other phenotypic changes during the course of evolution, a given structure (even a whole nucleus) may change its function. Comparisons from species to species on the basis of similar cell types, topography (including various landmarks such as sulci), and fiber connections must nonetheless remain fixed within the confines of homologous neural fields. This is a strong constraint and it makes functional extrapolation difficult. Moreover, it is well to remember that the nervous system evolved for adaptive action and reaction. Its glandular functions to maintain the interior milieu as well as certain aversive and appetitive features of motor responses were probably the chief bases for selection during its *early* evolution. We shall take up only a few such functional issues here, because they involve arguments from plausibility rather than solidly grounded hypotheses; in the interests of the theory, we are committed mainly to a consideration of the evolutionary origins of primary repertoires. Nonetheless, because natural selection is for behavior, it is important to show how variation in such repertoires can affect behavior, particularly in mapped systems, a task we shall take up at the end of the chapter.

The major reasons for considering any of these issues in the context of the theory of neuronal group selection are (1) to provide a basis for a discussion of the mechanism by which distributed systems (Mountcastle 1978) arose during neural evolution and (2) to show how degeneracy (Edelman 1978) may have emerged as a major principle governing the function of highly complex brains. We will say less about the evolution of the neuron itself; here, we may note that, from tunicates on, it is among the most ancient of highly differentiated cell types.

Certain useful generalizations important for the theory emerge from a long view of the evolution of vertebrate nervous systems from chordates to man. Unlike the principles governing earlier precursors, the grand themes are bilateral symmetry and progressive cephalization (Sarnat and Netsky 1981); subsidiary themes include decussation, metamerism, overlap, somatotopy, and parallelism (table 6.1). The development of increasing numbers of nuclei and laminae, of internal regulation, and of systems for appetitive food gathering appears to have been paralleled by the need to develop sensorimotor aversive responses to predators (Masterton et al. 1976b). The early basic layout around a muscular notochord (as in amphioxus) was bilaterally symmetrical, with repeated myotomes supplied by repetitive nerves from a spinal cord but with no evidence of special senses. This metameric theme of segmental sensory innervation in the periphery is constant throughout subsequent vertebrate evolution, but the arrangement of alternation between sensory and motor innervation (seen in cyclostomes) gives way

Table 6.1

Structural Themes in the Evolution of the Nervous System*

Main Themes	Concomitants
Bilateral symmetry	Orienting and aversive movements
Decussation	Sensorimotor coordinations
Metamerism (sensorimotor)	Modularity
Progressive cephalization	Special senses
	Fusion of structures
	Enlargement
	Repetition of microscopic structures (modularity)
Overlap of innervation	Degeneracy
	"Compaction" of tracts
Somatotopy	Mapping
Parallelism of multiple sensorimotor systems	Reentry (classification couples)
Increasing number of nuclei and laminae	Multilayered structures, vertical and horizontal circuit organization
	Variation and increasing numbers of cell types

*This table omits explicit consideration of musculoskeletal and motor ensembles in relation to posture and gesture. This subject is taken up in detail in chapter 8.

in terrestrial forms to dorsal and ventral roots that emerge in each segment at the same level.

Overlap is nonetheless a major principle, and no segment receives innervation strictly from one root only, an early form of degeneracy. This principle is crucial for understanding later central representations of the periphery in maps and is probably attributable to the selection of those forms that, as a consequence of this overlap, did not lose segmental innervation after local injury. Somatotopic representation is also seen in many central structures. From the earliest times, this is a basic feature in dorsal spinal nerves and their roots as well as in ventral horns and motor nerves; it appears later in cerebellar cortex and nuclei, retinal fields, and cortex. Overlap and somatotopy are in all likelihood related to the necessary continuity in small neighboring regions of the inductive cellular collectives that form during regulative development; in later evolution, separation and enlargement of derivatives of such regions would tend to maintain some degree of continuity, a fact of central importance for mapping.

With increasing cephalization, concomitant new developments emerge: special senses, enlargements of the brain, shifts in the position

of myotomes, shifts and fusions in the formation of cranial roots, alteration in the positions and number of branchial clefts, and, finally, growth
of the forebrain (Ebbesson and Northcutt 1976). While structures tend
to be bilaterally paired, asymmetries can be seen in structures such as
the habenula (related to feeding habits), in the vagus nerve, and, eventually, in the cerebral cortex; certain unpaired structures like the pineal
are also sustained.

Within the context of these developments, another general feature
appears early and is of great significance for neuronal group selection:
the emergence of reentrant systems in a series of developments presag-
ing the ultimate function of categorization. One sees the appearance of
similar or different *parallel* neural systems for sampling the environment or for reacting to it in an arrangement that provides a much richer
resource than does bilateral symmetry alone (table 6.1). This fundamental feature accompanies the development of all somatic and special
sensory systems as well as motor and autonomic systems. It makes
possible sampling by means of two or more different modalities or
submodalities simultaneously, an important development leading to
the creation of a new function or the modification of a function. In its
simplest form, it is dyadic, as may be seen in several cases: (1) in organisms with an olfactory bulb and an accessory olfactory bulb, for example, the vomeronasal system in snakes, lizards, and turtles (Graziadei
and Tucker 1970; Halpern, 1976); (2) in the development of the vestibular system; (3) in the concurrent maintenance of retinotectal and
retinogeniculate systems (Schneider 1969); (4) in the higher-order parallel arrangements seen in the spinothalamic and spinocerebellar tracts;
and (5) in the dorsal column system. As we shall see later, a dyadic
parallel arrangement is an essential *minimum* requirement for an
effective reentrant system of neuronal group selection. This arrangement is the so-called classification couple (see figure 3.4), to be described in detail in chapters 9, 10, and 11. The requirement for such
parallel arrangements is tied to the need for disjunctive sampling of
polymorphous sets in the stimulus domain in an adaptive manner, as
was discussed in chapters 1 and 3.

Another central feature related to bilateral symmetry that is seen in
a variety of species is the existence of crossed pathways in the presence
or absence of ipsilateral pathways. Sarnat and Netsky (1981) have reviewed the earliest progenitors available for study—crossed connections from singular neurons. These are the Rohde cells in amphioxus,
Mueller cells in cyclostomes (Rovainen 1978), and Mauthner cells in
teleosts (Bullock 1978; Faber and Korn 1978). Rohde cells are decussat-

ing interneurons in the spinal cord of amphioxus that mediate the aversive coiling reflex, and Mueller and Mauthner cells are brain stem neurons having dendritic synapses with vestibular and sensory neurons. Their axons are projected on the contralateral side of the cord to caudal segments mediating aversive and reflex tail movements. It has been proposed that the same selective pressures that gave adaptive advantage to aversive reflexes away from the threatened sides gave rise to decussation of optic nerves. Sarnat and Netsky (1981) have also pointed out that dorsal columns in higher animals are similar and that their connectivity resembles that of the so-called Rohon-Beard cells (Spitzer and Spitzer 1975; Spitzer, 1985), which are seen as transient sensory neurons in the tadpoles of certain amphibians. These multisynaptic cells send dendritic branches to muscle and skin. Their axons ascend ipsilaterally in the cord but synapse with decussating interneurons to relay impulses to motor neurons on the opposite side. In the case of dorsal column nuclei, the role is strictly sensory and the decussating interneurons are in the cells of the gracile and cuneate nuclei. Ebbesson (1980) accounts for these findings in a somewhat different fashion; the main point here is that the early overall patterns of decussation are either preserved in certain lines of descent or redeveloped by convergent evolution.

A number of other general morphological features (table 6.1) of neural organization also deserve special notice, particularly as they relate to ideas of somatic selection and reentry. The first is the fact that long ascending and descending tracts are not as compact in descendants of earlier vertebrates as they are in later vertebrates. This bears upon the evolutionary significance of degeneracy, a subject to be taken up later. A second general feature is found in the local organization of structures such as the cerebellum and various telencephalic derivatives: the presence of modular or repetitive structures such as those of the folia of the cerebellum or of cortical columns. It must not be assumed that these repetitive structures lack internal variance: as we mentioned in chapters 2 and 3, they are in fact a main matrix for quantitative as well as microscopic and chemical qualitative variations (Chan-Palay et al. 1981; Ingram et al. 1985) that provide a basis for the different repertoires postulated by the theory.

A third general feature (of particular pertinence to the theory of neuronal group selection) is the increasing tendency during evolution toward the development of reentrant connectivity. This feature is expressed in the development of the vestibular system for orientation in space and in the vestibulospinal tract, which is the first motor tract to

regulate spinal motor neurons. Such reentrant structures appear early
(just after amphioxus) in precursors of the true vertebrates. Eventually,
the tracts related to lateral line organs that had evolved for detection
of displacements in water currents became adapted for the auditory
system of the cochlea. Finally, with the development of cerebellar
structures, large numbers of reentrant pathways emerged (Sarnat and
Netsky 1981). The theme of reentry is also prominent in the independent development of dorsal thalamic structures for optic responses. The
dorsal column nuclei appearing in reptiles provide an early example of
reentrant long tracts; accordingly, there is a descending projection
from gracile and cuneate nuclei. By the time of advanced telencephalic
developments, reentry is a major feature of most complex systems of
afferent and efferent nuclei as well as of laminae, in the sense that they
have local modules connected to each other by mutual intrinsic connections.

What is the adaptive significance of reentrant connections? As the
theory of neuronal group selection implies, they are essential for the
temporal correlation of various inputs and for the development of new
functions by linkage of classification couples, as will be shown in chapters 9 and 10. The more conventional view has been that they are
"feedback systems" in the sense of control theory. The difficulty with
this view lies in its assumption that specific coded information is travel-
ing along each reentrant pathway. While there are certainly examples
of gross reentrant reflex arcs that subserve feedback functions, this
interpretation seems inadequate as a *general* explanation of function in
most major complex circuits. A more plausible general explanation is
that the existence of classification couples and the parallelism of higher-
order circuits both require coordinated adjustment of the responses of
interconnected subsystems at all levels of a parallel distributed system;
reentry provides such a means. As we shall see later in this chapter
when we provide a model of somatosensory maps, reentry uses mechanisms of selection rather than of feedback.

A NETWORK EXAMPLE

Many of the general principles in this brief evolutionary survey can be
illustrated by reviewing a circuit discussed by Ulinski (1980), who has
characterized the visual network (Hall and Ebner, 1970a, 1970b) of the
red-eared turtle *(Pseudemys scripta elegans)* in terms of its evolution-

ary bases and functional morphology (see figure 6.1). Ulinski makes a number of points: (1) The organization of the network is nonlinear, having two parallel routes to the dorsal ventricular ridge. (2) Not all pairs of nuclei are directly connected—the ventral lateral geniculate nucleus is not linked to the nucleus rotundus, for example. This is relevant to the evolutionary hypothesis of parcellation to be discussed later, but it also illustrates the notion that even locally, at the level of microcircuitry, n elements do not form n^2 connections. As rich as the connectivity of the central nervous system is, it is of a much lower order than would be implied by a complete graph. (3) On each side, the network is so arranged as to maintain a through path of connectivity that emphasizes signals from the contralateral eye. (4) Several connections are reciprocal and thus may be reentrant. (5) Nuclei close to the input side receive visual signals; those near the output side receive signals from several sensory modalities. (6) Although it has a single visual input, the network has two outputs—the first to the hypothalamus and hypophysis and the second, via the reticular formation, to motor neurons.

In considering the function of the projections to the tectum in this network, Ulinski (1980) also emphasizes the relationship between topologic properties, magnification factors, or metric properties, and the parallel temporal and reentrant properties of such a system. He points out the well-known topological continuity of the retinotectal map but stresses, too, the metric disparities that must have evolved—retinal measures are different from tectal measures, as is shown by the fact that there is a difference in area between the retinal surface and tectal surface. Because of this, the map is scaled so that a traverse of 1.0 μm of retinal surface per msec covers only 0.2 μm of tectal surface per msec. Such a map also has additional corticotectal projections which link to the basal dendrites and somata of deep radial tectal cells, in contrast to the retinal projection which links to the apical dendrites. Cortical receptive fields are much larger than those of retinal ganglion cells. In consequence, two spatiotemporal factors play upon function within this circuit arrangement: a cluster of deep cells in the tectum receives input representing a domain of visual space in coarse grain on basal dendrites, and simultaneously there is a representation in fine grain on apical dendrites. Moreover, the input from the retina arrives with 50 msec latency, a much earlier arrival than that from cortex, which has much longer latency. As Ulinski puts it, the time window for a given radial cell to function is determined by its convergent projections. When a fly moving at 10°/sec causes input at a given cluster of

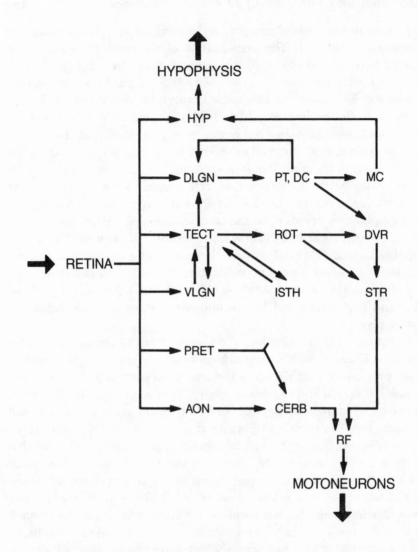

Figure 6.1

Visual network in Pseudemys, *a typical challenge to evolutionary analysis (Ulinski 1980). Interrelations between the structures known to be involved in the visual network in* Pseudemys *are diagrammed. It is likely that many structures, such as the pretectum, have additional connections, which are still unknown. Abbreviations: AON, accessory optic nuclei; CERB, cerebellum; DC, dorsal cortex; DLGN, dorsal lateral geniculate nucleus; DVR, dorsal ventricular ridge; HYP, hypothalamus; ISTH, nucleus isthmi; MC, medial cortex; PT, pallial thickening; PRET, pretectum; RF, reticular formation; ROT, nucleus rotundus; STR, striatum; VLGN, ventral lateral geniculate nucleus. As discussed in the text, this circuit contains components with different receptive fields, convergent receptivities, time delays, and dendritic spreads.*

the apical dendritic field to arrive over a period of 10 msec, the basal dendrites of the same cluster are receiving input about the same visual space more than 30 msec before the fly arrived.

This analysis points up the strong need for correlation in both spatial *and* temporal domains of signals in a parallel reentrant system. Tectal efferents from radial cells specify the interactions of the tectum in the whole network, and this necessitates coordinated mapped changes in all of the tectally connected nuclei in the network. This circuit example is a highly relevant instance illustrating the principles related to spatio-temporal continuity originally discussed in the first proposal of neuronal group selection (Edelman 1978). The means by which reentrant connections are actually coordinated in circuits is a major problem that will be considered in chapter 10.

To understand this circuit example, we must highlight several features of the phylogenetic data: (1) how cells segregate their inputs and outputs to define a nucleus or lamina; (2) how segregation of multiple nuclei can occur in parallel in relatively short evolutionary times; (3) how very rapid changes in size can occur in a particular structure (the primate cortex is the outstanding example). We will address the larger aspects of these issues in the last section of this chapter. But first we will turn to the variation of richly connected reentrant circuits among nuclei and laminae in different species. Their evolutionary origins will be explained in terms of the regulator hypothesis, and a structural and functional model will be proposed for the group selective behavior of such circuits in maps.

INTERSPECIES VARIABILITY: THE EVOLUTIONARY ORIGIN OF NUCLEI, LAMINAE, AND PARALLEL CIRCUITS

How do circuits such as the neuronal network we have just discussed arise, and what combination of developmental and evolutionary mechanisms is responsible for the emergence of the variety of nuclei and laminae in the brain? In a series of comparative studies, Ebbesson (Ebbesson et al. 1972; Ebbesson and Northcutt 1976; Ebbesson 1980, 1984) has addressed the question of how such structures arise through evolution from early forms. To account for the remarkable interspecies variability in otherwise homologous neural circuits, he has suggested a unifying idea, the parcellation theory (Ebbesson 1980). It is clear from what we have already said that the sensory and motor structures of a given phenotype result from *coevolution* of various nuclei, laminae, and connectivities in different species. Older systems in general persist and show increased cell numbers but are also supplemented by newer systems. There is a pattern of constancy but also one of diversity: brain stems of vertebrates have most structural features in common, but the tectal, thalamic, and telencephalic regions are more variable. What accounts, for example, for the presence of nine visual thalamic nuclei in the Tegu lizard and of two in the nurse shark while there are only three in most mammals (Ebbesson et al. 1972)?

Ebbesson's proposal (figure 6.2) is that neural systems evolve by *parcellation* (rearrangement and reconnection) of *already existing systems*, a process accompanied by increases in cell number. To quote his proposal (Ebbesson 1980), "Neural systems evolve not by the mixing of systems, not *de novo*, but by differentiation and parcellation which involves competition of inputs, the redistribution of inputs, and the loss of connections."

A

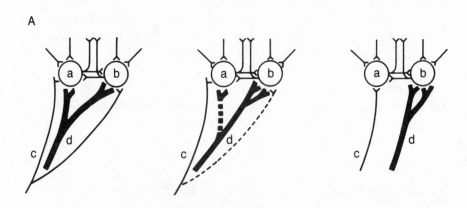

Figure 6.2
The parcellation theory of Ebbesson (1980). The parcellation process is thought to involve the loss of one or more inputs to a cell or aggregate of cells as new subcircuits evolve. A: The diagram shows how two identical neurons (a and b) in a hypothetical aggregate become less and less influenced by a given input, with the eventual outcome that cell a loses input d and cell b input c. Further parcellation of such clusters can occur if some cells lose other inputs or outputs. Collaterals or main axons may degenerate in response to various selective pressures. Certain cells can lose some of their dendrites as given inputs recede, and cell size decreases if axon collaterals or main projections are also lost. B: Another example. Schematic sequence (1–4) of hypothetical cell aggregates undergoing parcellation with the eventual production of two cell groups with different inputs.

The degree of parcellation depends upon the neural organization that obtained when new selection pressures were encountered and upon the strength of those pressures. Ebbesson (1984) provides evidence to reject competing notions that diversity is achieved by the merger of existing systems, by invasion of one system by the other, or by *de novo* mutations, any one of which might lead to the specific or direct creation of a new neural structure. The proposed mechanism of parcellation is, by contrast, one in which more or less diffusely connected early systems containing a potential range of patterns are restructured during natural selection by the *selective loss* of connections from daughter cell aggregates. Ordered complexity thus results from removal, and distributed systems result from the *redistribution* of connections.

Although Ebbesson does not claim that parcellation is the *only* mechanism for all evolutionary pattern, he proposes it to account for much of interspecies variability. In principle, parcellation can be closely coordinated with previously discussed developmental and genetic mech-

B

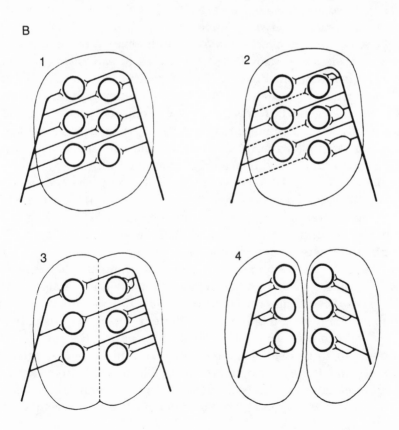

anisms as they bear upon evolution as well as upon neuronal group selection. Indeed, in view of its fundamental premise, which is a form of eliminative selection, it could provide one of the bases for the evolutionary origin and modification of degeneracy in even the most sophisticated nervous system. Nevertheless, as we shall discuss below, a detailed scrutiny of the facts prompts us to reject parcellation as too limited in scope to explain all the variations seen and as too closely grounded in recapitulationist ideas to be fully consistent with neuronal group selection. This does not imply, however, that mechanisms akin to parcellation do not occur in the evolution of certain portions of the nervous system.

Despite its limitations, the line of evidence that gave rise to this idea is extremely revealing and worthy of review. Ebbesson studied five systems by modern comparative methods: olfactory, visual, ascending spinal, and tectal and thalamic afferents. He employs the term "neocortical equivalent" to specify structures with connections similar to those of mammals. The use of modern methods led to the discovery that, contrary to some previous views, telencephalic regions in nonmammalian vertebrates receive a relatively small olfactory input; the major input comes from nonolfactory sources. Additional evidence indicated that a neothalamus exists in these vertebrates, in particular a somatosensory region ventromedial to the lateral geniculate. Ebbesson discovered neocortical equivalents in the shark representing visual inputs. Four basic telencephalic forms were found in different species: (1) laminated hemispheres (amphibians), (2) nonlaminar organizations (elasmobranch and birds), (3) a mixture of laminar and nonlaminar structures (reptiles), and (4) everted nonlaminar structures (teleosts).

In these systems, bilaterality is very variable: in the shark visual system, almost all the fibers are crossed, whereas in birds the tracts are 75 percent ipsilateral and 25 percent contralateral. Ebbesson suggests that the primitive condition was bilateral, with later loss of either of the other two alternatives. As is the case in mammals, in all of these systems there was considerable reentry of neocortical equivalents to the thalamus, tectum, red nucleus, reticular system, and dorsal column nuclei.

Although these studies revealed very similar distributions of a given system in all of the vertebrate classes, there was marked variability in the recipient zone of each system. Projections were to the same target and never to an unusual one, but they differed in size and degree of differentiation. For example, the tectum differed mainly in intratectal organization, not much in its afferent and efferent connections. Differentiation in structure in a particular region such as the tectum was found to be correlated with increased differentiation (or parcellation) in a connected structure such as the diencephalon. Increased differentiation, enlargement, and the proposed parcellation were usually reflected in greater segregation of inputs as well as in the specialization or cytodifferentiation of neurons. Comparisons of the tecta of nurse shark, squirrel, fish, and Tegu lizard, for example, revealed great variability both in cell types and in the segregation of inputs.

The proposed parcellation of retinotectal projections can explain the variation in number of visual thalamic nuclei, and it fits in well with the variation in neuronal overlap seen in structures such as the somatosensorimotor cortex (figure 5.7). Similar explanations can account for the breakup of the single cerebellar nucleus of the nurse shark during evolution to give four nuclei in mammals. The argument can be extended to the sharpening of the dorsal column nuclei with increasing discrimination from each other as limb development becomes more complex. In the cortex, the more parcellated a structure, the more it may *lack* certain connections, as is seen, for example, in the confinement of visual commissural connections to certain portions of well-developed, highly evolved systems.

Ebbesson distinguishes horizontal parcellation of nuclei from the vertical parcellation evident in the evolutionary development of laminated structures and microcircuitry. Segregation of inputs to layers may thus lead to biased selection of newly differentiated cell types during evolution. This would arise in response to the need for more accurate or precise adaptive categorization of real-world stimuli with appropriated refinement of behavior. It would in turn lead to more highly refined and specialized microcircuits; in forming such circuits, parcellation could obviously affect important cellular features such as the shift of synaptic contacts.

Parcellation events must occur during development. In considering the relationship of parcellation to ontogeny, Ebbesson points out how, after experimental injury, aberrant connections made by sprouting resemble certain ancestral projections that existed before parcellation in the evolution of a species. Although some events during development (reviewed in the preceding chapter) are consistent with parcellation as one possible evolutionary mechanism, this ontogenetic explanation smacks too much of recapitulationist views and is too narrow. Moreover, it does not take sufficient account of the nonlinear dynamics and constraints relating developmental genetics and evolution (Alberch 1982a; Edelman 1986b). By stressing recapitulation, it does not accord sufficient attention to heterochrony, the alteration through mutations in regulatory genes of the rates of developmental expression of traits possessed by ancestors. It ignores the fact that neural substrates of motor behavior can be organized in embryonic life without sensory experience in the world (Preyer 1885; Hamburger 1963, 1968; Bekoff et al. 1975; Bekoff 1978). It also ignores species-specific nonneural and behavioral changes in the phenotype that would influence ontogenetic change (Coghill 1929; Hamburger 1970; see discussion below).

According to the present theory, it is more likely that ontogenetic variants resulting from regulatory gene changes (particularly those bringing about various forms of heterochrony) led to the emergence of phenotypic variants having nervous systems with both new nuclei and new tracts that conferred selective advantage. This view calls upon a much wider range of primary processes as a source for evolutionary change than does parcellation. As we pointed out in the preceding chapter, modification of the morphoregulatory genes for CAMs so that the timing of expression of these molecules is altered could, for example, lead to the rapid emergence of new nuclei and to neuronal group organization in relatively short evolutionary times. This is consistent with data indicating that neural systems and their components advanced at different rates in different species, some maintaining earlier features while changing others.

In a review and critique of newer data on telencephalic evolution, Northcutt (1981) also rejects the notion of a linear theory such as Ebbesson's and emphasizes the likelihood that richer forms of explanation relating development to evolution will be required (for other critiques, see Ebbesson 1984). What can we offer as such an explanation?

DEVELOPMENTAL CONSTRAINTS AND EVOLUTIONARY CHANGE:
THE RELATIONSHIP OF THE REGULATOR HYPOTHESIS TO HETEROCHRONY

As a more far-reaching alternative to the parcellation hypothesis, we turn here to a selectionist view based on a mechanism (Edelman 1986b) for heterochrony, the variation in the time or rate of emergence during development of traits inherited from ancestors (Gould 1977). The position we will espouse is that, although parcellation can be made consistent with one particular kind of heterochrony and is thus not completely excluded, it is not sufficiently broad to account for neuronal group organization. In reviewing the molecular bases of morphogenetic movements and embryonic inductions in chapter 4, we described the regulator hypothesis but touched only briefly upon its implications for morphologic evolution. This hypothesis was in fact designed to provide a specific molecular framework in which to relate developmental genetics to evolution in terms that included a basis for heterochrony (Edelman 1984c, 1985b, 1986b). It specifically addressed (1) how a one-dimensional genetic code could specify a three-dimensional animal and (2) how such a mechanism could be compatible with large changes in form within related species occurring in relatively short periods of evolutionary time. As we saw, the hypothesis derived from an analysis of the interactive morphogenetic roles of cell division, cell movement, and embryonic induction during regulative development. It specified that the link between the code and the three-dimensional form of complex organisms rested in the epigenetic expression at appropriate developmental times of appropriately modulated CAMs as well as SAMs such as cytotactin (Crossin et al. 1986).

According to the hypothesis, the morphoregulatory genes for cell adhesion molecules (CAMs) are expressed in schedules prior to and largely independent of those of the historegulatory genes determining cytodifferentiation (see figure 6.3 for a summary of all the stages in the general hypothesis). The expressed CAMs and SAMs act as regulators of the overall patterns of those morphogenetic movements that are essential for inductive sequences or early milieu-dependent differentiations. It was suggested that, during evolution, natural selection eliminates those organisms in which variants of CAM or SAM gene expression or of genes affecting morphogenetic movements or of both result in interruptions in the inductive sequences that lead epigenetically to the bases for succeeding morphologic steps during ontogeny. Under this assumption, more than one (but not all) *covariant* combinations of these two variables could lead to stabilization of the order of inductive sequences and of the body plan in a variety of species. Small variations in the pattern of action of regulatory genes for CAMs in those organisms that are not selected against could lead to large changes in animal form and in neuroanatomy within relatively short periods of evolutionary time (figure 6.3).

Although the theoretical constructs embedded in the regulator hypothesis and in the neuronal group selection theory may appear unrelated at first glance, they are in fact closely linked. The regulator hypothesis (Edelman 1984c, 1985b) attempts to account at a molecular

Movement of mesenchymal cells and tissue sheets leads to border interactions with exchange of inductive signals between cells of different history. Signals alter gene expression affecting primary processes.

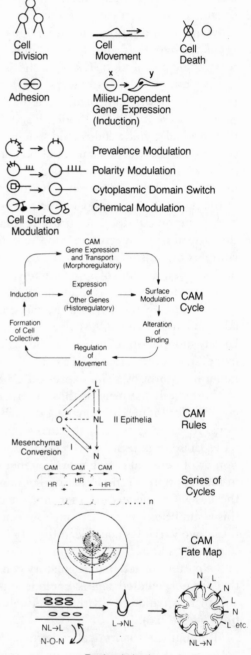

Cell Division

Cell Movement

Cell Death

Adhesion

Milieu-Dependent Gene Expression (Induction)

CAMs act to link epithelia, condense mesenchyme, and form borders (by cell surface modulation and different boundary specificity).

Prevalence Modulation

Polarity Modulation

Cytoplasmic Domain Switch

Chemical Modulation

Cell Surface Modulation

Expression of regulatory signals in each new milieu leads to successive expression of CAM genes according to rules and in parallel with the expression of historegulatory genes in a CAM cycle. Order of expression depends on historical trajectory of cells. Key notion is that signals depend on the formation of different bordering high-level collectives linked by CAMs.

CAM Gene Expression and Transport (Morphoregulatory)

Induction

Expression of Other Genes (Historegulatory)

Formation of Cell Collective

Surface Modulation

CAM Cycle

Alteration of Binding

Regulation of Movement

L

O ←---- NL   II Epithelia

Mesenchymal Conversion

N

CAM Rules

CAM   CAM   CAM

HR   HR   HR

...... n

Series of Cycles

Evolutionary selection for phenotype fixes body plan (as reflected in a fate map with CAM-determined borders, the result of a series of CAM cycles).

CAM Fate Map

During histogenesis, "syntactical" variants of the CAM rules and cycles are repeated at finer and finer scales, as exemplified by feather development.

NL→L
N-O-N

L→NL

NL→N

N L
N
L
N
L etc.

Feather Induction and Histogenesis

level for both the genetic and the epigenetic origins of constancy and variation of embryonic structures, including those of the brain. In addition, it provides a transformational mechanism to account for rapid evolutionary changes in complex organ systems. The neuronal group selection theory is based on the resultant evolutionary and developmental origins of anatomical structure and variation as they relate to adaptive neural function in the individual animal. The tie between the transformational and variational mechanisms proposed in each of these theoretical proposals is twofold: (1) The regulated expression of gene products such as CAMs and SAMs that mediate mechanochemical functions controls the constancy and constrained evolutionary change of higher-level form and anatomy as well as the individual microscopic variation in neuronal circuitry required for group selection. (2) The selection of those organisms having mutations in regulatory genes for such molecules provides a specific basis for heterochrony, which is a main means of

Figure 6.3

The regulator hypothesis. Cell adhesion molecules (CAMs) and substrate adhesion molecules (SAMs) play a central role in morphogenesis by acting through adhesion as steersmen or regulators for other primary processes, particularly morphogenetic movements. CAMs exercise their role as regulators by means of local cell surface modulation. Morphogenetic movements are resultants of the inherent motility of cells and of CAM expression as it is coordinated with the presence of SAMs such as fibronectin and cytotactin. These movements, which are regulated by CAM modulation, are responsible in part for bringing cells of different history together to result in various embryonic inductions. Genes for CAMs are expressed in schedules prior to and relatively independent of those for particular networks of cytodifferentiation in different organs. The CAM gene schedules follow rules that have "syntactical" variants. Control of CAM structural genes by morphoregulatory genes leading to border formation is responsible for the body plan as seen in fate maps. In the chick, this plan is reflected in a topological order: a simply connected central region of N-CAM surrounded by a contiguous, simply connected central ring of cells expressing L-CAM. Natural selection acts to eliminate inappropriate movements by selecting against organisms that express CAM genes in sequences leading to failure of induction. On the other hand, any variant combination of movements and timing of CAM gene expression (resulting from variation in morphoregulatory genes) that leads to appropriate inductive sequences with phenotypic function will, in general, be evolutionarily selected. This allows for great variation in the details of fate maps from species to species but at the same time tends to conserve the basic body plan. Small evolutionary changes in CAM regulatory genes leading to heterochrony that do not abrogate this principle of selection could lead to large changes in form and tissue patterns in relatively short evolutionary times.

effecting morphologic variation in evolution. Changes resulting from each of these mechanisms would yield more adaptive phenotypes containing new anatomical structures as well as more extensively variant repertoires of neuronal groups within these structures. In interpreting these remarks, we must remember again that evolution selects not only for morphologic variation but above all for *functioning* neuroanatomy, including repertoire variance within the overall phenotype.

The regulator hypothesis applies to all inductive systems and can account for certain aspects of CNS development during the inductive period as specified by N-CAM and other CAMs and SAMs. In a modified form, it can also account for certain aspects of evolutionary change that are important for the morphogenesis of nuclei and laminae and of sensory sheets and motor ensembles. As was mentioned in chapter 4, large changes in Ng-CAM distribution and N-CAM prevalence occur during formation and fixation of fiber tracts at a time when N-CAM is undergoing E-to-A conversion and myelination has begun. The data are compatible with the notion that feedback signals from postsynaptic cells and from glia alter the expression and chemical modulation of N-CAM and Ng-CAM. Genetic changes leading to early alterations in the periphery could lead to alterations in the timing of such feedback signals, with consequent changes in the CNS. Among these changes would be retraction of fibers, altered competition between fibers, different patterns of cell death, and new fiber tract connections, as was discussed in chapter 5.

Against the background of the regulator hypothesis, we may specifically relate the idea of alterations of CAM regulatory genes resulting in heterochrony to the independence of the primary processes described in chapter 5. For example, the fact that cell migration and process extension are largely independent allows for many variants as a consequence of changes in the timing of N-CAM expression or of Ng-CAM expression. A delay in one or the other could differentially affect these two processes. This might lead to alteration in the amount of competition (Purves and Lichtman 1983) for a target population of neurons or glia at a particular stage of epigenesis, changing subsequent signals to the next CAM cycle. Such events would in turn not only affect the number of cells surviving and undergoing cell death but also change the options for target population by the surviving cells. An example of this kind is seen in a recent experiment of Cowan's group (Stanfield et al. 1982; Stanfield and O'Leary 1985) in which it was observed that a projection to the spinal cord by visual cortical neurons in early development was retracted in later stages. If these same neurons at an earlier stage were transplanted to the environment of the motor cortex, they contributed to the spinal projection normal for that site but retained their connectivity at later stages. In like fashion, heterochronic changes based on the regulator hypothesis could also lead to similar alterations of site and target preference. If such alterations resulted in increased fitness, natural selection of those individuals with appropriately changed morphoregulatory and historegulatory genes would occur.

Such changes, which would be the result of graded effects and the continuous properties of CAM modulation, are entirely compatible with the CAM cycle and the dynamic cellular processes described in chapters 4 and 5. According to the dynamic principles outlined there, cytodifferentiation of neurons and new variant forms of neurons (which can arise by alteration of historegulatory genes independently of regulation of CAM genes) could then provide the basis for evolutionary selection of new microcircuitry.

It is useful to contrast the regulator hypothesis with the parcellation hypothesis. According to the former, the heterochronic change that is the fundamental basis of new morphogenetic evolution occurs as a result of parallel alterations in responses to local signals of *two* kinds of regulatory genes acting in the CAM cycle: those for CAMs (morphoregulatory genes) and those for other specific cellular proteins (historegulatory genes). The advantage of this view over the parcellation theory, which is narrower and recapitulationist, is that it makes it less difficult to imagine how the various coevolved phenotypic features of animal form *and* behavior could have emerged in a coordinate fashion with such apparently radical changes in neural networks. As we discussed in chapter 5, the somatic *variance* that provides the basis for the primary repertoire may allow the nervous system to make *immediate* accommodation to mutationally induced phenotypic change in form and function in the periphery. Subsequent *evolutionary* alterations of the CAM cycle in CNS development could allow further adaptation and improved performance. Contrary to Ebbesson's suggestion, the ontogenetic sequence does not show recapitulation; instead, it is compatible with altered developmental genetics of CAM modulation resulting in various forms of heterochrony that would affect *many* primary processes and that would give rise to numbers of individual variations. Thus, the regulator hypothesis is the basis not only for diversity and degeneracy in individual nervous systems but also for the evolutionary origin of distributed systems (Mountcastle 1978). These systems, particularly those seen in maps, are in turn the basis of the adaptive behavior upon which evolutionary selections are made.

EVOLUTIONARY MAINTENANCE OF DEGENERACY IN DISTRIBUTED SYSTEMS

We are now in a position to show a link between the formation of degenerate primary repertoires and the evolutionary formation of an adult map that results from behavior and that leads to further behavior.

The foregoing argument sees degeneracy as a natural consequence of a variety of evolutionary and developmental phenomena. Degeneracy originates from the biochemical variation and epigenetic mechanisms that accompany development. It is a key feature of the diffuse connectivity of early systems and is maintained as a result of the early evolutionary need for overlap in sensory distributions. It persists later in the microscopic variation of the modules and structural domains found in the brains of more highly evolved organisms. Degeneracy thus provides both an evolutionary substrate for neural specialization and a ground for variation in somatic selectional repertoires. If the premises reviewed here are correct and the regulator hypothesis is substantiated, overlapping axonal arbors and dendritic trees would remain as highly variable sources of three-dimensional microscopic diversity within the neural substrate, sources that have been maintained by natural selection and that provide a basis for somatic selection even in the most sophisticated nervous systems with multiple nuclei and laminae.

According to such an interpretation, a circuit of the kind shown in figure 6.1, as expressed in different individuals, contains degenerate elements at the level of both its modules *and* its reentrant loops. From the point of view of somatic function and phenotypic selection, such a circuit is both a bounded repertoire for group selection in somatic time and an influence upon the phenotype leading to natural selection. Considered as a result of evolution, such a circuit in a given species is a *redistributed* system in the description of which the classical idea of hierarchy becomes somewhat etiolated. At best, such a system is a heterarchy, the various regions of which have meaning only in terms of their relation to dynamics of input and output during behavior governed by phenotypic expression. Evolutionary selection acts strongly upon behavior, and the envelope of behavioral patterns in a species is affected by degeneracy in neural networks. Seen in this light, controversies over the localization of fixed functions restricted to named brain regions or portions of such networks are bootless: many levels of interaction are involved, and many different functions can be carried out by primary repertoires even within a given region.

Natural selection acts upon the phenotypic behavior of animals whose brains are made up of such systems, not upon the systems themselves. For this reason, it is important to show how *somatic* selection in a brain region in adult life can lead to functional maps, for such maps strongly constrain the behavior upon which natural selection acts. In other words, it is necessary to provide a detailed basis for understanding how phenotypic change resulting from alterations and interactions in both primary *and* secondary repertoires could lead to evolutionary fixation of altered morphoregulatory genes in a population. A detailed model of the local somatosensory maps that were described in the last chapter provides a useful example.

OVERLAPPING ARBORS AND REENTRANT MAPS

We may now usefully integrate the data and hypotheses in this and the preceding chapters into a model of mapping based on neuronal group selection that can account for map dynamics in adult life. The model (Edelman and Finkel 1984) is based on the data on the somatosensory cortex reviewed in chapter 5. The purpose of presenting this model after our review of the evolutionary data is to show that an explanation of adult plasticity in terms of neuronal group selection in primary *and* secondary repertoires can provide an understanding of how complex structural and functional variants in a population might be created to be acted upon by natural selection. According to the theory, factors related to those involved in this model must have played a major role in the evolution of mapped systems. A detailed model of this kind, posed in terms of neuronal group selection, should reveal the different levels upon which natural selection must act to relate nervous system evolution to the rest of the phenotype. Moreover, the model serves as an explicit case in which the concept of a neuronal group may be refined; a further refinement will come when we consider synaptic rules in chapter 7.

Unlike the parcellation hypothesis, which is strictly input-output driven and is recapitulationist, this model has as its major bases (1) the regulator hypothesis as a mechanism for heterochrony, (2) degeneracy with overlapping arbors, and (3) the reentrant coordination of circuits at *all* levels rather than in terms of simple input-output arrangements. After showing how the theory of neuronal group selection can account for Merzenich's findings on adult somatosensory cortex and thus for some of the phenotypic function upon which natural selection acts, we will be in a better position to consider how the principles of diversity, degeneracy, group competition, and reentry could constrain the evolutionary development of cortical laminae and subcortical nuclei.

The model we shall propose is designed to account for the data on cortical maps, but it is important to observe that a number of reports indicate that partial deafferentation also leads to reorganization in *subcortical* structures of the somatosensory system (see Kaas et al. 1983). These data are particularly significant because of the emphasis on reentry between cortical maps and such subcortical structures. A change in one part of such an interconnected network must perforce lead to reentrant alterations in other parts. Work on subcortical systems confirms that such changes can occur, for example, in the dorsal column nuclei (Devor and Wall 1981).

With these observations in mind, let us recapitulate briefly the effects on the cortex observed by Merzenich et al. (1983a; Kaas et al. 1983). Their data indicated the following: (1) normal maps vary in different individuals; (2) during reorganization, the overlap of receptive fields recorded within a distance limit of roughly 600 μm from the deafferented border is maintained while representational loci and magnifications of representations change dramatically; (3) there is an inverse relation between the magnification factor of a cortical representation and receptive field size; (4) continuity is maintained during the establishment of new maps; and (5) the cortical location of somatotopic map boundaries can shift over distances of many hundreds of microns. These findings suggest that each region of cortex is organized in such a way that it could support many different possible maps. In view of the topographic continuity of these maps at a very refined level of representation and given the overlap and distance limits, one may conclude that adjacent regions of anatomical input to the cortex (specifically, axonal arbors) must overlap extensively. At the same time, however, the rough somatotopic order of the input from the thalamus and, ultimately, from the periphery is still maintained.

The model proposes that the expressed map emerges as a result of a group selective competitive process acting upon a degenerate anatomical substrate that could give rise to numerous possible maps. The fundamental challenge is to explain how a given map is selected out of the degenerate primary repertoire in the behaving individual by suitable synaptic alterations. The detailed synaptic rules by which this could occur will be discussed in the next chapter. According to the model, a neuronal group in the cerebral cortex is functionally defined as an ensemble of cohesively interconnected cells, all of which express the same receptive field. Anatomically, groups are related to cortical columns (Mountcastle 1978) in that columns are made up of groups; however, groups must always be viewed in conjunction with their dynamical function. Group dynamics (formation and dissolution) depend upon both input *and* internal connectivity; together, these determine which of the afferents received by the group will have their inputs expressed as the group's receptive field.

A fundamental operation of neuronal groups is to compete with other potential groups in the secondary repertoire for domination of cell activity. This is achieved by the strengthening of synaptic connections between interacting cells in the group and any particular cell that might be captured by that group. As new cells are brought into a group, the balance of afferent inputs and internal connectivity is altered, and the newly constituted group may require different patterns of input for correlated activation. As long as significant activation is achieved, the group can continue to consolidate its "hold" on cells. But other groups are constantly competing for the same cells, and any weakening of connections because of decreased activation puts the group at risk either of losing a few cells or, in the extreme case, of being divided and conquered. According to this model, both thalamocortical and corticocortical synapses may be modifiable, but the burden of accounting for rapid switching and movement in cortical maps falls mainly on modifiable intracortical connections.

In the model, three population processes are proposed to give rise to fully functional cortical maps (figure 6.4). The first concerns an obligate limitation of group size, which is called *group confinement.* The primary repertoire consists of degenerate corticocortical connections, which are predominantly oriented vertically (Mountcastle 1978), an anatomical fact accepted since Lorente de Nó (1938) and consistent with established developmental events (Rakic 1977). Local inhibitory horizontal connections serve to funnel any activity into restricted cortical domains. As we shall show, this has the effect of limiting the expansion and contraction of cohesively connected cortical groups. The second process, *group selection,* arises from the distribution of afferent arbors, each of which spreads over a limited cortical region and extensively overlaps with neighboring arbors. Across these degenerate arbors, the play of spatiotemporally correlated peripheral stimuli leads to selection of groups according to a set of synaptic modification rules to be discussed at length in the next chapter. The final and highest-level process, *group competition*, concerns the competitive interactions among those groups that have arisen from confinement and are then selected. It is proposed that a hierarchical set of competition rules determines the readjustment of territorial control between different groups. These competition rules can include historical effects, as reflected, for example, in the notion that functioning extant groups can strongly influence the selection of new groups. Let us briefly consider these three processes in order (figure 6.4).

Group Confinement

One may conjecture that the average size of a neuronal group in the hand representation of SI is about 50 μm, although it may vary by a factor of two or more (see below). This area includes 165–200 cell bodies through the depth of the cortex, if we use the data of Rockel et al. (1980) on cell density in macaque somatosensory cortex. Let us choose the value 50 μm because it represents the upper bound for separated locations in cortex with identical receptive fields (Sur et al. 1980). Group size may vary somewhat in other brain regions. Nonetheless, a group extends over only a fraction of the extent of the arborization of a thalamic afferent. The size of a group depends upon all three of the processes mentioned; but before selection and competition of groups can occur, the group's initial size must be confined to a limited region. Confinement reflects the establishment of a stable size range for groups as a result of the interplay of excitatory and inhibitory corticocortical connections in different laminae.

We accept the postulate that pyramidal cells, particularly in the supragranular layers, receive excitatory connections on their spines from other pyramidal cells and from the layer IV spiny stellates (Szentágothai 1975; Winfield et al. 1981). In conjunction with the thalamic afferents, these excitatory interconnections are assumed to provide the "cell-catching" mechanisms of the group. Pyramidal cells that receive significant excitation (from thalamic, commissural, and associational afferents in addition to excitation from other nearby pyramidal cells and spiny stellate cells in layers directly below) are activated and strengthen their connections to the pyramidal cells that they excite in turn. Local inhibitory cells sharpen the dynamic response by lateral inhibition. As depicted in figure 6.5, the supra- and infragranular layers are sites of excitatory group expansion. But layer IV, the predominant thalamic recipient, is dominated by the inhibitory nonspiny stellates. As larger

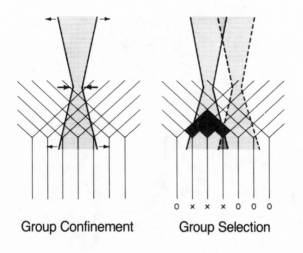

Group Confinement   Group Selection

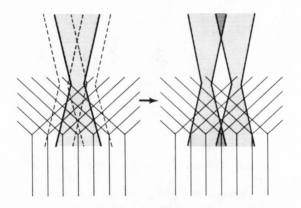

Group Competition

Figure 6.4

The three components of map formation according to the neuronal group selection theory. The cerebral cortex is used as our example. Ascending Y-shaped figures represent thalamic afferents; hourglass figures represent groups with narrow waists in layer IV. Group confinement (top left) restricts activity to local areas by the interplay of excitation in supra- and infragranular layers with inhibition in layer IV; see figure 6.5 for details. Coactive input in group selection (top right), denoted by the x's, selects the group on the left since it contains a region (blackened) that receives coactive input but not uncorrelated input (denoted by O's) from the adjacent afferents; see figure 6.6 for details. Group competition (bottom) between three previously selected groups leads in this hypothetical case to dissolution of the central group (perhaps because its receptive field does not overlap with those of the surrounding groups).

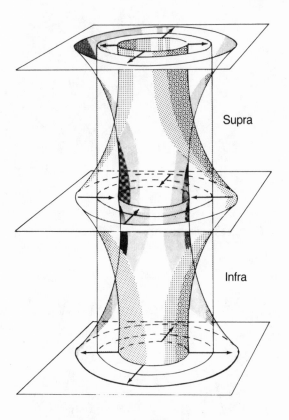

Figure 6.5

Schematic conceptualization of the hypothesized process of group confinement. Three different group configurations are demarcated by the three surfaces. A group will tend to expand in the supragranular layers because of excitatory horizontal connections. This expansion leads to increased inhibition in layer IV, leading to constriction of the group; contrariwise, constriction of the group in supragranular layers leads to expansion in layer IV. The intermediate cylinder represents an equilibrium configuration for the group. The supragranular portion is depicted as symmetrical with the infragranular, but in reality it probably differs because of the existence of direct supragranular input.

regions of layer IV are excited by thalamic input and by the increasing amounts of excitation in other layers, increasing inhibition is generated in IV, which tends to lead to tamponade of the source of excitation. The dynamic equilibrium that occurs between granular level "contraction" and supra- and infragranular "expansion," inextricably linked by predominant vertical connectivity, results in the initial formation and confinement of the group.

Group Selection

Group confinement is an intrinsic property of the cortex and assures that group size will not exceed certain limits; in itself, however, it provides little specificity. To achieve specificity for group selection, we must invoke temporally correlated inputs to the cells of a group. Figure 6.6 shows a highly idealized set of overlapping cortical afferents. The afferents marked X receive correlated stimulation from peripheral receptors, leading to correlated activity across the hatched area. Adjacent afferents marked O are not receiving correlated activation; thus, all regions outside the darkened box receive uncorrelated activity. Despite the wide arborization of the afferent terminals, there is just a small cortical region that receives maximal correlated activity but minimal uncorrelated activity. Only groups situated within this region are strongly selected by the correlated stimuli.

Group selection proceeds through synaptic modifications induced by the correlated activation of cells within a group. It is the time sequence of activity, in addition to its magnitude, that leads to synaptic modification. The threshold for synaptic modification is assumed to lie somewhere within the distribution of the activity produced by significant correlated stimulation. The exact mechanisms and rules for synaptic alteration are taken for granted here; details are given in chapter 7, in

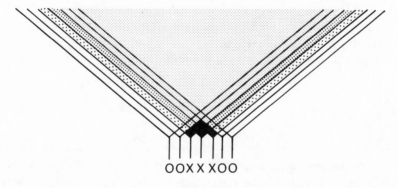

Figure 6.6
Highly idealized representation of overlapping thalamic afferent arbors. Afferents marked X *receive coactivated stimulation, whereas those marked* O *receive uncorrelated stimulation. The* three densities of stippling *indicate regions in which one, two, or three coactivated afferents overlap. The* darkened region *receives coactivated input, but no uncorrelated input.*

which a computer model of the process of group selection in the somatosensory cortex will be presented.

A group will be selected only if it is localized to a region showing a high percentage of overlap of those afferents mediating its receptive field. This is the region referred to above as receiving maximum correlated and minimum uncorrelated stimulation (figure 6.6). As the number of afferents receiving correlated stimulation increases, the area of cortex receiving correlated stimuli also increases. But the distribution of correlated activity over the cortical surface becomes progressively more peaked and less uniform, until the area exceeds roughly 600 μm, at which point the distribution flattens out again because of the lack of afferent overlap. This increase in correlated activity is matched by a corresponding decrease in uncorrelated activity in the region. These two effects combine with the highly nonlinear group dynamics to yield a restricted cortical region with a large ratio of correlated to uncorrelated input.

The arborization pattern depicted in figure 6.6 is obviously idealized. Real arbors would commonly have patches of higher and lower terminal density, branches could interdigitate in nonuniform ways, and arbor size and orientation could vary. Furthermore, we have assumed that the recipient cortical cells are homogeneously and isotropically arrayed with identical dendritic trees. Groups receive a distribution of connections that only approximate this simple idealized version in the statistical limit. In any event, whatever inhomogeneities and anisotropies exist only serve to skew the selection of the preexistent groups and do not affect the basic argument. We have not explicitly mentioned the role of the geometry of dendritic trees, having confined our analysis to the axonal arborizations. Clearly, both types of ramifications play a crucial role, and this simplified approach has, in effect, lumped the two together.

Group Competition

We may now consider the last of the three processes responsible for map organization, group competition. The treatment will necessarily be briefer than that of the other two mechanisms, inasmuch as the details of competitive interactions (which groups prevail under what circumstances) are exquisitely dependent upon the environment in which the competition takes place. Group competition is, nevertheless, perhaps the single most important process in determining what an actual map will look like. We will therefore examine those general properties that pertain to most competitive interactions in the cortex.

We suggest that, in addition to group confinement and selection, a Darwinian competition occurs between various groups for cortical representation space as different stimuli are successively encountered (figure 6.4). In general, within the constraints of peripheral innervation density, groups with smaller receptive fields would have the competitive edge as they receive correlated stimulation most frequently. A reasonable surmise is that there must be a set of hierarchy rules according to which groups can compete with others. A self-consistent set would include, for example, (1) group expansion beyond a certain size and contraction below a certain size are both unstable; (2) groups that overlap with neighboring groups within certain limits are favored; (3) cells that are at greater distances from those in the rest of the group are in greater danger of being captured by other groups; (4) extant groups have an advantage over incipient groups; (5) receptor density constrains the receptive field of a group, and thus its competitiveness; and (6) the most competitive groups are those that are associated with the most frequently stimulated peripheral locations.

A model composed of the three related and interactive mechanisms for group confinement, selection, and competition can explain most of the observations of Merzenich and his coworkers (Kaas et al. 1983). Local movement of map borders is accounted for by the trading of cells between adjacent groups. Larger movements of borders would take place because of dissolution of a group, which would occur only after major change in input, such as that which follows from nerve transection. The sharpness of map borders is a property of the size of the group and is a result of the competition of discrete groups with limited receptive field overlap. A border disappears only when the group disappears, at which point other groups will define the border. Continuity of the alteration in map boundaries is based on the extensive spread of arbors and on the fact that extant groups favor overlap of receptive fields; otherwise, in general, intergroup competition would be enhanced, resulting in a weakening of the connections of groups with nonoverlapping fields. The distance limit seen by Merzenich and his colleagues reflects the average anatomical limit of overlapping arbors—without a substrate in the primary repertoire, dynamic selection by particular inputs cannot occur. In turn, receptive field overlap is maintained by competition and is relative, but its limit of 600 μm is related to the distance limit. Group competition tends to preserve the normal percentage overlap and to yield an average optimal size depending on the average input.

The inverse relation between the size of receptive fields and the size of the cortical representation can be explained by the fact that, with fixed overlap, a greater number of smaller receptive fields are needed to cover a given area of periphery. This will require a greater number of groups, and since group size under confinement changes to only a certain small extent with receptive field size, a larger amount of cortex will be occupied by the greater number of groups. This is so because group confinement prevents expansion, and as group size increases, the *relative change* in the number of afferents increases appreciably only for groups that are small with respect to the overlapping arbors. Groups behave, according to this model, like species undergoing competitive exclusion—environmental variations (here seen as correlated or uncorrelated input) limit the packing of species, which will be packed more closely when environmental variations are smaller and more widely when variations are larger.

As shown in figure 6.7, because of the reentrant connectivity of the entire system from cortex to thalamus to dorsal column nuclei and cord, group rearrangements in the cortex will lead to appropriate shifts in the various nuclei at different levels. This is consistent with the need to maintain coordinate reentry in the entire functioning system.

This detailed model suggests that group selection within a degenerate anatomical substrate can lead to dynamic expression of local maps corresponding to environmentally relevant structures. A cortical group is a cooperative self-organizing unit whose mechanism of formation constrains all cells within it to share a receptive field. Group size can vary somewhat but is limited by the vertically mediated dynamic balance between a propensity to contract in layer IV and a tendency to expand in other layers (group confinement). Afferent expression requires that interconnected cortical cells receive connections from afferents that are simultaneously stimulated. The choice of exactly which afferents will be expressed depends upon the temporal correlation of peripheral activation stimulating these afferents through the various relays, and it operates under the constraints of previously established corticocortical synaptic efficacies (group selection). Every stimulus acts to alter the competitive balance between groups (group competition). The *functional* map represents the combined effects of group confinement, group selection, and group competition, and it is a key feature of the phenotype, the properties of which will obviously be reflected in behavior and thus be subject to natural selection. Consideration of this model indicates that such selection could occur through effects on the phenotype at a number of different levels from primary through sec-

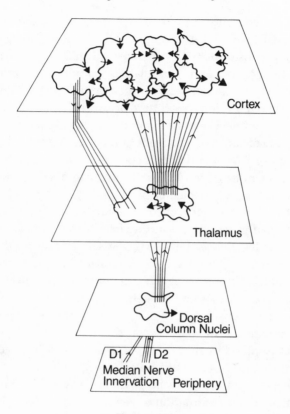

Figure 6.7
Schematic diagram of dynamic vertical and horizontal reentrant connectivity across a linked system of laminae and nuclei. Changes in any one level must result in readjustment of all "linked" levels.

ondary repertoires. Natural selection could influence maps as a result of variance in the periphery, in CAM mechanisms, and in synaptic structures or neurotransmitters.

MAP FUNCTION AND HETEROCHRONY

With this analysis as a modal example, it is valuable to consider again the process of natural selection of complex neural circuits within the phenotype. The first issue worthy of notice is that the proposed model bears directly upon the issue of categorization, inasmuch as it depends upon spatiotemporal correlation of inputs from regions of skin (particularly on the digits) that are used to explore the environment. Natural selection would favor those arrangements that gave the most refined discrimination consistent with other organismic needs of the phenotype. This idea, applied here to a relatively simple categorization, may be extended to other modalities. Within a projection for a given modality, there would be strong selection pressure for local coherence of dense neuronal connections and for overlapping projections of afferent arbors. Because of the group competition rules, there would be a tendency to select for wiring that allows coherency of groups of neurons up to certain size limits; beyond these limits, there would be too much degeneracy and loss of specificity of mapping.

The occurrence of a heterochronic delay (neoteny) in the mapping of some neuronal precursors, resulting from a mutation in a regulatory gene for molecules such as the CAMs or in those controlling expression of molecules involved in movement or neurite extension, could lead to a reduction of local connectivity. If cell death did not ensue and if the neurons involved found a new target, selection of organisms with this rewiring would be constrained by rules for reentry. Because of the need for coherent matching of coarsely continuous regions in two reentrant fields (a need imposed by shifts in input; see figure 6.7), projections that destroyed such matching would be selected against. If, on the other hand, a new projection opened the possibility of creating a new submodality by enhancing the formation of new classification couples, it would be selected for.

Because of the constraints of reentry or of created new function, heterochronic shifts based on the regulator hypothesis either would tend to be terminated by cell death or would be propagated by developmental changes in such a way that more than one new mapping could be established in relatively short periods of evolutionary time. Such heterochronic shifts would act either as isolating mechanisms for neurons in certain regions or as developmental mechanisms prompting migrations of neuronal precursors into new areas, depending upon competition. The variables that would constrain the process include requirements for degeneracy and overlap, coherency in reentry, and the overall functional responses to input of the ensuing map in adult life. These considerations would apply to the segregation of inputs and outputs defining nuclei as well as laminae, and, given the nonlinear effects of small changes of morphoregulatory genes on heterochrony, segregation of multiple centers could also occur in relatively short evolutionary times.

Because of the combinatorial nature of neuronal group selection and the general improvement in performance resulting from bounded increases in repertoire size (figure 3.1), there would be no problem in the rapid enlargement of a lamina or nucleus once founded, provided that other phenotypic changes in morphology were permissive. This problem has been dealt with for neuronal group selection, as it applies to the cerebral cortex, by Lumsden (1983).

The detailed model of the somatosensory cortex was elaborated here to demonstrate that isolated descriptions of anatomy or of physiology or of behavior alone are in themselves not sufficient for us to develop a cogent evolutionary explanation to account for the selection of brain circuitry. Two requirements related to primary and secondary repertoires must be met. There is a need for an hypothesis such as the regulator hypothesis to link mechanochemical events in the primary processes of morphogenesis with the expression of morphoregulatory genes controlling molecules such as CAMs and SAMs. Given such a hypothesis, a connection can be established between developmental genetics and evolution by providing a basis for the heterochrony leading to anatomical change. In addition, it is necessary to have a thoroughgoing theory relating the resultant morphology to physiological function and phenotypic behavior, as provided here by somatic synaptic selection in the model for somatosensory maps. Satisfaction of both of these requirements provides a reasonably complete and consistent mechanism for heterochrony, relating structure to function and function to natural selection.

Developmental variations that affect morphogenesis, such as those envisioned in the regulator hypothesis, can lead to the evolution of a different anatomical substrate (primary repertoire) upon which group selection can operate in the individual. Natural selection can then act upon the *range* of phenotypic expressions and altered behaviors that are generated. Over evolutionary time, this leads to increasing numbers of "neuroanatomical species" in the brains of different animal species, largely because of the isolations and alterations that arise by selectional means in ontogeny. In somatic time, the overall reentrant circuits that ensue must create functional maps by neuronal group selection as described here, following defined synaptic rules for populations of synapses, as we shall see in the next chapter. These rules do not necessarily lead to irreversible changes like those seen in the neuroanatomy; rather, they lead to formation of a secondary repertoire. Obviously, because somatic selection occurs in a synaptic change, mutations affecting synapses or transmitter type can have significant effects on mapping. In general, somatic selection for a secondary repertoire will result in the formation of *metastable* maps and to a certain steady-state population of functional neuronal groups that govern and are governed by behavior. Natural selection *on such behavior* will in turn ultimately lead to selection of the appropriate developmental variants. As we shall see in chapter 11, somatic selection upon certain primary repertoires exhibiting heterochronic delay in selection, as observed in certain songbirds, can lead to more stable maps because of species-specific learning.

At this point, we reach a culmination of the argument: perhaps one of the most powerful claims that can be made for the theory of neuronal group selection is that it solves the problem of the mapping of *peripheral* phenotypic structures that themselves arose by heterochrony (such as altered appendages or altered muscle insertions in ancestors of cichlid fish; see chapter 8) onto an already functioning brain. Inasmuch as neuronal group selection treats such new structures as part of the world to be categorized, it is not necessary to invoke mutation in genes specifying *simultaneous* neuroanatomical changes to match each phenotypic change in form. Of course, in time, mutations leading to gradual changes affecting neuroanatomy by the means we have described could and most likely would then occur to improve the adaptive performance of the organism.

The resemblances of the evolutionary emergence of defined neural structures to speciation and island geography, and of neuronal group selection to ecological events such as competitive exclusion (MacArthur and Wilson 1967), derive from the fact that these phenomena all arise under selective constraints in complex environments with competition. If the group selection theory is correct, there is a kind of neuroecology occurring at several complex levels of development and behavior. Neuronal groups must maintain stability and adaptability to novelty in a heterogeneous and changeable world. To do so, they must spread risk among variants, as is seen for surviving animal species (Wright 1932; den Boer 1982). In certain respects, groups within a region resemble a species subdivided into many races, each interacting mainly within itself, but occasionally crossbreeding. As was pointed out by Sewall Wright (1932), in evolving organisms such *intergroup* selection is much more effective in dealing with environmental variation and novelty than is intragroup selection.

One of the major epigenetic mechanisms governing this neuroecology at developmental and behavioral levels concerns the behavior of synapses as populations that leads to formation of the secondary repertoire; this will be the subject of the next chapter. Beyond these mechanisms lie the overall or global responses of the systems in which they occur. To see some of the detailed constraints governing such responses—in particular, the interactions of nuclei and laminae at higher levels beyond primary receiving areas and local maps—it will be necessary to consider together the interactions of peripheral inputs from sensory receptors and the motor ensembles that mediate output responses. At this point, the emphasis will switch from sensory to motor systems. It is the global response resulting from the interactions of these systems on which behavior in the phenotype is based. This will be the subject of part 3 of this book.

7

Synapses as Populations: The Bases of the Secondary Repertoire

INTRODUCTION

In the beginning of the present part, I described a series of epigenetic mechanisms to account for the formation of the primary repertoire. As expressed in the regulator hypothesis, the basic mechanisms were concerned with the developmental origins of variability and constancy in the connectivity of neural networks. We may now turn to a detailed discussion of the second set of pivotal epigenetic mechanisms fundamental for the theory: those concerned with synaptic change as the basis for selection of a secondary repertoire. These mechanisms are fundamental to the confinement-selection-competition model, discussed in the preceding chapter.

Synaptic mechanisms are also considered to be developmental in nature, and we have already seen that they play a functional role during development in the refinement of maps and in the formation of such structures as neuromuscular junctions. The formal discussion of synaptic rules for selection and variation presented here provides the additional epigenetic mechanism required for our final essay: to explain the origins of memory and learning within the framework of a selectionist theory of perceptual categorization.

The idea that modification of synaptic function can provide a basis for memory arose shortly after the first anatomical description of the synapse (Ramón y Cajal 1889, 1937; Foster and Sherrington 1897; Held 1897a, 1897b; Sherrington 1897; Auerbach 1898; for reviews see Granit 1967; Clarke and O'Malley 1968; Kandel 1976). Since that time, a number of models (Hebb 1949; Shimbel 1950; Hayek 1952; Eccles 1953; Kandel 1981) have been proposed in which various cognitive activities are represented by combinations of the firing patterns of individual neurons. In many of these models, learning or memory is presumed to be due to activity-dependent changes at *individual* synapses. The prevalent idea is that changes resulting from a particular pattern of neural activity preferentially enhance subsequent occurrences of that activity pattern.

In general, however, the complexity of the nervous system makes it highly unlikely that there is a simple relationship between changes at any individual synapse and changes in the behavior of the network. It is much more likely that multiple synaptic modifications occur simultaneously at various sites in the network, reflecting its degeneracy. This prompts the consideration of synapses as populations. The importance of this consideration is obvious: modification of synaptic function serves as the principal means for the selection of neuronal groups and for their competitive interactions that lead to the formation of the secondary repertoire.

To meet the requirements of the theory of neuronal group selection, a population model of synapses must answer two main questions: (1) How can populations of synapses yield continued specificity of responses (for input and output) within degenerate networks of groups committed to categorization without reducing variability to a level where selection could not operate? (2) How can the mechanisms proposed by such a population model of synapses at the same time yield properties consistent with the existence of short- and long-term memory?

Any model proposed to meet these requirements must include mechanisms for modifications in both presynaptic and postsynaptic cells. It is necessary to explain how the expression of these mechanisms is altered within different network contexts and how such modifications in turn alter the behavior of networks. In addition, the mechanisms for modification of synaptic efficacy must be consistent with the existence of various central neurotransmitters and modulators and, indeed, must account for their specificity and multiplicity. In view of the strongly biophysical flavor of synaptic mechanisms, the model to be proposed, which is centrally based on work with my colleague Leif Finkel (Finkel and Edelman 1985, 1987), will be described in more formal terms than other models that are satellite to the theory of neuronal group selection. Nonetheless, an attempt to synthesize a reasonable qualitative description will also be made, and a realization of neuronal group selection in the somatosensory cortex will be presented in a computer model to illustrate how formal rules can be incorporated in a simplified version of the model presented in chapter 6.

Background for a Population Model

This is not the place to review extensively the anatomical, physiological, and molecular aspects of various kinds of synapses, nor is it particularly germane to describe previous models in detail (see Hebb 1949; Shimbel 1950; Eccles 1953; Brindley 1967; Marr 1969; Changeux 1981; Kandel 1981; Koch et al. 1983; Changeux et al. 1984; Edelman et al. 1987a), except as they bear upon the construction of a population model. The main objectives here are (1) to propose synaptic modification rules based on known biochemical and biophysical mechanisms; (2) to consider the interactions between presynaptic changes and postsynaptic changes operating independently and simultaneously in a structurally defined network within which selection can occur; and (3) to examine how these interactions are constrained by the geometrical and population structure of the network. I will first consider detailed mechanisms for pre- and postsynaptic modifications of synaptic efficacy and then discuss how their interaction yields the desired properties.

Experimental evidence indicates that both presynaptic and postsynaptic (Llinás et al. 1976; Changeux 1981; Douglas et al. 1982; Magleby and Zengel 1982; Lynch and Baudry 1984; Smith et al. 1985) modifications occur at the biochemical and ultrastructural level (Fifková and van Harreveld 1977; Desmond and Levy 1981; Vrensen and Nunes-Cardozo 1981). Pre- and postsynaptic changes involving more than one cell can occur at the same synapse; an important issue is whether one kind of change depends obligately upon the other *at that synapse* or whether presynaptic and postsynaptic changes occur independently. In what we shall term an independent synaptic rule, not only do presynaptic modifications and postsynaptic modifications result from two different mechanisms, but no aspect of either one of these mechanisms is actually required for the other to operate *at the molecular level.* Such an assumption of independence stresses the individuality of each member of *any* pair of neurons involved in a synapse as well as the different contributions to the network that result from neuronal morphology and the asymmetry of the synapse.

Most theoretical work since the proposals of Hebb (1949) and Hayek (1952) has relied upon particular forms of dependent synaptic rules in which either pre- or postsynaptic change is contingent upon closely occurring events in both neurons taking part in the synapse. Such assumptions, which make the more or less simultaneous activity (or firing) of both cells necessary and sufficient for modification, confront empirical and theoretical difficulties. Evidence from studies of *Aplysia* (Carew et al. 1984) and the hippocampus (Wigstrom et al. 1982), for example, suggest that such firing is neither necessary nor sufficient. Even more tellingly, dependent rules cannot explain the occurrence of heterosynaptic modifications.

A heterosynaptic modification is a change in the efficacy of a synapse that is contingent upon the results of stimulation *to other synapses* on the same neuron; a homosynaptic change occurs when only direct stimulation of a given synapse is required (figure 7.1). It is important to note that an individual presynaptic input can be strengthened without inducing postsynaptic changes and that heterosynaptic facilitation can occur without simultaneous firing of various presynaptic inputs to a cell. One of our chief tasks is to show how independent population rules can account for such heterosynaptic facilitation.

For the reasons given above, it has been suggested (Finkel and Edelman 1985) that pre- and postsynaptic modifications are controlled by independent mechanisms described by different rules. Although rules for these modifications can operate concurrently and in parallel at each synapse and contribute jointly to its net change in efficacy, the different

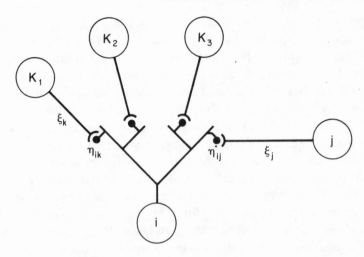

Figure 7.1

Schematic of inputs received by a neuron. Circles represent neurons; neuron i receives inputs on its dendritic tree. Presynaptic efficacy, ξ_j, is the amount of transmitter released by cell j for a given depolarization. Postsynaptic efficacy η_{ij} is the local depolarization produced at postsynaptic process for a given amount of released transmitter. Change in η_{ij} depends upon the statistical relationship between the firing of cell j and the firing of the heterosynaptic inputs k_1, k_2, k_3, etc. as given by equation 7.9 in text.

modifications are *functionally* indistinguishable at the level of that synapse. Nevertheless, the two rules differ greatly in their structural details, as does the geometric distribution of the modifications that result from their independent operation; such modifications can be distinguished by their different distributions in the synaptic population in relation to neuroanatomy as well as by their temporal properties. Consequently, the density of connectivity and the overall anatomical and pharmacological details of a particular network play major roles in determining synaptic interactions, as one might expect in a selection system with population properties.

We shall consider explicit examples of a presynaptic rule and a post-synaptic rule. These examples are intended to be illustrative of a class of mechanisms; they by no means represent the only possible synaptic processes in operation. Their choice has nevertheless been dictated by the available experimental data, and their formulation will allow us to consider some principles of how independent rules interact. At this point, it may be useful to state the two synaptic rules baldly before considering each in some formal detail.

The postsynaptic rule states that coactivated heterosynaptic inputs to a neuron alter the states of ion channels at a given synapse in a *state-dependent* fashion, thereby changing the susceptibility of these channels to local biochemical alterations. The ensuing change in the population distribution of local channel states affects the postsynaptic potential produced at that synapse by subsequent inputs. In general, this rule applies to relatively short-term changes at specific individual synapses.

The presynaptic rule applies to long-term changes in the whole neuron, resulting in an altered probability of transmitter release. It states that if the long-term average (over times of the order of 1 sec) of the instantaneous presynaptic efficacy as determined by transmitter release exceeds a threshold, then the baseline presynaptic efficacy determining that release is reset by the cell to a new value. Because of neuroanatomical constraints, the presynaptic rule affects large numbers of synapses (defined by the connectivity of the neuron in question), and these are in general distributed relatively nonspecifically over a large population, depending upon the morphology of the neuron (extent of arborization, arbor overlap, other aspects of degeneracy, etc.).

The detailed formal analysis of the two synaptic rules that follows is ultimately aimed at determining their properties in a network with group structure. This analysis will show that these dual rules operating independently over the same period of time can account for both heterosynaptic and homosynaptic changes. Moreover, the operation of the rules results in stable network changes over several different time scales; long-term and short-term changes can coexist in the same network and can be related to each other through network anatomy despite the independent biochemical mechanisms underlying the two different rules. Finally, it will be shown that the dual operation of these rules fulfills the need in a selective system for a continual source of variance in the synaptic couplings of a network.

A FORMAL EXAMPLE OF THE POSTSYNAPTIC RULE AND AN APPLICATION TO MAPPING

Because of the geometry of neurons in networks, the postsynaptic rule is the one likely to govern early changes in those synapses that receive specific projections and short-term correlations of signals. This is so because neuroanatomy determines that changes at a postsynaptic locus are not *necessarily* reflected elsewhere, as are those obeying the presynaptic rule. Nonetheless, effects on a given synapse of other synapses on the same neuron cannot be neglected.

The postsynaptic rule involves a family of local biochemical alterations of postsynaptic structures triggered by modifying substances or enzymes. In its most general form, this rule states that it is the positional pattern and the timing of heterosynaptic inputs to a neuron in relation to the homosynaptic inputs to a given synapse that govern the change in postsynaptic efficacy induced by a modifying substance at that synapse. Various mechanisms may be responsible for communication of heterosynaptic effects: intracellular diffusion of modifying substances or messengers, paracrine diffusion, cell surface modulation, and active or electrotonic conduction. Any one or more of these mechanisms are compatible with the postsynaptic rule and with a combined model of interactions of different independent rules within a network. I shall discuss the last mechanism (electrotonic conduction) in detail because it is exemplary; its plausibility depends most critically on temporal and morphological constraints, and many of these constraints apply to the other mechanisms.

In this specific example of the postsynaptic rule, homosynaptic inputs give rise to a substance that modifies local voltage-sensitive channels, but the susceptibility of these channels to modification is altered by heterosynaptic inputs (figure 7.2). It is assumed that the result of the biochemical modification is a change in the voltage-dependent probability of switching between *functional states* of the channel—for example, open, closed, inactivated (Catterall 1979; de Peyer et al. 1982; Huang et al. 1982; Siegelbaum et al. 1982; Huganir et al. 1986). Such a modification would alter the postsynaptic potential evoked by subsequent homosynaptic inputs as well as the sensitivity to heterosynaptic inputs.

The main assumption is that the local biochemical modifications are *interdependent:* the probability of modifying a channel depends upon its functional state. Conducted voltages from other synapses will transiently alter the ratio of voltage-sensitive channels in the different possible functional states (i.e., will alter what we may call the channel population distribution) and thereby alter the number of channels susceptible to modification (Catterall 1979). Without the critical assumption of state dependence, heterosynaptic effects would be nonspecific: conducted voltages would increase the probability of modifications at many postsynaptic sites, regardless of the state of activity of the synapses corresponding to these sites.

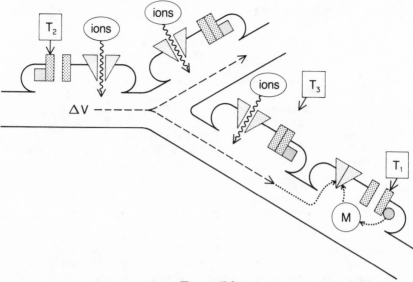

Figure 7.2

*Proposed postsynaptic mechanism. Schematic of four synapses on a branching
dendritic tree.* Shaded triangles *represent voltage-sensitive channels (VSCs),
and* shaded rectangles *represent receptor-operated channels (ROCs). Transmitter T_1 has bound to synapse* (lower right), *leading to the opening of the
ROCs and also to the production of modifying substance M through activation
of a membrane-associated protein* (small shaded circle). *M modifies VSCs,
which are in the modifiable state. More recently, a potentially different transmitter T_2 has bound to the leftmost synapse, opening local ROCs and VSCs.
The resulting change in membrane potential (ΔV) is propagated through the
dendritic tree* (dashed line), *changing the states of VSCs as they are reached.
If the potential reaches the bottom-right synapse* (dotted line) *at a time (see
figure 7.3) when the concentration of M is still high, the fraction of VSCs in
the modifiable state at the synapse will be altered and, consequently, so will the
number of channels modified by M. Synapses that have not yet bound transmitter (e.g., T_3), and synapses not yet reached by the potential, will not be
affected.*

Under these assumptions, it is important to show that the magnitude
of electrotonically conducted voltages can be sufficient to affect local
modifications. Consider first the constraints on the relative timing
(Baranyi and Fehér 1981) of inputs such as those shown in figure 7.2.
Suppose that homosynaptic inputs lead to production of modifying substance persisting for a time t_M after a lag time of t_L, and that conducted
heterosynaptic inputs produce a local change in membrane potential
persisting for a time t_V after a conduction delay of t_D (figure 7.3). Then

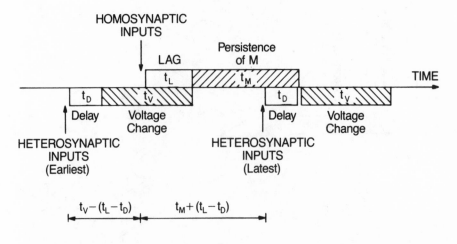

Figure 7.3

Timing constraints for postsynaptic modification. Time axis showing the time window before and after a homosynaptic input during which the occurrence of heterosynaptic inputs can lead to modification. After a barrage of homo-synaptic inputs, a biochemical cascade of duration t_L *leads to production of modifying substance* M, *which persists for a time* t_M. *Heterosynaptic inputs lead to a depolarization (or hyperpolarization) at the local synapse that begins after a conduction delay* t_D *and then persists for* t_V. *Arrows indicate the earliest and latest the heterosynaptic inputs can occur with respect to the homosynaptic inputs so that the effect of the conducted voltage temporally overlaps with the prevalence of* M. *Depending on the values of the time con-stants* t_V, t_M, *etc. (see text), heterosynaptic inputs may be constrained exclu-sively either to follow or to precede the homosynaptic inputs in order to achieve modification.*

a necessary constraint on modification is that heterosynaptic inputs occur *within* a time window starting $(t_V - (t_L - t_D))$ before the homosynaptic inputs, and ending at a time $(t_M + (t_L - t_D))$ after them. If either of these quantities is negative for a given synapse, presentation of the inputs in that particular order will not lead to a modification.

The state-dependent aspect of the biochemical modification can be represented by the simple two-state model shown in figure 7.4, where M is the concentration of modifying substance. A represents the active state and I the inactive state of a channel; we suppose in this example that only channels in the inactive state can be modified. Decay of the modification may also be state-specific, but for simplicity we assume that it is not: thus, $K_{b2} = K_b$. We assume that the time constants for state transitions, $(a + b)^{-1}$, are small with respect to the time constant

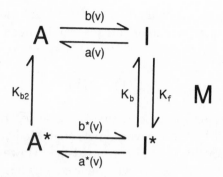

Figure 7.4
Kinetics of state-dependent modification using a two-state model for a channel as an example. A represents lumped activated states; I represents lumped inactivated states, which we take to be the modifiable states. Channels in state I can be modified in the presence of modifying substance M, to modified state I*. Forward and backward rate constants for modification are k_f and k_b. Effect of modification is to change voltage-dependent state transition probabilities governed by parameters a(v) and b(v) to modified parameters a*(v) and b*(v). Modification is short-term, and decays from I* according to k_b and from the activated state by a potentially different constant k_{b2}.

for biochemical modification, $(K_f + K_b)^{-1}$. We also assume that the channels are at their equilibrium distribution during the modification. Thus,

$$dN^*(t)/dt = K_f \cdot [I(t) \cdot M(t)] - K_b \cdot [I^*(t) + A^*(t)] \qquad (7.1)$$

$$= K_f \cdot [(N - N^*) \cdot (b(V)/(a(V)+b(V))] \cdot M(t) - K_b N^*. \qquad (7.2)$$

where N is the total number of channels, N^* of which are modified. To find the steady-state fraction of modified channels we let $dN^*/dt = 0$, yielding an equation similar to the Michaelis-Menten equation:

$$N^*/N = M \cdot (b/(a+b)) / (M \cdot (b/(a+b)) + K_b/K_f). \qquad (7.3)$$

The plausibility of this postsynaptic mechanism rests upon the magnitude of the change in the postsynaptic potential resulting from channel modifications. Consider the case in which a single species k of voltage-sensitive channels undergoes modification, and suppose the N_k^* out of the total number N_k, of channels of species k are modified. Assuming that the change in capacitive currents can be neglected, the change in local current due to the modification is given approximately by

$$\Delta I_L = N_k^* \cdot (g_k^*(V) - g_k(V)) \cdot (V - E_k), \qquad (7.4)$$

where g_k is the voltage-dependent conductance, g_k^* is the modified conductance, and E_k is the reversal potential. Modification of the conductance will alter the local input impedance. However, if we assume that the impedance of the nonsynaptic region is large compared with the modified synaptic impedance, we may, to a first approximation, write the relative change in the postsynaptic potential (PSP) as

$$\Delta V/V = (N_k^*/N_k) \cdot (\Delta g_k/g_k). \qquad (7.5)$$

Values of N^*/N can be estimated from equation 3. Using values of $b(V)$ and $a(V)$ from the Hodgkin-Huxley model (1952), a depolarization of 20 mV gives a change in the value of N^*/N on the order of 0.05 for the inactivated state of the regenerative sodium channels. $\Delta g/g$ has been estimated to be between 1 and about 20, on the basis of reports regarding shifts in current-voltage curves due to biochemical modification (Kupfermann 1979; Haas and Konnerth 1983; Hawkins et al. 1983) and therefore the change in the PSP might be as little as 5 percent and as much as 100 percent of its original magnitude.

It is clear that postsynaptic modifications depend upon (1) the number and intensity of heterosynaptic inputs occurring during the modification period; (2) the timing of the heterosynaptic inputs relative to the homosynaptic inputs; (3) the spatial distribution of synapses on the postsynaptic cell (attenuations and conduction delays); and (4) the types of transmitters, receptors, and ion channels present. These factors apply not only to the electrotonic mechanisms detailed here but also to the other mechanisms (diffusion of modifier, cell surface modulation) through which the postsynaptic rule might also operate.

To illustrate how an independent postsynaptic rule can act in populations of synapses to yield group structure in a secondary repertoire, we may briefly give a computer realization of group selection from preexisting neuroanatomy in a model of somatosensory cortex. A sketch of this model is given here; for details, the reader may consult the original publication (Pearson et al. 1987). The model itself represents a somewhat simplified version of the confinement-selection-competition model described in the preceding chapter.

The computer model incorporates detailed simulations at three levels of neural organization: neural architecture, neuronal properties, and synaptic plasticity. The neural architecture consists of interconnected excitatory and inhibitory cells (typically 1500 cells) and an input array that represents sensory receptors on the glabrous and dorsal surfaces of the hand. The receptors of the input array project topographically onto the network. Each cell in the network receives inputs from a large area of the hand on *both* dorsal and glabrous surfaces. In this fashion, the network captures key details of real cortical tissue.

A degree of realism is also realized at the level of both excitatory and inhibitory individual neurons. Excitatory and inhibitory cells differ in their connection patterns and in their modifiability. At the synaptic level, the model incorporates the effects of synaptic saturation, shunting conductances, and the modification mechanisms of the postsynaptic rule.

Some typical results of the model are given in figure 7.5. Initially, the strengths of the synaptic connections are assigned randomly according to a Gaussian distribution, as shown in figure 7.5, *A*. It has been shown that the initially unorganized network organizes into neuronal groups under a remarkably broad set of stimulation conditions, according to which the input array receives stimuli of various shapes, areas, and positions. A typical example of group formation is shown in figure 7.5, *B*. Note that cells within each group are strongly interconnected *(yellow, red)* but are only weakly connected *(purple, blue)* to cells outside the group. The differences between the patterns in panels *A* and *B* of figure 7.5 are the result of changes in both intrinsic and extrinsic connections. It is the heterosynaptic property of the postsynaptic rule that coordinates these separate synaptic changes and ties the structural and functional properties of the groups together.

The functional properties of a group are exemplified in the model by the properties of the receptive fields of the component neurons. After stimulation, all cells in a group were found to have very similar receptive fields—such cells are exclusively glabrous or exclusively dorsal, and they are highly overlapped spatially. Figure 7.5, *C*, shows the receptive field map of the network after group formation. Initially, the map is topographic, but all cells have receptive fields on both glabrous and dorsal surfaces, and most cells are equally driven by inputs from the two surfaces. After the formation of groups, the receptive field map (figure 7.5, *C*) organizes into compact regions in which cells are driven exclusively by only one surface, dorsal or glabrous. The resulting map corresponds closely to that seen in area 3b of the squirrel monkey (see figure

Figure 7.5

Computer visualization of a model of somatosensory map plasticity employing the postsynaptic rule (Pearson et al. 1987). Results of simulations performed on an IBM 3090 computer of a neural network containing 1024 excitatory and 512 inhibitory cells. An excitatory cell contacts 17 nearby excitatory cells and also contacts 69 inhibitory cells that are located, on the average, slightly farther away. Inhibitory cells contact only nearby excitatory cells. The network receives two superposed topographically ordered projections from an input array, representing the projections from the glabrous and dorsal surfaces of the hand. The postsynaptic rule is used to modify the strengths of extrinsic connections from the hand as well as the intrinsic connections between excitatory cells in the network. The extent of a group is limited by the underlying anatomical connectivity; group size is constrained physiologically by competitive inhibition. The postsynaptic rule acts to strengthen synaptic efficacies between cells that receive coactivated input. This results in the formation of groups that have lesser extents than that allowed by the anatomical connectivity. Once formed, groups adjust the synaptic strengths of the extrinsic connections they receive by the same postsynaptic mechanism. A: Display of initial connection strengths. The strength of synaptic connections between excitatory cells in the network is displayed by color-coded lines that are drawn between synaptically connected cells; the color code is given by the key below. The initial distribution of synaptic strengths is Gaussian. B: Formation of neuronal groups by selection after stimulation. The initial network shown in A was repeatedly stimulated with small focal stimuli in a random sequence of locations on the hand. Display shows the connection strengths between excitatory cells, color coded as in A. Connections between cells in a group are strong (yellow, red), while connections between cells in different groups are weak (blue, purple). Most cells belong exclusively to one group. C: Receptive field map corresponding to the network shown in B after group formation. The receptive field of each excitatory cell in the network is coded according to the color at the position of the center of its receptive field on the hand (right). The hand has four fingers and a palm; surface shown is the glabrous surface. The dorsal surface is denoted by corresponding darker shades of the same color (e.g., glabrous digit 1 is yellow, dorsal digit 1 is dark yellow, etc.). The normal receptive field map shown in C closely resembles those found experimentally. This map is devoted mainly to glabrous representations with small islands of dorsal representation. D: Results after repeated tapping of first digit: receptive field map after the glabrous surface of digit 1 was repeatedly tapped with a small focal stimulus in cycles, denoted by yellow lines in figure (right). The representation of the stimulated area has expanded (light yellow region), while the representations of digits 3 and 4 are largely unaffected. E: Simulation of results after transection of nerve supplying digits 1 and 2 (yellow and orange, respectively). Receptive field map after transection of the fibers from the glabrous digits 1 and 2 and the underlying medial palm (gray-black area in hand at right). The representation of the de-afferented glabrous surface has been replaced by an ordered, topographic representation of the corresponding dorsal surface. After the transection, both glabrous and dorsal surfaces were lightly stimulated in a random fashion. Shortly after the cut, some regions of the network remained unresponsive to any stimuli (black cells); however, with time, most cells in the affected region regained receptive fields on the dorsum (not shown). Note: The color code in panels C, D, and E has a reference different from that used in panels A and B.

5.4 for comparison). This organization of the receptive field map results from the functional dynamics of the neuronal groups—cells in the same group have similar receptive fields, and the borders between different representational areas are sharper as a result of the sharpness of the group borders.

The computer simulation indicates that with a simple but fairly realistic network incorporating the postsynaptic rule, the network will organize into groups under a wide range of stimulation conditions. Once formed, groups can organize the receptive field map through group competition. This exemplifies the cortical dynamics proposed in the confinement-selection-competition model presented earlier, and it shows how the postsynaptic rule coordinates the different classes of inputs retained by individual cells in a more global map organization.

The network has been used to simulate several experiments that have been reported in the literature (see Merzenich et al. 1984b for comparison). The first, shown in figure 7.5, *D,* involved repeated tapping of the glabrous surface of digit 1. The area of representation of glabrous digit 1 expanded dramatically into areas formerly representing digit 2, dorsal digit 1, and the median palm. This result closely resembles that found experimentally (Merzenich et al. 1984b) and demonstrates that the magnification factor of a representation in a self-organizing network of this kind depends upon the balance of local activation in a competitive manner. Connections that were formerly subthreshold have been strengthened by means of the postsynaptic rule largely because the coactivated input from the periphery has overwhelmed the previous sources of coactivated input. The groups involved have shifted their receptive fields accordingly to reflect the new balance of environmental input.

The second simulated experiment shows the same principle as it applies to the loss of input. In figure 7.5, *E* is shown the receptive field map of the network after the input fibers from the median half of the glabrous surface of the hand (i.e., fibers of the median nerve) were transected. The former area of glabrous representation is now completely devoted to a dorsal representation. The exact location of the borders between digits 1, 2, and 3 and the palm differs from that on the pre-lesion map (figure 7.5, *C*), yet they retain the organizational features of a topographic map.

These simulated experiments demonstrate how well-defined maps can arise out of the degenerate anatomy as a result of selection organized through the correlated input mediated by a postsynaptic rule. Neuronal groups act as "degeneracy breaking" structures picking one from among many representational possibilities. Competition and coordination between groups then dynamically balance the functional map with the ambient conditions in the external environment. The postsynaptic rule is ideally suited for making such complex, context-dependent modifications because it can allow responses to heterosynaptic impulses.

A FORMAL TREATMENT OF PRESYNAPTIC MODIFICATIONS

Now we may consider changes in presynaptic efficacy, the amount of neurotransmitter released in response to depolarization of a presynaptic terminal. The key feature of the presynaptic rule is a long-term shift in the level of transmitter release at all presynaptic terminals of a neuron as a result of large fluctuations in the time-averaged instantaneous values of presynaptic efficacy (figure 7.6). The regulation of transmitter release depends upon a number of incompletely understood complex cell biological processes, and therefore the model for presynaptic change is formulated at the level of the macroscopic observables—facilitation and depression.

Several separate macroscopic components of increased transmitter release (Magleby and Zengel 1982) and of decreased transmitter release (Bryan and Atwood 1981) have been reported. In order to simplify the model, however, use is made here of only a single component of increased release, a generic "facilitation," and a single component of "depression." For the facilitation

$$dF_i/dt = \epsilon \cdot S_i(t) - \lambda \cdot F_i(t), \tag{7.6}$$

where $F_i(t)$ is the degree of facilitation in a presynaptic terminal, λ is the decay time constant, $S_i(t)$ is the firing rate of the neuron at time t, and ϵ is the increase in facilitation per spike.

Synaptic depression is described by a similar equation,

$$dD_i(t)/dt = \kappa \cdot \xi_i(t) \cdot S_i(t) - \beta \cdot D_i(t), \tag{7.7}$$

where $D_i(t)$ is the degree of depression in the presynaptic terminal, β is the decay time constant, $\xi_i(t)$ is the presynaptic efficacy of neuron i, and κ is the constant of proportionality between release and depression. The first term indicates that depression increases linearly with the amount of release and that substantial levels of evoked release can occur only at times when significant depolarization has taken place, presumably because of diffusion of calcium away from the release site during interspike interval. The second term represents the decay of depression because of replenishment of depleted transmitter, reactivation of release sites, or return to equilibrium of whatever molecular process is actually involved.

The key assumption of the presynaptic rule is that long-term modification takes the form of a shift in the baseline amount of transmitter release, ξ_i° (see figures 7.1 and 7.6). Long-term modification of ξ_i° results from biochemical responses to time-averaged fluctuations, both facilitatory and depressive, in the presynaptic strength $\xi_i(t)$; this response could include changes in gene expression with synthesis of controlling proteins, increased transmitter synthesis, or changes in the ultrastructure of release sites. This baseline change alters the dynamic behavior of the neuron in response to subsequent inputs.

Given these considerations, the fundamental presynaptic equation

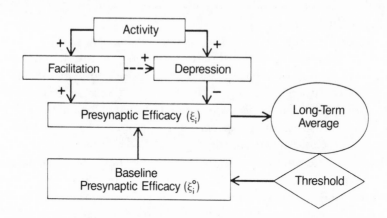

Figure 7.6
Flow chart illustrating operation of the presynaptic rule. Activity increases the degree of both facilitation and depression, which are also coupled inasmuch as greater facilitation increases depression (see the fundamental presynaptic equation 7.8 in the text). Facilitation increases and depression decreases presynaptic efficacy ξ_i, which also depends on the baseline presynaptic efficacy ξ_i°. The presynaptic rule states that a long-term average is kept of ξ_i as it fluctuates because of the temporal pattern of activity. If this average reaches a threshold, the baseline value of presynaptic efficacy is reset to a new value. This changes the response of the cell to future inputs.

relates the amount of release to this baseline level and the degree of facilitation and depression:

$$\xi_i(t) = \xi_i^\circ \cdot (1 + F_i(t))^3 \cdot (1 - D_i(t)). \qquad (7.8)$$

Note that F can range between 0 and an arbitrary maximum value, while D ranges from 0 to 1. It is conceivable that, aside from ξ_i°, changes in other parameters (ϵ, λ, κ, or β) can also underlie long-term modifications. Magleby and Zengel (1982) found that raising the facilitatory term to the third power resulted in a better fit to their data. This nonlinearity also agrees with the cubic relationship found by Smith and colleagues (1985) for the dependence of PSP magnitude on calcium current.

The stability properties conferred by these relationships are significant: stronger synapses will be harder to strengthen and easier to weaken. As ξ_i° increases, the degree of facilitation is unchanged (equation 7.6), but the amount of transmitter released increases, leading to a greater degree of depression (equation 7.7) for a similar sequence of stimulation. The stability property follows from the choice that large net facilitatory fluctuations give rise to an *increase* in ξ_i°, while net depressive fluctuations result in a *decrease* in ξ_i°.

There are two reasons for postulating that long-term modification occurs on a total cell basis rather than independently at individual synapses of a cell: (1) We have assumed that presynaptic modifications are dependent upon the firing of the cell; while a single neuron may have several quasi-independent functional domains for output as well as for input, a large number of presynaptic terminals of a neuron would in general be expected to fire together. (2) We implicitly assume that certain long-term modifications must involve a change in gene expression (Greengard and Kuo 1970). Given the inherent time lags in the production and transport of newly synthesized gene products, there is no currently known way to route the new material selectively to individual synapses at particular branches of the presynaptic neuron.

A major consequence for considering possible effects on networks is that, according to the rule, *all or most of the terminals* of the presynaptic neuron are influenced, *regardless of which correlated inputs* (following the postsynaptic rule) were responsible for the change in ξ_i°. Thus, the consequences of presynaptic changes are temporally stable but are *distributed* by axonal ramifications over a large number of synapses throughout the network. Of course, local constraints could affect the degree to which any particular synapse would be affected.

POPULATION EFFECTS ARISING FROM DUAL RULES IN A NETWORK

We now come to the two remaining key issues mentioned at the beginning of this chapter: how pre- and postsynaptic rules interact to produce functional changes in network behavior, and how network characteristics affect the operation of the rules. A detailed formal analysis has been given elsewhere (Finkel and Edelman 1985, 1987); we can give the gist by examining a model of short-term postsynaptic and long-term presynaptic modifications. The results of this analysis are directly pertinent to neuronal group selection and show that, given the dual rules model, (1) short-term changes in a neuronal group can lead to long-term changes primarily within that group; (2) group structure is sufficient to ensure that long-term changes arising from short-term changes in a particular group will differentially affect future short-term changes in that group; and (3) long-term changes can increase the variability of subsequent short-term changes, especially in other groups.

In order to demonstrate these points, we introduce several simplifying assumptions. These simplifications diminish the richness and generality of the actual postsynaptic rule; nonetheless, the analysis shows that this weaker version is sufficient to address the above three points relating the rules to group structure. Consider networks consisting of groups of only a single type of neuron with a single type of transmitter and receptor, and assume that the attenuation of voltages between any pair of synapses on a neuron is identical. For postsynaptic modification to occur, only a statistical relationship between coactive inputs is sufficient; one can ignore the details of timing and the voltage attenuation factors discussed above and calculate only the mixed second-order moment between the weighted activities of the heterosynaptic inputs and the time-averaged homosynaptic input.

The resultant simplified formal version of the postsynaptic rule is

$$\Delta\eta_{ij} = c_1 \langle \eta_{ij}\xi_j \overline{S_j}(t) \cdot \sum_k \eta_{ik}\xi_k S_k(t) \rangle - c_2(\eta_{ij} - \eta_{ij}^\circ), \qquad (7.9)$$

where $\cdot$ represents a time average, and n_{ij} is the strength of the postsynaptic connection from neuron j to neuron i, $\Delta\eta_{ij}$ is the change of n_{ij}, and n_{ij}° is its baseline value, ξ_j is the presynaptic strength from neuron j, $S_j(t)$ is the activity of neuron j at the time t, $\overline{S}_j(t)$ is this same activity averaged over some time period, and c_1 and c_2 are constants. The terms in the equation can be appreciated by reference to figure 7.1. The first term is the mixed second-order moment at the time t between the amount of modifying substance present at the jth synapse and the magnitude of the conducted voltage (depolarizing or hyperpolarizing) from all other synapses on the cell. The second term in equation 7.9 represents the short-term decay of the modification. The net strength is taken to be the product of post- and presynaptic strengths $\eta \cdot \xi$. This is equivalent to assuming for the simplest case that transmitters and receptors interact with first-order kinetics. In addition, it is assumed that ξ changes slowly with respect to η and that both change slowly with respect to changes in activity S; thus,

$$\Delta \eta_{ij} = c_1 \eta_{ij} \xi_j \sum_k \eta_{ik} \xi_k <\overline{S_j}(t) \cdot S_k(t)> - c_2(\eta_{ij} - \eta_{ij}^{\circ}). \qquad (7.10)$$

Now consider neurons that are segregated into groups (figure 7.7). Let capital letters, for example, I, J, and K, denote groups, rather than individual neurons; let N_{IJ} be the number of connections from group J to group I, and N_{II} the number of intragroup connections in group I. All connections between the same pair of groups are assumed to have

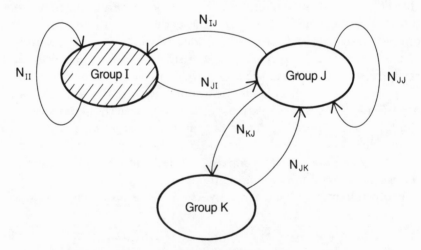

Figure 7.7

Classes of connections among groups. Ellipses represent neuronal groups, and arrows represent intra- or intergroup connections. A long-term change in presynaptic strengths of cells in group I differentially affects subsequent short-term changes in the postsynaptic strengths of these various classes of connections (see text).

the same pre- and postsynaptic strengths. We are interested in post-synaptic modifications of the connections both within and between various groups as shown in figure 7.7. The modification of connections from any group M to any group L (where M, L, and H are dummy variables, and C_1 and C_2 are lumped constants) is given by

$$\Delta\eta_{LM} = C_1\eta_{LM}\xi_M\sum_H N_{LH}\eta_{LH}\xi_H<\overline{S_M}(t)\cdot S_H(t)>$$
$$- C_2(\eta_{LM} - \eta^\circ_{LM}). \tag{7.11}$$

Consider that, because of short-term fluctuations, a long-term pre-synaptic modification has occurred in one group, for example, in group I: $\xi_I \to \xi_I + \delta_I$ where δ_I is a constant. Long-term modifications in other groups or in several groups could be treated similarly. It is reasonable to assume that the modification in group I does not significantly affect the statistical relationship between firing of neurons in different groups. The effect of the long-term change on subsequent modifications ($\Delta'\eta_{LM}$) can be found by substituting $\xi_I + \delta_I$ into equation 7.11 and keeping only first-order terms in δ_I, we find that after a long-term modification in group I, the change in subsequent short-term modifications of the various classes of connections between groups, $\Delta^2\eta_{LM}$, (figure 7.7) is given by

$$\Delta^2\eta_{LM} \equiv \Delta'\eta_{LM} - \Delta\eta_{LM}$$

$$= \delta_I c_1 [N_{LI}\eta_{LI}\eta_{LM}\xi_M<\overline{S_M}(t)\cdot S_I(t)>]$$

$$+ \begin{cases} \eta_{LI}\sum_H N_{LH}\eta_{LH}\xi_H<\overline{S_I}(t)\cdot S_H(t)> & \text{if } M = I \\ 0 & \text{if } M \neq I. \end{cases} \tag{7.12}$$

There are three conditions jointly sufficient to guarantee that $\Delta^2\eta_{II}$ is the biggest change, that is, that short-term changes in that group experiencing the long-term modification are maximally affected:

(i) $N_{II}\eta_{II} > N_{JI}\eta_{JI}$.

(ii) $<\overline{S_I}(t)\cdot S_I(t)> > <\overline{S_J}(t)\cdot S_I(t)>$.

(iii) $\sum_H N_{LH}\eta_{LH}\xi_H<\overline{S_I}(t)\cdot S_H(t)> \approx 0$.

These conditions are as follows: (1) connectivity within a group is stronger than between groups; (2) neurons in the same group fire together more often than neurons in different groups; and (3) on the average, input from different groups is statistically unrelated. Within the context of this simplified model, these conditions are the same as those that define the necessary attributes of a neuronal group (Edelman and Finkel 1984); that is, a set of more or less tightly connected cells that fire predominantly together and constitute the smallest neural unit of selection. Note that these conditions are *not* met if the network is randomly connected.

Given these group conditions, we can rank the classes of connections in a hierarchy, according to the magnitude of the change in subsequent short-term modifications. The intrinsic connections of group I—namely, $\Delta^2\eta_{II}$—are always affected to the greatest extent; connections between other groups ($\Delta^2\eta_{JK}$) are always affected the least; and the three remaining classes of connections are affected to different relative extents, depending upon the relative values of N_{II}/N_{JI}, $\eta_{II}/\eta_{JI}/\eta_{JJ}$, and $<\overline{S_IS_I}>/<\overline{S_JS_I}>$. We would usually expect $\Delta^2\eta_{JJ}$ to be the smallest of the three, $\Delta^2\eta_{II}$ to be the largest for a few select groups J that are highly correlated in input with group I, but $\Delta^2\eta_{JI}$ to be largest for most other groups J.

CONSEQUENCES OF A POPULATION MODEL OBEYING DUAL RULES

The major consequence of this model is that the organization of a network into neuronal groups provides a sufficient condition for long-term changes in a given group to result in a hierarchy of changes in subsequent short-term modifications among various groups, but with the greatest change occurring in the group itself. Computer simulations have been carried out in a model system shown in figure 7.8; the workings of each of the rules are shown in operation in figure 7.9. Further simulations of both rules acting together indicate (Finkel and Edelman 1987) that a long-term change in one group increases the variability in subsequent patterns of short-term changes both in that group and in all other groups that receive connections from that group (figure 7.10). This leads to competition between groups: the differential enhancement of particular short-term changes in each group because of long-term changes in that group is opposed by nonspecific variation of all

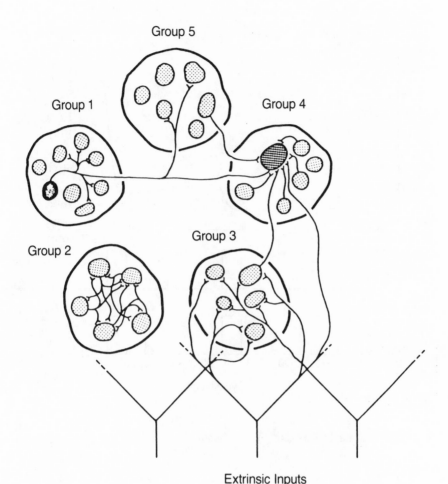

Group 5

Group 1

Group 4

Group 2

Group 3

Extrinsic Inputs

Figure 7.8

Schematic network connectivity used in computer simulations of each rule acting alone and of rules acting simultaneously. Five groups (dark outlines) are shown with some of their cells indicated. Each group illustrates one aspect of the connectivity. Group 1 illustrates that each cell contacts cells in its own group and in other groups. Group 2 illustrates the dense internal connectivity of groups. Group 3 illustrates that each group also receives inputs from a set of overlapped extrinsic inputs that can be selectively stimulated. Group 4 shows that each cell thus receives inputs from cells in its own group, from cells in other groups, and from extrinsic sources. The computer simulation allows observation of changes in presynaptic and postsynaptic efficacies of the various connections after different stimulation paradigms shown in figures 7.9 and 7.10.

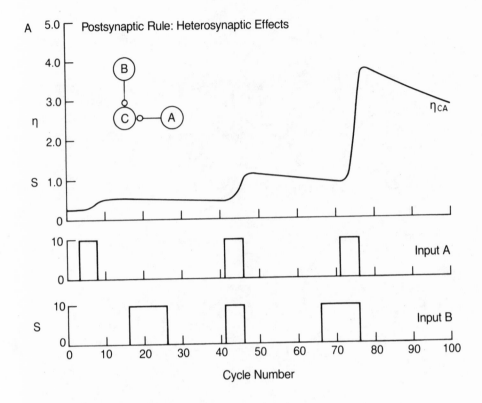

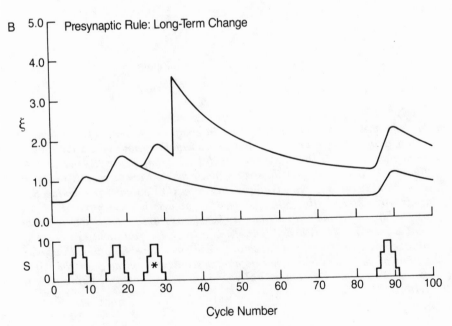

short-term changes in that group resulting from long-term changes in other groups. Such continuing generation of variability in the population is a valuable property of any rich selective system.

It is an important consequence for the theory that some of the properties arising from interaction of these rules in a network consisting of populations of neurons can be density-dependent. For example, organization into locally connected groups with higher densities of connectivity can increase the probability of a recursive relationship between the connectivities of those neurons having long-term changes and those neurons in the network that suffered the short-term alterations that initially caused these long-term changes. The effects of this recursive interaction would tend to outweigh nonspecific variation arising from long-term changes in other groups.

It is illuminating to contrast this population model with dependent models such as the Hebb (1949) rule. The population model differs from the Hebb rule—in the model, the correlated firing of neuron j and neuron i is neither necessary nor sufficient to change the postsynaptic strength η_{ij} of the connection from j to i. Rather, η_{ij} is modified when the time-averaged firing of neuron j is temporally associated with the firing *of a large number of other neurons k*, which make synapses with neuron i. In this way, synaptic alterations are governed by *population effects* in the network. Indications of such effects have been reported in several preparations involving heterosynaptic effects in the hippocampus and cerebellum (Ito et al. 1982; Wigstrom and Gustafsson 1983).

Figure 7.9

Computer simulation showing effects of synaptic rules. Panel A: *Heterosynaptic effects of the postsynaptic rule. Postsynaptic efficacy, η_{CA}, of input from cell A to cell C as a function of stimuli from cell A and from heterosynaptic input (cell B). Stimulus burst to cell A increases η_{CA}; a lone heterosynaptic burst has no effect; paired homosynaptic and heterosynaptic bursts produce a larger increase in η_{CA}. However, a large heterosynaptic burst with appropriately timed homosynaptic burst (final pair) produces a much larger increase, demonstrating that heterosynaptic inputs can modulate local postsynaptic modifications.* Panel B: *Long-term presynaptic change. Two superposed plots of presynaptic efficacy ξ_i versus number of cycles; bottom panel shows the applied stimulation. Two stimulus bursts (without *) produce the lower curve, which does not achieve a long-term change and which shows a response to test burst at cycle 85 that is virtually identical to initial response. Three stimulus bursts (including the burst marked with *) give rise to a long-term change* (upper curve), *manifested as increased baseline presynaptic strength. Test burst at cycle 85 produces an enhanced response.*

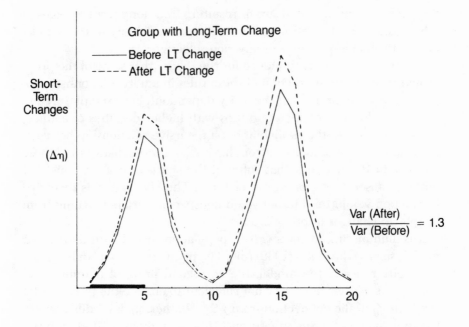

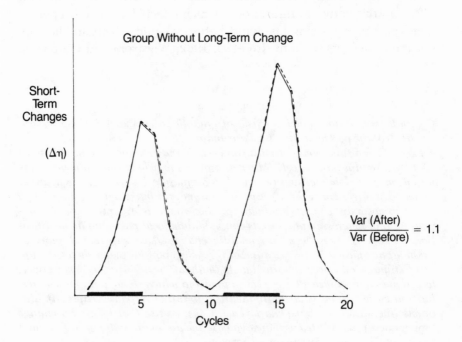

TRANSMITTER LOGIC

In addition to the ensuing continual generation of variability under constraints of competition, the view of synapses as populations also provides the possibility of increases in the number of specific means of connecting subnetworks in the population to yield a variety of circuits. This is a result of the postsynaptic rule: instead of dividing inputs into only two classes—excitatory and inhibitory—and thinking of neuronal operations in Boolean terms, we might rather consider a kind of "transmitter logic" in which each transmitter (in association with its postsynaptic partners) can lead to characteristic modifications of synapses receiving only certain other transmitters and located only on certain other parts of the dendritic tree. This occurs because of the connection between location, channel population distribution, and differing time constraints (see figures 7.2 and 7.3). Such a system would generate a great diversity of classes of synaptic modifications, all specific, but varying with respect to magnitude, time course, origin, and target. The key point is that this diversity would depend upon the number and types of transmitters and receptors. Despite the already great extent and detail of connectivity in the CNS reflected in the primary repertoire, such an arrangement between combinations of channels and transmitters would make it evolutionarily advantageous to have increasing numbers of modulators and neuropeptides for behavioral selection of various secondary repertoires. Such increases would result in a much larger set of functional subnetworks of groups that can contribute to

Figure 7.10

Illustration of long-term changes leading to variance as a result of the operation of dual rules. Plots of the magnitude of the change in postsynaptic efficacy η versus time (iteration). Two groups were chosen at random and were stimulated (darkened bar on abscissa) in turn for five cycles, allowed to rest for five cycles, then stimulated again for five cycles. The solid line shows the resulting short-term changes. One group (top) was then repeatedly stimulated for fifty cycles to produce a long-term presynaptic change in some of the cells in the group. After allowing fifty cycles of rest, the initial stimulation sequence (five cycles stimulation/five cycles rest/five cycles stimulation) was given again. The short-term changes are shown by the dashed line. Only the group that received the long-term change shows an alteration in subsequent short-term changes (compare top and bottom panels). Also shown is the ratio of the variance in Δη of the group (measured at cycle 15) before and after the long-term change. The variance increases in both groups.

combinatorial interactions in that repertoire. A rich pharmacology thus assures a very rich set of functional network variants. One of the most powerful aspects of the dual rules model is the rich structure-dependent or context-dependent nature of its consequences. This context dependence is similar to that seen in the epigenetic realization of CAM rules and cycles generating a primary repertoire. In both cases, biochemistry, pharmacology, and neuroanatomy are joined to create both common structure and rich diversity.

THE RELATION OF SYNAPTIC CHANGE TO MEMORY

One of the outstanding challenges to any general brain theory is to explain the structural basis of long- and short-term memory. This challenge is actually multiple. What must be explained is (1) how the same network can carry out short-term changes affecting perceptual categorization and learning in a continuing fashion while accruing long-term changes; (2) how both kinds of changes can be *distributed* in the network and how they are related to input and output; and (3) how long-term changes can last so long (up to the lifetime of an individual, conceivably as long as one hundred years). These issues bring us back to those raised at the very beginning of this chapter and prepare us for the detailed considerations of global changes in the next part of the book. The previous discussion has shed light on the first two issues but has not related synaptic mechanisms to the stabilization of memory.

It is important to recognize that the time constraints of synaptic change do not *necessarily* relate directly to those of memory: in a selection theory, there is no direct or isomorphic relationship between a physical event, its effect on synapses, and the ability to be recalled by categorization. Inasmuch as it is the *procedure* by which memory operates that determines the issue, and in view of the assertion that memory is a form of recategorization based on global mappings (chapter 9), long-term synaptic changes do not necessarily correspond to long-term memory. Nonetheless, it must be shown how, on the average, a categorical memory with durations up to years can be constructed from less long lasting synaptic changes in the network.

Given the assumptions of the theory, memory cannot be stored *simply* in molecular patterns. Protein turnover is great, fixed unchanging structure is rare, and no evidence exists that polynucleotide structures that *can* be repaired faithfully have any connection with memory storage. According to the alternative view adopted in the theory of neuronal group selection, a categorical memory (see chapter 9) requires the following:

1. Group structure *with degeneracy* organized in global mappings with interconnections between network hierarchies of such global mappings to give a variety of classification couples capable of dealing with polymorphous sets in the signal domain. As will be explained in detail in the next chapter, a global mapping consists of multiple classification couples from different local maps linked in an input-output system, as seen for example in sensorimotor systems.
2. *Relatively* long-term changes at the *cellular* level (months to years).
3. Continuing creation of variance in certain synapses while keeping certain *cells* that have undergone long-term presynaptic changes in stable states of gene expression.

We have already touched on aspects of the first of these requirements and will expand on it extensively in the next several chapters. The last two requirements are met by the synaptic model presented here. Long-term changes instituted by the presynaptic rule can last the lifetime of a cell because they involve gene expression. At the same time (and in the same network), short-term postsynaptic changes can still occur more or less independently in the groups stimulated by correlated input, partitioning their responses into subsets that, while influenced by presynaptic change, are not completely dominated by such change. The diversity of this specific postsynaptic response would be enhanced by the existence of transmitter (or modulator) logic.

This picture relates the rules to the possibility of categorization but still does not explain how long-term memories can last for years and even for the lifetime of the organism. But if, as we shall suggest later, memory is recategorization based on the degenerate responses of multiple nonisomorphic structures in groups, and if the paths of reentry to the responding groups are highly diverse, a long-term synaptic change lasting months and up to a year can be converted to a lifetime response. The reason is clear: the likelihood of the death of *all* of the neurons that have undergone a presynaptic change in *all* the degenerate networks yielding a classification couple is extremely small. The combination of synaptic change in neuronal populations with reentrant classification couples involving degenerate groups would be sufficient to create isofunctional responses that could last effectively for the lifetime of a normal brain.

The interesting question in such a system is not so much whether categorical memory can be stabilized but, rather, whether the existence and growth of categorical memory compromises the continuing need for the ability to categorize in response to novelty. A population theory of synapses, with its competitive balance between long-term and short-term change and between fixation of responses and introduction of variability, provides a plausible answer to this question: dependent upon need and shifting competitive demands, categorization can continue even in secondary repertoires in which extensive selection has already occurred.

PART THREE

GLOBAL FUNCTIONS

8

Action and Perception

INTRODUCTION

Given the principles of somatic selection and epigenetic mechanisms for the establishment of both primary and secondary repertoires, arranged largely but not solely in the form of maps, we must show how interactions of the resulting structures lead to global functions. By "global functions," I mean those activities leading to categorization, memory, learning, and behavioral performance permitting adaptation and survival—activities that require the concerted functioning of multiple areas in large parts of the brain together with the peripheral sensorimotor apparatus. Such activities depend as much upon the morphology of nonneural structures in the phenotype as upon the brain. In this chapter, the argument pursued in the preceding part is extended to include a consideration of motor activity and its relation to perception and neural mapping within a selective system. This will lead to the notion of a global mapping, a dynamic structure that contains multiple reentrant local maps, both motor and sensory, which interact with nonmapped regions to form a spatiotemporally continuous representation of objects or events. Through motor activity, a global mapping alters the sampling of the environment by sensory sheets. Each repertoire within the local maps of a global mapping disjunctively samples various aspects or features of the environment. Connection of these local maps (see chapter 5) in a global mapping serves to link these samples by reentry so that the various representations of features are *correlated* in space and time. None of the local maps alone would be adequate for perceptual categorizations or generalizations. A global mapping provides the minimal unit capable of such function, and it depends upon continual motor activity, both spontaneous and learned.

Of all the systems discussed in this essay, perhaps the most riddled with apparent paradoxes is the motor system. Although the motor system was considered particularly by Head (1920; see Oldfield and Zangwill 1942a, 1942b, 1942c, 1943), by Sherrington (1906, 1925, 1933, 1941), and by Sperry (1945, 1950, 1952) to be at the very center of capacities related to higher brain functions such as perception and memory, its relation to the sensory system and the fundamental means by which it operates have either remained vaguely specified or have been viewed mainly in terms of information processing (for a review, see Brooks 1981). The alternative view taken here, that motor and sensory structures can be understood only as a coordinated selective system, leads to a sharply defined position concerning the relative roles of early signals in development and so-called higher events in the CNS: selection by early signals in both motor and sensory systems acting *together* in a global mapping is considered to be crucial in solving the problem of adaptive perceptual categorization. The degree of coupling of motor and sensory systems to meet the requirements for adaptive categorization and behavior depends upon various evolutionary and ecological constraints. This can be seen, for example, in the work of Coghill (1929) and Hamburger (1970; see also Bekoff 1978), which shows that the relationship between sensory and motor responses in behavioral embryology and postnatal behavior can vary widely across different taxa.

While sensation and perhaps certain aspects of perception can proceed without a contribution of the motor apparatus, perceptual categorization depends upon the interplay between local cortical sensory maps and local motor maps; these, together with thalamic nuclei, basal ganglia, and cerebellum, interact to form the global mappings that permit the definition of objects as a result of continual motor activity. In the process of global mapping (which, as I shall argue further, constitutes the *minimal* basis for categorization and memory), multiple events of selection and reentry occur in a dynamic loop that includes the matching of gesture and posture to sensory signals. The strongest consequence of this assumption is that categorization cannot be a property of one small portion of the nervous system: a global mapping as a minimal basis for categorization is already a very large and complex neural structure. This consequence in turn bears strongly upon the interpretation of the concept of a distributed neural system (Mountcastle 1978).

In this view, selective matching between sensory and motor systems is not the result of independent categorization by the sensory areas, which *then* execute a program to activate motor activity, which is in turn controlled by feedback loops. Instead, the results of motor activity are considered to be an integral part of the original perceptual categorization. I will describe two analyses that support this notion. The first is evolutionary; it indicates that while certain musculoskeletal changes are canalized during evolution, even small phenotypic changes in other parts of the motor apparatus (see Dullemeijer 1974; Alexander 1975) require that concomitant functional changes occur *immediately* in the CNS to assure overall adaptive behavior. These changes must be related to gestures or patterned functional complexes of motion that are adaptive to a *given phenotype* and not to individual types of motion or previous phenotypic functions of evolutionary precursors. The second analysis is physiological and psychological; it stems from the proposal of Bernstein (1967) on the matching of central neural activity to gestures that result from so-called synergies or classes of movement patterns, a position that has been related to perception in theories such as the revised motor theory of speech of Liberman (Mattingly and Liberman 1987). Both the evolutionary and the physiological analyses suggest that selection among gestures by a reentrant system provides a basis for perceptual categorization and for motor learning. This is an *active* process in which behavioral action provides a continual test of new environments as well as a means of rehearsal for older mappings.

This idea requires an enlargement of our view of the mapping problem—input mapping based on local maps (considered in chapters 5 and 6) must be related to the mapping of output in a global mapping. An understanding of such mapping must start with a consideration of the structure and evolution of the musculoskeletal system. In the latter portion of this chapter, we will consider a detailed hypothesis on how a linked reentrant system can allow the formation of global mappings that serve to categorize gestures and also to correlate input and output. But first we must consider the components of motor activity.

The Motor Ensemble

The brain evolved for adaptive action and obviously could not have done so independently of the musculoskeletal system and its constraints upon the phenotype. We must therefore consider certain aspects of the evolution of the musculoskeletal system and, above all, note the extraordinary consequences of even small changes in that system (Dullemeijer 1974; Liem 1974; Alexander 1975; Oxnard 1968; Ulinski 1986). It is particularly important to recognize that throughout evolution various taxa encountered *different* problems related to motion within their econiches and that natural selection has accordingly solved these problems in different ways. These solutions are based both on morphogenetic factors and on selection for overall behavior. The analysis of motion must therefore focus to a great extent upon several problems related to habitat and to functional adaptations of phenotypes rather than upon any simple idea that muscles move bones and that the nervous system excites muscles.

Axial motions of swimming, postural adaptations, brachiation, mastication, and appendicular specializations for fine digital control all pose separate problems of this type (Grillner 1975; Brooks 1981; Evarts et al. 1984). It is true that in a highly evolved creature they are superimposed and melded one upon the other. Nonetheless, it is important for the theory to correlate the *separate adaptations* of the appropriate musculoskeletal structures to the *coevolution* of the appropriate central neural structures that must function together with them in an adaptive mode. This evolutionary qualification makes it clear that no single generalized explanation of motion—be it reflexes, central pattern generators, hierarchical control (Gallistel 1980), or feedback systems—is likely to be general enough to account for all aspects of the evolution of the adaptive motor responses that are integrated during the evolution of an organism such as *Homo sapiens.*

We will call the entire system (muscles, joints, proprioceptive and kinesthetic functions, and appropriate portions of the brain) the motor ensemble, to emphasize the point that they must all evolve and function as a unit. Interpretations of the functions of the motor ensemble vary widely from author to author. One approach attempts to explain motor activity in terms of detailed analyses of reflexes, pattern generators, and feedback loops with superimposition of hierarchical organization (Gallistel 1980). Another considers that the kinetic ensembles constituting limbs, for example, do not operate solely in this mode but are instead in a coordinative relationship with the CNS that is in constant flux, does not depend upon *fixed* pattern generators, and operates not *for* central structures but *with* them (Bernstein 1967; Kelso and Tuller 1984). Reconciliation of these extreme views is further complicated by findings that the activity of musculotendinous receptors (see Sherrington 1900) cannot be correlated *simply* with length, force, velocity, viscosity, tension, or stretch of particular muscles (Roland 1978; Matthews 1982). There is evidence that musculotendinous receptors signal in a feed-forward fashion both the force and the extent of voluntary movements, but the locus of control acting on such signals is not clear (Roland 1978; Burgess et al. 1982; Matthews 1982). Furthermore, the nature of particular connections of elastic muscles to whole ensembles of joints, bones, ligaments, and tendons makes it difficult to consider in general that the activity of any single muscle is essential or, in some cases, even of major consequence in a given patterned movement—the number of degrees of freedom is simply too great (Bernstein 1967). These conclusions and classical analyses of the integration of neuromuscular behavior (Weiss 1936, 1941; Stein 1982) suggest that neither the ordinary physical variables nor the particular subunits of a motor ensemble are the key elements guiding the formation of any central neural construct for motion.

All of these observations, especially those of the Soviet school (Gelfand et al. 1971) pioneered by Bernstein (1967), which will be discussed below, indicate that there is a major problem in explaining the connection of motor activity to sensory input, central control, and memory. This bears upon the issue of how global mappings are constructed. What is in fact mapped when a motion is planned, selected, executed, and remembered? Only a thorough consideration of the evolution and development of the structural bases of motor responses as well as a functional analysis of motor coordination will begin to shed light on this central question.

EVOLUTIONARY CONSIDERATIONS

Before examining the functional aspects of central motor structures, let us extend certain of the evolutionary arguments pursued in chapter 6. We will survey evolutionary trends in motor-sensory systems and consider how some musculoskeletal adaptations can simplify the problem of neuromuscular interactions whereas others can radically alter a species' entire evolutionary responses to environmental demands. The requirements on the CNS to meet these demands, particularly those related to changes in the sequence, pattern, speed, and intricacy of responses, are among the most complex faced by the organism. Our main argument will be that the coevolution of the appropriate neural structures to meet these demands depends upon neuronal group selection.

The initial question to be considered is how neural structures can evolve with the musculoskeletal system in a coordinate fashion. Muscles must be matched to bones, the two must be matched to function, and the CNS must coordinate (and be coordinated by) these variables. Two factors appear to be of key significance in mitigating the difficulties of matching. The first is the requirement during ontogeny that neural activity and neuromuscular interaction occur in order to ensure the appropriate innervation of muscle (Hamburger 1970). The second is the structural adaptability of muscle and bone to altered stresses in adult function (Alexander 1975). Both of these factors, which show elements of degeneracy and the operation of stochastic processes, provide leeway in the match between the brain and the motor apparatus. The fact that the first is unrelated to adult function and that the second is completely dependent on such function after all of the motor connections are already set suggests in itself that there is a considerable variation in the modes of linkage between the CNS and the motor system. An evolutionary shift in a muscle insertion may have strong effects on the ontogenetic patterning of neuromuscular networks as well as indirect effects on the evolution of the CNS through adult behavior. Developmental shaping mechanisms (Hamburger 1970; Changeux and Danchin 1976; Korneliusen and Jansen 1976; Van Essen 1982) and adult plasticity (Evarts et al. 1984) must both play major roles in the duplex rearrangements required for adequate function.

In trying to understand how the CNS could have developed adaptive structures for coordinating sensory and motor functions, we must also appreciate how a few stable evolutionary solutions to a structural problem with many degrees of freedom can change the adaptational picture. We shall mention a few examples from a variety of species to give some flavor to the argument that small changes may require remarkable somatic and evolutionary adaptation by central neural structures. One case (Liem 1974) will show that enormous diversity can arise from a small phenotypic change; another (Oxnard 1968) will show the convergent and canalized nature of certain musculoskeletal adaptations in a variety of very different species.

These issues have been considered insightfully by Alexander (1975), who has shown that the strength of bone and the forces of muscles must be integrated and that small changes in relative sizes of organs such as the jawbones of piranha fish may entail large-scale rearrangements in the structure of the head and of muscle insertions. This entails changes in the cranium, the shape of the brain, and the position of the eyes. Perhaps the most extraordinary example of the evolutionary consequences of such changes when they occur in the presence of varying and rich prospective adaptive zones in the environment is the development of the pharyngeal jaws of cichlid fish (Liem 1974). In the course of evolution, these fish develop a synarthrosis of the lower pharyngeal jaws, an all-important shift of the insertion of the fourth levator externi muscles, as well as synovial joints in the upper jaws. Such structural changes allow these fish to prepare food and transport it in a way that frees the premaxillary and mandibular jaws to evolve different specializations for very diverse foods in different species (figure 8.1). Electromyograms of the fourth levator muscles in percoid fish (figure 8.1, A) and in cichlid fish show completely different temporal activities and phasing of function. The changes allowing separation of the activities of food grasping, mastication, and deglutition resulted in an explosive and adaptively successful radiation of cichlid fish, with concomitant rich morphologic variation. Thus, while only slight reconstruction of existing structures can force complex changes in local organs (Alexander 1975), it can also lead to opportunities for rapid morphologic adaptation to large shifts in various zones of the environment.

More to the point of the present exercise is that clear-cut selective changes made during the ontogeny of a musculoskeletal apparatus can lead to large-scale behavioral changes in a species. This would be expected eventually to have major effects on the evolution of the brain, particularly of its motor control systems. The electromyograms (Osse 1969; Liem 1974) of jaw muscles that *reverse* their function after morphologic change (levator ext. 4, figure 8.1, A, C) show temporal sequences of response that adapt them efficiently for their new roles. The pattern of firing of nerves supplying branchial muscles changes, but without major rearrangement of motor sensory or proprioceptive senses in the CNS. Even though the evolutionary changes leading to the structural changes might have been gradual, it is likely that, at the time of the first changes leading from percoid to cichlid fish, the brain had to adapt *somatically* to the musculoskeletal change with altered firing patterns, without simultaneous mutations leading to appropriately altered brain structure. This example, as well as the analysis of alterations

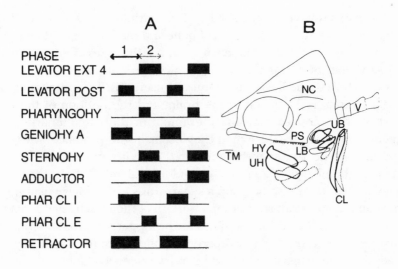

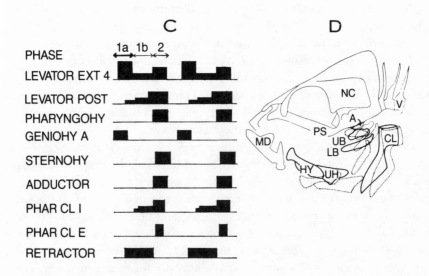

Figure 8.1

Comparison of jaw muscle electromyographic activity and jaw movements of percoid and cichlid fish (Liem 1974). A: Diagram of active periods of branchial and hyoid muscles of unanesthetized and unrestrained Pristolepis fasciatus *feeding on live crickets. B: Diagram of movements of pharyngeal jaws, as revealed by sequence of successive X-ray pictures in the generalized percoid fish* Pristolepis fasciatus. *C: Diagram of active periods of muscles of unanesthetized and unrestrained* Haplochromis burtoni *feeding on* Gammarus *sp. D: Simplified diagram of movements of the pharyngeal jaws of a generalized cichlid* of the premaxilla in boas and pythons by Frazzetta (1970), shows that relatively small variations during ontogeny based on the need to adjust for individual epigenetic variations can lead to large adaptive changes in evolution. Some of these may be based on preadaptions (Bock 1965) and gradual evolutionary change, but others must depend upon the brain's ability to adjust by somatic selection.

In this and other examples lurks an apparent capacity for diversification in structure so immense that it is difficult to see how any singular adaptive solution can be achieved. That this may not be so taxing an issue can be understood by realizing that there are strong morphological constraints on evolution (Alberch 1980, 1982a, 1985). An example pertinent to the musculoskeletal system and its central nervous control is provided by a consideration of the factors determining the shape of the scapula and the architecture of the shoulder. The studies of Oxnard (1968) suggest that the function of the shoulder in locomotion during evolution sharply constrains the myriad possible shapes of mammalian shoulder girdles into two or three major classes. He found that nine osteometric features of the scapula and its connections could be grouped under three variates. The first separates different monkeys and apes in relation to the tensile forces that the shoulder can withstand. The second statistical variate separates arboreal and terrestrial mammalian forms. A third variate separates man, baboons, and ungulates from all other forms. Variate 1 seems closely related to arm raising and weight bearing in arboreal monkeys; variate 2, to the advantage of placing the shoulder joint more laterally with the greater mobility required in trees; variate 3, to the need to shift the scapula more distally on the trunk either for extension (as is seen in flying squirrels) or for greater extension of the limb segment (as in ungulates, for running). In man, the scapula is more proximal than in any other form—its relation

---

fish, as revealed by successive X-ray pictures. Compare with B, and note differences in phases of activity of levator externus 4. Bold lines (phase 1a): food preparation (mastication). Thin lines (phase 1b): food transport (swallowing, deglutition). Broken lines (phase 2): protraction-abduction. Abbreviations: ADDUCTOR, fifth adductor; GENIOHYA, geniohyoideus anterior; LEVATOR EXT 4, fourth levator externus; LEVATOR POST, levator posterior; PHAR CL E, pharyngocleithralis externus; PHAR CL I, pharyngocleithralis internus; PHARYNGOHY, pharyngohyoideus; RETRACTOR, retractor pharyngeus superior; STERNOHY, sternohyoideus. A, pharyngeal process (apophysis); CL, cleithrum; HY, hyoid; LB, lower pharyngeal jaw; MD, mandible; NC, neurocranium; PS, parasphenoid; TM, tip of mandible; UB, upper pharyngeal jaw; UH, urohyal; V, vertebra.

to prehensile function and tactile function remains to be explained.

The major suggestion stemming from this work, which stands in contrast to the example of the cichlid fish, is that a structure like the shoulder may have relatively simple functions *in a wide range of animals*—and that this may constrain the convergent structural solutions found even in unrelated animals. The unforeseen and uncorrelated factors that appear in evolution have led convergently to only a few stable "solutions" for the shape of the scapula; clearly, developmental constraints (Alberch 1982a; Edelman 1986b; Shubin and Alberch 1986) must play a major role in restricting the evolution of such phenotypic variants.

Given these restrictions, an all the more striking aspect of the evolution of motor sensory systems is that, *along with* locomotor sophistication, there is an almost explosive *parallel* emergence of special senses (table 6.1). In amphioxus, where axial wriggling is carried out by means of paired myotomes and a muscular notochord, no special senses, not even those for balance, are seen. But in freely swimming hagfishes and lampreys, lateral line systems, systems of smell, and vestibular systems all are seen accompanying specializations of branchial nerves and a series of remarkable motor patterns driven by a pattern generator in the spinal cord (Grillner et al. 1982). By the time elasmobranchs arrived on the evolutionary scene, cerebellar systems and even primitive thalamic nuclei mediating separate modalities were probably present, along with extensive and exquisite musculature for swimming in sharply demanding situations of rapidly changing currents in three dimensions. The interesting evolutionary development is the rapid *parallel* specialization of all of these features and the corresponding need to coordinate them. If one sense is good, several at once appear to be excellent (see table 6.1).

Radiation onto the land and the movements of terrestrial animals add the complexities of the evolution of limb girdles, alterations of centers of mass, and the need for sequential coordination of gait. The ensuing musculoskeletal plan for limbs with monopod, zeugopod, and stylopod structures and for the limb girdles is a general one (Hinchliffe and Johnson 1980; Shubin and Alberch 1986). In amphibia, the movements of the girdles are superimposed on the remnants of axial motion reminiscent of that of fish. Only with various reptiles do we see an independent set of specializations, from bipedalism to flying, with a remarkable specialization in certain functions of the forelimb and hindlimb in coordination with motion of the tail. By the time that true bipedalism is assumed in primates, the fine specializations of digital control and of brachiation call for even more refined control of perceptual relations between motions of the head, neck, and eyes and for an exquisite interrelation between patterns of walking, grasping, and feeding (Grillner 1975, 1977).

It is important not to confuse the different evolutionary stages of what *appear* to be similar movements with each other, particularly as these stages are reflected by modifications in the CNS. Rhythmic movements can be carried out in amphioxus without a vestibular system or cerebellum. By the time that cyclostomes had evolved, a much greater axial flexibility and adaptability was accompanied by evolution of vestibular nuclei and the cerebellum. In teleosts, the cerebellum is highly developed. Although a sharply defined ascription of functions of the vermis to axial coordination and those of the flocculonodular lobes to visuomotor coordination would be simplistic (Armstrong 1978; Ito 1984), it is clear that extensive development of the lateral lobes accompanies the evolution of the ability to carry out distal fine movements (Armstrong 1978; Sarnat and Netsky 1981). Evolutionary changes in other areas involved in motor function far exceed those of sensory areas: as Ulinski (1986) has pointed out, the largest single evolutionary change between therapsid reptiles and mammals is not in the development of extensive thalamocortical reorganization but in the relation of the basal ganglia to the cortex. Specifically, what is most striking about this transition is the extensive development of motor nuclei and intralaminar nuclei of the thalamus, and of reentrant connections between the cortex and basal ganglia.

These various observations suggest that the movements of different body parts that must be coordinated in a highly evolved terrestrial species probably have different evolutionary origins. The data indicate that axial motions based on central pattern generators (for a review, see Gallistel 1980) are combined later with vestibular and cerebellar developments, with enhancements related to cerebellar control of appendages, and, finally, with the development of basal ganglia and lateral cerebellum as well as cortical areas for fine voluntary motion. Motion can be based upon *any* combination of axial, appendicular, and postural components that can carry out a given gesture. This implies *varying* contributions of reflexes, central pattern generators, and feedback as well as feed-forward loops. But in an advanced mammal or primate, these components with separate evolutionary origins are functionally merged or overlapped, obscuring to some extent the fact that postural, rhythmic axial, rhythmic appendicular, and voluntary digital movements call for different degrees of central control. The repertoires of neuronal groups that must selectively adapt to such a rich mixture must respond epigenetically in somatic time to these combinations.

This summary indicates that the movement systems of more highly evolved mammals may indeed retain connectivities related to the evolution of central pattern generators, as well as various reflexes and servomechanisms (Gallistel 1980). But by the time voluntary movement and planned movement are possible, these components are embedded in much more complex coordinative structures. Thus, while the brain stem reticular formation contains structures regulating pattern generators, the more variable and voluntary movement patterns emerge as a result of interactions between cortex, basal ganglia, and cerebellum, as we shall discuss shortly (Evarts et al. 1984). These observations are consistent with the view that a selection process by repertoires related to movement must take place to coordinate the movement *patterns* of an animal. This is a problem of *categorization* faced by each individual, and it is constrained by a variety of phenotypic idiosyncrasies in each individual.

The main burden of the evolutionary argument advanced here may now be summarized. No simple relationship of CNS changes in circuitry can be imagined to account for each of the phenotypic alterations in the musculoskeletal system that can occur. There is no single best *a priori* way in which specific matching can occur between musculoskeletal change and neural network change. The adjustment of the nervous system to evolutionary changes in the musculoskeletal system probably occurs first through neuronal group selection in early progenitors and later through mutation and selection affecting brain structure via epigenetic alterations in development as is postulated in the regulator hypothesis (see chapters 4 and 6), a process that probably involves synaptic stabilization during the later developmental period. Other adjustments in the secondary repertoire are also required to support the capacity of muscle and bone to adapt to load during active adult function.

According to these interpretations, the linkage between brain regions and muscles *cannot* be absolutely strict. This suggests that any fixed model of control loops for motor behavior is not likely to be generally correct, at least not for more complex nonautomatic movements. The units of action are not muscles or joints or simple feedback loops but functional complexes or synergies (patterns of movement) in the phenotype that are more akin to gestures, postures, and their transitions (Greene 1971; Kelso and Tuller 1984). Such gestures must be considered as *patterns to be recognized* by somatic selection in the nervous system. The evolutionary evidence reviewed here is most consistent with this idea and provides us with the background for a review of the concordant functional or physiological evidence.

FUNCTIONAL BASES OF GESTURES

One of the most direct and compelling cases for the existence of functional complexes or patterns was made in the now classical studies of Bernstein (1967; see also Whiting 1984) on the coordination and regulation of movements. Bernstein recognized that the large number of degrees of freedom in the skeletomuscular system and a series of kinematic and gravitational factors make it impossible that each muscle or movement can be controlled specifically at all times. He proposed, instead, that the various components of the motor system are linked into functional complexes or ensembles called synergies, which comprise *classes of movement patterns* or gestures (figure 8.2). Synergies are not controlled in a one-to-one fashion but are tightly constrained among themselves, sharply reducing the number of degrees of freedom of movement. Such synergies behave in a degenerate manner.

Bernstein saw that, in the complex movements of vertebrates, there is no unique relationship between a pattern of motor impulses and the movements that they accompany. This follows from the fact that, once a motion is initiated, components of the musculoskeletal system are independently subject to irreversible forces because of their kinematic linkage; moreover, they are subject to gravitational and inertial forces. As Kelso and Tuller (1984) have pointed out in a review of the position of the Soviet school, different contextual conditions may require very different patterns of activation to bring about the same kinematic movement (figure 8.2), whereas the same pattern of innervation may produce very different movement outcomes. This is one of the most compelling examples of degeneracy in the entire body of evidence on neural organization and function. The adaptive value of such degeneracy must be based on the need for the matching of function conditioned by the evolutionary factors discussed in the preceding section.

The covariance of activity of a set of muscles in a synergy is accompanied by appropriate covariances in neural signals. The key question is how this relational interaction between functioning synergies and central nervous activities is arranged. The thesis we shall pursue here is that this is done by selection of appropriate neuronal groups in reen-

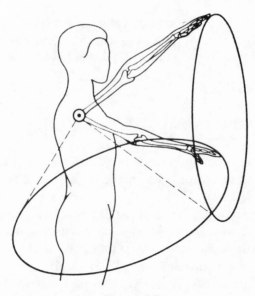

Figure 8.2

As indicated by Bernstein (1967), circular movements made with the arm extended in various positions are accomplished by completely different innervational schemes for trajectories of the same type.

trant systems. Nervous systems adapting to muscle synergies are faced with the same problems of categorization and of specificity versus range that must be faced by the overall perceptual system in dealing with sensory signals (see chapter 3). This implies that during motion a diversity of neurons in a population must accommodate their responses. Recent work by Georgopoulos and colleagues (Georgopoulos et al. 1984, 1986; Georgopoulos 1986) is consistent with this conclusion and indicates that production of movement in a particular direction is a function of the combined activity of multineuronal ensembles that are directionally heterogeneous in the sense that responses corresponding to preferred directions vary from cell to cell.

These findings and Bernstein's idea of the functional nonunivocality of connections between the CNS and the periphery are closely related to the notion of degeneracy. Bernstein (1967) identifies the sources of this many-to-one mapping as (1) anatomy—the number of degrees of freedom in complex kinematic chains, the multiplicity of action of muscles, the variation of action with the disposition of limb segments, and the impossibility of the existence of fixed antagonists; (2) the mechanical complexity of multisegmented kinematic chains, the activity of which leads to variant reactive forces following Newton's laws; and (3) the physiological variance in central effector impulses. The overall conclusion is that motor consequences of central impulses must be decided peripherally as well as centrally. Even in repetitive motion of limbs, for example, it cannot be that the brain *computes* the postural algorithm to accommodate for body recoil by Newton's third law. Selection must occur in such a fashion as to bring to lower values the number of degrees of freedom in the periphery. In their review of Bernstein's ideas, Kelso and Tuller (1984) remark upon the correspondence of some of the features of synergies or coordinative structures with the assumptions of neuronal group selection theory. They also point out in a qualitative manner the resemblance of such coordinative structures to the far-from-equilibrium behavior for dynamical ensembles in which symmetry breaking takes place. The resemblance between attempts to characterize developmental pattern-forming events in these terms (see Harrison 1982 and chapter 4) and Bernstein's insightful views of movements as problems in morphogenesis is not fortuitous.

Two related insights are particularly important in linking Bernstein's ideas of motor function to the neuronal group selection theory. The first is the understanding that the analysis of the biomechanics of limb motion is a problem in developmental biology. Movements of an organism are considered as morphological objects—they develop, react, and evolve in definite epigenetic patterns. Studies of walking and running (figure 8.3) in children through the use of cyclography and other techniques (Bernstein 1967) indicate that, through successive stages, the locomotor system reorganizes epigenetically, setting new problems for the CNS to which it must adapt. This process involves costs in energy that must be minimized. The second important idea is that a distinction must be made between the qualitative characteristics of movements and synergies and their quantitative metric properties. Those qualitative properties consisting of the *pattern* of spatial configurations and form of movements Bernstein calls topological (figure 8.4), in analogy to but not in strict equivalence with mathematical usage. He stresses that the movements of organisms are as much determined by topological properties as are perceptions. The metric properties are those having to do with relative length and scaling found in each individual. *Both* of these properties must be accommodated by appropriate adjustments in a selectional system.

Before considering the relevance of these views to neuronal group selection in more detail, we must place the contrary position in perspective. We may do this by citing a recent review. Gallistel (1980) has proposed that an arrangement of basic central patterns consisting of

Figure 8.3

Gait patterns in running at different ages (successive strips) according to Bernstein (1967). Schemes for positions of the body during phases of the step: $n_A(S)$, *downward push in the thigh of the rear leg;* $C(\pi)$, *thrust to the rear by the rear leg;* m_β, *limit of raising of the knee to the rear;* $D(p)$, *thrust to the rear;* $E(\pi)$, *the last dynamic element of the support period. The young child shows only slight differences between walking and running. The biomechanical reorganization with increasing age sets new problems for the CNS to which it must adapt.*

Figure 8.4

"Topology" according to Bernstein (1967). This term is adopted for all qualitative aspects of spatial configuration or forms of movements, in contrast to quantitative metric aspects. Examples include 1–5, topological class of five-pointed stars; 6, topological class of figure eights with four angles; 7–14, topological class of letters A.

reflexes, oscillators, and servomechanisms connected in a hierarchical fashion, with the more general control features at the top and more specific ones in the periphery, can account for the control of movement. The defect of this view is not that such structures do not exist but rather that they do not account for the unavoidable topological and metric characteristics of motor systems as described by Bernstein. Moreover, this view is subject to difficulties in explaining those postures and gestures that correspond to the functionally adaptive aspects of movement, particularly voluntary movement and above all in those gestures related to speech (Mattingly and Liberman 1987). Vaguely defined neural potentiation based on prior representation or information must be invoked *ad hoc* to account for the relation of the various elements in Gallistel's hierarchy. This is because, in his proposal, the problem of movement is not viewed as part of the more general problem of pattern formation and recognition.

A rejection of this hierarchical interpretation does not imply a denial of the existence of the components invoked by Gallistel as parts of an adequate explanation. As Grillner (1975) pointed out well before Gallistel's analysis appeared, there is considerable evidence for central pattern generators for rhythmic movement. This does not contradict the notion of synergy but in fact complements it. For example, axial rhythmic swimming movements do show evidence of automaticity, and appendicular movements in amphibia remain tied to such patterns but still have characteristics of synergies. Moreover, the later articulation of fine distal movements and the coordination of gait in more advanced vertebrates (Cohen and Gans 1975) are clearly consistent with the idea of synergies in a selective system exhibiting degeneracy. Even in simple invertebrate systems based on central pattern generators (Getting and Dekin 1985) it is clear that one simple network is capable of several different circuit and activity patterns leading to different swimming or aversive behaviors.

We conclude that in the performance of complex coordinated movements, it is gestures, synergies, or functional complexes that are the functional elements, and that these are categories or *classes* of patterns. Their degenerate properties, their kinetic (or far-from-equilibrium) states, and their requirements for matching with neural patterns are entirely consistent with and supportive of the notion of neuronal group selection. Indeed, it is difficult to imagine how a more fixed pattern (even one arranged in hierarchical "action systems") could accommodate even to gradual alterations in motion systems seen in evolution and in individual development, to the context dependence of gestures, and to the "degrees of freedom" problem as sketched by Bernstein and his school (Bernstein 1967; Greene 1971). Moreover, there is an intimate relationship between the problems of the evolution of the motor ensemble and those of individual somatic adaptation required to coordinate various synergies.

Gestures and Neuronal Group Selection

The foregoing discussion points up several issues related to the attempt to define neural structures capable of coordinating synergies. (1) What is the nature of the reentrant system that can adjust the degenerate repertoires of cortical and subcortical groups to the degenerate possibilities afforded by a synergy or gesture? (2) How does the working of such a system relate to the problem of local mapping as covered in previous chapters, and what is in fact mapped or stored as a result of selection upon *combined* sensory and motor activity? (3) What is the relationship of this selective process to the set or state of an animal's preparedness to act (Evarts et al. 1984) after some sensorimotor event? In other words, how does an internal pattern based on a sensorily determined pattern or a memory lead to the *choice* of the appropriate sequence of movements? These are profound questions the complete answers to which will require more data and more sharply posed experimental protocols than we currently possess. A synthesis consistent with the theory of neuronal group selection can nonetheless be proposed, one that may in fact help design the appropriate experiments.

We may start with a conjecture that has a bearing upon all three issues: the result of the combined action of synergies, tactile and visuomotor coordination, and vestibular and cerebellar action is the selection of neuronal groups leading to the *categorization* of gestures and postures and the transitions between them. By a "gesture," I mean the degenerate set of all those coordinated motions that can produce a particular pattern that is adaptive in a phenotype.

With this conjecture before us, we may attempt to sketch how neuronal group selection could account for the choice of gestures. For the sake of discussion, we shall pick one of the most developed examples, the interactive function of the motor cortex, cerebellum, and basal ganglia, inasmuch as many of the neuronal groups selected in various postures and gestures are connected in reentrant pathways linking basal ganglia with cortex and cerebellum with cortex. The evidence on the role of the basal ganglia is scanty, whereas that on the cerebellum's is extensive (Ito 1984); in any case, the definitive functions of these important structures are still not fully described. Evarts and coworkers (1984) have suggested that the cerebellum acts as an open-loop system controlling ballistic movements, whereas the basal ganglia participate as a closed-loop system regulating precise slow movements in much the same mode as the cortex. In waking monkeys, activity prior to a movement can be recorded in both the basal ganglia and the cerebellum. Cortical recordings also show activity that more immediately precedes a movement.

In the model adopted here, I shall assume that the cortex plays several roles. First, it must correlate selected populations of neuronal groups receiving the combined inputs of musculotendinous receptors (Roland 1978) with groups receiving both visual and tactile inputs. This can take place in mappings from visual and sensorimotor receiving areas to parietal cortex (Mountcastle et al. 1975, 1984; Motter et al. 1987; Steinmetz et al. 1987). Second, by means of frontal motor fields and connections with basal ganglia, the activities of such neuronal groups must be correlated with those of groups representing the combined effects of gestures.

This set of linkages constitutes a global mapping—a dynamic system consisting of *multiple* reentrant local maps correlating sensory input *and* motor activity and interacting with nonmapped regions to form a representation of objects and events (figure 8.5). Global mapping results in a coordinated interaction of those cortical groups representing a

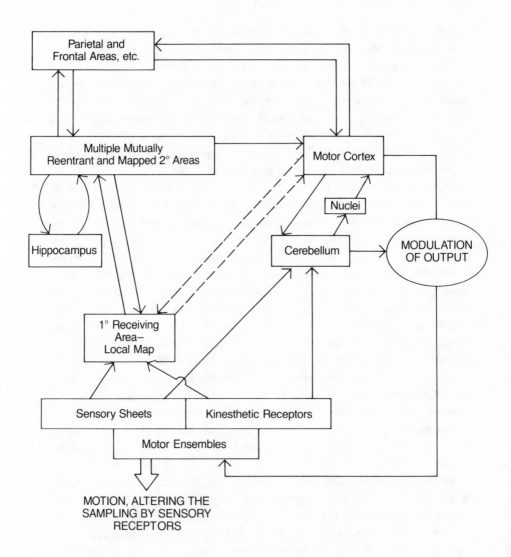

Figure 8.5

A schematic diagram of some components contributing to a global mapping. The essential components are (1) sensory sheets tied to separate motor ensembles capable of disjunctive sampling, such as the retinae in the eyes linked to the oculomotor system, or receptors for light touch or kinesthesia linked to fingers, hand, or arm; (2) a local mapping of the sensory sheets to appropriate primary receiving areas forming local maps; (3) a profusion of mapped secondary areas for each modality to carry out various submodal responses to disjunctive samples—these are linked to mapped motor areas; (4) extensive reentrant connections among various maps of each order, with ultimate reentry back to the primary local map for maintenance of spatiotemporal continuity; (5) subcorti-

gesture. In this system, the basal ganglia form a major link between gestural *sequences,* parts of which are composed in the frontal motor areas, those in sensorimotor cortex that are coordinated by the cerebellum, and motivational circuits in the limbic system (see chapter 11).

A main function of the cerebellum is to link sequentially the sensorimotor components of a synergy in a feed-forward fashion. In this sense, it is a rehearsal center for successive components of alternative gestural activities that arise in different reentrant loops. Another function of the cerebellum in this scheme is proposed to be largely negative: in fast movements, inappropriate synergies differing from the gestural goal that is abstracted and categorized in cortex (the coordinative linkage of whose components has already been rehearsed by the cerebellum) are suppressed. Of course, the cerebellum also has several functions not directly related to this proposed censoring role. One of the key consequences of the assumption that the cerebellum is a censor is that it has a major function in early behavior by regulating the *initial* development of appropriate reentrant relationships among selected neuronal groups in the cortex and spinal cord. Upon repeated selection, however, this activity of the cerebellum may be needed only for occasional reinforcements or slight corrections. In this view, the cerebellum, like the hippocampus (see chapter 9), does not store specific patterns for motion but, rather, serves to link successive unpredicted parts of synergies constructed in a global mapping. It may be pertinent that the cerebellum, despite its highly repetitive structure, is organized into cortical microzones and corticonuclear complexes (Ito 1984) that have many of the characteristics of neuronal groups.

The reentrant nature of all of these systems permits the selection of a degenerate set of groups connecting different areas in such a way that their responses correspond to prototypical gestures or to what Bern-

---

cal areas (e.g., hippocampus, cerebellum) for ordering sequential events or switching output; and (6) appropriate postural or orienting changes by the output of the mapping to alter the position and sampling of sensory components of the motor ensemble. Movement of the sensory sheets can lead to feature correlation at the time when these same sheets are carrying out feature detection. A given global mapping can consist of varying contributions by each of the different components and involves input-output correlation. It is therefore a dynamic structure that is altered as the sampling by different sensory sheets and the input-output correlations are changed by motion or behavior. Each alteration can alter neuronal group selection within the components. Notice that a global mapping constitutes a distributed system.

stein (1967) termed a motor field. Selection "carves" out effective motions from the large set of postural and gestural components, ranging from the mechanical and muscular components of the motor ensemble to the complex neuronal adaptations that are the components of reentrant maps. It is important to recognize that the two sets of these otherwise disparate mechanical and neural components mix to create a gesture or synergy. The degeneracy of each component of the system allows a variety of selective constraints to be placed upon the large number of degrees of freedom in synergies. At the same time, the selective nature of neural interactions with such synergies allows them to be treated in the same way the sensory systems treat signals from the environment: categorical and associative relationships can be *built up* centrally (mainly in the cortex; see Mountcastle et al. 1984) from repeated multimodal and motor responses.

The action of various synergies, in conjunction with concurrent sensory input, can result in the selection of constellations of active neuronal groups that define boundaries and objects. This view considers synergies and gestures from the standpoint of neuronal group selection theory as major sources of *feature correlation* that define environmental conditions and environmental objects. Feature correlation through motor activity allows connection of the individual features of objects into coherent sequences. The topological flavor of feature correlation follows, as Bernstein pointed out (1967), from the physical property of *continuity* that is inherent in motion and in the activity of the motor ensemble.

In its ability to define objects, this global capacity of feature correlation in synergies far exceeds that of the feature detection that is a major property of sensory systems. A motion as defined by synergies thus forms a major concomitant to sensory feature-detecting systems. It is essential not only to the determination of the continuity of object boundaries but also to the correlation of the more minute and locally directed feature detections carried out in parallel by sensory systems during categorization and generalization. The construction and shaping of a global mapping are thus driven by ongoing motor activity, building upon the result of past activities and learning (see chapter 11). Such a mapping is dynamic, and it depends epigenetically upon unceasing exploratory movements and constant motor rehearsals in interactions with the environment (see Jeannerod 1985).

According to this view, the motor sequences and global mappings leading to synergies and gestures are *essential* elements in forming categorizations. Nonetheless, it is obvious that the detailed categorization and individuation of objects obligately requires concomitant and parallel sensory input from the elements that are driven by synergies. Before taking up the problem of global mapping in further detail, we must therefore reconsider some sensory systems from this point of view.

MOTOR ACTIVITY AFFECTING SENSORY SHEETS: FEATURE CORRELATION AND PARALLEL SAMPLING

The introduction of single unit recording and the refinement of psychophysical techniques have brought into dominance a detailed view of thalamic and cortical neurons based on their properties as feature detectors. This has been particularly true in vision (Hubel and Wiesel 1977). Thus, there are X, Y, and W cells in the retina (Stone 1983), each with different properties, as well as various orientation-specific cells in area 17, or striate cortex. This work has clarified our views of the degree to which the properties of a network can be expressed in the response of a single cell (for continuing theoretical views, see Rose and Dobson 1985). But it is well to remember that such cells exist in *populations* and that it is this property as well as morphology, connection pattern, and biochemistry that give the individual cell its characteristics. Sensory systems in general consist of multiple populations of receptors in the receptor sheet, multiple populations of ganglion cells with characteristic properties, and multiple representations of the receiving surface in the cord, brain stem, and cortex leading to variance in receptive fields. This is consistent with the fact that sensory systems also contain multiple parallel pathways and extensive reentrant connectivity. We discussed in chapters 5 and 6 the degenerate and dynamic nature of the local maps that are formed in such systems.

One of the striking evolutionary aspects of the special senses that emerged from this discussion is the early development of parallelism and the almost explosive simultaneous appearance in evolution of multimodal pathways and specialized receptors. The proposed hypothesis is that this development enormously increased the possibility of adaptive categorization of significant events in the environment by means of different movements and disjunctive sampling. Two aspects of such categorization are particularly pertinent to our discussion of global mapping. The first is that *separate* channels in the same modality or a different modality provide the opportunity to construct classification couples. Each channel can sample a different part of the environment as a result of movement and position and, according to the properties of sensory receptors at the two-dimensional receptor sheet, may extract different features in the respective sample. Further enhancement or suppression of this abstraction can occur in subsequent portions of the sensory network. The main point, however, is that the simultaneous *correlation* of the different kinds of disjunctive samples form a polymorphous set that emerges from the selection of neuronal groups that are themselves connected in reentrant loops in a global mapping.

The second essential aspect of categorization is the *definition of an object* (and, above all, its continuity properties) by the responding organism. This is a particularly salient issue—the categorization of surfaces or textures (Julesz 1984) is necessary but not sufficient to define objects, inasmuch as the continuity properties of a contour are not inherently definable topologically by a static receptor sheet. There are several ways in which an "object" may be categorized via motion or depth cues, however. For example, the systematic relative motion across a visual background of one object upon another can serve as a cue to the continuity of its contour. This seems to happen in young infants of four months who have not yet developed directed grasping (Kellman and Spelke 1983). Similarly, small changes in depth cues also can serve to define a border.

It is in connection with object definition that the relation of various forms of motor activity to sensory input comes to the fore. The evolutionary development of eye movements, head and neck movements, and coordinated evolutionary patterns of correlation of these movements with limb extension are key adaptive features. They not only prepare animals for appropriate responses but also serve to relate feature extraction by sensory sheets to the global feature correlation that accompanies the definition of an object. This is a key point in relating movement to categorization.

Perceptual responses thus require both special parallel structures in sensory modalities and a series of sampling events guided by motor responses *in continual actions* to yield the adaptive categorization that is the basis of generalization. The minimal structural requirements for carrying out such activity may be listed as follows:

1. The existence of motor ensembles, sensory sheets, and their neuronal substrates to carry out feature correlation as outlined above. Such neuromuscular ensembles are considered essential for the determination of systematic relative motion either of things that move together ("ob-

jects") or of the organism itself. They also provide the basis for continuity properties—the scale-free gestural equivalences that Bernstein (1967) called topological properties (figure 8.4). The carrying out of gestures with such properties reflects inherent capacities in the musculoskeletal system and the underlying neural substrate—they are not learned in the strict sense but precede learning as part of perceptual categorization. In contrast, metric features of objects and of parts of the organism's body as well as its treatment of near space (Mountcastle et al. 1984; Motter et al. 1987; Steinmetz et al. 1987) must be learned.

2. The existence of *multiple* parallel feature-detecting sensory sheets on *mobile* structures, along with appropriate neural substrates subserving several modalities. The particular features extracted are evolutionarily determined to a great extent by the receptors and transducers of the sheet and their relative arrangements on the limbs, head, and trunk.

3. Reentrant connections between neuronal groups subserving the motor system and those subserving the sensory system. This allows particular gestures to be related to the correlated definition of an object that is the result of motion (Ullman 1979). It is this *combination* in a global mapping that provides a basis for the abstract storage of the categorization corresponding to a gesture or a posture in terms of synaptic change.

4. The development of complex connections between *sequences* of action as learned responses and the resultant refinement of sampling of the environment by sensory sheets. This will be described further in chapters 9 and 11.

Several key aspects of this scheme deserve further emphasis. The first is the extraordinary degree of parallelism in even a single sensory system. According to this view, the mammalian eye and its associated receiving areas constitute an *assembly* of parallel sampling systems—for contrast, contour, color, disparity, and movement (Zeki 1969, 1971, 1978b, 1981, 1983; Van Essen 1979; Cowey 1981). The result of the selection of appropriate neuronal groups is a covariance, *not* an image or a sketch (see Marr 1982 for the contrary point of view). The existence of at least thirteen separate visual centers in cortical and subcortical regions, for example, does *not* require a central "scratch pad," as is implied by certain psychophysical or computational theories (Marr 1982). Instead, reentrant connectivity within this system and connectivity to higher-order neuronal groups relating feature to gesture is sufficient to provide adaptive responses.

Another consequence of this scheme is that there is no single inherent referential coordinate origin for an object or for the organism itself. While sampling systems and motion systems are inherently Euclidean (O'Keefe and Nadel 1978), there is no *single* object-centered axis or organism-centered axis. Instead, coordinate axes are defined as necessary, depending upon the properties of the sensory channel or the act.

For example, the definition of a vertical relationship to gravitation by the vestibular system can provide an independent axis in respect to others simultaneously determined by the organism. But the definition of an object in terms of its systematic *relative* motion across or behind another object is sufficient to free the categorization of that object from a particular position of its image on the retina. There exist a series of simultaneous and independent or quasi-independent coordinate origins defined by each modality, submodality, and channel. In considering such coordinate systems, one must note the order of different *scales* in motor and sensory tasks—posturally the scale is at the level of the whole organism, gesturally it is at the level of its appendages, and sensorily it can be *much* smaller. These scales are obligately linked by reentry according to the combined view adopted here. (This holds as well for temporal scales; see the evolutionary discussion of the visual system of *Pseudemys* in chapter 6.)

According to this interpretation, the categorical response of an organism depends to a very large degree upon the particular physical features of its receptor sheets and their positions on body parts as developed during evolution. This is not meant in the banal sense that if cones were not present, color would not be sensed. Rather, it is intended to imply that the physical structure of rods and cones or of the cochlear apparatus, for example, are already adapted by evolution to abstract major adaptive properties and that the function of higher-order neural networks is not to "compute" but to correlate these abstracted properties by further reentrant selection among selected populations of particular neuronal groups, as driven by motion. Given the possibility of neuronal group selection, with its rich combinatorial possibilities, the nature of the transducers and of the relation to the motor ensemble puts by far the single greatest constraint upon the capacity of such a system to categorize and generalize.

Some of the views taken here may appear to be consistent with aspects of the notions of affordances and ecological optics developed by Gibson (1979) and others (Turvey 1977). Nevertheless, there are profound differences between the neuronal group selection theory and so-called direct perception (for a criticism of the latter view, see Ullman 1980). Neuronal group selection is a complex and highly indirect process, and the theory, unlike Gibson's, is primarily concerned with the structure and character of responses of the neural substrate as determined by an animal's behavior. Moreover, the central issue in neuronal group selection is categorization and generalization driven by action.

This requires definition of objects prior to their *extensive* characterization in terms of features. Gibson's theory (1979) places emphasis upon *information* in texture patterns, optic flow, and general geometric aspects of the environment. In neuronal group selection, these aspects may provide signals—in the same sense that preattentive vision provides the basis for texton patterns (Julesz 1984)—but the key event is the discrimination of objects by combining in a global mapping the *feature correlations* arising from gesture with the *feature extractions* arising from the coordinated responses of moving sensory sheets.

The ecological viewpoint has served an important function in directing attention to those adequate combinations of stimuli that simultaneously excite different receptor sheets. But it bypasses the problem of categorization and ignores the issue of the nature of the neural systems and the continual motor sampling (Held 1961, 1965) constituted by evolution to solve this paramount problem of adaptation. Subsequent views of the processing of signals adequate for vision, such as those of Marr and his colleagues (Marr 1982), have greatly refined the Gibsonian position without necessarily agreeing with the idea that sufficient invariance exists in the structure of the world to allow direct perception (see Ullman 1980). But the present proposal also differs strongly from the computationalism of Marr: it rejects the idea that the nervous system computes a function. The selective behavior of ensembles or neuronal groups may be *describable* by certain mathematical functions; it is clear, for example, that the physical properties of receptors can be so described. But it seems as unlikely that a collection of neurons carries out the computation of an algorithm as that interacting lions and antelopes compute Lotka-Volterra equations. As we have already mentioned, imaging in a direct sense is also not assumed by the theory of neuronal group selection, and it appears misleading to use the idea of a sketch (Marr 1982) to embody the notion of complex correlations of different channels of feature detectors or extractors in a local map. Such correlations in themselves are essential, but they are highly abstract, are represented in multiple differently located populations of neuronal groups, and cannot by themselves constitute categorizations of objects. What, then, is the *overall* operation by which such categorization takes place and what structures carry it out? The theory asserts that the operation is carried out by global mappings.

GLOBAL MAPPINGS

In previous chapters, we considered the origin and nature of the local maps in the CNS, such as those found in the somatosensory cortex. In the present chapter, we have taken the position that both synergies *and* sensory inputs driven by synergies are required in parallel to give a sufficient basis for adaptive categorizations in a selective system. In applying this idea to neuronal group selection, we asked several questions about the relationship of this viewpoint to mapping. One question concerned the selective responses of neuronal groups to synergies and has already been discussed. We are now in a position to take up again the question of how internal maps and group constructs can lead to the choice of appropriate movements. This will prepare us to examine in later chapters the question of what is stored as a result of perception accompanying posture and gesture.

It is useful at the outset to point out a fundamental asymmetry inherent in sensory and motor maps. Operationally, a sensory map is constructed by recording responses of neurons to input. A motor map is constructed by stimulating neurons directly at the cortex or colliculus or in other regions directing impulses to motor assemblies or by recording from such neurons during activity (Evarts et al. 1984; Georgopoulos et al. 1984). The two mappings define somatotopic orders, but by two entirely disparate procedures. Nevertheless, the basis of what is locally mapped is a place (say, in cortex) to which reentrant correlations can be made. This is particularly significant because, in a multiple reentrant system, it is important to correlate the *disjunct* responses that are correlated with the spatiotemporal continuity of objects. Without *loci* for the neural correlation of both sensory input *and* motor responses with the continuity properties of the input signal, various separate parallel features that are correlated through motion could not be connected in real time even in a reentrant system.

Several additional interactions that do *not* preserve local topology or object characteristics appear to be necessary. These interactions take place in projections to *zonal* but not strictly somatotopically mapped systems such as basal ganglia and cerebellum, and they also occur in the *mixing* of multimodal secondary inputs to neuronal groups in mapped areas such as the parietal cortex (Mountcastle et al. 1975, 1984; Mountcastle 1978). Presumably, it is in these regions that the major correlations and recategorizations of parallel inputs are carried out. It is im-

portant, however, to note that such areas are always connected by reentrant loops to strictly mapped regions in primary receiving areas,
to sensorimotor cortex, or to nuclei that have somatotopic order; without such reentrant mapping, spatiotemporal continuity could not be
preserved.

Within such reentrant networks, there exist sequences of signals from
mapped to nonmapped to mapped regions. By reentrant correlation in
such networks of successive neural signals in time, a relationship can be
maintained with the coherent signals arising in a particular temporally
stable portion of the environment as they eventually reach primary
receiving areas. The resultant global mapping includes both sensory
input and the results of motor gestures, defining both the topology and
a metric for the individual animal (figure 8.5). The dynamic structure
of a global mapping is maintained, refreshed, and altered by continual
motor activity and rehearsal.

We can now consider global mapping as the basis for set-dependent
responses (Evarts et al. 1984). Inasmuch as both sensorily extracted
features and motor gestures are combined in inputs to higher-order
neuronal groups, a particular categorization is made in terms of both.
Relationships between frontal cortical groups, the basal ganglia, and
sensorimotor cortex would be expected to activate groups in the sensorimotor cortex that together would coordinate their responses to particular motor activities. The *initiation* of responses of the appropriate
groups in sensorimotor cortex rests with the frontal cortical and basal
ganglion signals. Particular signals to proximal muscle groups and the
subsequent responses of the system to connect successive portions of
synergies are tailored by cerebellar coordination and inhibition and
must represent *learned* associations (see chapter 11) within this complex reentrant path.

What is related among the groups linked by this path is a form of
categorization—an embodiment of the accompaniment of gestures
with a variety of features. What is learned and what is stored is either
relationships between activities of selected and reentrantly connected
neuronal groups made coherent by the presence of an object or relationships realized by the triggering of previously established linkages
between appropriate groups in the different local maps making up the
global mapping. In this view, perception, motor response, and recall are
all obligately linked by reentrant connections between several different
nuclei and laminae; the function of this global mapping is to provide
continuous dynamic sensorimotor recategorizations of objects. As we

shall see in chapter 11, choice or set-dependent behavior must result from the differential activation of such global mappings, an activation based upon evolutionarily established values and upon learning.

SUMMARY

As a preliminary to the discussion of categorization and memory in the next chapter, it may be useful to summarize the hypothesis on action and perception advanced in this chapter. According to the theory of neuronal group selection, the units of action are functional complexes for gestures and postures, the musculoskeletal components of which form a degenerate set. Matching between elements in this set and degenerate reentrant circuits is considered to be the main basis of patterned action. Gestures, the sets of all coordinated motions that produce a particular pattern, have to confront the same problems of specificity and range as those confronted by sensory signals. In this view, action is fundamental to perception, and sensory sheets and motor ensembles must operate together to yield a sufficient basis for perceptual categorization. Discrimination of objects occurs (at least initially) by combining feature correlations arising from those sensory signals that are coupled to gestures with the feature extractions arising from the coordinated multimodal responses of sensory sheets.

Structural, evolutionary, and functional considerations suggest that information processing models of motion based on control loops in which the units of action are muscles, joints, or the hierarchical arrangement of feedbacks are inadequate. A major or additional difficulty of such models is that they must invoke vaguely defined neural "potentiation" on the sensory side in order to account for the choice of actions (Hebb 1949; Bindra 1976; Gallistel 1980). In contrast, choice in the present model is based on differential selection of global mappings. As we shall see in chapter 11, this selection results from the interaction between ethological variables and conventional learning, an interaction that requires the prior existence of perceptual categories based on the activities carried out by both the sensory and the motor components of global mappings.

The major and essential contribution of motor ensembles to perception is feature *correlation,* which arises out of the *continuity* properties of motion and the continual focusing of sensory signals by creating postural and gestural movements. As has been suggested by Liberman

(Mattingly and Liberman 1987), the correlations of gestures provide essential bases for speech recognition, perhaps the most sophisticated form of perceptual categorization.

The minimal neural basis for perceptual categorization is considered to be a global mapping consisting of (1) multiple reentrant systems containing cortical loci mapping sensory input and motor responses that occur in parallel in real time; (2) connections from such strictly local mapped regions to nonmapped regions (such as basal ganglia) and back to mapped regions; (3) correlation by phasic reentrant signaling of successive neural signals in real time, maintaining a relationship between local maps in primary receiving areas and coherent signals arising in a portion of the environment as a result of ongoing motor activity. The manner in which feature correlation can arise from motion to yield neuronal group selection in maps will be further illustrated in the performance of a selective recognition automaton in chapter 10. During perception, categorization of features correlated continuously by gestures serves to define an equivalent of an object, which is simultaneously related to features extracted by sensory sheets. Continuous coordination occurs through reentry and parallel sampling in the global mapping, and these allow the recognition of a polymorphous set; a limited but highly specific functional instance of such coordination will also be taken up in chapter 10.

As was indicated in the evolutionary discussion, different components that might contribute to particular global mappings are enlarged or diminished in different species. The central point of this discussion is that the existence of global mappings alleviates the evolutionary difficulties of matching central responses to phenotypic changes in motor ensembles: neuronal group selection involving global mapping allows immediate matching in somatic time to evolved sensorimotor changes in the periphery, relaxing what might otherwise be an impossibly restrictive developmental constraint.

The coordination required for categorization by global mapping in a given species occurs in time and requires memory. According to the theory, perception, motor response, and recollection are intimately tied together by means of the activity of global mapping in a continual process of recategorization of objects that, we will contend in the next chapter, is the major basis of memory.

9

Categorization
and Memory

INTRODUCTION

The states of the world are remarkably varied, and so are those of the
behaving animal whose needs for survival require a system for adaptive
matching between states within itself and those of the environment.
This matching requirement becomes most sophisticated in relation to
the so-called higher brain functions. So far, the thesis on the structural
bases of higher brain functions that is pursued in this book can be
summarized roughly as follows. The epigenetic processes of development lead to structures within evolved nuclei and laminae that are
highly and individually variant in their intrinsic connectivity. These
structures provide the basis for the formation of large numbers of degenerate neuronal groups in different repertoires linked extrinsically in
ways that permit reentrant signaling. Mapping and somatotopic ordering arise evolutionarily from the need to maintain a reference for the

spatiotemporal continuity of objects as they interact with reentrant systems. Functionally, variant brain structures emerge during evolution to match the phenotypic changes that gave rise to alterations in sensory sheets and motor ensembles among different taxa. The enormous degree of parallelism in the global mappings formed within this system leads to increasingly refined independent sampling of the environment by separate submodalities, different modalities, or combined sensorimotor interactions. In interacting with signals from such mappings, the motor ensembles required for adaptive behavior provide a means in the nervous system for feature correlation, categorization of topological invariances, and continuities that are intimately related to the detailed sensory abstractions based on the feature detection that occurs in parallel and that is driven by motor activity. Whatever the form of their storage, repertoires changed by the sensory signals that reflect motor topology in global mappings must be "decorated" with parallel sensory signals of higher resolution. The components of global mappings must be able to deal with novelty while retaining the effects of favorable selections; this is accomplished in part by the operation of synaptic rules that enhance correlated short-term changes by means of long-term changes while assuring a continuous source of variance in network operation.

This summary points up the central issue of global brain function: What is the nature of categorization, generalization, and memory, and how does their interaction mediate the continually changing relationships between experience and novelty? The word "memory" and its connotations and denotations have been applied to a great variety of levels of system operation, from molecules to the grand semantic abstractions of social organisms. At the functional level, memory has been classified as procedural or declarative, semantic or nonsemantic, and short-term or long-term (see Norman 1969; Nilsson 1979; Neisser 1982; Squire and Butters 1984). It has been discussed mechanistically in terms of neural plasticity, sprouting of termini, chemical changes at synapses, and conditioning without very clear-cut distinctions of the levels of discourse in applying the different terminologies (Thompson et al. 1983).

In this chapter, I will take a radical view and suggest that memory is the enhanced *ability* to categorize or generalize associatively, not the storage of features or attributes of objects as a list. The minimal unit capable of carrying out such "recategorical memory" is a global mapping buttressed by learning (chapter 11), both of which are related to the satisfaction of systems linked to evolutionary survival. This implies that the necessary and sufficient bases of memory reside not only in global mappings but also in neural structures serving the hedonic or value-ridden aspects of behavior. In order fully to understand memory as recategorization in terms of neural structures, it will therefore be necessary first to understand categorization (the task of the present chapter), then to consider a concrete example of a selective network emulating a global mapping and therefore capable of serving this function (chapter 10), and finally to take up the relationship of categorization to learning (chapter 11). Not until all these tasks are complete will the notion of memory as recategorization be fully detailed.

This new notion of memory proposed in the theory rests centrally on two pillars: the structure of global mappings in a selective system and the nature of perceptual categorization itself. We dealt with the first in the preceding chapter and shall relate it further to memory in chapter 11, on learning. Before returning, however, to the idea of memory as recategorization in greater detail, we must devote most of the present chapter to the nature of categorization itself, for it is my contention here that the basis of memory is mainly in those neural structures that are responsible for categorization. This contention will require some justification, for most memory research does not accord categorization a position of prominence. Instead, a large body of research on memory is cognitive in nature and relates to information processing, language, consciousness, and notions of self; in other words, it is concerned with declarative memory which has a large semantic component (Neisser 1982; Squire 1982; Squire and Butters 1984). The complexity of the relatively unexplored *conceptual* mechanisms underlying such cognitive memorial performances would make any attempt to relate them to specific neural structures highly speculative; for this reason, we will direct the discussion here mainly to operations more akin to what has been called procedural memory. In any case, the issues may not be far removed from each other: the two major amnesic syndromes (diencephalic and bitemporal) do not fall easily into the categories of failures of retrieval (Squire 1982). Instead, they appear to be related to failures of performance connected with incoming signals, suggesting that even so-called declarative memory may have a procedural base related to such signals.

RESTRICTIONS AND DEFINITIONS

For our present purposes, the subjects of memory and categorization must be delimited and more sharply defined before the details of their interrelationship are considered. This is necessary because our major task is to define the *minimal* requirement that must be met by the neural apparatus in order for it to be capable of carrying out adaptive categorization.

The constrained position to be adopted here is as follows: (1) The term "memory" will be used to describe the *repeated* operation during categorization of whole circuits of neurons—for example, global mappings—and particularly to describe behaviors depending upon or attributable to such circuits. In the absence of detailed knowledge of circuitry, the term shall be used in connection with such behaviors and not in connection with the molecular events underlying synaptic rules. (2) The main emphasis will be upon procedural memory; this means ipso facto that we will focus upon alterations related to perceptual and motor acts. (3) The hypothesis will be entertained that memory of this kind *obligatorily* involves categorization (which will itself be defined shortly). (4) While this kind of memory is essential, additional neural events that are separate from categorization and that involve association and conditioning (see chapter 11) are considered to be essential, particularly for the behavior that is based on perceptual-motor memory. (5) Short- and long-term memory will be considered only within this limited context. Their operation will be related to the function of regions such as the hippocampus that, according to the theory, serve to assure real-time linkage in successive orders of various classification couples. As detailed in chapter 7, the mechanism of long-term storage is considered in terms of the workings of the set of independent synaptic rules operating on degenerate collections of neuronal groups in global mappings. Special care must be taken not to conflate this notion of storage with memory itself. In such a deliberately restricted view of memory, categorization is assumed to play a determinant role; that is, no molecular alteration of a metastable or stable type is deemed to be consequential for memory if there is no indication that concomitant categorization has taken place.

Obviously, this narrow or constrained view does not include much that is ordinarily considered to be consequential in the memory process. Even at the level of the neural substrate, it is only one of the bases for higher-order functions—including, for example, a variety of other functions carried out by structures such as the hippocampus (O'Keefe and Nadel 1978; Milner 1985). Its major focus is on perceptual categorization. Until recently, the study of categorization has been linked to the performance of semantically adept, acculturated individuals (Rosch and Lloyd 1978), or it has been considered solely as a philosophical issue (Ryle 1949; Wittgenstein 1953; Pitcher 1968; Quine 1969; see also Ghiselin 1981). Following Epstein (1982), we may define a "category" as a group of nonidentical objects or events that an individual treats as equivalent. This somewhat noncommittal definition will be refined later in the section entitled "Critical Summary." Here it is important to note that the activities subsumed under this weak definition would include so-called stimulus and response equivalence, generalization, and adaptive classification (Staddon 1983). In addition to the semantic and cognitive difficulties already mentioned in connection with memory, the traditional difficulties surrounding these processes relate to the question of whether categorization occurs mainly at the perceptual or the conceptual level. The position adopted here restricts the issue to the perceptual and motor sphere, ignores issues of consciousness and related perceptual experience, and focuses for the time being upon behavior. Data that fall into the conceptual domain will be used, but with due caution and warning. If this program is successful, it may serve later as a base for speculating upon the origins of declarative memory.

In deliberately restricting our theoretical task to the neuronal bases of memory as a form of recategorization, we shift away from cognitive issues to a concern with the evolution of neural structures adapted for coping with particular aspects of the econiche in which an individual of a species finds itself. We focus attention on the means by which a choice is made by the individual among the very large number of ways in which that niche may be partitioned in terms of adaptive perceptual categorization. To understand the prior conditions and grounds that might affect such a choice, we must take up the problem of categorization in detail.

CATEGORIZATION

Researchers studying categorization have used mainly adult human subjects, for obvious reasons: given the difficulties of the subject, results are more readily obtained from adults within a culture using the language of that culture. As has been pointed out by one of the pioneers in this arena, E. Rosch (1977, 1978; Rosch and Mervis 1975; Rosch et al. 1976; Rosch and Lloyd 1978), the aim of such research is not to develop models of how categorizations are achieved by neural processes. It is nevertheless useful initially to consider the adaptive functions served by categorization in terms of the work of these researchers, work that points up the enormous richness of categorical processes (for a critical view, see, e.g., Armstrong et al. 1983).

Categorization allows the individual to correlate properties in the world and thus to go beyond the immediate or given stimulus. To be of adaptive value, categorization must entail generalization, or the ability on the basis of a few stimuli to respond or recognize a much larger range of stimuli. To the degree that such generalization takes place, it allows the individual to deal with novel instances and to ignore other stimuli within a behavioral context. And, as has been pointed out by Rosch (1978), as seen from the standpoint of conventional views of memory, it results in cognitive economies—it relieves the organism of the burden of storing large numbers of single instances.

The question that must be confronted is whether perceptual-motor categorization has similar advantages and whether it can be studied in the absence of semantic and self-referential memory (see Macmillan et al. 1977; Smith and Medin 1981). We shall advance here, as a main thesis of the neuronal group selection theory, the notion that perceptual-motor categorization is *essential* for the development of learning in complex organisms and that it has adaptive advantages similar to those of conceptual categorization, to which it is obviously prior. There are two major instances in which perceptual categorization has been studied extensively without the additional complexities of linguistic issues: in pigeons and in human infants. Before considering such studies, we will do well, despite our strictures, to review some conclusions of category research on adults in the conceptual domain, mainly to provide a basis for later discussions of the nature of adaptive categories as they pertain to the function of neuronal groups.

Research on categorization carried out with articulate human subjects suggests that, at the level of conscious choice and language, subjects do not define categories by the classical method of lists of singly necessary and jointly sufficient attributes. Instead, they employ more probabilistic means, often calling upon nonnecessary features, various stimulus dimensions, or holistic properties. In other words, the classic (see Smith and Medin 1981) idea that a concept is a summary description of features, with the defining features cast in terms of subordinate concepts, is not supported. Instead, classification appears to be more disjunctive in nature. Individuals categorize *typical* members of a set more efficiently, do this in terms of family resemblance, use nonnecessary features, and do not necessarily follow strict superordination or subordination in assigning categories.

The analysis of conceptual categorization by Smith and Medin (1981) suggests that individuals use featural or dimensional descriptions but relate features to concept membership only probabilistically. In certain instances, individuals additionally perform classifications according to separate descriptions of exemplars of a concept. This last procedure accounts in part for the use of nonnecessary features, and it is consistent with the disjunctiveness of the categorization process and, to some degree, with the typicality effects that have been measured.

These authors point out that although these two ways of categorizing both admit of disjunction, the exemplar view requires explicit disjunction and large "storage capacity," whereas the probabilistic view allows disjunction to arise as a result of characterization and thus may require less "storage capacity." The greater the number of properties shared in a class, the more likely that a summary will be used rather than exemplars. Finally, these authors indicate that in certain circumstances the two components—probabilistic summary and exemplars—may be used together.

Other authors (Armstrong et al. 1983) have pointed out that the methodological bases of defining or assessing family resemblance or typicality are not always completely sound; exemplars of categories often yield graded rather than all-or-none responses from subjects. Such authors have suggested that certain concepts may have a core description "stored" in memory and possess an additional simple and ready identification method that leads to comparisons in degrees. They also suggest that it is not at all clear how features are chosen in the first place; this issue is intimately tied as well to perceptual categorization and to ethological constraints on natural categories (see Fagan 1979; Owings and Owings 1979; Marler 1982). Whatever these difficulties may be, and whatever their biological origin, it is clear that, at the level of concepts, categorization is carried out neither by rigorous, nor by logical, nor by universal criteria. Indeed, there may be no single general means by which categories are formed at this level.

Is there any evidence that one fares better at the perceptual level, particularly in considering the behavior of animals that lack language? Two kinds of animals have been studied: those that have no language possible because they have no evolved brain structure capable of subserving that function (e.g., pigeons) and those that have the brain structures necessary for language but have not yet fully acquired language (e.g., human infants below four months of age). An understanding of the problem of perceptual categorization is sharpened by studies in both cases.

PERCEPTUAL CATEGORIZATION

We shall consider here perceptual categorization by pigeons and object recognition as well as phonetic recognition by human infants. In both arenas, the data are only suggestive and require much supplementation. Nonetheless, they are sufficiently controlled and challenging to warrant serious attention. They indicate that some language-free organisms are capable of generalization and that language-based organisms inherently possess a number of categorization processes that are quite complex and that arise prior to language acquisition without formal tuition or learning paradigms. Both sets of findings, as well as others on the acquisition of bird song (Konishi 1978; Gould and Marler 1984; Marler 1984), provide strong evidence for selectionist theories of brain function. A major task of these theories is to sketch how such capabilities can arise within the neural structures of each of the species and to relate these capabilities to the capacities of associative memory and learning. Before undertaking this aspect of the theoretical task, let us briefly consider the data.

Generalization in Pigeons

The studies providing the most startling results are those of Herrnstein (1982, 1985; Herrnstein et al. 1976) and of Cerella (1979). Herrnstein's experiments involved exposing individual pigeons in an operant chamber to specifically or randomly chosen Kodachrome slides projected on a screen. When a positive pattern was projected, pecking on a key was reinforced; negative patterns received no reinforcement. Recognition was taken to be swift responses to positive patterns and no responses to negative patterns. The pictures were chosen in a variety of ways and on a variety of subjects. In one series (figure 9.1), forty pictures of trees in a variety of perspectives, distances, collective numbers, and types were mixed with forty irrelevant pictures. Reinforcement of a small number of tree scenes led to rapid recognition and few errors on a variety of other tree scenes. Controls consisting of tree-like

Figure 9.1
*Tree discrimination experiment by Herrnstein (1982). Black-and-white repro-
ductions of eight of the color slides that were correctly classified as trees or
nontrees by at least three of four pigeons tested. Trees are in the upper four
pictures; nontrees, in the lower four. The bottom left nontree shows a vine
climbing on a cement wall; the bottom right, a clump of celery.*

objects such as the sides of geometrically decorated buildings, vine-like
patterns, or lampposts were not recognized.

Trees are part of the pigeon's natural environment, and it might be
surmised that such capabilities have an evolutionary or ethological base.
But fish are not commonly in a pigeon's environment, and a series of

slides of fish in underwater scenes were positively discriminated, provided that the views were side or three-quarter views. These pictures, like those of trees, varied greatly in context, distance, color value, and presence of confusing cues. Perhaps most dramatic was a set of experiments on a particular woman photographed in a variety of views, clothes, backgrounds, and distances. After reinforcement, most pigeons had no difficulty recognizing views of this woman, and they rejected views of another woman dressed in her clothes and photographed on the same street.

A number of controls were carried out to exclude the possibility of hidden cues, learning of sequences, and similar variables. The order of the slides varied from test to test and from day to day. The range of generalization and the specificity were impressive. As far as could be discerned, there were no systematic bases for explaining the performance of the pigeons in terms of the specific learning of irrelevant cues. If this were the case, it would seem an astounding feat in itself, but there was no indication that any hidden cues beyond the original operant reinforcement in early views were present.

The studies of Cerella (1979; see figure 2.4), though similar, employed "simpler" and more abstract patterns and were aimed at analyzing some of the mechanisms underlying the pigeons' performance. Using a series of computer-generated distortions of a training figure, Cerella showed that the pigeon is sensitive to any alteration of a graphic pattern, confirming earlier work. Alterations included translations, truncations, deformations, rotations, and dilations. In addition, the studies of Blough (1973) demonstrated that pattern recognition in the pigeon can be position invariant. In the work of Cerella (1979), there was a suggestion that discrimination decreased with increasing degree of distortion from prototypes. Some studies by Anish (1978) of natural scenes, such as trees or close-ups of twigs and leaves, showed significant responses to test slides after training slides of a similar type were presented. These studies resembled those based on abstract figures and were simpler versions of those by Herrnstein (1979; Herrnstein and Loveland 1964; Siegel and Honig 1970; Poole and Lander 1971; Herrnstein and de Villiers 1980).

Cerella (1979) suggested that his results might reflect matching by flexible templates, provided it was understood, for example, that a view of a person was not the thing matched; instead, his notion was that such a view was first broken up into a series of disjunctive subviews. Each of these subviews would be learned independently. Cerella realized, however, that this hypothesis could not accommodate the finding by

Herrnstein (1979) that a probabilistic reinforcement schedule worked: tree slides in the fifth session that had never been reinforced elicited as strong a response as those reinforced in every instance. Thus, while the template theory required the learning of many individual slides, the facts indicated that this was not necessary. Moreover, a relatively small set of apparent exemplars was sufficient. Cerella (1977, 1979, 1980) has attempted to rescue a template theory by suggesting that the "capture ratio" of templates is large—that is, that just a few examples of a category contain sufficient cues to account for all subsequent performances on a large number of disparate instances. So far, this assumption has received no strong support from the available data.

Cerella's additional studies have, however, cast the problem of generalization in a sharper light, and they put limits on the kind of generalizations that can be carried out by pigeons. He first used figures from the Charlie Brown ("Peanuts") cartoon series and showed that, provided the early views did not have too complex a background, pigeons readily recognized each figure regardless of the degree of variation in pose or clothes. He then truncated, scrambled, or inverted the views of Charlie Brown and found that such incomplete and distorted figures were recognized as well as those of the intact cartoon personality. He also permuted head, trunk, and feet in haphazard orders and found little or no perturbation of recognition. He recognized that these results augured poorly for any simple template theory and suggested that perhaps pigeons used mainly local features as cues, making decisions on the basis of a sufficiency of such cues (i.e., some number over a threshold). Significantly, he showed that pigeons could *not* distinguish very extensively between two classes of patterns (such as projections of cubes) when these patterns differed only in three-dimensional structure but not in local features.

In other studies, it was found that pigeons could distinguish oak leaves from nonoak leaves but not individual oak leaves from each other. This suggests an inability even in two dimensions to generalize in fine detail—that is, the pigeons did not discern specific relations between features, at least not in these examples. If a pigeon sees Charlie Brown as a set of features, then, consistent with the findings on projections, scrambling does not disturb recognition, because at least some relations between features are not critical; moreover, any subset of features would seem to be sufficient, as the truncation experiments indicate.

Cerella has pointed out that these conclusions suggest that only some part of a test image need match some part of a framing image. He relates this conclusion to the work of Rosch and Mervis (1975) and

Rosch and others (1976) on concept formation and categorization in nongraphical categories. He is critically aware, however, that the pigeon's apparent limitations may reflect some limitations of the methods: (1) The images were static. Movement systems of vision were not explicitly tested and may not show such limitations. (2) Graphic images were used and not objects, halftones, or color slides. (3) Hidden relational propensities such as connectedness and sidedness were not tested. (4) Blank backgrounds were favored, and the effect of "visual noise" was not tested.

In addition to demonstrating these limitations of generalizing power, these studies also yielded some important positive findings. Rotational invariance was preserved in several kinds of contexts. In cartoon scenes, the presence of backgrounds was annoying and destructive to early retention, whereas they were irrelevant in natural scenes such as those of Herrnstein (1979). These results suggest that the list of bases upon which pigeons generalize may change, depending upon the context and type of material.

These remarkable studies, while incomplete, suggest equally remarkable powers of generalization in an animal that has no language system. Formal tuition or forced learning are not at issue here: it is clear that the pigeon can discern parallel presentations of disjunctive features, use some of them in a set to recognize others connected with new features in another set, and, to a large (but not absolute) degree, ignore great variations in context.

Before attempting to interpret such findings in the light of brain structure and the theory of neuronal group selection, let us turn to an organism that has not yet acquired language but has the capability to do so—the very young human infant.

Object and Auditory Recognition in Infants

It may seem discordant to jump from the subject of how pigeons divide up their visual world to that of the recognition of object coherence in human infancy and categorization in infant perception of speech. Despite vast differences in evolutionary history, in brain size, and in the capabilities of their subjects, however, these studies on different species confront the same puzzle: the structural basis of generalization in neural and motor systems.

In the last decade, a number of studies of very young infants have revived interest in the question of their capacity to integrate, categorize, and generalize without formal tuition. We shall mention only two areas of this burgeoning and important field (see Bower 1967, 1982; Wolff and Ferber 1979; Aslin et al. 1981; Gallin 1981; Harris 1983; Brainerd and Pressley 1985) as they bear upon the concerns of this chapter. We begin with object perception. Spelke and her colleagues (Kellman and Spelke 1983) have investigated whether a very young infant can determine the unity of an object occluded by a second object, whether such an infant can be aware that parts of the world move as units, and whether he or she can determine that two adjacent surfaces lie on the same or different objects. We shall consider the experimental results in summary form only; the details may be seen in the original publications.

The experimental paradigm involved the observing of infants four months old while they watched stationary and moving objects and visible and occluded objects (figure 9.2). If two originally colinear rods occluded behind a block were moved separately, the infant registered the occluded rods as two separate objects. But if the rods moved systematically with their ends always transitionally colinear relative to the occluding block, they were viewed as a single object. The test was based on the tendency of infants to look, after the first presentation of objects, only at novel things, not at familiar ones. A large series of tests and controls were done to determine whether the results depended on forms or colors. The capacity to see systematically moving entities did not depend on simplicity or regularity in shapes or colors: objects of irregular shapes were also seen as one with the rod if they moved with it. There was no evidence of *Prägnanz*, as defined by Gestalt psychologists (Wertheimer 1958; see Kubovy and Pomerantz 1981). The infants did not seem to perceive scenes in terms of a mosaic related to visible fragments of surfaces, and thus they do not appear to construe the world as Gibson (1979) proposed; this ability to see object coherency appears before infants can act coherently *upon* objects in terms of coordinated grasping.

Adjacent contiguous objects lying in the same plane were seen by these infants as one unit; those separated in depth were seen as two objects. The major conclusions of this work (Kellman and Spelke 1983) suggest that very young infants see the world as made up of spatially connected and separately moveable "objects." Infants do not seem to recognize textures in precedence over unitary systematic relative motion and do not tend to classify objects as uniform in substance or regular in shape. They do not respond simply to surfaces or sensation. It is not clear whether infants are born with the notion of an object—but if these observations are confirmed, it *is* clear that vision and relative

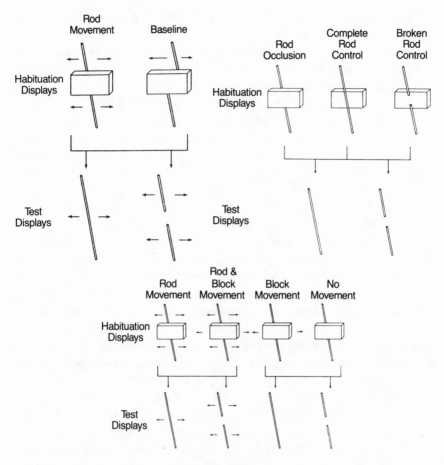

Figure 9.2

Examples of displays used by Kellman and Spelke (1983) to test perception of partly occluded objects by four-month-old infants. Infants were habituated to an object whose top and bottom were visible but whose center was occluded by a nearer object. They were then tested with a visible continuing object and with two visible object pieces showing a gap where the occluder had been. The boundaries of a partly hidden object were perceived by analyzing the movements of the surfaces, and a connected object was perceived when its ends moved in a common translation behind the occluder. There was no evidence that decisions were made by analyzing colors or the form of any objects.

motion can lead to a primitive categorization of things that move together as "objects." By and large, the continuity properties implied by motion carry over into these capabilities of categorization.

Before integrating these results on vision with those on other forms of categorization, we shall turn briefly to an auditory example concerned with evidence for the capacity of very young prelinguistic infants to show perceptual categorization. We focus upon the ability of infants to perceive at the phonetic and acoustic level and upon the fact that such infants can carry out such categorical perception in the face of considerable variation in the rates of speech.

The work of Eimas et al. (1987; Eimas and Miller 1981; Eimas 1982) and Aslin et al. (1981) and their reviews of other investigators' work provide the basis of this survey. Speech categorization by infants has been studied in terms of (1) the infant's capacity to categorize variations in coarticulation, speaker differences, and differences in intonation patterns (so-called equivalence class formation); and (2) the infant's capacity to define categories in terms of temporal variations of articulatory mechanisms (so-called categorical perception). Basically, both of these are forms of categorization. Eimas and coworkers point out an important limitation: it is not possible to detect whether infants perceive two instances of the same category as *identical* events. But one can observe whether an infant responds *as if* physically different occurrences of the same category are equivalent experiences. It has been shown in respect to equivalence classes that four-*day*-old infants can form such classes on the basis of varied vocal quality (Jusczyk et al. 1980). In other studies, infants were shown to be able to distinguish fricative contrasts in initial and final syllable positions produced with different vowels and speakers. Similarly, evidence was obtained for stops versus nasals.

In most of these experiments, the annotated observations were for head-turning responses. Another test procedure is based on the high-amplitude sucking response; differences in sucking rate to a new stimulus relative to control rates are used as a basis for recognizing categorization. Synthetically generated speech sounds could be used. Small differences in voice onset time, in spectral composition of formant transitions, and in manner of articulation all are distinguished categorically by infants to greater or lesser degree. This categorical perception is based upon multiple cues and is strongly context-dependent. Infant listeners can compensate for changes in rate of speech, changes that can be shown separately to lead to ambiguities in distinguishing between stop consonants (short transitions) and semivowels (long transitions), for example, in [b] versus [w]. Yet, adults and infants both handle this ambiguity by "processing" the transition duration in relation to the duration of the syllable, a duration that in fact reflects speech rate. This ability, called by Eimas et al. (1987) a procedure for "normalizing speech for rate of speech," is a form of categorization.

Many other examples of evidence for categorical response may be cited. But perhaps it is more to the point to cite the proposal of Eimas et al. (1987) that the infant comes to the world biologically endowed with the ability to categorize some of the phonetic distinctions used in natural languages. This capacity is not restricted to speech but is also seen in perception of nonspeech sounds, as it is in visual object recognition. In addition to showing coherent object recognition (discussed previously), infants can categorize a form presented in different orientations at six months of age (McGurk 1972), can distinguish characteristics of human faces, age, and sex at five months (Fagan 1976; Fagan and Singer 1979), color categories (Bornstein et al. 1976), and prototype averages (Strauss 1979). Miller et al. (1982) suggest that at the prephonetic level of processing, categories are also defined in terms of prototypical categories. Eimas et al. (1987) conjecture that the categories formed by infants may be based on prototypes that cut across sensory modalities—that is, that, in the neural construct, particular procedures exist for relating modalities in a manner that produces similar category boundaries.

This is not the place to discuss the relation of these findings to the formation of phonetics and a lexicon (see Eimas et al. 1987). But, for the purposes at hand, we can conclude that infants have a considerable ability to sort out an auditory world before the acquisition of language, that this ability is likely to be one of the bases of language acquisition, and that the fundamental problem is to determine the nature of the underlying biological mechanism. It is important to recognize, however, that the claims for a special or separate form of processing of speech sounds (Liberman et al. 1972; Liberman and Studdert-Kennedy 1978; Eimas et al. 1987; Mattingly and Liberman 1987) have not yet been fully validated. Indeed, recent work has suggested that whatever mechanisms are in play, they are initially tuned to acoustic, not phonetic, information. The later work of Aslin and coworkers (1981; Walley et al. 1981) and Jusczyk (1981; Jusczyk et al. 1977, 1983) suggests that categorical perception is not limited to speech signals. Moreover, in line with our previous arguments, categorical perception is not limited to human (linguistic) perception. Chinchillas show a discrimination of stop consonants similar to that of humans (Kuhl and Miller 1975, 1978). Language may exploit such properties of perceptual systems, but it obviously does not precede them. These conclusions are in accord with our proposal that perceptual categorization is a reflection of the general properties of reentrant degenerate repertoires.

In dealing with the essential problem of speech perception—namely, how a listener redefines an acoustical signal in such a way as to map a phonetic segment and finally give it lexical meaning—an infant appears to come into the world well but obviously not completely equipped (Liberman et al. 1972; Liberman and Studdert-Kennedy 1978; Mattingly and Liberman 1987). This is extraordinary, for the categorization mechanisms for speech sound are quite complex—segmentation is not sequential, there is evidence that anticipation is occurring during coarticulation, there is overlapping information for individual segments, and this overlapping is not limited to word boundaries. There is a many-to-one mapping between acoustic signal units and their analyses at the phonetic level, even as acoustic properties change with context, rate of speech, and the speaker. All of these properties show inherent variability, and yet, to some extent, an infant can categorize them and detect invariances.

The remarkable fact is that despite the difficulties of segmentation, multiple cues, context changes, and inherent variability, the speech signals *are* categorized. Indeed, the evidence supports the existence of constrained systems that are not based initially, or at least not completely, upon learning or formal tuition. The parameters of constraint are fixed very early if not at birth. Yet, considerable flexibility exists, and the features *emphasized* by an organism may be shifted in different contexts or sequences. In making categorizations, organisms thus must make some kind of decision about what to dwell on and what to overlook. In some cases (McGurk and MacDonald 1976), one modality dominates over the other, and this kind of decision may be affected accordingly.

CRITICAL SUMMARY

For categorization to be carried out at very early ages, there must be a good deal of initial constraint in the structural and functional aspects of neural organization. Before we try to formulate a possible neural basis for generalization and categorization in terms of neuronal group selection, it may help to separate the critical issues and to attempt some syntheses on the basis of the different studies reviewed so far. These syntheses suggest that a major function in categorization is disjunctive sampling in parallel channels and that the capabilities of animals go beyond the weak definition of categorization (page 244) with which we started.

First, it is important to notice that in both visual and auditory tasks, parallel and simultaneous processes are occurring—segmentation is not merely sequential in speech, nor are features grasped one at a time. There is coarticulation as well as "copresentation," and physically defined signal properties also overlap various partitions or segmentation boundaries. Moreover, there are multiple properties with many-to-one mappings, for example, in the phonetic distribution of a consonant sound in the presence of a vowel. In addition, there is great variability in multiple presentations across multiple properties. Recognition does *not* depend upon a fixed order in a sequence, and, in many cases, local features can themselves be grasped as an unordered set. Nonetheless, practically all of the situations reviewed above show strong context dependence.

While most instances of patterns discussed here are not polymodal, the use of different sensory modalities may greatly enhance the power of generalizing systems. In many instances, it is hard to ignore motor involvement—eye movements, object movements, manipulation, or action upon the object. Parallel systems, such as the two visual systems (Schneider 1969), may be involved, one of which is strongly dependent upon motion. Considered in connection with memory, this is reminiscent of Henry Head's motor schema (Head 1920; Oldfield and Zangwill 1942a, 1942b, 1942c, 1943), and it suggests the presence of different salience hierarchies, depending upon the current or previous state of the organism's motor system as reflected in global mappings. It also suggests that what matters in interpreting motion is the systematic relative displacement of objects in relation to the organism. What the CNS may be doing with eyes, muscles, and limbs is categorizing patterns of actions or gestures. Bernstein (1967), Spelke (Kellman and Spelke 1983), and Herrnstein (1979) may not be far apart.

Despite the evidence for recognition of local features, some kind of overall "object distinction" (not necessarily veridical) is made by the generalizing organism. In infants, the evidence suggests the existence of processes that guarantee internal coherence, boundary persistence, and grouping of three-dimensional movements of surfaces. Pigeons are apparently deficient at this latter task but perhaps succeed in other groupings of salience, such as color and tonality. This may explain the apparent discrepancy between Cerella's (1979) and Herrnstein's (1979, 1982) results. Whatever their grouping, targets in images are clustered as objects. Suppression of attributes like color, brightness, and texture can occur (at least in infants) as readily as segmentation.

All of these observations indicate that novelty cannot be reduced to any simple or single closed description on a set of stimuli. Categorization involves more than stimulus generalization (i.e., variation along any single dimension or spread of effects among wider ranges of stimuli). It is multidimensional. There is evidence for the establishment of hierarchies and for the existence of several stages in both motion and object detection and in speech perception. Object detection, for example, involves at the minimum (1) perception of the three-dimensional layout and movement of surfaces and (2) grouping of surfaces. Speech involves (1) anticipation and coarticulation of sounds and (2) grouping of sounds after normalizing for syllable length. Generalization can involve common features, common responses, or common history, any *one* of which may act independently of the others. Moreover, generalization involves nonlinear processes; as a result, small biases in internal states can lead to large changes in responses.

There is no evidence for the use of Gestalt properties (Wertheimer 1958) or of surface properties (Julesz 1984) directly or *per se* in early generalization. There is some evidence throughout for prototypicality effects (Strauss 1979), suggesting that two functions are occurring simultaneously: assignment of objects to classes and assignment of uniqueness to objects. But prototypicality effects can be modulated by graded dimensions and conjunction effects, as has been shown by Armstrong et al. (1983). In all cases, errors occur but are surprisingly rare; everything seems to be responded to more or less well. However, most of the experiments done so far do not distinguish topological from metrical invariances.

All of these observations lead to the important conclusion that the idea of discrete case learning fails as a general explanation for categorization—even if such learning is well developed, it flies in the face of the facts of generalization. Moreover, as was mentioned previously, it places enormous demands upon any system of memory. The proposal of the existence of extreme prototypicality or of unitary exemplars plus template variation also fails; there must be at least some mediation between, or some mixture of, these two processes. The world may not be amorphous, but it does not come in fixed or predesignated categories. This does not mean, however, that certain "natural categories" cannot be fixed during the evolution of a species within a relatively stable econiche (Marler 1982). Nevertheless, categorization and generalization cannot be explained sufficiently on the basis of conventional learning and reward plus ethological variables fixed by evolution.

The failure of prototypicality alone as an explanation, the contradictions that cannot be explained by models of simple feature detection, the strong influence of context, and the highly parallel nature of the inputs all suggest that there is no general *closed* solution to the problem of categorization. This may confute certain attempts to carry out linguistic analysis in terms of rules and representations, but it is not disturbing to a selectionist considering the problem at the perceptual level. At this level, the key question may be how an animal disjunctively chooses local criteria (not just features) to guide category inclusion in a given instance. By local criteria, I mean a *few* grouped features or correlates of features. In some cases, both *local feature detection* and *global feature correlation* occur simultaneously and in variable degrees. Perhaps within the context of an animal's common history and responses, it is the combination of the two processes, abstracted from the object in different ways, that determines which subset of attributes the animal picks. Partitioning the world by a determination of apparent object boundaries may be the first key step. As in evolution itself, parallelism and the possibility of convergent and equivalent solutions may allow the choice to be made in a number of ways.

Finally, as was suggested in the discussion of conceptual categorization, although there are vast differences in their complexity, "simple" perceptual categorization and culture-bound "top-down" categorization based on advanced natural languages (Chomsky 1980) may themselves have much in common. As the study of phonetics indicates, the one may provide a base for determining the other (Liberman and Studdert-Kennedy 1978; Mattingly and Liberman 1987).

NEURAL ORGANIZATION AND THE PROCESS OF GENERALIZATION

We are now in a position to consider some possible neural organizations that may lie behind the capacity to categorize and generalize. Because of the complexity of these processes, we can only sketch candidate structures and minimal models; nonetheless, the model that can be formulated is satisfyingly consistent with selectionist theories. A detailed test of the self-consistency of the model sketched here will be presented in chapter 10, in which the performance of an automation based on the model is described. The neural organizations to be proposed provide the structural basis for a description of memory as recategorization.

It is illuminating to begin by examining certain issues related to the environment and signals or stimuli. While the world is not amorphous and the *properties* of objects are describable in terms of chemistry and physics (Pantin 1968), it is clear that, at the macroscopic level, objects do not come in predefined categories, are variable in time, occur as novelties, and are responded to in terms of relative adaptive value to the organism rather than of veridical descriptions. This lends a relativistic and disjunctive flavor to the categorization of objects by animals: things are partitioned according to those factors that are significant for and available to the perceiving animal. Feature shaping occurs according to the particular sets of saliencies, cues, and contexts presented at some time and in some sequence. There is a fundamental ambiguity in classifying objects under such constraints as those shown in figure 9.3, modified from Bongard (1970): depending upon context, an animal might classify the large figures as either ellipses or large objects.

Inasmuch as any particular presentation of an object does not exhaust its features and feature relationships, we have to consider which features are sampled and which are considered characteristic. We have seen that studies of conceptual categorization show evidence that subjects use both probabilistic feature ensembles and exemplars. In per-

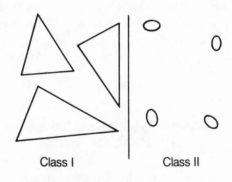

Class I   Class II

Figure 9.3
Ambiguities of classification according to Bongard (1970). If the large ellipse is presented for test after objects in class I and II, three decisions are possible: (1) Class I, "big"; (2) Class II, "ellipse"; and (3) "trash," that is, irrelevant.

ceptual categorization, we have also seen evidence for prototypicality effects, although they do not dominate all decisions.

These characteristics show that there is no closed definition either of a universal or of a universal in absence ("a memory") by the nervous system; in confronting stimuli, there is no definition in terms of singly necessary and jointly sufficient features. Instead, the choices mimic Wittgenstein's (1953) family resemblances or his definition of games: a game is not described by a fixed features list, nor is it true that each game is defined arbitrarily by nominalistic designation. Instead, it is clear that games do not necessarily have anything in common except that they are games. (Translation: if n is the size of an arbitrarily long list of attributes of games, a list that is not closed, any m out of the n attributes would suffice to make a particular activity a game.)

This is in effect a definition of a polymorphous set (see figure 2.5). Dennis and others (1973) constructed visual sets of this type and found that it was extremely difficult for university students to find the designators that distinguished Y from N (figure 2.5). In the example shown, the rule according to which Y was constructed and the objects in it were characterized as follows: at least two of circular or dark or symmetric. In effect, a polymorphous set is characterized by a disjunction of the possible partitions (in the sense of probability theory) of objects or of features. This can be seen in the diagram of figure 9.4. Degeneracy, as we have defined it in repertoires of neuronal groups, also consists of disjunctions, here of partitions in neural nets—that is, the variety of functional ways that neurons can be connected nonisomorphically in groups to give more or less equivalent responses under some threshold condition. Such a network arrangement is admirably suited to responding adaptively to a world that is to be partitioned in a disjunctive manner. The question is, How may this network arrangement be coupled *specifically* in its neuroanatomy to yield generalization?

An analysis based on the theory of neuronal group selection suggests that six properties are necessary in such an arrangement: (1) The presence of extensive local variability and degeneracy of neuronal groups at all levels. (2) Evolutionarily determined structures serving as abstractors in sensory sheets and acting in concert and simultaneously with motor ensembles in an adapted phenotype. (3) Neuronal networks and CNS structures that are connected to sensory sheets to carry out local feature detection. Those networks that are connected to sensorimotor ensembles have evolved for the determination of either object-centered or organism-centered axes, for the determination of the continuity of an object, and for the detection and representation of system-

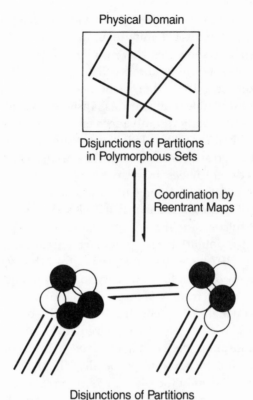

Figure 9.4

The selection of partitions of neuronal groups as a result of reentrant mapping of disjunctions of partitions in polymorphous sets of signals. Disjunctions involve nonexclusive OR functions, and, outside of rough somatotopy and point-to-area mapping, higher repertoires in global mappings show no isomorphism with the signal domain.

atic relative motion. (4) Map structures and sequences similar to those described in previous chapters: local maps leading from somatotopic representations to nonmapped polymodal structures and, finally, to a motor output map; together, these constitute a global mapping. (5) Reentry among levels and between maps—the first to accommodate dynamic shifts and readjust the mapping (see figure 6.7) and the second to create derivative maps resulting in classification couples (figure 9.5). Reentrant connections assure that the patterns of neuronal groups responding to unique features in one map can be associated simultaneously with correlations of features associated in another map to yield invariant patterns. Such invariances are established by topological representations similar to those for sensorimotor ensembles, described in the preceding chapter. (6) The reentrant functions of such maps can at different moments have different degrees of local and global flavor, depending upon whether the feature-detecting or the feature-correlating aspects of the system are emphasized.

A system of global mappings constructed in this way can deal with polymorphous sets. As shown schematically in figure 9.4, the system does so by mapping those disjunctions sampled according to adaptive criteria onto the disjunctions of partitions represented by selections of

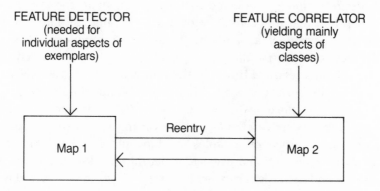

Figure 9.5

Diagram of classification couple using reentry. Neurons—those in the visual system, for example—act as feature detectors (inheriting that capacity as a result of evolution). They map on the left (map 1) to some higher-order lamina in the brain. Other neurons—for example, those related to light touch on a moving finger—act as feature correlators, tracing an object by motion, as shown on the right. These neurons map to another lamina (map 2). The two maps project onto each other by reentrant connections, so that groups in one map may excite groups in the other. This allows the parallel simultaneous sampling of disjunctive characteristics constituting a polymorphous set in the stimulus; because of the reentrant connections, these characteristics can be connected in the responses of higher-order networks. In this way, certain more general characteristics of an object representation can be connected with other, particular characteristics. By means of synaptic change, particular patterns of responses in map 1 will be linked to independently sampled patterns of responses in map 2 as a result of the reentrant connections. Generalization can occur on the basis of any combination of local features or feature correlations resulting from disjunctive sampling of signals from objects not encountered before. The reentry will link the responses to these combinations to previous patterns of responses. To some extent, the notion of a classification couple is a limiting case: there is every reason to suspect that, in general, more than two maps interact, forming classification n-tuples.

degenerate sets of neuronal groups coupled in series and in parallel (figure 9.5). Of course, this sampling is limited by the phenotypic properties of the sensorimotor apparatus and by the ethological bases (Marler et al. 1981; Gould and Marler 1984) of behavior.

It is essential to recognize that such a system is neither complete nor error-free—a threshold response leading to adaptive behavior is sufficient. The reason the system can generalize is that it trades off completeness and error-free operation for a sufficient mapping between locally sampled feature properties and global object definitions attained through feature correlation (notice the similarity in feature correlation to infant object definition). The specificity and potential variability of feature detection is connected by these means with the invariance of independent feature correlation over a wide range of different object properties. Inasmuch as sampling for these two functions occurs more or less separately in parallel and in real time, each function may fluctuate widely at a series of times. In the neural structure, the efficacies of associative higher-order connections may also fluctuate greatly, but in the presence of the object they are repeatedly reinforced by reentry as it occurs in successive chunks of time during which the sampling by classification couples or n-tuples is taking place. As we shall discuss later, while conventional associative learning links such a system to responses and rewards, it can never be responsible for the *initial* generalization carried out by the system. Nonetheless, such learning assures both the output to arbitrary behavior and the linkage of neuronal group selection to rewards having adaptive advantage for the entire animal. An example of how such a learning system might operate at the whole animal level is discussed in chapter 11.

Depictions of specific detailed neural structures that might be responsible for such activities are ignored in figures 9.4 and 9.5. Clearly, an assignment to specific neural nuclei and laminae and to particular neuroanatomy is essential; just as clearly, with the exception of the structures mentioned in previous chapters, detailed assignments are lacking and await the design of suitable experimental protocols. Some of these protocols will be outlined in the last chapter; here, we must appeal to an argument from sufficiency, which is obviously not fully persuasive. The specific instantiation in circuits given in chapter 10 will at least deal with the self-consistency of these ideas and show how generalization can take place following initial categorization.

The system we have outlined could not function if events were not reflected by alterations in populations of synapses, as was described in chapter 7. In order to exhibit generalization from a sequence of test objects to other objects seen in later times as a string of novelties, the properties of memory are also needed. Let us reconsider some aspects of the key problem of memory as seen in terms of the findings on categorization and generalization that have been reviewed here.

THE PROBLEM OF MEMORY RECONSIDERED

In the first part of this chapter, we adopted the tactic of avoiding the issue of semantic memory. Instead, we chose to examine *what* is remembered and *how* it is *first* defined at the perceptual level. The key issue to be confronted at this level is, Is memory replicative? In other words, is what is stored something like a systematic (albeit transformed) set of particular features, attributes, and properties, stored in the same way a computer stores lists of gray values in a matrix in order to represent a scene?

Our considerations in this chapter suggest that this is not the case. Instead, we have taken the position that perception, categorization, generalization, and memory are necessarily intimately linked. According to this view, memory is a form of recategorization based upon current input; as such, it is transformational rather than replicative, although alterations corresponding to exemplary features may be reflected in synaptic changes in various parts of a classification couple.

This assumption—that memory is a form of recategorization resulting from the enhanced ability to categorize and generalize—is not too far from some aspects of Head's motor schema (Head 1920; Oldfield and Zangwill 1942a, 1942b, 1942c, 1943) and Bartlett's later views (1964). But besides confronting the issue at the level of neural organization, the present proposal differs in several specific additional ways. It limits itself to the level of perceptual categories and directly confronts the nonverbal aspects that are central to constructing any more ambitious model of memory. It is explicit in its assumption that the essence of memory involves generalization (not just associative learning), and it is equally explicit about the selective nature of the neural organizations that contribute to such memory. Finally, it proposes that a specific neural process or form of organization (a global mapping; see figure 8.5) is *required* for recategorical memory and that this substrate is the *minimal* one required to carry out such a function.

According to this view, the relation of memory in the brain to information and the notion of finite storage (Pierce 1961) must both be rigorously reexamined. Inasmuch as the recategorization carried out by classification couples has a variable element and because categorization is a continually *active* selective process of disjunctive partitioning of a world that exists "without labels," the static idea of information as it is used in communication theory is not very appropriate. It is true that, as the amount of categorization of members of a set increases, there is an accrual of adaptive behavior and of response generalization; it is also likely that this is accompanied by a decrease in degeneracy in the neural circuits mediating the response. But inasmuch as there is always a trade-off between specificity and range in selective systems (see chapter 2), and because there is, in general, no prior prefixed or coded relation between an animal's behavior and objects and events in its present environment, it is not illuminating to talk of information (except *a posteriori,* as an observer). It is equally fruitless to attempt to measure the capacity of such a system in information theoretical terms: reaching a response that even vaguely categorizes a stimulus by trading some specificity for range puts an animal in a reasonably good position for adaptive behavior. If that behavior is rewarded, the gain or loss in the amount of "information" is an *ex post facto* judgment the efficacy of which is dubious.

Such a view of the perceptual basis of memory alters the idea of storage and its relation to synaptic change; it also modifies our understanding of certain related but more abstract ideas concerning images and propositions. Storage occurs by alteration of synaptic strengths (see chapter 7) and leads to connections of whole systems or populations of neuronal groups responding to unique features, with separate populations of groups acting to correlate features and yielding more or less invariant response. The number of ways of entering such a dynamic network is very large, but, in general, a particular large set of local features assignable to an object is *not* stored. It is sufficient to "store" only those synaptic alterations related to procedures yielding exemplary combinations, most frequent combinations, and disjunctive aspects in a degenerate fashion (Fuster 1984). And of course, a full representation of an object is *not* stored. If presentation of an object calls up any sufficient subset of neuronal groups in a classification couple, the rest of the groups that are related either to necessary *or* nonnecessary features in a global mapping have an increased probability of responding.

It is the entire sensorimotor system and its repetitive activity and responses coordinated with the function of classification couples (figure 9.5) in global mappings (figure 8.5) that leads to memorial response.

With this view, we can understand both the probabilistic and the exemplary nature of this mixed system. The strong procedural flavor of such a system is also evident. *It is the complex of capacities to carry out a particular set of procedures (or acts) leading to categorization that is recollected.* This occurs through internal associations resulting from confrontations with objects and properties shared in polymorphous sets, buttressed by the results of associative learning (chapter 11).

The foregoing has considered the general structure of the *necessary* neural substrates for perceptual categorization but has ignored the question of how these substrates are *linked* to form a coherent set corresponding to events in time. In the confrontation of a variety of signals, a number of classification couples (and n-tuples) distributed in various cortical and subcortical areas are engaged. The key question is how this disperse collection can reflect the continuity in time and the properties of succession that are characteristic of events and objects and their recall in motions concerned with attack and defense, for example. One of the chief characteristics of memory related to perceptual categorization and action is this dynamic continuity. Where is it established?

The theory requires that there be such an area or brain region and that it be able to deal with overall succession and linkage of classification couples. This area, however, should not be one in which classification of disjunctive properties is taking place; rather, it should be one in which various classification couples can be subsequently connected and ordered for time periods one order of magnitude larger than the maximum time for an animal to move its body away from threat. Clearly, this is a strong evolutionary requirement—it is obviously useful, for example, in receiving and responding to series of auditory signals, but it is also meaningful in situations of visually observed attack.

While extrapolation and assignment of function to particular brain regions and structures is hazardous, it is a fruitful speculation that medial temporal regions, the hippocampus, and the amygdaloid complex are reasonable candidates for such a role. Recent work in neuropsychology (see Squire 1986 for a review) and a series of ablation studies in monkeys (Mishkin 1982; Mishkin et al. 1984) based on classic work (Milner 1985) have shown that these regions play a major role in the mediation of short-term memory but are not loci for direct recall of such memory. Thus, although removal of one or more of these regions leads to severe failures in short-term memory, the bulk of evidence suggests that these structures do not serve as the loci for categorization *per se.*

At present, there is only sufficient information for us to speculate that the hippocampus (Isaacson and Pribram 1975; Weiskrantz 1978) may play a role in modulating sensory aspects of perception similar to that played by the cerebellum (Ito 1984); for motor aspects, see chapter 8. Both structures have repetitive neuronal architectures with characteristic convergent-divergent connectivity, both are highly reentrant, and, at the synaptic level, both undergo long-term potentiation (for the hippocampus, see Lynch et al. 1976, 1977, 1982; Andersen 1977, 1980; Lynch and Baudry 1984) or long-term depression (for the cerebellum, see Ito et al. 1982). Such metastable synaptic effects in these structures (see figure 8.5) may be necessary for a global mapping to act as a selective filter in timing relationships and for the successions of events that may be required to induce further long-term change in cortical areas.

Like the hippocampus, the cerebellum is assumed to act as a real-time rehearsal system to connect various unforeseen portions of synergies in a smooth sequence; however, unlike the hippocampus, it proceeds to coordinate output for action. In both cases, there is a "feed-forward" aspect to their basic function, and in neither is there *direct* mediation of the functions that they make coherent by their action. There is in the structure of both the hippocampus and the cerebellum an input-output circuit arrangement that would seem ideal for making sequential linkages with a strong temporal component. Such linkages could then direct secondary connections, ensuring synaptic changes in the cortex between classification couples in the sensory system and between such couples and other nonmapped regions in the motor system. According to this speculation, the hippocampus is an on-line real-time rehearsal center for the linkage, in succession or in ordered sequences, of the activity of the distributed classification couples (present mainly in cerebral cortex) that are related to disjunctive categorization. In this view, the connectivity of these regions to the limbic system for the establishment of value related to learning is not fortuitous and, as will be discussed in chapter 11, is essential for learning. In this system (Mishkin 1982; Mishkin et al. 1984), the amygdala plays a key role in polymodal interactions.

Failure of the coordination establishing succession or of the linkage of classification couples could lead to failure of representative linkages in the sensory systems of the cortex and thus prevent coherent short-term memory. However, after consolidation of short-term memory and after establishment of secondary intracortical connections between cortical classification couples, there would be no need for real-time sequencing by the hippocampus. Long-term memory, in this view, can be established by secondary connections, and, in such associative memory, succession can be a *derived* property, with no need for rehearsal of the kind presumed to require the hippocampus.

This view has three consequences. The first is that the same classification couples used in short-term memory can be fixed for long-term memory in whole or part by means of synaptic changes outside of the hippocampus. The second is that while, by virtue of the physics of perception, continuity in the very short term would be maintained even among couples that are not linked and in the absence of the action of the hippocampus, the hippocampus would serve to link repetitious but variant events or contrasting abrupt changes in events in a time scale perhaps ten times to a hundred times longer than that of the organism's motor response times. The third consequence, depending upon the degree of consolidation, is that long-term memory would avail itself of some or all of the classification couples used in short-term memory. In contrast to short-term memory, however, it would show no *obligate* succession in the linkage of such structures and no direct dependence on the hippocampus. In animals with impoverished frontal lobes, any combination of classification couples linked by secondary connections through learning would be adequate for responses of flight or defense (categorization is often order-free). In animals with frontal lobes, secondary connections that actually imposed particular sequences could be learned. And obviously in animals with language, such learned sequences would be present but could be rearranged or overridden according to other demands.

Finally, we may ask, What is the relation of this constrained notion of perceptually based memory to declarative memory (Squire 1982)? Because declarative memory depends upon semantic capacities, notions of self, consciousness, and culturally induced transmission, we must defer an extended discussion of the issue here. If the current theory is correct, however, memory as recategorization is a necessary but obviously not sufficient basis for the perceptual *experience* underlying such declarative memory; associative learning (see chapter 11) is also required. This notion, which does not at first appear very rich, is made more impressive by the consideration that the powers of recategorization increase dramatically with the number of independent classification couples operating together in real time. Moreover, as the number of such neural arrangements increases, the distributed nature of memory becomes inevitable. Inasmuch as what is stored is not replicative of the category or event, but is rather the capacity to generalize and then to narrow consequential behavior to achieve appropriate rewards, there is no single, specially privileged locus for a "memory" or a "trace" (Lashley 1950). Recategorical memory is dynamic, transformational, associative, and distributed—its procedures are *representative* of categorizations, but they are not necessarily representations (see Rortblatt 1982).

The critical tests of the *sufficiency* of these ideas on the neural bases of memory are to show how synapses can change their properties as populations in a selective network in a fashion consistent with the function of one or more classification couples and to show how such couples can actually function in detail to aid in learning. The discussion in the next two chapters will attempt to meet these challenges by exemplifying categorization in classification couples in a testable model and by analyzing the relation between memory (as defined here) and learning. The *necessity* of these ideas is, of course, an empirical issue to be pursued by experiments, some of which will be suggested at the end of this book.

10

Selective Networks and Recognition Automata

INTRODUCTION

The proposal that perceptual categorization depends upon classification couples acting concertedly in global mappings and the view that memory is recategorization together provide a cogent description essential to the theory, but they do not necessarily guarantee performance. Moreover, while the three major premises of the theory of neuronal group selection (developmental transformation leading to a primary repertoire, synaptic selection to yield a secondary repertoire, and reentry) can all be stated reasonably simply, their actual operation in interacting nonlinear networks is highly complex. For both of these reasons, it would be useful to be able to explore such interactions in model systems. This bears upon the self-consistency of the theory: Can a prewired network or congeries of networks based on selective principles and reentry respond stably and adaptively to structural inputs to yield pattern recognition, categorization, and association without prior instructions, explicit semantic rules, or forced learning? Can we exemplify in a functioning model the proposals embodied in the last chapter?

In order to explore these questions, an automaton called Darwin II has been devised and simulated in a large digital computer by George

N. Reeke, Jr., and myself (Edelman and Reeke 1982; Reeke and Edelman 1984). This model embeds the major premises of the theory, but it is not an explicit model of either the whole or the parts of real nervous systems. Analysis of such a model nonetheless can help focus certain experimental questions and allow one to explore the power of selective networks to solve real problems of categorization, and it points the way to the construction of artificial pattern-recognizing systems employing the principles of selection theories. Although the actual automaton, Darwin II, is quite limited, it is a novel machine that acts as a classification couple in that it can function without a program and without forced learning to recognize two-dimensional "visual" stimuli, classify them, and form associations between them. It has many of the features of a global mapping implicit in its design. The model also serves to give an explicit example of one kind of reentry as it acts in a classification couple.

There is a dilemma in modeling the degree of complexity underlying the function of higher neural networks. On the one hand, any representation in a machine must be very limited as compared with real neural networks. On the other hand, the internal design of even a highly simplified and minimal model of a classification couple such as Darwin II must be highly complex as compared with computer logic. This is so because of the minimal size requirements on repertoires, the parallelism of classification couples, the nonlinearity of the network behavior, and the deliberate avoidance of semantic or instructional components in the design of the machine. The main purpose of describing Darwin II here is heuristic: the exercise is designed to demonstrate in explicit terms how part of the selection theory, particularly that described in the last several chapters, can be embedded in a functioning self-organizing network.

THE SYSTEM DESIGN OF DARWIN II

In devising Darwin II, we were guided by a number of ground rules (table 10.1). It was obvious that the system should be a network. The nodes of this network are the recognizing elements of the model, corresponding to the groups of neurons postulated by the theory. We decided to model these groups at the functional level, not at the level of detailed electrophysiological properties. Each group in the model has a state corresponding to its level of activity. The state of a group is

Table 10.1

Ground Rules for Designing a Recognition Automaton

The system must be a network.

Network nodes are recognizing elements corresponding to groups of neurons.

The activity of each group depends only on its inputs and past history.

Groups can signal their activity to other groups along network connections ("synapses").

Connectivity, once established, cannot change (one-way dogma).

Connection strengths do change in response to the activity of one or both of the groups connected (synaptic rules).

No specific information about stimuli is built in, and no forced learning takes place in the initial stages of categorization (neuronal ignorance; selective system).

---

dependent only upon its present inputs and past history. The groups are able to transmit values of their state variables to other groups along the connections of the network, which are analogous to the synapses in a nervous system. Before discussing the overall system design, we will describe a group. A group (figure 10.1) formally represents a connected assembly of neuron-like units, although the connections among such units constituting the group are not explicitly specified in the simulation. The legend to figure 10.1 gives an overall account of group function; the details appear in the equations below.

Groups have multiple inputs that may come from various other groups in the same or different networks. The state of each group is characterized by a single time-dependent scalar variable s, which is determined from the inputs and past history of the group according to a nonlinear response function,

$$s_i(t) = \sum_j c_{ij} \left(s_{l_{ij}} - \theta_E\right) - \sum_k \beta(S_k - \theta_I) + N + \omega \cdot s_i(t - 1), \quad (10.1)$$

where $s_i(t)$ is the state of the ith group at time t; c_{ij} is the connection strength of the jth input to group i ($c_{ij} > 0$, excitatory; $c_{ij} < 0$, inhibitory); $s_{l_{ij}}$ is the state of the group specified by l_{ij} (i.e., of the group connected to the jth input of group i); θ_E is the excitatory input threshold (only inputs with $s_{l_{ij}} \geq \theta_E$ are included); β is a fixed inhibition coefficient; s_k is the state of the group defined by k, which ranges over all groups within a specified inhibitory neighborhood around group i; θ_I is the inhibitory input threshold (only inputs with $s_k \geq \theta_I$ are included); N is a noise term drawn from a normal distribution with chosen mean and *SD*; and ω is a persistence parameter ($\omega = e^{-1/\tau}$, where τ

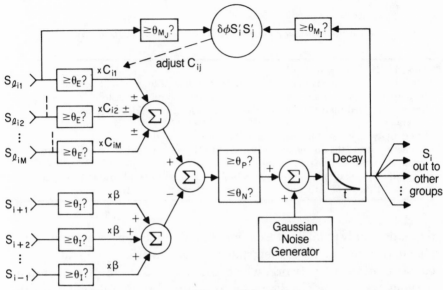

Figure 10.1

Logical structure of a group in Darwin II. All the repertoires in the automaton are made by connecting together groups that have a common logical structure, as summarized in figure 10.2. There are two classes of input connections. Specific connections (upper left) may come from the input array or from groups in the same or other repertoires. The sources of all these connections are specified by lists ("evolutionary specifications"), the construction of which differs from one repertoire to another. There are also short-range inhibitory connections (lower left) having a function corresponding to lateral inhibition in neural nets. These connections are geometrically specified and nonspecific. The level of activity at each input connection, if it exceeds a given threshold level, is multiplied by a weight corresponding to the strength of its particular synapse. The weight establishes how important the particular input is in determining the overall response of the entire group. The weighted inputs are all combined by adding the contribution from the excitatory inputs and subtracting the contributions from the inhibitory inputs. The combined input must exceed a second excitatory or inhibitory threshold in order to have any effect on the group's activity. If not, the previous level of activity simply undergoes exponential decay. In either case, a varying amount of noise is added to the response of the group by analogy with the fluctuations found in real neuronal networks. The final response obtained by combining all of these terms is made available to whatever other groups may be connected to this one (arrows at right). See equations 10.1 and 10.2 in the text for definition of symbols.

is a characteristic time constant). The first and second terms of the response function are ignored unless their sum exceeds a positive firing threshold (θ_P) or is less than a negative inhibitory threshold (θ_N). (Provision is also made for groups to have a refractory period following suprathreshold excitation.) The number of groups in each repertoire and the number of connections to each group can be varied at will; a maximum of about 10^6 connections, distributed in any way among the various repertoires, is permitted by the available computer memory.

The amplification function, which is designed to alter the "synaptic strength" or efficacy c_{ij} of a connection according to the activity of the pre- and postsynaptic groups, is

$$c_{ij}(t + 1) = c_{ij}(t) + \delta \cdot \phi \ (c_{ij}) \cdot (s_i - \theta_{M_I}) \cdot (s_j - \theta_{M_J}), \qquad (10.2)$$

where δ is the amplification factor ($0 \leq \delta < 1$); $\phi(c)$ is a saturation factor to prevent $|c_{ij}|$ from becoming larger than 1 [$\phi(c) = 1 - 2c^2 + c^4$ if $c \cdot (s_i - \theta_{M_I}) \cdot (s_j - \theta_{M_J}) > 0$; $\phi(c) = 1$ if $c \cdot (s_i - \theta_{M_I}) \cdot (s_j - \theta_{M_J}) \leq 0$]; and θ_{M_I} and θ_{M_J} are amplification thresholds for postsynaptic groups i and for presynaptic groups j. A total of $3^4 = 81$ amplification rules can be constructed by taking δ to be positive, negative, or zero, according to whether s_i and s_j are greater than or less than the thresholds θ_{M_I} and θ_{M_J}, respectively. (In terms of real neuronal function, only a few of these would be sensible. In most of the examples in this chapter, δ was zero if $s_i \leq \theta_{M_I}$ and $s_j \leq \theta_{M_J}$; otherwise δ was positive.)

Before discussing the overall plan of Darwin II, we should point out that, aside from changes in their parameters, in this automaton all groups are alike. In the connecting of the groups in networks, there is much leeway; nonetheless, as in the adult central nervous system, the one-way dogma holds—the connectivity of the network, once established, is not changed. However, the connection strengths can change, and it is these changes that provide the mechanism for the selective amplification of response required by the theory. Finally, one of the most important rules, one that distinguishes Darwin II from systems based on digital computers or artificial intelligence, is that there can be no specific information about particular stimulus objects built into the system. Of course, *general* information about the kinds of stimuli that will be significant to the system is implicit in the choice of feature-detecting elements within the automaton—this is akin to the choices built into organisms by their evolutionarily determined programs and phenotypes.

A schematic overall plan of Darwin II is shown in figure 10.2. At the top is an "input array," where stimuli are presented as patterns of light and dark picture elements on a lattice. (One may use letters of the alphabet on a 16×16 grid, but any two-dimensional pattern is acceptable.) The system proper is below the input array. It consists of two parallel concatenations of networks, each with several subnetworks or repertoires (indicated by boxes). These operate in parallel and "speak" to each other by reentry to carry out a function not possessed by either set alone. The two sets of networks, which together form a classification couple, are for convenience arbitrarily named "Darwin" and "Wallace," after the two main figures in the description of natural selection.

The Darwin network *(left)* is designed to respond uniquely to each individual stimulus pattern and very loosely corresponds to the exemplar approach to categorization. The Wallace network *(right)*, on the other hand, is designed to respond in a similar fashion to objects belonging to a class and loosely corresponds to the probabilistic matching

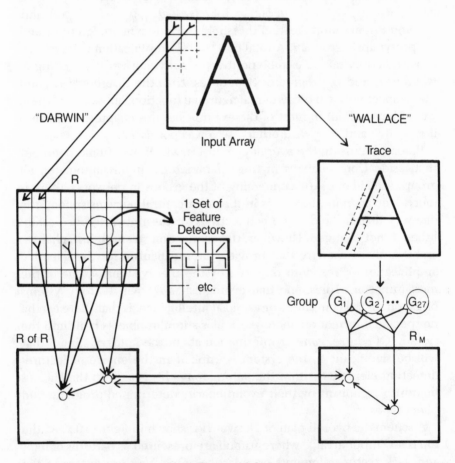

Figure 10.2

Simplified construction plan for Darwin II. For detailed explanation see text. Notice general resemblance to a classification couple (see figure 9.5).

approach to categorization. Darwin and Wallace have a common level structure. Each has connected to the input array (or "world") a level that deals with features; above that, there is an abstracting or transforming level that receives its main input from the first level.

The first level of Darwin is the R, or "recognizer," repertoire. It has groups that respond to local features on the input array, such as line segments oriented in certain directions or having certain bends, as is suggested by the inset (figure 10.2). Sets of these feature detectors are connected topographically to the input array so that the patterns of response in R spatially resemble the stimulus patterns. Connected to R is a higher-level transforming network called R of R ("recognizer of recognizers"). Groups in R of R are connected to multiple R groups distributed over the R sheet, so that each R-of-R group is capable of responding to an entire pattern of response in R. In the process, the topographic mapping of R is not preserved; as a result, R of R gives an abstract transformation of the original stimulus pattern. (Note that if the stimulus undergoes a change, such as a translation to a new position on the input array, the pattern of response in R of R will be quite different. It is Wallace that deals with this translation problem and the need to maintain invariance. R of R is concerned with *individual* properties of a stimulus through feature detection events; without further specification, these include the relation of a stimulus to the background.)

Wallace, acting as a feature correlator, begins with a tracing mechanism designed to scan the input array, detecting object contours and tracing along them to give correlations of features that reveal both the presence of objects as single entities and their continuity properties; such a trace can respond to some of an object's characteristics, such as junctions between lines of various types. In this respect, Wallace works somewhat as the eye does in rapidly scanning a scene to detect the objects present or as a finger does in tracing an object's edges. The result of the trace is that a set of "virtual" groups (G_1, . . . , G_{27} in figure 10.2) is excited according to the topology of the input pattern. These groups are called "virtual" because, *in the simulation,* their input does not involve ordinary synaptic connections but is instead connected to a computer simulation of the scanning and tracing function. Nonetheless, they function as *bona fide* groups. These virtual groups are connected in turn to a higher-level abstracting network, R_M ("recognizer of motion"), that responds to patterns of activity in the trace in much the same way as R of R responds to patterns of activity in R. Because the trace responds to the presence of lines or junctions of lines with only slight regard for their lengths and orientations, R_M is insensitive to both rigid and nonrigid transformations of the stimulus object and tends to respond to class characteristics of whole families of related stimuli (see Bernstein's "topology," figure 8.4).

The R of R and R_M networks are connected together by the reciprocal cross-connections shown in the figure *(bottom center)*. These connections are reentrant in that they reciprocally connect one part of the system to another part of itself rather than to the outside and phasically exchange signals; they provide the mechanism needed for the system to display associative recall by allowing Darwin and Wallace to interact with each other and act as a classification couple.

To the extent that different groups are constructed with similar input connection lists and connection strengths, repertoires of these groups will have the required degeneracy. The specificities of the groups are implicit in their connection strengths—the best response is obtained when the most active inputs are connected to synapses with high connection strengths. The way in which these connection strengths are changed during the course of selection is suggested in figure 10.1 for a typical connection. As we already mentioned, Darwin II permits any of eighty-one possible rules to be chosen for each type of connection. These rules have in common that the change in connection strength depends on the activity of either or both of the pre- and postsynaptic activities and on the preexisting value of the connection strengths, but not on any other variables. Within the limits of this simplified model, it is not too important exactly what synaptic rule is used, as long as it is recognized that connections must be able to decrease in strength as well as increase—otherwise, all synapses are eventually driven to maximum strength, and the system ceases to show selectivity.

In order to keep the realization of the automaton within certain bounds of complexity, the rules for synapses did not incorporate the population model discussed in chapter 7. Instead, the early versions of the machine used presynaptic change alone, postsynaptic change alone, or a rule resembling the Hebb rule: if a particular group responds strongly, and the input to one of its synapses is simultaneously active, the strength of that synapse is strengthened so that later applications of the same input will give a still stronger response. If the input is strong and the output weak, or vice versa, the synapse is weakened. It is important to understand that while this simple rule limits the performance of the machine, it does not radically alter the basic character of its overall response, to which we now turn. Moreover, because of the connectivity patterns and the group selective nature of the machine, even such simple rules do not operate to transfer explicit information from neuron to neuron.

THE RESPONSES OF DARWIN II

In examining the results obtained with Darwin II, we employed three criteria (table 10.2) of success: (1) in Darwin, the generation of individual representations, comprising unique responses to each different stimulus and the same but stronger response to repeated presentations of the same stimulus; (2) in Wallace, the generation of class representations, that is, similar responses to different stimuli having common class characteristics; (3) in the complete system, these individual and class representations were required to interact by reentry to give associative recall of different stimuli in a common class.

In figure 10.3 are shown the responses of the individual repertoires under conditions in which the reentrant cross-connections between Darwin and Wallace were *not* functioning. It can be seen that the R responses are topographic, generally resembling the stimulus letters except for some occasional noise responses. The responses in R of R, as expected, are individual and idiosyncratic, and not at all topographic, because features from different parts of R are being correlated. The responses to the two A's appear to be no more similar than the response to an A is to the response to an X, although statistics do show a somewhat greater degree of similarity between similar shapes, as we shall see

Table 10.2

Criteria for Successful Performance

"Darwin"
  Individual representation—unique response to each different stimulus; same response to repeated presentation of same stimulus, but stronger.

"Wallace"
  Class representation—similar response to different stimuli having common class characteristics.

"Darwin II" (Complete System)
  Interaction of individual and class representations to give associative recall of different stimuli in a common class.

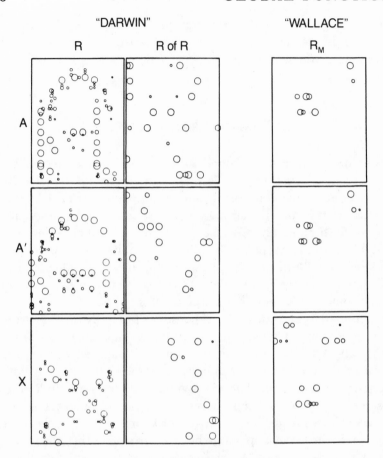

Figure 10.3

Responses of individual repertoires (R, R of R, and R_M; names at top) to a tall, narrow A (top row), a lower, wider A (middle), and an X (bottom). Circles represent groups responding to 0.5 (small circle) or more of maximal response (large circles). Groups responding at less than half of maximal response are not shown, leaving blank areas in the repertoire plots.

later. The situation in Wallace is entirely different. The responses in R_M are very similar for the two stimuli that are in the same class (the two A's of different shape), and are not at all sensitive to the idiosyncratic features of each letter. Moreover, the response is independent of any rotation or translation of a letter.

When selection is allowed to occur, in which synaptic strengths are modified in accord with an amplification rule, the responses become more specific (see figure 10.4). These response frequency histograms show the distribution of responses when a particular stimulus is first presented and again after it has been presented for some time. Initially, most groups respond weakly, but a few happen to respond very well. After selection, more good responders have been recruited from among the groups that had earlier been medium-strength responders, but large numbers of nonresponders remain available, able to respond to other stimuli not used in this experiment.

Such behavior exemplifies recognition, that is, an enhanced response to a stimulus experienced previously. If this same type of experiment is done with several different kinds of stimuli, the overall system is

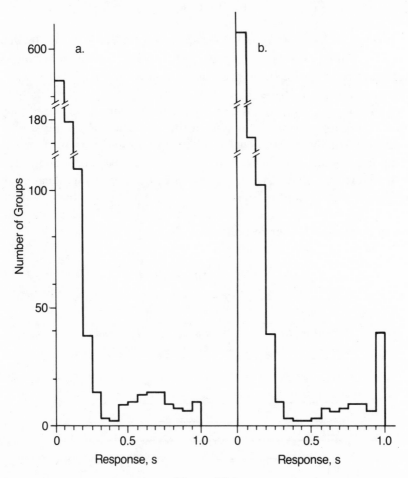

Figure 10.4
Response frequency histograms. A: Initial response to a novel stimulus. B: response to same stimulus after selection has proceeded for a time. Abscissae: response levels s, expressed as a fraction of maximal response. Ordinate: numbers of groups responding at level s.

capable of limited classification (table 10.3). The similarity of the responses of a repertoire to any two letters can be measured by counting the number of groups that respond to both of the letters and dividing it by the number that would have been obtained by chance if the same total number of responding groups had been distributed evenly over the repertoire. Classification can be assessed by examining ratios in which these similarity measures, obtained for pairs of letters (or patterns) in the same class, are divided by the corresponding similarity measures for pairs of patterns in different classes. Obviously, the class memberships of the different letters used are specified by the experimenter and are not available to Darwin II.

In table 10.3 are presented values of this ratio for R of R and for R_M at the beginning of a typical experiment and after selection had been allowed to progress for three presentations of each stimulus. For these stimuli, groups in Wallace (R_M) were ninety-one times more likely to respond to both of two stimuli if they were in the same class than if they were in different classes. The system thus classifies by giving similar responses to different letters of the same kind. As was indicated earlier, a minimal amount of classification is also seen in Darwin, as suggested by the value of 1.21 for the initial ratio. After selective modification of the connection strengths, the classification gets better, even though there is no feedback from the environment that would permit the system to "learn" which responses are "correct."

Table 10.3

Classification in Darwin II

Number of Groups Responding to Stimuli in Same Class/Number Responding to Stimuli in Different Classes	
DARWIN (R of R)	*WALLACE* (RM)
Initially	
1.21	90.93
After Selection	
1.41	241.30

Repertoires: R, 3840 groups; others, 4096 groups; no Darwin-Wallace connections.
Stimuli used: 16 (4 each of 4 classes).
Amplification: 3 series of 4 stimuli/run, 8 cycles/stimulus.

These results can be extended to stimuli not included in the training set (the set presented during selection) to yield generalization (table 10.4) in both R_M and R of R. In R_M, this is a direct consequence of the class-responding characteristics of that repertoire, but in R of R it is not, and in fact generalization can be obtained only if reentrant connections from R_M to R of R and within R of R are present. These connections permit R_M to influence the activity of R of R, supporting common patterns in the response to disparate stimuli that have similarities in their R_M response by virtue of their common class membership.

As shown in one particular experiment (table 10.4), the ratio of similarity of intraclass responses to interclass responses in R of R for a test set of letters not previously presented was 6.10 after selection based on other letters of the same kind (the training set), whereas it had been only 1.77 initially. The results for a control set of unrelated letters show that this effect is specific and that it is not due to a general increase in similarity of response to all stimuli.

Although these results serve to illustrate how the Darwin and Wallace networks fulfill their design criteria, we wished to use them together as a classification couple and show that reentrant connections between them can work to give associative recollection of responses to stimuli that the system places in the same class by virtue of the similar responses they elicit in the Wallace network and, to a lesser extent, those they elicit in the Darwin network. The setup of the system for an association experiment is shown in figure 10.5. Just two stimuli are used:

Table 10.4

Generalization in R of R

	Intraclass/ Chance	Interclass/ Chance	Intraclass/ Interclass
		Initially	
Training set	2.09	0.72	2.90
Test set	2.89	1.63	1.77
Control set	—	1.96	—
		After Selection	
Test set	6.10	1.00	6.10
Control	—	1.00	—

Repertoires: R, 3840 groups; others, 1024 groups.
Connections to each R of R group: 96 from R, 64 from R of R, 128 from R_M.
Amplification: 4 series of 16 stimuli each, 4 cycles/stimulus.

an X and a $+$, chosen because their responses in R of R are quite different, while their responses in R_M are very similar (obviously because each consists of a pair of lines crossing near their centers). When the X is first presented (figure 10.5, *left panel*), R *(center left)* gives the expected topographic response; R of R gives a unique pattern characteristic of that stimulus (for clarity, only a single group is shown responding in the figure, with stimulation via pathway 1).

At the same time, a trace occurs in Wallace, eliciting an appropriate pattern of response in R_M. Cross-connections are present in both directions between R of R and R_M; connections that happen to join responding groups in the two repertoires are strengthened by the normal modification procedure (pathway 2). In the center panel of figure 10.5, the X is removed and a $+$ is presented. The groups active in the response to the X are now no longer active *(open circles)* although the connections between them remain strengthened *(solid lines)*. New groups in R and R of R become active in response to the $+$ *(filled circles);* connections between these groups are strengthened as before *(dashed lines, pathways 1)*. In Wallace, the trace pattern is the same as

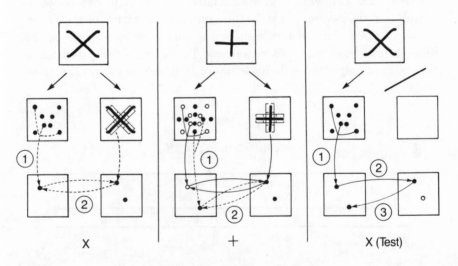

Figure 10.5

Schematic views of Darwin II, showing three stages in an associative recall experiment for explanatory purposes. Filled circles *represent active groups;* open circles, *inactive groups.* Solid lines *between groups represent connections selectively strengthened;* dashed lines *represent connections activated for the first time.* Numerals enclosed in circles *label pathways activated at successive times. For discussion, see text.*

for the X, eliciting a response in R_M very similar to that obtained before. Connections between the $+$ responding groups in R of R and these same responders in R_M are therefore strengthened. An indirect associative pathway is thus established via R_M between groups involved in the two patterns of response in R of R.

The third panel in figure 10.5 shows how the association is tested. The trace mechanism is turned off so that the association will be based entirely on past experience with the stimuli, not on any immediate correlation occurring during the test. When the X is presented under these conditions, R and R of R give responses very similar to those obtained originally with the X. R_M receives input only from R of R via the previously strengthened pathways 2, eliciting the common pattern of response appropriate to both the X and the $+$. Pathways 3 then permit R_M to stimulate in R of R the pattern originally associated with the second stimulus, (the $+$), even though the $+$ is not then present on the input array. Depending on the time constants chosen, this associated response can occur together with the X response or later.

Results of a typical experiment of this type are presented in figure 10.6. Upon presentation of an initial stimulus, completely different groups responded to an X and a $+$ (figure 10.6, A). After repeated amplifications upon exposure, responses are plotted as a function of time for a number of individual R-of-R groups. In figure 10.6, B *(left)*, are seen the results when the test stimulus was the X. The groups at the top are ones that responded to the X during the first presentation of that letter; the groups at the bottom are ones that responded to the $+$ during the first presentation of that letter. As expected, these $+$ responders do not respond immediately when the X is presented. After four cycles of stimulation, the R repertoire is switched off *(arrow)*, so that it no longer dominates the R-of-R response and there is now no outside input to either Darwin or Wallace. Under these conditions, the response of some of the X responders *(top)* begins to decay away (see, e.g., groups 77, 85, and 91), while some of the $+$ responders now become active as a result of the stimulation they receive through the reentrant connections from R_M (see, e.g., groups 28, 34, and 95). Thus, the system, presented with an X, recalls elements of the response proper to the $+$; these two stimuli have become associated.

A separate, reciprocal experiment is shown on the right in figure 10.6, B, in which the same groups are plotted for the case where the $+$ is the test stimulus. Now it is the $+$ responders *(top)* that begin responding immediately but decay when R is switched off *(arrow)*, and it is the X responders *(bottom)* that come up in associative recall when the stimu-

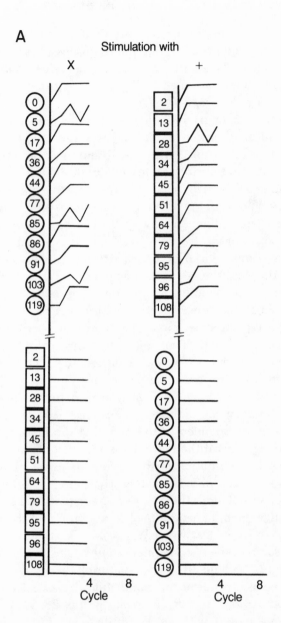

Figure 10.6
Responses of individual R-*of-*R *groups in an associative recall test.* A: *Groups responding to stimulation with an* X *(left) or a* + *(right) before test; note that no groups are common to the two stimuli. Each group is labeled by its serial number in the repertoire. A serial number is enclosed in a* circle *if the group responded initially to an* X *or in a* box *if the group responded initially to a* +. B: *"Training response" of each group is plotted as a function of time,*

B

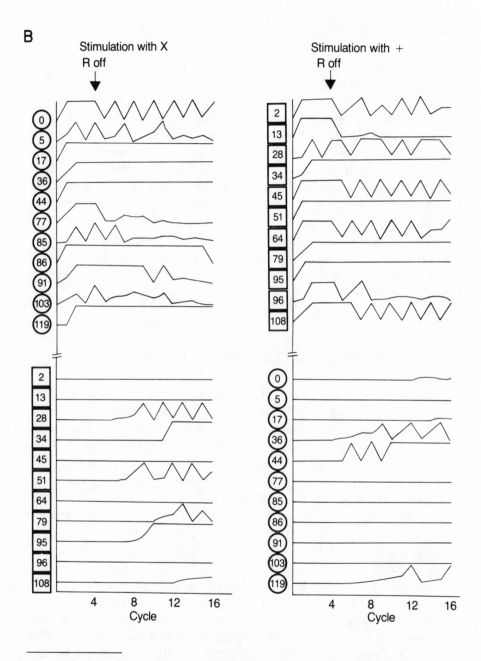

measured in cycles of the model (scales at bottom). Arrows (top) *indicate time (after fourth cycle) at which all input to system was cut off.* Left panel: *Stimulation with an* X. Right panel: *Stimulation with a* +. *Note the dynamic oscillatory nature of the responses and the partial recollection and association in the degenerate response.*

lus is removed. Thus, the association is bidirectional—the + is associated with the X, and the X is associated with the +. No association occurs if the original stimuli have no common response in Wallace, for example, an A and an X.

In this experiment, letters are associated in Wallace in a trivial way because their responses are very similar to begin with. In Darwin, however, their responses are not the same but have individual character. The association obtained in Darwin in this experiment could not have been obtained without Wallace, but at the same time it goes beyond what Wallace could have done alone, because in Darwin the individual character of the responses to the two stimuli is preserved. Acting as a classification couple, Darwin and Wallace illustrate how pattern recognition is enhanced by the interaction of two basic methods of category formation, one based on a strategy loosely similar to the use of exemplars, the other based on a statistical strategy emphasizing common class features.

PERFORMANCE LIMITATIONS AND PROSPECTS

The construction of Darwin II was prompted by three related aims (Edelman and Reeke 1982; Reeke and Edelman 1984): (1) to test the self-consistency of the notion of group selection in nonlinear degenerate repertoires made up of neuron-like groups that have preassigned connectivity and connection strengths; (2) to design networks capable of making unique representations of individual objects by means of local feature detection, as well as networks for making relatively invariant representations of objects within a class by means of global feature correlation; and (3) to arrange reentrant interactions of the two networks carrying out these separate operations in parallel so that an associative memory linking individual representations within a class is developed. Effectively, Darwin II behaves as a classification couple, and it also embeds several key features of a global mapping.

While Darwin II is not a model of an actual nervous system, it does set out to approach one of the problems that evolution had to solve in forming complex nervous systems—the need to form categories in a bottom-up manner from structures in the environment. Five key features of the model make this possible: (1) Darwin II incorporates selective networks whose initial specificities enable them to respond without instruction to unfamiliar stimuli; (2) degeneracy provides multiple possibilities of response to any one stimulus, at the same time providing functional redundancy against component failure; (3) the output of Darwin II is a *pattern* of response, making use of the simultaneous responses of multiple degenerate groups to avoid the need for very high specificity and the combinatorial disaster that this would imply; (4) reentry within individual networks vitiates the limitations described by Minsky and Papert (1969) for a class of perceptual automata (perceptrons) lacking such connections; and (5) reentry between intercommunicating networks with different functions gives rise to new functions, such as association, that each network alone could not carry out.

Neither the representative transformations nor the limited generalizations performed by Darwin II require the direct intervention of a classifying observer, either through instruction or through forced learning. These capabilities arise instead from the selective principle embodied in the network by means of feature detection, reentry, and differential amplification. Selection permits the system to make certain discriminations on the basis of internally generated criteria. If the system is allowed to evolve according to its experience, these criteria become correlated with the relevant physical properties of the outside world.

Even the limited performance of this recognition automaton suggests the possibility of extended development in this area. Obvious extensions include adding networks that would allow motor output of a suitably constituted "arm" or "head"; introducing networks that would give the capability to deal with multiple stimuli that are in motion, an ability that probably precedes the ability of real organisms to deal in detail with stationary stimuli; giving the machine the capability to deal with one or another of multiple stimulus objects through some form of attentional mechanism or rules; and giving it a means of responding to an innate value network while receiving feedback from the world so that it can learn conventional associations.

Such capabilities, which require further systems of global mappings, are currently being incorporated into a new machine, Darwin III. The capacity to deal with conventional learning or arbitrary associations would be built upon the base of categorization already inherent in the automaton, and its acquisition would promote Darwin II from being a solipsistic machine to being one with a wider adaptive range and an ability to communicate with other similarly constituted automata. It is clear that advances in this arena of network automaton theory (which might be called "textoretics," after the Latin *textor*, "weaver," and *rete*, "net") will depend upon such additions and also upon the development of further insights into the mathematical behavior of nonlinear systems. Textoretics differs fundamentally from current instructive approaches to network modeling (see Cooper 1974; Kohonen 1977; Murdock 1979; Anderson and Hinton 1981) in that it requires no *a priori* semantic conventions or assumptions in establishing the categories that lead to adaptive or memorial responses of the automata with which it is concerned.

Darwin II is not an explicit model of either the whole or a part of any nervous system. Nevertheless, it was designed heuristically with nervous systems in mind, and it would not be surprising if it reflected some aspects of their performance. In any case, its performance serves to demonstrate the capabilities of group selection among repertoires of neuron-like groups, illustrates the ideas of reentry, classification couples, and global mappings, and—even in its present, limited form—establishes the self-consistency of the ideas of group selection and reentry in multineuron networks capable of categorization. Having shown that such a primitive network can carry out limited categorization, we are in a position to turn in the next chapter to the relationship between perceptual categorization and learning in selective systems, specifically emphasizing their mutual adaptive advantages for the organism. This will in turn allow us to develop a richer notion of memory as recategorization.

11

Selection, Learning, and Behavior

INTRODUCTION

The foregoing discussion of factors bearing upon neuronal group selection dealt with the evolution and development of sensorimotor systems and brains but did not emphasize the actual behavior that arises from perceptual categorization. Natural selection works, however, not upon perception but upon those phenotypes that give rise to behavior that is adaptive. Following the injunctions of Tinbergen (1942, 1951, 1963), we must therefore inquire into the functions, causes, development, and evolution of behavior as they touch upon the theory. The tack taken here will stress the first three issues, leaving many of the important ethological or evolutionary aspects relatively untouched. Evolved innate behavior patterns (Gould 1982) can be quite complex and obviously have fundamental significance, but more extensive consideration of their origins would bear only indirectly upon the somatic selection processes that are the focus of this book. We shall, however, consider certain aspects of bird song (Marler 1982, 1984) because this subject shows particularly well how evolutionary factors and somatic shaping by learning through selection can interact.

Why is learning so much more powerful than perception alone? One reason is that the brain evolved for adaptive action and behavior, not merely to register representations. Moreover, perceptual categorization alone, while centrally important and essential for learning, is insufficient to generate adaptive behavior. In any complex environment containing combinations and juxtapositions of fortuitous events that may nonetheless affect survival, learning must take place to assure successful adaptation. Learning is *necessarily* bounded by value systems that have been selected during evolution for survival of a particular species.

The most successful components of evolved or innate behavior are those that render the organism increasingly *independent* of the short-term fluctuations of the environment. But much that is in the environment cannot be dealt with in this fashion alone. Novel adaptive responses (Staddon 1983) are required that can engage those short-term changes in an animal's niche that may themselves be adventitious, heterogeneous, unique, complex, or novel. For these, we must consider the various local changes related to a series of adaptive functions: habituation, facilitation, pseudo-conditioning, or true learning in both classical and operant modes.

Inasmuch as our thesis relates to animals with complex brains in rich environments, the discussion will focus mainly upon true learning. The thesis is that true learning depends upon the prior ability to carry out perceptual categorization. Because of the increased adaptive capabilities of systems of specific learning and the enhanced possibilities of learning in systems capable of rich categorization, the development of more sophisticated primary and secondary repertoires should in general be selected for during evolution. Adopting this thesis implies that the "conditioning" of various neural systems (Thompson 1986), while a component of true learning, is not equivalent to it. According to the theory, true learning must be linked to the behavior of the whole animal, and therefore its linkage to ethological factors cannot be neglected.

In our discussion of learning, we shall first consider experiential factors, using classical and operant conditioning as a main example, and then consider heritable and developmental factors as they relate to learning, using the acquisition of bird song as an example. A minimal model of the neural bases of learning will subsequently be presented.

In this model, learning alters the linkage of global mappings to hedonic centers through synaptic changes in classification couples, some of which may be species-specific. Such changes yield a categorization of complexes of adaptive value under conditions of expectancy. With this model in hand, we will be in a position to understand how neuronal group selection is compatible with the emergence of information processing in individuals and species.

THE MODERN INTERPRETATION OF LEARNING EXPERIMENTS

Most students of the subject of learning currently agree (see Jenkins 1979, 1984; Staddon 1983) that a *general* theory of learning (Dickenson 1980) across species—as based on classical studies of the kind performed by Thorndike, Pavlov, Hull, or Skinner—is not tenable. More recent ethological studies (Marler and Terrace 1984) and analyses of the evolution and development of human language (MacPhail 1982; Gleitman 1984) point up the fact that very special evolutionary features conditioned by niche strongly influence the learning and behavior of individual species. Moreover, although the basic paradigms of classical and operant conditioning remain robust (Mackintosh 1983), the interpretation of their significance has changed. The old view that the contiguity and precedence relations of a conditioned stimulus and an unconditioned stimulus are sufficient has had to be abandoned. The analyses of conditioned emotional responses (CERs) by Estes and Skinner (1941), of food aversion by Garcia (Garcia et al. 1955, 1973), of context sensitivity by Rescorla (Rescorla 1968, 1976; Rescorla and Skucy 1969; Rescorla and Wagner 1972), and of autoshaping (Hearst and Jenkins 1974; Schwartz and Gamzu 1977; Locurto et al. 1981), among other examples, have made clear the indirectness of the processes being observed and interpreted. The studies by Rescorla and Wagner (1972) and by Kamin (1969) suggest that contiguity of stimuli is not the major issue in learning; rather, it is the correlation of context with the predictive value of the conditioned stimulus that is significant. This leads to the important conclusion that an animal in a species develops a representation or knowledge of a learning situation on the basis of differential expectancies; that is, certain stimuli show stronger interactions than others. Obviously, such knowledge must be based in part upon the perceptual categorization that is characteristic of that species.

In addition to this important conceptual shift, the modern view recognizes that the ingredients of classical conditioning are also required for operant conditioning. In this interpretation, performance and learning are not coextensive and principles of association are not alone sufficient to account for behavior. This poses the key problem of how learning is to be translated into performance. Finally, as we mentioned already, the modern position recognizes the importance of an animal's niche and species (Marler and Terrace 1984) and insists that one must reconcile ethological studies with laboratory behavior.

The tasks suggested to theoreticians by these emerging viewpoints are first to show how the contents of learning can be represented in terms of expectancies within the animal and then to show how they can lead to observed behavior. The converse is also a challenge: If performance underestimates knowledge (Staddon 1983), how are the so-called representations constituting that knowledge to be embedded in a theory of learning?

According to the position taken here, the only reasonable explanation must proceed from a theory of mechanisms and processes dealing with the neural substrate, describing how the structure and function of that substrate make perceptual categorizations possible in a given species. The obverse view, that psychological experiments may be pursued in the absence of such considerations, while obviously important for functional interpretation (see Staddon 1983), can only lead from phenomenological descriptions at the functional level to a virtually infinite set of possible neural interpretations. Furthermore, any generalized faculty psychology derived from a functionalist view runs against ethological evidence for species-specific behavior as well as against evolutionary evidence indicating that nervous systems and adaptations in different taxa are quite different. These issues, more than any others so far considered, bring us into direct confrontation with the tasks described in the preface of this book.

The purpose of this chapter is to address these issues squarely and to provide an interpretation of the problems suggested by modern findings on learning in terms of neuronal group selection theory. I will begin by defining learning in a provisional way and then discuss some modern interpretations of conditioning experiments. An attempt will be made to show how the requirement for expectancies in learning entails prior perceptual categorization. The resulting interpretation of expectancies as categorizations coupled to needs will require us to reexamine the interactions of classification couples in global mappings.

Further consideration of the development of such mappings will then allow us to relate general aspects of conditioning to development in species-specific cases like that of bird song.

LEARNING AND SURPRISE

As has been pointed out by Staddon (1983), learning is a specific form of acquired change, one that connects present to past behavior in an adaptive fashion so that the positive or negative outcomes of events serve as signals for something else. Adaptation of this kind requires selection upon variation according to a set of rules that are related in a complex fashion to categorization, spatiotemporal continuity and contiguity, individual history, and a series of ontogenetic and phylogenetic constraints. Although learning is not a single process, in general, it is not defined to include habituation or sensitization. It is specific to a *context,* which consists of the internal state of the animal (ultimately its brain state) as it responds to the appearance of certain objects and events in the world. A stimulus constitutes a very specific event leading to a change in this internal state; such a change stochastically determines both the next state and the response, which is jointly determined by the stimulus and the preceding internal state. In the real world, a series of stimuli lead to a history of state changes and responses. This defines the context of learning; insofar as history is involved in this process, so is memory. In view of the discussion in the preceding two chapters, however, no assumption is made that memory is a stored *replication* of an animal's actual history.

The criteria for learning are a set of matches to changes in the environment that have a specific value and that lead to adaptation in a dynamic manner. Learning can be observed only indirectly, inasmuch as it connects present to past and general methods are lacking for simultaneous parallel measurements of all relevant brain activity. For this reason, most learning theory (or the interpretation of conditioning experiments) is cast in terms of functional explanations, as has been pointed out clearly by Staddon (1983), whose excellent analysis provides the basis for much of the description in this portion of the chapter. Our task is to go beyond this description and relate it to neural structure.

This is not the place to discuss the vast area of learning experiments in detail. But it is pertinent to stress again that, in the modern view, classical, or Pavlovian, conditioning involves more than mere association or contiguity: it also involves signification. Certain aspects of events signify food, predict danger, stand for the passage of time, and so forth. This signification is connected with value—reward and punishment that is related ultimately to Darwinian inclusive fitness (see Sober 1984). Value in a particular species is relative to the current state, past knowledge, and evolutionarily innate characteristics of animals in that species. Put in a summary way, classical conditioning occurs only when the conditioned stimulus (CS) predicts the unconditioned stimulus (US) in a context related to value. As Staddon has pointed out, this implies that the animal must act *as if* it carries out a *kind* of inference (expectation or prediction) on the basis of an internal set of states or a representation. In our discussion here, we will consider this representation to be a global mapping in the brain of the animal that is connected to brain regions (limbic regions, hypothalamus, etc.) in the function of which certain evolutionarily determined values, usually related to consummatory activity or fear responses, are embedded.

Most important for our argument is the fact that animals initiate true learning only when an element of novelty, surprise, or violation of expectation is present; the first occurrence of such a surprise in real time is critical (Rescorla 1975; Dickenson 1980). Surprise involves the spatiotemporal ordering of real objects or events in connection with value, not just in connection with stimulus dimensions. It is in this sense that surprise implies a discrepancy between such an ordering and the current state of an animal.

Within this functional framework, we may attempt to connect our previous arguments with the results of some key experiments on learning. The macroscopic world consists of events and objects presented in a dynamic, irreversible, and fluctuating set of arrangements and interactions. If an animal is to learn or to match its brain states (involving synaptic efficacies, motor responses, etc.) to signals representing relationships between objects and events and then develop adaptive behavior, how can it recognize these objects and events? Clearly, the answer involves perceptual categorization, the neural basis of which must already exist in the animal. According to our earlier argument, this basis is in neuronal group structure and selection and in the satisfaction of continuity requirements by appropriate global mapping and reentry.

The ability to learn thus requires that these means for perceptual categorization first be in place. Perceptual categorization in itself is clearly not sufficient, however, to fulfill adaptive needs in either evolutionary or somatic time. The ability to define objects to some extent by

these means is based upon certain innate capacities to carry out disjunctive characterization of various stimulus objects. But events and the
arrangements of objects in an animal's niche can be fortuitous by category and occasion (winds may blow down trees, water may inundate
food, etc.). Some *conventional* adaptive means must be at hand to deal
with the sampling of such events according to contingency, to their
juxtaposition in time, and to their assumed relation to cause. This means
is learning.

The main point to be made in this chapter is that neuronal group
selection could not occur *adaptively* without behavior that can deal
with such event contingencies. This is so both because neuronal group
selection cannot occur efficiently without variance in behavior (inasmuch as it depends upon variation in brain states) and because, in a
varying environment, adaptation requires learning. In other words, it
is learning that makes categorization adaptive. This is not a circular
argument—the apparatus capable of perceptual categorization must be
built by evolutionary means into the structure of the brain and nervous
system *before* the events of learning ever take place. The basic embryological facts (Weiss 1955) support such a view: development of a primary repertoire does not require any behavior of the kind that occurs
in postnatal life (Hamburger 1970).

BEHAVIOR AND CONDITIONING

Although interpretations of experiments on learning use functional explanations, the data nonetheless point inexorably to the existence in the
animal and its brain of means of classifying objects and events. Before
sketching these means in more detail, we must show how the two forms
of conditioning are related to the sensorimotor apparatus used in adaptive categorization. Following Staddon's argument (Staddon 1983; see
also Mackintosh 1983), we can usefully summarize the relation between
classical and operant conditioning. Learning is a specific change in the
animal related to a positive or negative outcome, using an event or its
absence as a signal for something else. Classical conditioning involves
reliable presentation of a neutral conditioned stimulus (CS) prior to a
hedonic stimulus (the unconditional stimulus, or US); the CS is a predic-
tor or signal for the US, and the animal reacts to the CS as if it is in
anticipation of the US. In contrast to this classical, or Pavlovian, conditioning, operant conditioning involves two phases. The first is behavior

that leads sooner or later to reward or punishment, a kind of control by consequences (Skinner 1981). The second phase consists of recurrence of adaptive behavior when the animal is again presented with the original situation.

These two forms of conditioning are closely related: the selection of the behavior in a Pavlovian response depends upon the animal's ability to predict on the basis of the relation between the particular CS and the US; in the operant situation, the discriminative stimulus consists of all those environmental features (leading to categorization) that can control behavior. In both cases of conditioning, a change in expectancy, signaling a change in internal state based on categorization, is required.

A way of summarizing the difference in the two modes is to say (Staddon 1983) that classical conditioning is open-loop (or a procedure for assigning value to a *neutral* stimulus); in contrast, operant conditioning is closed-loop and leads to a change in the priority of action. While in this latter case action *is part of the animal's categorical representation,* classical procedures relating contingencies are nonetheless required to reinforce operant behavior. It is the Pavlovian mode that allows an animal to define a situation according to values depending upon prior innate and previously formed associations. In the operant mode, the animal must not only select candidate stimuli related to value but also select stimuli to allocate behavior. Given our view of global mappings and of gestures as part of categories, this does not represent an extraordinary shift in interpretive point of view.

The recurrences and variabilities in learning performances are remarkable. Reinforced responses arise from what appears to be a variety of activities, but they occur in a nonetheless definite fashion. Conditioning functions to determine action by sampling the available innate evolutionary, ontogenetic, and knowledge structures. Clearly, a rapid sampling of a large enough set of possibilities is important for success. This set of possibilities requires memory of large numbers of categorization functions, both motor and sensory. An animal's interim behavior that seems aimless to an observer may in fact involve sensorimotor rehearsals involving a large number of global mappings. In such rehearsals and in attentional and aroused states, the selection of responses depends also on the selection of those stimuli that both define an event and are targets for responses.

Variability and selection are thus central themes of behavior; the key importance of movement and action in mediating the two is in accord with our earlier discussions on the function of global mappings. Staddon (1983) has elegantly summarized this set of characteristics. He proposes that reinforced learning proceeds through four repeating stages: (1) novelty or surprise → (2) "inference" → (3) action → (4) new environmental situation → surprise. Various protective and exploratory responses alter representations and values as the animal carries out assessments of salience, of causal or prior relations to valued events, and of temporal proximity to a hedonic stimulus (Dickenson 1985). This repeated process continues until the historical pattern leads to a stabilizing response in which there is little or no categorical surprise.

In this fashion, the animal presumably uses its limited resources for categorization and response in as efficient a way as it can. An animal (even a "higher" animal) can, however, do only one or a few things at a time (Neisser 1967). In addition, it must sample variation with intervening actions at the same time as it is exploiting various gains, and these two activities must be balanced. This requires means of resource allocation—relationships between arousal and attention and the ability to shift attention, giving preference to stimuli that are predictive of value while separating object properties from hedonic consequences. Because of the historical and the nonequilibrium nature of the procedure, different animals will pick different patterns of control in representing a situation, in updating knowledge by various selections and procedures, and, finally, in "automatizing" their response.

Despite this individuality, behaviors within a given species generally converge in a similar situation. Thus, a kind of degeneracy also occurs in the mechanisms of behavior, possibly reflecting underlying mechanisms constraining neuronal group selection in sensorimotor ensembles making up global mappings. The processes in both cases are developmental, and, as I have already mentioned, they obey principles strikingly similar to those of morphogenesis.

Staddon's (1983) argument for the close linkage of the two main processes of conditioning is consistent with the view of sensorimotor ensembles proposed in earlier chapters. In the classical open-loop situation, the need for categorization procedures and for the recategorization provided by memory is evident. Selection of response is guided by temporal relationships between acts and reinforcing stimuli and by innate factors as well as past memorial experience. In part, such selection is negative—ineffectual variants of behavior are selected against. As we noted in connection with classical and operant conditioning modes, the selection of responses depends upon the selection of what it is valuable to know. Such selection occurs as a combined result of many levels of inheritance, development, and experience.

We have mainly discussed certain aspects of experience in this section. What can we say of the other factors? In considering inheritance and development, and species-specific aspects of learning, I shall pick song learning in birds as a key example because it emphasizes the importance of niche selection and because it involves all of the components presumed to be necessary to assure the formation of global mappings. With this example and that of conditioning in hand, we may attempt to connect the two in a model based on neuronal group selection.

HIERARCHIES OF SELECTION IN DEVELOPMENTAL LEARNING: BIRD SONG

Song learning in birds provides a specific example that appears structurally to be in contrast to the situations seen in conditioning. Moreover, at the level of song production, it seems to have selectional aspects that have been interpreted (Marler 1984) as direct evidence of neuronal group selection. For these two reasons, it is valuable to discuss bird song, for it can be analyzed profitably in terms of neuronal group selection, allowing us to disentangle the various kinds of selection that occur in such behavior.

As has been shown by Marler (1984) and Konishi (1984), song learning and production consist of three phases: (1) a sensory phase in which young birds hear a song during a critical period and memorize at least some of its components; (2) a sensorimotor phase in which they rehearse and vocalize the song (the bird's hearing its own voice is essential in this vocal reproduction); and (3) a phase of automatic production of the finally "crystallized" song. At least in some species, vocalization and auditory feedback are used to prevent deviation from the memorized pattern. The feedback involves trial and error, and in these species song is thus an acquired motor skill.

That this is a very special skill can be seen from an examination of Marler's results. His work shows that there are innate species differences in the song-learning process, that there are innate triggers of learning, that there is context-dependent cue specificity, that there is resistance to reversal (after the stage of crystallized song is initiated), and that the process occurs in the absence of apparent reward. Significantly, there is suggestive evidence for the preexistence of at least some plastic brain circuitry (Nottebohm 1980, 1981a, 1981b) committed to this type of learning.

Perhaps the issues most relevant to our concerns are those connected with the suggestion that the acquisition of song skills represents selective learning with both stereotyped and variable features that emerge in an epigenetic program (Marler 1984). The components of this program include the following: (1) *Central motor programs* that can develop even in deaf birds, generating simple versions of singing behavior. (2) *Auditory mechanisms* providing so-called syntactical templates; in their absence and in birds raised in isolation, the fine structure of notes and syllables is abnormal. (3) *Imitation*, in which conspecific songs (which *can* be learned) are rejected over intraspecific songs. This is an active process occurring selectively for both fine structure of notes and whole-song patterning. (4) *Memorization* followed by *sensorimotor invention and improvisation*. This progresses in stages of amorphous subsong production, plastic song production, and then full song. Models are not produced exactly but are decomposed into syllables, phrases, or notes. Sometimes inventions and deviations are interspersed. Selective attention is suggested as a partial basis for song variation. (5) This trial and error activity is finally succeeded by a *fixed motor program.*

Different song segments can have different developmental bases, some subject to dialect, some to imitation, some to invention. The cues triggering song acquisition include not only acoustic components but also other cues of overall structure that must be learned.

Marler (1984) proposes that species-specific auditory templates are involved not just in the sensorimotor phase but also in the earliest phases of the process of song acquisition. He suggests that the production of new motor patterns by experience involves permutation and alteration of a species-universal set of vocal gestures. He suggests a selective picture based on the existence of three kinds of "templates"— specialized active templates that can influence development without specific auditory stimulation, specialized latent templates requiring triggering by matched environmental auditory templates, and generalized auditory templates with broader capabilities involving heterospecific and environmental sounds capable of guiding vocal imitation. The two specialized templates are used in commitment to memory and in memory consolidation; active templates emerge normally in isolated birds, but latent ones do not. In normal experience, both kinds of templates are selected.

This entire description of song learning differs greatly from that of conditioning. Nonetheless, because both kinds of learning can occur in a single species, any theory of learning based on neural structure must also accommodate both. Before suggesting how that may be done, we

must again take up certain characteristics of critical periods and epigenesis (see chapter 5 for our discussion of these topics in terms of maps).
The emergence of crystallized bird song provides an example of an
epigenetic event in which a defined sequence of developmental stages
must be traversed before fixation is reached. Such neural and behavioral epigenetic sequences differ from those seen during embryogenesis
(Hamburger 1970) in the sense that they have components of true
learning associated with them at particular points or critical periods in
the sequence. Although such behavioral routines are self-terminating,
they require learning for adaptive integration. Similar, though less well
detailed, sequences appear in the assembly of appropriate components
of copulatory behavior by male rhesus monkeys (Mason 1968), in maturation of food-burying routines in squirrels (Ewer 1965), and in bird
mating calls (Immelmann 1984).

The most detailed anatomical example of a critical period in relation
to perception is seen in the development of binocular vision in cats and
monkeys (Wiesel and Hubel 1963a, 1963b; Hubel and Wiesel 1970;
Wiesel 1982), although in this case the learning components, if present
at all, have not been so successfully detailed. Deprivation can lengthen
the critical period for both bird song and binocular vision, but the
termination of this period cannot be postponed indefinitely. The importance of the visual case is that it shows clear-cut neuronal competition
and plasticity in a cortical area (see chapter 5). This raises the possibility
that many of the epigenetic learning events might combine the acquisition of learning with the connectional maturation of committed but
plastic neural centers.

While such neural centers seem highly specialized by evolution,
there is every reason to believe that they are neurally coupled to groups
of cells and circuits that participate in conditioning responses. We have
already seen that the connectivity of primary repertoires in certain
circuits, such as those for binocular vision and in the retinotectal projection, can be influenced by activity (see chapter 5). We may call learning
in critical periods neotenic learning to emphasize that delay of fixation
of circuitry may be involved. Neotenic learning, unlike the usual learning by conditioning, may occur during postnatal formation of new patterns of connections and influence those patterns.

All of the data recapitulated above are consistent with the hypothesis
that song learning is neotenic: it is selective, it has a critical phase, and
it must contain innately specified triggering stimuli. Classic reinforcers
fail to alter the morphology of the song. Nonetheless, components of
selective learning and epigenetically based programs probably still in-

volve associative learning (Jenkins 1979, 1984). It would therefore be a mistake to conclude that, because selective learning occurs in particular species, certain general features of conditioning are not shared as an evolved trait of nervous systems in that species. Moreover, contrary to Marler's (1984) suggestion, the existence of selective learning is in itself neither proof nor disproof of neuronal group selection. Although the latter is consistent with the former, the levels of organization at which selection occurs in each are vastly different, and selective learning could come about through means other than neuronal group selection. What, then, is the connection between neuronal group selection and the various forms of learning?

NEURONAL GROUP SELECTION IN LEARNING

For our purposes, the main significance of learning in critical periods is the challenge it poses to the neuronal group selection theory: How can neuronal group selection explain both conditioned learning, which is evolutionarily widespread, and selective learning in critical periods, which is species-specific? And how can both occur in an interactive mode? To answer these questions, we have to construct a learning model based on neuronal group selection that is consistent with *both* aspects of development.

With these questions in mind, we may state that an adequate theory of learning must have the following main goals: (1) The theory must be pitched at the neural level and concern itself with neural mechanisms and processes. (2) It must specify how conditions and situations can lead to the formation of categorical representations (or knowledge) on the basis of evolutionarily determined values underlying the differential expectancies and surprise included in such knowledge. (3) It must show how such representations can be translated into performance. (4) It must show how the neural bases of representation are compatible with species-specific learning, that is, with the remarkable niche adaptation that leads to particular evolved specificities of learning.

These requirements make it obvious that such a theory must be a developmental theory. This is so for a number of reasons. It is highly unlikely that one may go directly from observations of learning and its functional interpretations to deduce the history of the correct neural mechanisms. Given the existence of selective and epigenetically bounded learning (of which neotenic learning is a case), one cannot avoid developmental sequences in any adequate explanation. More-over, it is difficult to see how conditioning and selective or neotenic learning can be satisfactorily related in a detailed fashion without a consideration of development.

We have already seen that although the capacity for perceptual cate-gorization is necessary for learning, it is not sufficient. If the world does not come prelabeled, categorization must be carried out by selection utilizing classification couples and global mappings (see figure 8.5). In order, however, for the resultant representations (and the recategoriza-tions implied by memory) to take part adaptively in learning, the un-derlying global mappings must be coupled to portions of the brain related to appetitive, consummatory, and hedonic control—the amyg-dala, the hypothalamus and brain stem, and portions of the limbic system.

We may now outline a model for learning. I propose that the funda-mental neural structures for learning are neuronal groups tied in clas-sification couples within global mappings, linked in reentrant fashion to hedonic centers, which provide a basis for the assignment of value. In other words, a large number of groups acting in classification couples (sampling the environment through several modalities) and linked through reentrant connections with limbic circuits, as well as to output, provide a system that can fulfill the requirements for learning. These reentrant couples relate categorizations to sets of neuronal groups in the limbic system fulfilling various set points established evolutionarily in that system. At the same time, the connection to groups in global mappings subserving motor output allows revision by search until the input fulfills expectancies based on the preceding categorization ("memory") and reduces the reentrant drive from the limbic system. (For a neural account of a consummatory behavior in terms of neuronal group selection theory, see Mobbs and Pfaff [1987] and Pfaff and Mobbs [1987].)

Inasmuch as there is a great deal of flexibility in the linking of classifi-cation couples to each other through the synaptic rules, a rich tapestry of categorizations is possible. Couples in global mappings usually in-volve a hierarchical order of networks, with the higher-order networks reentrant among themselves (see chapter 10), lending enormous flexi-bility to the linkage of categorical responses. Their value (deviation from fixed points based on limbic state and memory) is established in a dynamic fashion. The number of classification couples or n-tuples, their higher-level reentry, and their degree of connectedness will de-termine the "openness" of the conditioning program. This model can account for variations of conditioning as well as for the importance of surprise.

In order to accommodate selective or neotenic learning into this scheme, we need only note that heterochrony or a developmental delay (see chapter 6) in the connectional pattern of some of the higher-order networks involved in particular couples in certain species would allow their ultimate morphological development and patterns of connection to come under selective influence of *external* signals. Their fixation of connections under the appropriate signals would then lead to closed programs (Marler 1984). Selective learning in this view is a form of neoteny—the connectional maturation of certain neural systems is delayed until certain postnatal inputs are received. Neotenic learning thus resembles metamorphic events (Alberch 1980, 1982a, 1982b) in the sense that certain developmental programs are held "in escrow" and only activated at particular times of confrontation with the environment.

The different kinds of learning can be related to the organization of the classification couples in maps and to their degree of fixation through development. In the case of situations such as the acquisition of song, fixation represents a kind of neoteny in neural circuitry that can be influenced by experience from without. This form of epigenesis is perhaps the most sophisticated known, inasmuch as it can be influenced by learning and somatic events in a manner that embryological sequences cannot (Hamburger 1970). In other cases of involuntary conditioning (Thompson 1986) where wiring is complete, the influence is solely through synaptic efficacy changes, and the function in learning is general. Both arrangements are subject to marked evolutionary change, and they overlap in the sense that all of the subcomponents are influenced by factors discussed in earlier chapters.

The evolutionary choices within such a system are very rich—the couples that are linked, the sensory modalities that participate in the couples, and the level and timing of group selection for the fixation of synaptic efficacy (or for the "closing" of certain wiring patterns, in the case of selective learning) are all elements upon which natural selection can act independently through the phenotype. The need for the efficient polling of a large number of networks of groups in somatic time is fulfilled by the linkage to motor responses, and these responses would improve sampling by particular couples, thus increasing the probability of reducing expectancies. In some cases, severe constraints would be put on the sensorimotor sampling systems; in others, a strong linkage would occur to neuronal groups concerned with hedonic systems fixed by evolution (accounting for the precedence of certain conditioned stimuli); finally, in others, the order of certain motor programs would be evolutionarily constrained.

According to this model, what is altered in learning is the linkage of global mappings with hedonic centers and with motor responses through the synaptic change of classification couples (some of which must be species-specific). The whole operation of such a circuit of networks leads to a categorical description of "value" under conditions of expectancy. In such networks, learning (and knowledge) must always exceed performance which is *selected* from the repertoires comprising components of couples in global mappings.

It is important to stress again that the proposed structures providing the basis for learning constitute complex and large subsegments of the nervous system (see John et al. 1986). This is not surprising given the fact that learning is obligately dependent upon prior categorization. Such a network system is not a simple reflex arc or even a conditionable subsystem (Thompson 1986). Views of conditioning based on such simple neural loops are consistent with old ideas of learning by contiguity and with the behavior of very simple organisms, but not with the modern view that expectancy and representation provide major bases for true learning in the whole behaving animal. What, then, can we make of the observations that neural subsystems *can* be isolated that do respond to paradigms akin to conditioning (Tsukahara 1981; Thompson 1986)? The answer must lie in the fact that the whole network we have described may contain *many* such systems. If only one system is activated and altered in the intact animal, or if only a few are, it still may not yield changes in global *behavior*. Indeed, if the function of such neural subsystems is inconsistent with the expectancies set by the workings of higher-order neuronal groups, their coupling to action may even be suppressed. Under other circumstances, however, one may envision that an increasing number of such "conditionable subsystems" might be changed by the events of learning so that if the minimal conditions of expectancy are met, these subsystems are rapidly used. In that case, one would expect to see evidence that many of these systems are altered by learning. The similarity to motor ensembles under central control and the ideas of set (Evarts et al. 1984) is striking. We conclude that the finding of a "conditionable" subsystem does not provide a sufficient model of learning; such a subsystem is only a small part of a much larger system in the whole behaving animal. It must be pointed out that this conclusion supplements but does not contradict observations that "association learning" can occur in neodecorticated animals (Oakley 1979, 1980).

The rationale of the model of learning based on the neuronal group selection theory may now be summarized: (1) It proceeds "bottom up" from neural elements to learning. (2) By means of classification couples and global mappings, it meets the needs of representation derived from conditioning experiments. (3) It deals with expectancy through the neural linkage of these structures to limbic "value" systems and through memory as a recategorical system. (4) It links operant behavior through the feedback action of motor groups to change the sampling ("polling") of the environment by lower-level networks of classification couples. (5) It allows for epigenetic change and ethological patterns in certain species through "teachable neoteny" within global mappings, allowing for alteration of connection patterns by experience at certain critical periods.

This picture is in accord not only with ethological data but also with the idea that conditioning is a *general* evolved feature of nervous systems present in many species. It is based on the recognition that networks dedicated to learning systems need to deal with conventional or arbitrary contingencies in ways that classification couples alone could not. Categorization can deal with objects through the sampling of some physical properties; only learning can lead to rich behavior. In other words, only learning can yield significance and survival value in the face of otherwise fortuitous juxtapositions of events and "causes" that occur at a macroscopic scale. Nonetheless, inasmuch as learning requires prior perceptual categorization, which in turn requires global mapping, there is an intimate connection between the phenotype in a given species and the kind of learning of which that species is capable. This is so because the sensorimotor components in global mappings are very dependent upon particular aspects of morphology and the motor ensemble, and also because of the obligate linkage of these mappings to neural systems evolved to realize species-specific consummatory states. In this sense, the neural substrate for perceptual categorization obliges specific linkages between conditioning and species-specific behavior.

Evolutionary change acting on behavioral phenotypes in a population can select which classification couples are linked and which networks in such couples undergo heterochronic change. The degree of species-specificity of networks dedicated to learning may thus be modified while much of their generality is preserved. Comparative psychology and developmental psychology are joined at this structural level through natural selection. Niche occupation in evolution is a form of higher-order categorization, and so is learning. The view taken here is that the development of neural networks capable of perceptual categorization through neuronal group selection makes possible a whole spectrum of adaptive phenotypic changes, from general conditioning to species-specific selective learning involving neoteny.

From Selective Reentrant Networks to Information Processing

Given this neuronally based model of learning, it is pertinent to consider further some general questions related to the adaptive value of neuronal group selection: How can a brain operating upon a world without labels by means of neuronal group selection *ultimately* process information, as it certainly must do in human beings? An explanation is necessary because, however powerfully supported a selectionist theory is by the facts on neuronal structure and function, it cannot by its various mechanisms alone give rise to a system in an individual animal that could process information. Perceptual categorization, as reflected by the variations in selected degenerate neuronal groups, is by itself only "solipsistic." Indeed, in certain situations, two different animals of the same species would each be expected to perform the same adaptive (and even novel) behaviors by means of different combinations of neuronal groups. As long as the categorizations based on neuronal group selection are sufficiently rich and stable, successive events can be coupled by neuronal associations leading to forms of learning that might be unique to each individual. Perceptual categorization in a single animal can obviously provide a basis for *individual* learning in which surprise or rupture of expectation is followed by reward or punishment. For two such animals of a species responding to a similar environment, however, the neural bases of similar categorizations may be different—indeed, are likely to be so. Such animals could never communicate those behaviors *solely* as a result of neuronal group selection, nor could the individual behaviors be established in a given species by evolutionary selection of the neural variants determining those behaviors. This is so because neuronal group selection, like natural selection, is *a posteriori,* and it can occur with equal efficacy in many different ways.

Although one might conceive that individual learning in the strict sense can take place in some species without shared information processing, we know with certainty that information processing *does* occur, at least in species capable of true learning buttressed by communication or social transmission. To resolve the issue in a general fashion requires linking neuronal group selection to information or learning transmitted *between* individuals, and ultimately linking such selection to the social transmission and extensive information processing that actually occurs in species such as humans. The linkage (by means of communication) of categories that have nothing necessarily in common in neural structure but whose association may be particularly adaptive is a form of learning. I shall call this communicated learning, to indicate that it must be established by communicative linkages of adaptive value (see, e.g., Cheney and Seyfarth 1985) rather than directly through implicit neural characteristics or representational categories that are *necessarily* shared by two animals. Communicated learning thus requires some form of exchange between at least two, and usually more than two, organisms.

According to this argument, to account for the evolution of true information processing that can deal with novelty, several processes must be added to the perceptual categorization of which reentrant networks of degenerate groups are capable. In order to account for the ability to handle information, these processes include true learning, communicated learning, and certain ethological and evolutionarily determined features of behavior within a species. What is required to connect the theory of neuronal group selection via true learning to information processing is the emergence of a *sequence* of dependent processes during evolution. These processes are (1) perceptual categorization via neuronal group selection; (2) adaptive learning based on imitation or convention communicated between at least two individuals of a species, constituting information processing; and (3) evolutionary selection of those individuals whose repertoires of neuronal group selection make possible the quickest or most efficient adaptive learning of this kind.

After the occurrence either of ethological change (Gould and Marler 1984) or of individual adaptation by conditioning with such communicated learning, information can be acquired by both the individual and the species. Its most developed evolutionary form is seen in the emergence of symbol-forming systems and language. It is the thesis of the neuronal group selection theory that natural selection, in giving rise to this transcendent development, operated on individuals whose nervous systems were already capable of categorization because of rich systems of somatic selection. A diagram illustrating various relation-

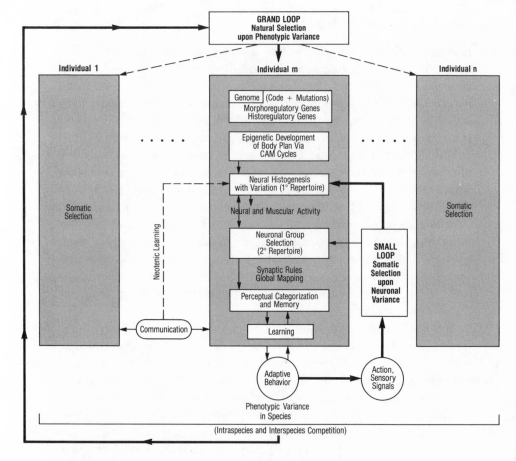

Figure 11.1

A schematic illustrating some interactions between evolution (the "grand loop") and various developmental constraints imposed by embryological events and by somatic neuronal group selection in individuals (the "small loop"). All processes within the vertical rectangular boxes (l, m, n) are assumed to take place within individuals in a species. Adaptive behavior and learning depend upon perceptual categorization established in the small loop. This leads to somatic variance that is unique to each individual. Phenotypic variants that are most adapted on the average undergo differential reproduction. Resultant changes in gene frequencies occur in a large collection of historegulatory genes and in a smaller collection of morphoregulatory genes (the regulator hypothesis), setting up new evolutionary opportunities for somatic selection in the small loop. Communication in species with changes leading to delays in primary repertoire formation can lead to neotenic learning that can be fixated in a population. Species developing true social transmission can carry out information processing.

ships between natural selection (the grand loop) and somatic selection (the small loop) is shown in figure 11.1. Obviously, behavior within each species differs in the degree to which it is ethologically determined and the degree to which it is determined by neuronal group selection in each individual. Whatever their relative contributions, the major point is that mechanisms of intraspecies communication (Boyd and Richerson 1985) and mechanisms of neuronal group selection *interact* to yield information processing systems. The recognition that this interaction can affect evolutionary selection has very rich consequences, some of which will be mentioned at the end of this book.

PART FOUR

CONCLUSION

12

Summary, Predictions, and Implications

INTRODUCTION

A useful theory should have explanatory power, make predictions, and point out directions for further experimental inquiry and refinement. A theory about complex systems necessarily has to contain a number of partial theories and models. The neuronal group selection theory is such a theory. In view of the intricacies of neural function, the likelihood is great that certain mechanistic details in the models subsumed under the main theory will turn out to be incorrect. It is therefore useful to ask stringently what the essential components are and to point out those that must remain robust in a minimal version for the theory to survive and be useful. In this chapter, we will review the key ideas in this book, emphasizing the essential components of the theory, falsification of which would require its abandonment. This will provide the opportunity for some further refinements of these ideas and for an analysis of the limits of their explanatory power. We may then take up some of the considerable number of predictions made by the theory.

Finally, it may be appropriate briefly to consider some of the more general implications of the theory, on the admittedly bold assumption that it is fundamentally correct.

According to the theory, perceptual categorization is a precondition for all conventional learning of any nontrivial degree of richness. Perception leading to categorization is adaptive and not necessarily veridical in its assignments. The macroscopic world (the collection of "objects" and events considered at a scale comparable to the physical limits of perception) is neither precategorized, named, nor ordered in an *a priori* fashion except as follows from the laws of physics. Stimuli are samples from polymorphous sets composed from objects and events in the world, the size and disjunctive partitions of which are limited by adaptive shaping during the natural selection of both sense organs and musculoskeletal systems.

Given these views, there are three main questions in neuroscience. The central biological question is, How did connected neurons evolve along with the rest of the phenotype to give richly adaptive behavior in complex, highly variable econiches? In chapters 6, 8, and 11, an attempt was made to provide a provisional answer to this biological question by showing how the developmental constraints on the evolution of the nervous system acted to yield variant repertoires in different neural regions that are linked in reentrant systems and that provide the substrate for such behavior.

Two subsidiary questions emerge from the central biological question. The psychological question is, How can initial perceptual categorization and generalization be carried out by the neural and motor systems of an individual animal? The ethological question is, How did such categorization become adaptive for true learning and species-specific learning, each yielding enhanced fitness within a taxon or species? Implicit in the latter two questions are the assumptions that the fundamental operation central to categorization is generalization and that the fundamental operation central to adaptive learning is association based on prior categorization of value under conditions of expectancy. Any theory invoked to answer these two questions must present an account formulated strictly in terms of the material arrangements and dynamic properties of neuronal populations in a given species, thus satisfying the biological question. No mentalistic notions (Sperry 1969, 1970; Popper and Eccles 1981) may be invoked.

Two contrary views can be taken within the boundaries of these constraints:

1. The organism receives information from its surroundings and processes it in a fashion similar to but obviously not identical to that of a computer. Although the brain is not organized in the same way as a digital computer, it carries out computations or algorithmic operations. These provide the basis for conditioned and operant responses and for conventional learning. This is the instructionist paradigm.

2. Alternatively, the organism receives stimuli from its environment or econiche as polymorphous sets. As a result of action, stimuli select among various dynamic nervous system states and arrangements that have already been established prior to the receipt of these stimuli, leading to enhancement of some states and suppression of others. Such stimulus sets constitute information, in the instructionist sense, only *after* selection, response, and memory have occurred; and information processing, in the larger and more specific sense of the term, occurs only *after* social transmission has emerged as an evolutionary development.

It is this second view that is espoused in the theory of neuronal group selection. The distinctions between these alternative views should not be abandoned or blurred because of the existence of special constraints on each. It is important, for example, to distinguish between evolutionarily determined behavioral responses and those dependent upon individual variation in somatic time within a species. In somatic time, the first view implies instruction—information from the environment *fundamentally* determines the order of functional connectivity (although not necessarily that of physical connectivity) in the nervous system. The second alternative is selection—groups in preexisting neuronal repertoires that form populations determined by phylogeny and ontogenetic generators of diversity are *selected* by stimuli to yield highly individual response patterns. In such a system, perceptual categorization can be defined clearly only in terms of the adaptive requirements and phenotypic restrictions of a particular species. While certain general principles may underlie such categorization, its instantiations are *always* special-purpose.

To account for perceptual categorization, we must provide a theory to explain generalization in responses during somatic time to stimuli that did not *necessarily* shape the taxon by natural selection in evolutionary time. A theory of somatic selection devised for this purpose must fulfill certain general requirements. (1) It must account for the formation of neuronal repertoires during development. This requires an explanation of the epigenetic origin of the connectional and chemical diversity of such repertoires. (2) It must provide a means by which stimuli constituting polymorphous sets can be sampled by independent parallel channels; this sampling must provide access to a sufficiently large segment of the various neuronal repertoires in particular anatomical regions. (3) The theory must include adequate synaptic mechanisms of selection, yielding differential amplification of selected neuronal subpopulations and suppression of competitors. At the same time, it must allow for continued generation of diversity. (4) It must provide mechanisms for mapping the parallel samples of stimuli onto neural populations to yield a continuous representation or representative procedure expressible in terms of neural response and motor activity that finally emerges as adaptive behavior.

The theory of neuronal group selection explicitly attempts to meet these requirements. It proposes the following:

1. Primary neuronal repertoires are established within a given species during development; the cellular constitution (neuronal types) and the gross connectivity of such repertoires are determined by evolution. The epigenetic means by which neural morphogenesis occurs in ontogeny is specified by the regulator hypothesis, which states that CAMs and SAMs act as regulators of morphogenetic movement and as linkers of cell collectives at particular places in the developing network. Because this morphogenetic principle is dynamic and epigenetic, it results in obligate variance at the level of the finest ramifications of the neuronal network. CAM modulation altering primary processes by epigenetic means provides the necessary origin of diversity in neural connectivity.

2. Multimodal input into mapped systems supplies a basis for independent sampling by classification couples of polymorphous sets in the stimulus domain according to individual features and feature correlation.

3. The sampling of stimuli by independent sensorimotor channels occurs in such a fashion that certain degenerate sets of neuronal groups respond under competitive circumstances more effectively than others, leading to selection and formation of secondary repertoires. A specific confinement-selection-competition model for groups in the cerebral cortex has been described as a paradigm for this process. The proposed epigenetic mechanism for the selection of such secondary repertoires invokes independent pre- and postsynaptic rules for changing synaptic efficacy over greater or lesser times. These rules operate to enable correlation of stimuli in time with receptor sheet space in such a way as to favor the responses of certain groups of neurons. At the same time,

the rules also act to bias certain short-term responses by long-term responses; this bias emerges from the recursively connected neurons in groups obeying both rules. While this increases the likelihood that certain groups will respond upon repeated stimulation, the long-term presynaptic changes can at the same time enhance the variability of synaptic efficacy within connected domains, generating additional diversity. The degree of variability is determined by the operation of the rules and is constrained by the degree of competition offered by different *correlated* stimuli affecting other groups in these domains. This process provides not only a basis for both novelty and generalization but also a continuous source of variation.

4. The constitution of a procedure or of a representation of categories in a spatiotemporal order occurs by mapping and reentry among parallel channels. While the *minimal* neuronal structure capable of carrying this out is a classification couple, in general, such couples do not act in isolation. Instead, they are embedded in large collections of parallel mapped channels, including reentry to and from nonmapped regions as well as to motor output systems. The collection of such components forms the smallest unit capable of a rich categorical response, called a global mapping. The emergence of global mappings as a result of action provides a critical part of the answer to the psychological question inasmuch as they provide the substrate for perceptual categorization.

According to these proposals, representations in a global mapping are procedural; that is, memory in the system constitutes a procedure of recategorization in which a particular output may be achieved repeatedly by many different (degenerate) combinations of group activity. Such recategorization can be enhanced by greater or lesser degrees of decoration and disjunctive detail provided by the patterns of group responses from independent reentrant systems. The collection of global mappings with such memorial properties provides the main basis for generalization and categorization, enhancing the possibility of adaptive learning as such maps are linked to hedonic systems. Thus, particular alterations (both evolutionary and somatic) in the properties of repertoires of neuronal groups (size, connectivity, synaptic responses, degree of variation, etc.) can have adaptive value for the organism as well as for the species if they increase the opportunities for parallel categorical responses that extend the range of learning.

The theory of neuronal group selection provides the base for the representations or representative procedures that are necessary to account for the role of surprise in determining the direction of learning.

While this is essential for classical and operant conditioning, it does not preclude the possibility that morphogenetic variants arising in ontogeny can be selected for during evolution to yield certain built-in patterns and species-specific categorizations. These ethologically significant patterns are more rigidly defined than learning responses based on individual categorization and can in certain environments obviously increase fitness. Some of these patterns offer the opportunity for neotenic learning, an intermediate case following developmental rules of selection for *patterns of circuitry* at the level of global mappings, as in bird song. This selection is environmentally guided, and the opportunity for its action is provided by a delay in the fixing of neural connections in certain regions during postnatal development. This is in contrast to but not in conflict with conventional learning, which operates solely by selection upon synapses in already fixed circuits. This overall picture of learning provides an answer to the ethological question.

Within certain species, conventional learning combined with social interactions can lead to the development of information processing systems. In this broad sense, *certain* nervous systems are capable of becoming information processors in the strict sense. But the path toward this development must proceed inexorably in the direction of evolution: ontogeny → primary repertoires → secondary repertoires by selection on synaptic populations → categorization by mapping and generalization → conventional learning → social interactions having adaptive value (possibly with neotenic learning) → information processing. Thus, the emergence of information processing is strongly related to the positively adaptive value of enhanced conventional learning under conditions of social transmission. In this view, information processing (strictly defined) in nervous systems arises primarily by communication in a taxon.

In the creation of a neural construct, motion plays a pivotal role in selectional events both in primary and in secondary repertoire development. The morphogenetic conditions for establishing primary repertoires (modulation and regulation of cell motion and process extension under regulatory constraint to give constancy and variation in neural circuits) have a counterpart in the requirement for organismic motion during early perceptual categorization and learning. In other words, the shape and capacity of a nervous system capable of adaptive categorization depend upon the motor capacity of cells yielding embryonic induction and upon the incessant motor capacity of whole organisms to give a continuous basis for representation by synaptic selection in a reentrant system.

Adequacy

With this summary description in hand, we may ask which parts of the theory are essential as described and which are inessential, in the sense that their falsification will not leave the theory hopelessly crippled. The essential components are (1) the existence of a source of connectional diversity during ontogeny; (2) a set of selection rules for changes in synaptic efficacy within synaptic populations leading to selection and additional variations; (3) the existence of functional reentrant circuits between maps to provide spatiotemporal continuity; (4) the parallel arrangements of such maps to yield classification couples or n-tuples for sampling of independent attributes; and (5) the final construction of global mappings containing motorsensory ensembles that are the smallest units capable of perceptual categorization. If our assumptions about the need for any one of these major components are falsified, the theory will be severely weakened. This list of essential components of the theory serves to stress that the mere application of any general idea of selection to the nervous system, while suggestive, is inadequate; specific mechanisms and structures must be proposed. This statement is *a fortiori* true of selection by Platonic reference (Jerne 1967), eliminative selection (Young 1965, 1973, 1975), and various mechanisms of microselection (Changeux and Danchin 1976) at the level of synapses that do not define a higher-order unit or offer a detailed consideration of the relationships necessary and sufficient to yield categorization.

In discussing the component mechanisms and structures of an adequate theory, we have had to construct from the available evidence certain partial theories and detailed models. These include the *regulator hypothesis* as the basis of the origin of morphologic diversity, the *dual rules model* for synaptic selection, and the *confinement-selection-competition model* for neuronal groups as the basis of maps. Given the present state of the evidence and the intricacies of their part processes, it would be surprising if these models turned out to be correct in all of their details. Even if these models had to be replaced by other models meeting similar requirements of the overall theory, however, the theory would remain robust. It would nevertheless be a mistake to confound principles with mechanisms and indulge glib analogies between the theory of neuronal group selection and evolution, or between the neuronal theory and clonal selection in the immune system. Particular mechanisms are unique to each of these selectionist theories and are essential to their further development.

What can the theory of neuronal group selection explain, and what does it predict? Deferring the latter issue to the next section, we may say that the theory resolves many of the paradoxes discussed in chapter 1 by providing bases for developmental diversity and individuality, for the formation of neural maps and their dynamics, for procedures of categorization, for short- and long-term procedural memory, and for the occurrence of surprise as a determinant in the initiation of learning. It explains how all of these performances can come about evolutionarily in various species, with only minimal genetic encoding of behavioral repertoires. Given these bases, it is not difficult to understand the origins of differences in performances and learning in different individuals and with differences in age.

A particularly satisfying explanatory aspect of the theory concerns the evolutionary diversity of nervous systems. The regulator hypothesis provides a definite basis for relating developmental genetic change to neural morphogenesis and also gives a definite basis for heterochrony. In doing so, it allows for matching between neural function and evolutionary changes in phenotypic traits of overall animal form, including various musculoskeletal capacities. Alterations of a muscle insertion, of limb morphology, or of cutaneous appendages do not require immediate parallel or simultaneous genetically determined changes in neural connectivity. Such peripheral alterations would be treated as defining new stimuli for selection from neural repertoires in somatic time. Later neural adaptations could occur gradually by mutation and selection. The theory thus offers a rich basis for understanding the development of new neural structures, and it constitutes an important part of the answer to the fundamental biological question of neuroscience. The major success of the theory must, however, remain its ability to explain the origins of adaptive perceptual categorization in somatic time within a variety of taxa as a result of interactions with an unlabeled world and without assumptions of homunculi.

It is important to point out here, as we did in the preface, that the theory, while providing an *initial* basis for the consideration of higher brain functions related to concept formation and language, has been deliberately confined to specific considerations of perception and perceptual categorization. Any less rigorous constraint would lead to vagueness; should the basic idea turn out to be right, it can be extended without major change to the more evolutionarily recent and complex brain functions.

PREDICTIONS

The theory of neuronal group selection attempts to unify a number of areas of neuroscience, ranging from development through synaptic function and from neuroanatomy through evolution of the phenotype, culminating finally in certain considerations of the relation of psychology to brain structure. Consequently, it provides the bases for a large number of predictions. These may be arranged in a number of ways according to subject matter. One arrangement that may serve to highlight the selective nature of neural systems is first to consider predictions based on the developmental and synaptic selection mechanisms providing for diversity and competition, then to consider those related to mapping arrangements and reentry, and finally to consider predictions connected with perceptual categorization and learning. Perforce, this arrangement has many of the defects of a terse list; its main value is summary and heuristic, and it is undoubtedly incomplete.

Selection Mechanisms

The first prediction relates to the regulator hypothesis: neural structure will arise epigenetically by the kinetically constrained driving forces of cell division, cell motion, and cell death. A major constraint will be provided by a relatively few CAMs and SAMs (numbering perhaps at most in the dozens) under the control of local signals generated by synaptic interactions and other interactions of neuronal collectives. The entire set of cell-cell interactions will thus require only a relatively small set of CAM or SAM specificities. As a result of the dynamic character of this model, vast amounts of connectional variability will be found at all places in the nervous system, but particularly at the level of axonal and dendritic arbors in their finest ramifications. This ensures individuality—while identical twins may have closer neuroanatomical structures than outbred individuals, it is predicted that they will nonetheless be found to have functionally significant variant wiring.

In particular regions of the central nervous system, very high degrees of overlap between arbors will be demonstrated by microneuroanatomical methods. This has not yet been shown experimentally for two adjacent arbors; when this is accomplished and analyzed in several locations, it will be found that this overlap results in a great deal of variation in the exact placement of synapses at targets as well as *en passant*. While connectivity can be restricted to particular regions of dendritic trees, such as is seen in the cerebellum and the hippocampus, the number of variant connections will nevertheless be very high.

After variant neuroanatomy has been set up, selection occurs according to synaptic rules. The theory predicts that *neuronal ignorance* will be confirmed: in general, a neural code corresponding to prior information processing will not be found. The Hebb rule will be found to be incorrect, and independent synaptic rules will permit signal correlation at the population level of neuronal groups, not at the level of individual synapses. *In general,* synaptic change will operate effectively only in populations. Pre- and postsynaptic modifications will occur independently through separate mechanisms; in no case will they be found to be contingent *only* upon correlated firing across individual synapses.

The *dual rules model for populational changes* in synapses explains heterosynaptic effects and allows for a wide variety of potentiations or depressions of synaptic efficacies with different temporal properties. It leads to a number of predictions that, in view of their specificity, warrant explicit listing: (1) Each class of biochemical modifications will primarily affect channels or receptors that are in a particular conformational state. Such modifications will lead to measurable changes in the magnitude and time course of the PSP, shifts in the current-voltage curve, and, possibly, to measurable changes in the time course of state transitions. This prediction could be tested by controlling the voltage across a patch-clamped postsynaptic membrane, then studying the relationship between the voltage level and the degree of channel modification (either conductance changes, transition probability changes, or phosphorylation, etc.) as a function of iontophoresed transmitter. (2) Heterosynaptic interactions will be found to be dependent on the relative timing of inputs, relative position of synapses on the postsynaptic neuron, and the types of transmitters, receptors, and channels present. The details of the constraints on the timing of inputs depend upon the distance between the synapses and the duration of the depolarization as well as upon the persistence of the modifying substance. The longer the depolarization or the persistence of modifying substance, the greater the distance over which heterosynaptic effects can take place. (3) Long-term presynaptic modifications will be found to occur on a cellwide basis. (4) After long-term presynaptic modifications, however, stronger synapses will be found to be more difficult to strengthen and easier to weaken. For short-term postsynaptic modifications, strong synapses will in general be found to be easier to strengthen. (5) Both short-term and long-term modifications will be found differentially distributed over the same neuronal population. (6) The presence of neuronal groups will be correlated with the observation that long-term modifications will locally and differentially enhance the short-term changes that led to those modifications.

According to the theory, the proposed selection rules will work on an anatomical substrate that is clearly provided *a priori;* in no case will neuronal sprouting substitute for the operation of the rules. Inasmuch as there is no predefined molecular specificity and no addressing, absolute substitution of connectivity patterns is excluded; the best that sprouting can provide is a new substitute for a damaged primary repertoire. The same restriction holds for models of learning based on sprouting. Regenerative systems such as the olfactory bulb and certain centers for bird song that are constructed seasonally will obey these principles. The same will be found true for "neotenic" learning. In other words, the *"one-way dogma"* holds (chapter 2), and in general there is system irreversibility.

The dual rules synaptic model provides a rationale for the existence of a relatively large number of neurotransmitters together with a small number of second messengers. Neurotransmitters and hormones will be found to be "information free" (not specifically targeted for only one function), but because the "transmitter logic" proposed in the synaptic model greatly increases the number of subcircuits and groups usable in a fixed network, an increasing number will be found in more complex nervous systems. Accordingly, in species with such nervous systems, the model predicts that an increasing number of instances of dynamic selection of subcircuit function resembling that seen in similar systems such as *Tritonia* (Getting and Dekin 1985) and lobster stomatogastric ganglion (Marder et al. 1987) will be found.

Mapping Arrangements and Reentry

Predictions about the intersection of anatomical and physiological response (primary and secondary repertoires) can be made in relation to various anatomical sites. The cerebral cortex will serve as a main focus in the present account, in which a series of predictions regarding group organization, pharmacological interactions, and reentrant circuitry will be briefly presented.

In accord with the *confinement-selection-competition model* (chapter 6), neuronal groups having extents of 60–100 μm, extending through all cortical layers and containing neurons with a common receptive field, will be found in the cortex, specifically in primary receiving areas. With respect to map borders, it is likely that multiple disparate afferents will be organized into stripes if they form a topographic map; most groups within a stripe will be interconnected. The receptive field overlap of groups within a stripe will have an upper bound, and repetitive stimulation by correlated input will be found to lead to smaller receptive fields and larger representations. The major site of modification will be the corticocortical synapse, not the thalamocortical synapse. In a corresponding fashion, groups having degenerate broadly tuned projective fields will be found in motor areas.

As was mentioned in connection with the dual rules model, the diversity of central neurotransmitters should reflect the decomposability of groups and their interconnections, as well as the possibility of new subcircuits created by transmitter logic. Given the proposed necessity for an initial stage of group confinement, one would expect a series of pathologies after blocking the action of various cell types by pharmacological agents (see table 12.1 for examples).

Most of the above considerations relate to map borders. In terms of map interactions, reentrant circuits will be found to dominate at all levels. As an example of that domination, map alterations that occur either because of distortion of correlated input or because of local changes in one of a pair of reentrantly connected maps will result in readjustments of receptive fields or coherent projections, so that the two maps are coordinate. Such coordinative map responses to map alterations at a different level will occur at all levels of projection.

In reentrant circuits, temporal correlates will be consistent with group size. In registered reentrant systems such as the corticothalamic system, correlations occurring in time ranges of 60–100 msec will be found, and the destruction of such correlations will lead to a loss of capacity for representation.

Perceptual Categorization and Learning

According to the theory, nonidentical early abstracting networks that operate simultaneously and in parallel in real time are necessary to form the basis for representations and associative memories. The system of memory operates as a form of associative recategorization using global mappings. While definite patterns of group firing can occur, the emphasis is on reentrant *processes* leading to recategorization in dynamic maps. While one would not expect a whole system of reentrant short-term memory to be correlated strictly with the postsynaptic rule, nor long-term memory with the presynaptic rule, these rules operate together in the process of consolidating short-term into long-term

Table 12.1

Predicted Pathological Effects of Alterations in the Activity of Various Cortical Cell Types

Cell Type	Transmitter*	Predicted Effect
Nonspiny stellate cells	(GABA)	No group confinement; huge receptive fields with enormous overlap; continuous shift of receptive fields of surrounding groups toward affected region
Double bouquet dendritic cells	(GABA)	Lessens group confinement; adds to above
Pyramidal cells	(Glutamate)	Groups fall apart, no longer have common receptive fields; noncompact receptive fields difficult to fire; some shift of receptive fields of surrounding groups
Spiny stellate cells	(Unknown)	Lose vertical (interlaminar) coupling; receptive field of surrounding groups shifts
Bipolar cells	(VIP, CCK)	Supragranular layers relatively unaffected; receptive fields of infragranular layers shift from surrounding groups
Thalamic afferents	(Unknown)	Effects similar to those observed in the experiments of Merzenich et al. as described in the text

*The diversity of central neurotransmitters provides a variety of pharmacological approaches to specific perturbation of subsets of cells within groups and of their interconnections.

memory. Long-term memories will in general reflect presynaptic and postsynaptic alterations; short-term memories will largely (but not exclusively) reflect postsynaptic alterations. Syndromes featuring an abnormality of a particular type of memory will be associated with a corresponding locus of neuronal pathology related to the pre- and postsynaptic rules. Amnesic syndromes with semantic or linguistic defects will be found to have *underlying* defects in related procedural aspects of recategorization.

According to the theory, learning of any degree of richness in a taxon or species requires perceptual categorization. Because such categorization requires the operation of global mappings with memorial functions and because adaptive learning requires evolutionarily developed value schemes, triangle networks of classification couples, motor ensembles, and limbic structures will be found to play a key role in learning events. Such networks will consist of very large numbers of neurons, and while subnetworks may show the properties of classical conditioning when isolated, only the entire network involving hedonic centers and a global mapping will have the capability of defining a direction of learning in terms of surprise and novelty. The behavior that ensues from the operation of such triangle networks will have a stochastic element because of the degeneracy of groups, the varying trade-off of time constraints, and the dynamic nature of associative reentrant systems. This balance between stereotypy and fluctuation in motor activity will provide elements necessary to poll new neuronal groups in repertoires as well as to search new environments in learning activity. Alterations of map boundaries, of motor or musculoskeletal ensembles, or of limbic stimuli should lead to the development of new global mappings; in the absence of the formation of such maps, learning deficits should be severe. Alterations of coordinated reentry in various maps may contribute to the severe perceptual alterations seen in psychotic states.

UNFINISHED BUSINESS AND GENERAL IMPLICATIONS

Formulation of the theory of neuronal group selection in a focused form subject to pragmatic test has required a rather severe restriction of the domains of higher brain function to be explicitly considered. In the effort to provide an account of how certain fundamental psychological functions could be interpreted in terms of brain organization, the decision was made to focus first on perception. Even with this deliberate restriction, very large bodies of facts in a great variety of fields have had to be interrelated. The proposed structures mediating perceptual categorization turn out to be remarkably complex in terms of both the proximal and the distal elements involved—a global mapping requires a very large number of neurons, musculoskeletal structures, more than one sensory channel, and, usually, various polymodal interactions.

Until the restricted form of the theory is tested in terms of such structures and objects, it will be almost fruitless to attempt a consideration of the basis in brain function of higher-level concepts, thinking (Bartlett 1982), or other related cognitive matters. Above all, the issue of language remains to be addressed along with notions of self-consciousness and awareness that lead to perceptual experience. Despite the lack of any direct consideration of such subjects, the theory, if validated at the level of its present ambitions, would not be beyond further extension. The structures provided by classification couples, global mappings, and the process of selection acting upon repertoires of groups are all highly dynamic. It is not difficult to imagine how they could be incorporated into information systems based on social transmission. But prudence suggests that to do so now would extend the theory beyond any present capabilities of test.

If extension to such issues finally turned out to be feasible, then it would not be surprising if, to some extent, every perception were considered to be an act of creation and every memory an act of imagination. The individualistic flavor and the extraordinary richness of selective repertoires suggest that, in each brain, epigenetic elements play major and unpredictable roles. Categorical genetic determinism has no place in such systems; neither has instructionist empiricism. Instead, genetic and developmental factors interact to yield systems of remarkable complexity capable of an equally remarkable degree of freedom. The constraints placed on this freedom by chronology and by the limits of repertoires, while definite, do not seem as impressive as the unending ability of somatic selective systems such as the brain to confront novelty, to generalize upon it, and to adapt in unforeseen fashions.

At the end of *On the Origin of Species,* Darwin (1859) commented upon the extraordinary richness and complexity of evolved life from "so simple a beginning." From the first emergence of replicating systems in prebiotic times, through the emergence of enzymic activities and systems of molecular complementarity, to cellular organizations with their nonlinear regulatory systems, one sees the play between constancy and variation. At certain transcendent (Stebbins 1982) stages, this play is given further reach. One of these stages certainly was the development of metazoan organization in which cellular motions during development led both to organismic order and to epigenetic fluctuations. Another was the emergence of neural networks regulating motion, sensing the environment, and interacting with chemical mechanisms of internal endocrine control. A third was the emergence of selective immune mechanisms, the other greatly elaborated somatic selective system resulting from natural selection.

The theory of neuronal group selection contends that a fourth transcendent step was the emergence in nervous systems of repertoires of groups obeying somatic selection rules. With this emergence came the possibility of rich perceptual categorization and enhanced powers of conventional and associative learning. And with this development, somatic selective systems reached new heights of complexity and speed as the precursors of enhanced social transmission systems came into being.

As one might expect in an evolutionary system, with time the complexity of operation of such systems increased: selection against complexity was undoubtedly considerable, but selection against simplicity was even greater. Out of the increase in complexity of evolutionary systems, more sophisticated somatic selection systems emerged. With the further increase in the complexity of somatic systems and their linkage to so many aspects of the phenotype, richly linked categorization and novel responses emerged. And finally, out of the interaction of individuals in species capable of social transmission (Boyd and Richerson 1985), informational systems emerged. At this level of transcendence, Lamarckian characteristics are superimposed upon a fundamental Darwinian base.

The degree of complexity of such transmission systems is apparently endless: the number of sentences in a language is infinite. That ultimate degree of complexity is nonetheless obligately based on the emergence of versatile systems of somatic variation and constancy underlying nervous systems capable of perceptual categorization. From so complex an emergence, no obvious end can be visualized. At the end of the simplification achieved when we finally understand brain function, we will still have before us the endless new possibilities emergent from somatic selection at all levels—developmental, synaptic, and cultural.

REFERENCES

Abbreviations of Scholarly Journals

Acta Physiol. Scand.	*Acta Physiological Scandinavica*
Adv. Biochem. Psychopharmacol.	*Advances in Biochemical Psychopharmacology*
Adv. Cell. Neurobiol.	*Advances in Cellular Neurobiology*
Am. Nat.	*American Naturalist*
Am. Zool.	*American Zoologist*
Anat. Rec.	*Anatomical Record*
Ann. N.Y. Acad. Sci.	*Annals of the New York Academy of Sciences*
Annu. Rev. Biochem.	*Annual Review of Biochemistry*
Annu. Rev. Cell Biol.	*Annual Review of Cell Biology*
Annu. Rev. Neurosci.	*Annual Review of Neuroscience*
Annu. Rev. Physiol.	*Annual Review of Physiology*
Arch. Anat. Physiol., Anat. Abt.	*Archiv für Anatomie und Physiologie, Anatomische Abteilung*
Arch. Exp. Zellforsch.	*Archiv für Experimentelle Zellforschung*
Arch. Mikrosk. Anat. Entwicklungsmech.	*Archiv für Mikroskopische Anatomie und Entwicklungsmechanik*
Behav. Brain Sci.	*Behavioral and Brain Sciences*
Biblio. Biotheoret.	*Bibliotheca Biotheoretica*
Biol. Rev. Cam. Philos. Soc.	*Biological Reviews of the Cambridge Philosophical Society (London)*
Br. J. Psychol.	*British Journal of Psychology*
Brain Behav. Evol.	*Brain Behavior and Evolution*
Brain Res.	*Brain Research*
Bull. Math. Biophys.	*Bulletin of Mathematical Biophysics*
Cell Tiss. Res.	*Cell and Tissue Research*
Child Dev.	*Child Development*
Cognit. Psychol.	*Cognitive Psychology*
Cold Spring Harbor Symp. Quant. Biol.	*Cold Spring Harbor Symposia on Quantitative Biology*
Commun. ACM	*Communications of the Association for Computing Machinery*
Comp. Biochem. Physiol.	*Comparative Biochemistry and Physiology*
Comp. Psychol. Monogr.	*Comparative Psychology Monograph*
Dev. Biol.	*Developmental Biology*
Dev. Brain Res.	*Developmental Brain Research*
Exp. Brain Res.	*Experimental Brain Research*

Exp. Cell Res.	*Experimental Cell Research*
Exp. Neurol.	*Experimental Neurology*
Harvey Lect.	*Harvey Lectures*
Infant Behav. & Dev.	*Infant Behavior and Development*
Int. J. Man Machine Stud.	*International Journal of Man-Machine Studies*
Int. Rev. Physiol.	*International Review of Physiology*
J. Acoust. Soc. Am.	*Journal of the Acoustic Society of America*
J. Biol. Chem.	*Journal of Biological Chemistry*
J. Cell Biol.	*Journal of Cell Biology*
J. Comp. Neurol.	*Journal of Comparative Neurology*
J. Comp. Physiol. Psychol.	*Journal of Comparative Physiology and Psychology*
J. Embryol. Exp. Morphol.	*Journal of Embryology and Experimental Morphology*
J. Exp. Anal. Behav.	*Journal of Experimental Analysis of Behavior*
J. Exp. Child Psychol.	*Journal of Experimental Child Psychology*
J. Exp. Psychol. Animal Behav. Processes	*Journal of Experimental Psychology: Animal Behavior Processes*
J. Exp. Psychol. Hum. Percept.	*Journal of Experimental Psychology: Human Perception and Performance*
J. Exp. Zool.	*Journal of Experimental Zoology*
J. Gen. Physiol.	*Journal of General Physiology*
J. Hum. Evol.	*Journal of Human Evolution*
J. Mind Behav.	*Journal of Mind and Behavior*
J. Morphol.	*Journal of Morphology*
J. Neurocytol.	*Journal of Neurocytology*
J. Neurophysiol.	*Journal of Neurophysiology*
J. Neurosci.	*Journal of Neuroscience*
J. New Ment. Dis.	*Journal of New Mental Disorders*
J. Physiol. (Lond.)	*Journal of Physiology (London)*
J. Theoret. Biol.	*Journal of Theoretical Biology*
J. Zool.	*Journal of Zoology*
Mar. Behav. Physiol.	*Marine Behavioral Physiology*
Neurol. Zentralbl.	*Neurologische Zentralblatt*
Neurosci. Biobehav. Rev.	*Neuroscience and Biobehavioral Reviews*
Neurosci. Lett.	*Neuroscience Letters*
Nobel Symp.	*Nobel Symposium*
Pattern Recogn.	*Pattern Recognition*
Percept. Psychophys.	*Perception and Psychophysics*
Perspect. Biol. Med.	*Perspectives in Biology and Medicine*
Philos. Trans. R. Soc. Lond. [Biol.]	*Philosophical Transactions of the Royal Society of London B [Biological Sciences]*
Physiol. Behav.	*Physiology and Behavior*
Physiol. Rev.	*Physiological Reviews*
Postgrad. Med. J.	*Postgraduate Medical Journal*
Proc. Natl. Acad. Sci. USA	*Proceedings of the National Academy of Sciences of the United States of America*
Proc. R. Soc. Lond. [Biol.]	*Proceedings of the Royal Society of London B [Biological Sciences]*
Proc. Sixth Int. Congr. Genet.	*Proceedings of the Sixth International Congress on Genetics*
Psychol. Rev.	*Psychological Review*
Psychonom. Sci.	*Psychonomic Science*
Q. J. Exp. Physiol.	*Quarterly Journal of Experimental Physiology*
Q. Rev. Biol.	*Quarterly Review of Biology*
Sci. Am.	*Scientific American*

Symp. Int. Union Physiol. Sci.	*Symposium of the International Union of Physiological Sciences*
Symp. Soc. Exp. Biol.	*Symposium of the Society for Experimental Biology*
Syst. Zool.	*Systematic Zoology*
Trends Neurosci.	*Trends in Neurosciences*
Z. Tierpsychol.	*Zeitschrift für Tierpsychologie*
Z. Zellforsch. Mikrosk. Anat.	*Zeitschrift für Zellforschung und Mikroskopische Anatomie*

Alberch, P. 1979. Size and shape in ontogeny and phylogeny. *Paleobiology* 5:296–317.
———. 1980. Ontogenesis and morphological diversification. *Am. Zool.* 20:653–67.
———. 1982a. Developmental constraints in evolutionary processes. In *Evolution and development,* ed. J. T. Bonner, pp. 313–32. Berlin: Springer-Verlag.
———. 1982b. The generative and regulatory roles of development. In *Environmental adaptation and evolution,* ed. D. Mossakowski and G. Roth, pp. 19–36. Stuttgart: Gustav Fischer.
———. 1985. Problems with the interpretation of developmental sequences. *Syst. Zool.* 34:46–58.
———. 1987. The evolution of a developmental process. In *Marine biological laboratories lectures in biology,* ed. R. A. Raff and E. Raff, pp. 23–46. New York: Alan R. Liss.
Alexander, R. M. 1975. Evolution of integrated design. *Am. Zool.* 15:419–25.
Altman, J. S., and N. M. Tyrer. 1977. The locust wing hinge stretch receptors. II. Variation, alternative pathways, and "mistakes" in the central arborizations. *J. Comp. Neurol.* 172:431–39.
Andersen, P. O. 1977. Specific long-lasting potentiation of synaptic transmission in hippocampal slices. *Nature* 266:736–37.
———. 1980. Possible mechanisms for long-lasting potentiation of synaptic transmission in hippocampal slices from guinea-pigs. *J. Physiol. (Lond.)* 302:463–82.
Anderson, J. A., and G. E. Hinton. 1981. Models of information processing in the brain. In *Parallel models of associative memory,* ed. G. E. Hinton and J. A. Anderson, pp. 9–48. Hillsdale, N.J.: Lawrence Erlbaum Associates.
Anderson, J. R. 1981. *Cognitive skills and their acquisition.* Hillsdale, N.J.: Lawrence Erlbaum Associates.
Anish, D. S. 1978. The natural concept tree: A study on learning in pigeons. Undergraduate honors thesis, Harvard College.
Armstrong, P. M. 1978. The mammalian cerebellum and its contribution to movement control. *Int. Rev. Physiol.* 17:239–94.
Armstrong, S. L., L. R. Gleitman, and H. Gleitman. 1983. What some concepts might not be. *Cognition* 13:263–308.
Arthur, W. 1984. *Mechanisms of morphological evolution.* New York: Wiley.
Aslin, R., J. R. Alberts, and M. R. Petersen. 1981. *Development of perception: Psychobiological perspectives.* Vols. 1 and 2. New York: Academic.
Attardi, D. G., and R. W. Sperry. 1963. Preferential selection of central pathways by regenerating optic fibers. *Exp. Neurol.* 7:46–64.
Auerbach, L. 1898. Nervenendigungen in den Centralorganen. *Neurol. Zentralbl.* 17:445–54.
Baldwin, J. M. 1895. *Mental development in the child and the race.* New York: Macmillan.
———. 1902. *Development and evolution.* New York: Macmillan.
Banker, G. A., and W. M. Cowan. 1977. Rat hippocampal neurons in dispersed cell culture. *Brain Res.* 126:397–425.
———. 1979. Further observations on hippocampal neurons in dispersed cell culture. *J. Comp. Neurol.* 187:469–94.
Baranyi, A., and O. Fehér. 1981. Intracellular studies on cortical synaptic plasticity. *Exp. Brain Res.* 41:124–34.
Bartlett, F. C. 1964. *Remembering: A study in experimental and social psychology,* Cambridge, England: Cambridge Univ. Press.
———. 1982. *Thinking: An experimental and social study.* Westport, Conn.: Greenwood.

Bastiani, M. J., S. du Lac, and C. S. Goodman. 1985. The first neuronal growth cones in insect embryos: Model systems for studying the development of neuronal specificity. In *Model neural networks and behavior*, ed. A. I. Selverston, pp. 149–74. New York: Plenum.

Bekoff, A. 1978. A neuroethological approach to the study of the ontogeny of coordinated behavior. In *The development of behavior: Comparative and evolutionary aspects*, ed. G. M. Burghardt and M. Bekoff, pp. 19–41. New York: Garland.

Bekoff, A., P. S. G. Stern, and V. Hamburger. 1975. Coordinated motor output in the hindlimb of the 7-day chick embryo. *Proc. Natl. Acad. Sci. USA* 72:1245–48.

Berg, D. L. 1982. Cell death in neuronal development: Regulation by trophic factors. In *Neuronal development*, ed. N. Spitzer, pp. 297–332. New York: Plenum.

Bernstein, N. 1967. *The coordination and regulation of movements.* Oxford: Pergamon.

Bertolotti, R., U. Rutishauser, and G. M. Edelman. 1980. A cell surface molecule involved in aggregation of embryonic liver cells. *Proc. Natl. Acad. Sci. USA* 77:4831–35.

Bindman, L., and O. Lippold. 1981. *The neurophysiology of cerebral cortex.* Austin: Univ. Texas Press.

Bindra, D. 1976. *A theory of intelligent behavior.* New York: Wiley.

Blough, P. M. 1973. Visual acuity in the pigeon. II. Effects of target distance and retinal lesions. *J. Exp. Anal. Behav.* 20:333–43.

Bock, W. J. 1965. The role of adaptive mechanisms in the origin of higher levels of organization. *Syst. Zool.* 14:272–87.

Bongard, M. 1970. *Pattern recognition*, ed. J. K. Hawkins. New York: Spartan Books.

Bonner, J. T., ed. 1982. *Evolution and development.* Berlin: Springer-Verlag.

Bornstein, M. H., W. Kessen, and S. Weiskopf. 1976. Color vision and hue categorization in young infants. *J. Exp. Psychol. Hum. Percept.* 2:115–29.

Bower, T. G. R. 1967. The development of object-permanence: Some studies of existence constancy. *Percept. Psychophys.* 2:411–18.

———. 1982. *Development in infancy.* 2d ed. San Francisco: Freeman.

Boyd, R., and P. J. Richerson. 1985. *Culture and the evolutionary process.* Chicago: Univ. Chicago Press.

Brainerd, C. J., and M. Pressley. 1985. *Basic processes in memory development.* New York: Springer-Verlag.

Brindley, G. S. 1967. The classification of modifiable synapses and their use in models for conditioning. *Proc. R. Soc. Lond.* [*Biol.*] 168:361–76.

Brodal, A. 1981. *Neurological anatomy in relation to clinical medicine.* New York: Oxford Univ. Press.

Brooks, V., ed. 1981. *Handbook of physiology.* Sect. 2, *The nervous system.* Vol. 2, *Motor control.* Pts. 1–2. Bethesda, Md.: American Physiological Society.

Bryan, J. S., and H. L. Atwood. 1981. Two types of synaptic depression at synapses of a single crustacean motor axon. *Mar. Behav. Physiol.* 8:99–121.

Bullock, T. H. 1967. Signals and neuronal coding. In *The neurosciences: A study program*, pp. 347–52. New York: Rockefeller Univ. Press.

———. 1978. Identifiable and addressed neurons in the vertebrates. In *Neurobiology of the Mauthner cell*, ed. D. S. Faber and H. Korn, pp. 1–12. New York: Raven.

———. 1984. Comparative neuroscience holds promise for quiet revolutions. *Science* 225:473–78.

Burgess, P. R., J. Y. Weis, F. J. Clark, and J. Simon. 1982. Signaling of kinesthetic information by peripheral sensory receptors. *Annu. Rev. Neurosci.* 5:171–87.

Burnet, F. M. 1959. *The clonal selection theory of acquired immunity.* Nashville: Vanderbilt Univ. Press.

Burns, B. D. 1968. *The uncertain nervous system.* London: Edward Arnold.

Buskirk, D. R., J.-P. Thiery, U. Rutishauser, and G. M. Edelman. 1980. Antibodies to a neural cell adhesion molecule disrupt histogenesis in cultured chick retinae. *Nature* 285:488–89.

Carew, T. J., R. D. Hawkins, T. W. Abrams, and E. R. Kandel. 1984. A test of Hebb's postulate at identified synapses which mediate classical conditioning in *Aplysia*. *J. Neurosci.* 4:1217–24.

Catterall, W. A. 1979. Binding of scorpion toxin to receptor sites associated with sodium channels in frog muscle—Correlation of voltage-dependent binding with activation. *J. Gen. Physiol.* 74:375–91.

Cerella, J. 1977. Absence of perspective processing in the pigeon. *Pattern Recogn.* 9:65–68.

———. 1979. Visual classes and natural categories in the pigeon. *J. Exp. Psychol. Hum. Percept.* 5:68–77.

———. 1980. The pigeon's analysis of pictures. *Pattern Recogn.* 12:1–6.

Changeux, J.-P. 1981. The acetylcholine receptor: An "allosteric" membrane protein. *Harvey Lect.* 75:85–254.

Changeux, J.-P., and A. Danchin. 1976. Selective stabilization of developing synapses as a mechanism for the specification of neuronal networks. *Nature* 264:705–11.

Changeux, J.-P., T. Heidmann, and P. Patte. 1984. Learning by selection. In *The Biology of learning*, ed. P. Marler and H. S. Terrace, pp. 115–37. New York: Springer-Verlag.

Chan-Palay, V., G. Nilaver, S. L. Palay, M. C. Beinfeld, E. A. Zimmerman, J.-Y. Wu, and T. L. O'Donohue. 1981. Chemical heterogeneity in cerebellar Purkinje cells: Existence and coexistence of glutamic acid decarboxylase-like and motilin-like immunoreactivities. *Proc. Natl. Acad. Sci. USA* 78:7787–91.

Chan-Palay, V., S. L. Palay, and J.-Y. Wu. 1982. Sagittal cerebellar microbands of taurine neurons: Immunocytochemical demonstration by using antibodies against the taurine-synthesizing enzyme cysteine sulfinic acid decarboxylase. *Proc. Natl. Acad. Sci. USA* 79:4221–25.

Cheney, D. L., and R. M. Seyfarth. 1985. Social and non-social knowledge in vervet monkeys. *Philos. Trans. R. Soc. Lond.* [*Biol.*] 308:187–201.

Chomsky, N. (1980) *Rules and representations.* New York: Columbia Univ. Press.

Chuong, C.-M., and G. M. Edelman. 1984. Alterations in neural cell adhesion molecules during development of different regions of the nervous system. *J. Neurosci.* 4:2354–68.

———. 1985a. Expression of cell adhesion molecules in embryonic induction. I. Morphogenesis of nestling feathers. *J. Cell Biol.* 101:1009–26.

———. 1985b. Expression of cell adhesion molecules in embryonic induction. II. Morphogenesis of adult feathers. *J. Cell Biol.* 101:1027–43.

Chuong, C.-M., K. L. Crossin, and G. M. Edelman. 1987. Sequential expression and differential function of multiple adhesion molecules during the formation of cerebellar cortical layers. *J. Cell Biol.* 104:331–42.

Clarke, E., and C. D. O'Malley. 1968. *The human brain and spinal cord: A historical study illustrated by writings from antiquity to the twentieth century.* Berkeley: Univ. California Press.

Coghill, G. E. 1929. *Anatomy and the problem of behaviour.* Cambridge, England: Cambridge Univ. Press. Reprint. New York: Hafner, 1965.

Cohen, A. H., and C. Gans. 1975. Muscle activity in rat locomotion: Movement analysis and electromyography of the flexors and extensors of the elbow. *J. Morphol.* 176:177–96.

Cooper, L. N. 1974. A possible organization of animal memory and learning. *Nobel Symp.* 24:252–64.

Coren, S., and J. S. Girgus. 1978. *Seeing is deceiving: The psychology of visual illusions.* Hillsdale, N.J.: Lawrence Erlbaum Associates.

Cowan, W. M. 1973. Neuronal death as a regulative mechanism in the control of cell number in the nervous system. In *Development and aging in the nervous system*, ed. M. Rockstein, pp. 19–41. New York: Academic.

———. 1978. Aspects of neural development. *Int. Rev. Physiol.* 17:150–91.

Cowan, W. M., and R. K. Hunt. 1985. The development of the retinotectal projection: An overview. In *Molecular bases of neural development*, ed. G. M. Edelman, W. E. Gall, and W. M. Cowan, pp. 389–428. New York: Wiley.

Cowan, W. M., and E. Wenger. 1967. Cell loss in the trochlear nucleus of the chick during normal development and after radical extirpation of the optic vesicle. *J. Exp. Zool.* 164:267–80.

Cowey, A. 1981. Why are there so many visual areas? In *The organization of the cerebral cortex*, ed. F. O. Schmitt, F. G. Worden, G. Adelman, and S. G. Dennis, pp. 395–413. Cambridge, Mass.: MIT Press.

Crossin, K. L., C.-M. Chuong, and G. M. Edelman. 1985. Expression sequences of cell adhesion molecules. *Proc. Natl. Acad. Sci. USA* 82:6942–46.

Crossin, K. L., S. Hoffman, M. Grumet, J.-P. Thiery, and G. M. Edelman. 1986. Site-restricted expression of cytotactin during development of the chicken embryo. *J. Cell Biol.* 102:1917–30.

Crossin, K. L., G. P. Richardson, C.-M. Chuong, and G. M. Edelman. 1987. Modulation of adhesion molecules during induction and differentiation of the auditory placode. In *Functions of the auditory system*, ed. G. M. Edelman, W. E. Gall, and W. M. Cowan. New York: Wiley (in press).

Cunningham, B. A., Y. Leutzinger, W. J. Gallin, B. C. Sorkin, and G. M. Edelman. 1984. Linear organization of the liver cell adhesion molecule L-CAM. *Proc. Natl. Acad. Sci. USA* 81:5787–91.

Damsky, C. H., K. A. Knudsen, and C. A. Buck. 1984. Integral membrane proteins in cell-cell and cell-substratum adhesion. In *The biology of glycoproteins*, ed. R. J. Ivatt, pp. 1–64. New York: Plenum.

Daniloff, J. K., C.-M. Chuong, G. Levi, and G. M. Edelman. 1986a. Differential distribution of cell adhesion molecules during histogenesis of the chick nervous system. *J. Neurosci.* 6:739–58.

Daniloff, J. K., G. Levi, M. Grumet, F. Rieger, and G. M. Edelman. 1986b. Altered expression on neuronal cell adhesion molecules induced by nerve injury and repair. *J. Cell Biol.* 103:929–45.

Darwin, C. 1859. *On the origin of species by means of natural selection or the preservation of favoured races in the struggle for life.* London: Murray.

———. 1872. *The expression of emotions in man and animals.* London: Murray.

de Lacoste-Utamsing, C., and R. L. Holloway. 1982. Sexual dimorphism in the human corpus callosum. *Science* 216:431–32.

den Boer, P. J. 1982. On the stability of animal populations or how to survive in a heterogeneous and changeable world. In *Environmental adaptation and evolution*, ed. D. Mossakowski and G. Roth, pp. 211–32. Stuttgart: Gustav Fischer.

Dennett, D. C. 1978. *Brainstorms: Philosophical essays on mind and psychology.* Montgomery, Vt.: Bradford Books.

Dennis, I., J. A. Hampton, and S. E. G. Lea. 1973. New problem in concept formation. *Nature* 243:101–2.

de Peyer, J. E., A. B. Cachelin, I. B. Levitan, and H. Reuter. 1982. Ca^{++}–activated K^+ conductance in internally perfused snail neurons is enhanced by protein phosphorylation. *Proc. Natl. Acad. Sci. USA* 79:4207–11.

Deregowski, J. B. 1980. *Illusions, patterns and pictures: A cross cultural perspective.* London: Academic.

Desmond, N. L., and W. B. Levy. 1981. Ultrastructural and numerical alteration in dendritic spines as a consequence of long-term potentiation. *Anat. Rec.* 199:68A–69A.

D'Eustachio, P., G. Owens, G. M. Edelman, and B. A. Cunningham. 1985. Chromosomal location of the gene encoding the neural cell adhesion molecule (N-CAM) in the mouse. *Proc. Natl. Acad. Sci. USA* 82:7631–35.

Devor, M., and P. D. Wall. 1981. Effects of peripheral nerve injury on receptive fields of cells in the cat spinal cord. *J. Comp. Neurol.* 199:227–91.

Dichter, M. A. 1978. Rat cortical neurons in cell culture: Culture methods, cell morphology, electrophysiology and synapse formation. *Brain Res.* 149:279–93.

Dickenson, A. 1980. *Contemporary animal learning theory.* Cambridge: Cambridge Univ. Press.

———. 1985. Actions and habits: The development of behavioral autonomy. *Philos. Trans. R. Soc. Lond. [Biol.]* 308:67–78.

Dodwell, P. C., and T. Caelli. 1984. *Figural synthesis.* Hillsdale, N.J.: Lawrence Erlbaum Associates.

Douglas, R. M., G. V. Goddard, and M. Riives. 1982. Inhibitory modulation of long-term potentiation: Evidence for a post-synaptic locus of control. *Brain Res.* 240:259–72.

Dullemeijer, P. 1974. *Concepts and approaches in animal morphology.* Assen, Netherlands: Van Gorcum.

Easter, S. S., Jr. 1983. Postnatal neurogenesis and changing connections. *Trends Neurosci.* 6:53–56.

———. 1985. The continuous formation of the retinotectal map in goldfish with special attention to the role of the axonal pathway. In *Molecular bases of neural development,* ed. G. M. Edelman, W. E. Gall, and W. M. Cowan, pp. 429–52. New York: Wiley.

Easter, S. S., Jr., and C. A. O. Stuermer. 1984. An evaluation of the hypothesis of shifting terminals in goldfish optic tectum. *J. Neurosci.* 4:1052–63.

Easter, S. S., Jr., D. Purves, P. Rakic, and N. C. Spitzer. 1985. The changing view of neural specificity. *Science* 230:507–11.

Ebbesson, S. O. E. 1980. The parcellation theory and its relation to interspecific variability in brain organization, evolutionary and ontogenetic development and neuronal plasticity. *Cell Tiss. Res.* 213:179–212.

———. 1984. Evolution and ontogeny of neural circuits. *Behav. Brain Sci.* 7:321–66.

Ebbesson, S. O. E., and R. G. Northcutt. 1976. Neurology of anamniotic vertebrates. In *Evolution of brain and behavior in vertebrates,* ed. R. B. Masterton, M. E. Bitterman, C. B. G. Campbell, and N. Hotton, pp. 115–46. Hillsdale, N.J.: Lawrence Erlbaum Associates.

Ebbesson, S. O. E., J. A. James, and D. M. Schroeder. 1972. An overview of major interspecific variation in thalamic organization. *Brain Behav. Evol.* 6:92–130.

Eccles, J. C. 1953. *The neurophysiological basis of mind.* Oxford: Oxford Univ. Press.

Edelman, G. M. 1973. Antibody structure and molecular immunology. *Science* 180:830–40.

———. 1974. The problem of molecular recognition by a selective system. In *Studies in the philosophy of biology,* ed. F. J. Ayala and T. Dobzhansky, pp. 45–56. London: Macmillan.

———. 1975. Molecular recognition in the immune and nervous systems. In *The neurosciences: Paths of discovery,* ed. F. G. Worden, J.-P. Swazey, G. Adelman, pp. 65–74. Cambridge, Mass.: MIT Press.

———. 1976. Surface modulation in cell recognition and cell growth. *Science* 192:218–26.

———. 1978. Group selection and phasic reentrant signaling: A theory of higher brain function. In *The mindful brain: Cortical organization and the group-selective theory of higher brain function,* by G. M. Edelman and V. B. Mountcastle, pp. 51–100. Cambridge, Mass.: MIT Press.

———. 1981. Group selection as the basis for higher brain function. In *Organization of the cerebral cortex,* ed. F. O. Schmitt, F. G. Worden, G. Adelman, and S. G. Dennis, pp. 535–63. Cambridge, Mass.: MIT Press.

———. 1983. Cell adhesion molecules. *Science* 219:450–57.

———. 1984a. Modulation of cell adhesion during induction, histogenesis, and perinatal development of the nervous system. *Annu. Rev. Neurosci.* 7:339–77.

———. 1984b. Cell surface modulation and marker multiplicity in neural patterning. *Trends Neurosci.* 7:78–84.

———. 1984c. Cell adhesion and morphogenesis: The regulator hypothesis. *Proc. Natl. Acad. Sci. USA* 81:1460–64.

———. 1985a. Neural Darwinism: Population thinking and higher brain function. In *How we know: The inner frontiers of cognitive science,* Proceedings of Nobel Conference XX, ed. M. Shafto, pp. 1–30. San Francisco: Harper & Row.

———. 1985b. Expression of cell adhesion molecules during embryogenesis and regeneration. *Exp. Cell Res.* 161:1–16.

———. 1985c. Evolution and morphogenesis: The regulator hypothesis. In *Stadler genetics symposium series on genetics, development and evolution,* ed. T. Gustafson, L. Stebbins, and F. J. Ayala, pp. 1–28. New York: Plenum.

———. 1985d. Cell adhesion and the molecular processes of morphogenesis. *Annu. Rev. Biochem.* 54:135–169.

———. 1985e. Specific cell adhesion in histogenesis and morphogenesis. In *The cell in contact: Adhesions and junctions as morphogenetic determinants,* ed. G. M. Edelman and J.-P. Thiery, pp. 139–68. New York: Wiley.

———. 1985f. Molecular regulation of neural morphogenesis. In *Molecular bases of neural development,* ed. G. M. Edelman, W. E. Gall, and W. M. Cowan, pp. 35–59. New York: Wiley.

———. 1986a. Cell adhesion molecules in the regulation of animal form and tissue pattern. *Annu. Rev. Cell Biol.* 2:81–116.

———. 1986b. Molecular mechanisms of morphogenetic evolution. In *Molecular evolution of life,* Chemica Scripta, vol. 26B, ed. H. Baltscheffsky, H. Jörnvall, and R. Rigler, pp. 363–75. Cambridge, England: Cambridge University Press.

Edelman, G. M., and C.-M. Chuong. 1982. Embryonic to adult conversion of neural cell adhesion molecules in normal and *staggerer* mice. *Proc. Natl. Acad. Sci. USA* 79:7036–46.

Edelman, G. M., and L. H. Finkel. 1984. Neuronal group selection in the cerebral cortex. In *Dynamic aspects of neocortical function,* ed. G. M. Edelman, W. E. Gall, and W. M. Cowan, pp. 653–95. New York: Wiley.

Edelman, G. M., and G. N. Reeke, Jr. 1982. Selective networks capable of representative transformation, limited generalizations, and associative memory. *Proc. Natl. Acad. Sci. USA* 79:2091–95.

Edelman, G. M., and J.-P. Thiery, eds. 1985. *The cell in contact: Adhesions and junctions as morphogenetic determinants.* New York: Wiley.

Edelman, G. M., W. J. Gallin, A. Delouvée, B. A. Cunningham, and J.-P. Thiery. 1983. Early epochal maps of two different cell adhesion molecules. *Proc. Natl. Acad. Sci. USA* 80:4384–88.

Edelman, G. M., W. E. Gall, and W. M. Cowan, eds. 1984. *Dynamic aspects of neocortical function.* New York: Wiley.

———, eds. 1985. *Molecular bases of neural development.* New York: Wiley.

———, eds. 1987a. *Synaptic function.* New York: Wiley.

———, eds. 1987b. *Functions of the auditory system.* New York: Wiley.

Eimas, P. D. 1982. Speech perception: A view of the initial state and perceptual mechanisms. In *Perspectives on mental representation,* ed. J. Metzler, E. C. T. Walker, and M. Garrett, pp. 339–60. Hillsdale, N.J.: Lawrence Erlbaum Associates.

Eimas, P. D., and J. L. Miller, eds. 1981. *Perspectives on the study of speech.* Hillsdale, N.J.: Lawrence Erlbaum Associates.

Eimas, P. D., J. L. Miller, and P. W. Jusczyk. 1987. On infant speech perception and the acquisition of language. In *Categorical perception,* ed. S. Harnad. New York: Cambridge Univ. Press (in press).

Epstein, R. 1982. A note on the mythological character of categorization research in psychology. *J. Mind Behav.* 3:161–69.

Estes, W. K., and B. F. Skinner. 1941. Some quantitative properties of anxiety. *J. Exp. Psychol.* 29:390–400.

Evarts, E. V., Y. Shinoda, and S. P. Wise. 1984. *Neurophysiological approaches to higher brain functions.* New York: Wiley.

Ewer, R. F. 1965. Food burying in the African ground squirrel. *Z. Tierpsychol.* 22:321–27.

Faber, D. S., and H. Korn, eds. 1978. *Neurobiology of the Mauthner cell.* New York: Raven.

Fagan, J. F., III. 1976. Infants' recognition of invariant features of faces. *Child Dev.* 47:627–38.

———. 1979. The origins of facial pattern recognition. In *Psychological development from infancy: Image to intention,* ed. M. Bornstein and W. Kessen, pp. 83–113. Hillsdale, N.J.: Lawrence Erlbaum Associates.

Fagan, J. F., III, and L. T. Singer. 1979. The role of simple feature differences in infant's recognition of faces. *Infant Behav. & Dev.* 2(1):39–45.

Fifková, E., and A. van Harreveld. 1977. Long-lasting morphological changes in dendritic spines of dentate granular cells following stimulation of the entorhinal area. *J. Neurocytol.* 6:211–30.

Finkel, L. H., and G. M. Edelman. 1985. Interaction of synaptic modification rules within populations of neurons. *Proc. Natl. Acad. Sci. USA* 82:1291–95.

———. 1987. Population rules for synapses in networks. In *Synaptic function,* ed. G. M. Edelman, W. E. Gall, and W. M. Cowan, pp. 711–57. New York: Wiley.

Fischbach, G. D. 1970. Synaptic potential recorded in cell cultures of nerve and muscle. *Science* 169:1331–33.

———. 1972. Synapse formation between dissociated nerve and muscle cells in low density cell cultures. *Dev. Biol.* 28:407–29.

Foster, M., and C. S. Sherrington. 1897. *A text book of physiology.* 7th ed., pt. 3, p. 929. London: Macmillan.

Fraser, S. E. 1985. Cell interaction involved in neural patterning: An experimental and theoretical approach. In *Molecular bases of neural development,* ed. G. M. Edelman, W. E. Gall, and W. M. Cowan, pp. 481–507. New York: Wiley.

Fraser, S. E., B. A. Murray, C.-M. Chuong, and G. M. Edelman. 1984. Alteration of the retinotectal map in *Xenopus* by antibodies to neural cell adhesion molecules. *Proc. Natl. Acad. Sci. USA* 81:4222–26.

Frazzetta, T. H. 1970. From hopeful monsters to Bolyerine snakes. *Am. Nat.* 104:55–72.

Friedlander, D. R., M. Grumet, and G. M. Edelman. 1986. Nerve growth factor enhances expression of neuron-glia cell adhesion molecules in PC12 cells. *J. Cell Biol.* 102:413–19.

Fuster, J. M. 1984. The cortical substrate of memory. In *Neuropsychology of memory,* ed. L. R. Squire and N. Butters, pp. 279–86. New York: Guilford.

Gallin, E. S., ed. 1981. *Developmental plasticity: Behavioral and biological aspects of variations in development.* New York: Academic.

Gallin, W. J., E. A. Prediger, G. M. Edelman, and B. A. Cunningham. 1985. Isolation of a cDNA clone for the liver cell adhesion molecule (L-CAM). *Proc. Natl. Acad. Sci. USA* 82:2809–13.

Gallin, W. J., C. M. Chuong, L. H. Finkel, and G. M. Edelman. 1986. Antibodies to L-CAM perturb inductive interactions and alter feather pattern and structure. *Proc. Natl. Acad. Sci. USA* 83:8235–39.

Gallistel, C. R. 1980. *The organization of action: A new synthesis.* Hillsdale, N.J.: Lawrence Erlbaum Associates.

Garcia, J., D. J. Kimeldorf, and R. A. Koelling. 1955. A conditioned aversion towards saccharin resulting from exposure to gamma radiation. *Science* 122:157–59.

Garcia, J., J. Clarke, and W. G. Hankins. 1973. Natural responses to scheduled rewards. In *Perspectives in ethology,* vol. 1, ed. P. G. Bateson and P. Klopfer, pp. 1–41. New York: Plenum.

Gaze, R. M., and S. C. Sharma. 1970. Axial differences in the reinnervation of the goldfish optic tectum by regenerating optic nerve fibers. *Exp. Brain Res.* 10:171–81.

Gelfand, I. M., V. S. Gurfinkel, S. V. Fomin, and M. L. Tsetlin, eds. 1971. *Models of the structural-functional organization of certain biological systems.* Cambridge, Mass.: MIT Press.

Georgopoulos, A. P. 1986. On reaching. *Annu. Rev. Neurosci.* 9:147–70.

Georgopoulos, A. P., J. F. Kalaska, M. D. Crutcher, R. Caminiti, and J. Massey. 1984. The representation of movement direction in the motor cortex: Single cell and population studies. In *Dynamic aspects of neocortical function,* ed. G. M. Edelman, W. E. Gall, and W. M. Cowan, pp. 501–24. New York: Wiley.

Georgopoulos, A. P., A. B. Schwartz, and R. E. Kettner. 1986. Neuronal population coding of movement direction. *Science* 233:1416–19.

Getting, P. A., and M. S. Dekin. 1985. *Tritonia* swimming: A model system for integration within rhythmic motor systems. In *Model neural networks and behavior,* ed. A. I. Selverston, pp. 3–20. New York: Plenum.

Ghiselin, M. T. 1981. Categories, life and thinking. *Behav. Brain Sci.* 4:269–313.

Gibson, J. J. 1979. *The ecological approach to visual perception.* Boston: Houghton Mifflin.

Gilbert, C. D., and T. N. Wiesel. 1979. Morphology and intracortical projections of functionally characterized neurons in the cat visual cortex. *Nature* 280:120–25.

———. 1981. Laminar specializations and intracortical connections in cat primary visual cortex. In *The organization of the cerebral cortex,* ed. F. O. Schmitt, F. G. Worden, G. Adelman, and S. G. Dennis, pp. 163–91. Cambridge, Mass.: MIT Press.

Gleitman, L. R. 1984. Biological predispositions to learn language. In *The biology of learning,* ed. P. Marler and H. S. Terrace, pp. 553–84. Berlin: Springer-Verlag.

Goodman, C. S., K. G. Pearson, and W. J. Heitler. 1979. Variability of identified neurons in grasshoppers. *Comp. Biochem. Physiol.* 64A:455–62.

Gottlieb, G. 1979. Comparative psychology and ethology. In *The first century of experimental psychology,* ed. E. Hearsted, pp. 147–71. Hillsdale, N.J.: Lawrence Erlbaum Associates.

Gould, J. L. 1982. *Ethology.* New York: Norton.

Gould, J. L., and P. Marler. 1984. Ethology and the natural history of learning. In *The biology of learning,* ed. P. Marler and H. S. Terrace, pp. 47–74. Berlin: Springer-Verlag.

Gould, S. J. 1977. *Ontogeny and phylogeny.* Cambridge, Mass.: Harvard Univ. Press.

Granit, R. 1967. *Charles Scott Sherrington: An appraisal.* New York: Doubleday.

Graziadei, P. P. C., and G. A. Monti Graziadei. 1978. Continuous nerve cell renewal in the olfactory system. In *Handbook of sensory physiology,* vol. 9, ed. M. Jacobson, pp. 55–83. Berlin: Springer-Verlag.

———. 1979a. Neurogenesis and neuron regeneration in the olfactory system of mammals. I. Morphological aspects of differentiation and structural organization of the olfactory sensory neurons. *J. Neurocytol.* 8:1–18.

———. 1979b. Neurogenesis and neuron regeneration in the olfactory system of mammals. II. Degeneration and reconstitution of the olfactory sensory neurons after axotomy. *J. Neurocytol.* 8:197–213.

Graziadei, P. P. C., and D. Tucker. 1970. Vomeronasal receptors in turtles. *Z. Zellforsch. Mikrosk. Anat.* 105:498–514.

Greenberg, M. E., R. Brackenbury, and G. M. Edelman. 1984. Alteration of neural cell adhesion molecule (N-CAM) expression after neuronal cell transformation by Rous sarcoma virus. *Proc. Natl. Acad. Sci. USA* 81:969–73.

Greene, P. H. 1971. Introduction. In *Models of the structural-functional organization of certain biological systems,* ed. I. M. Gelfand, V. S. Gurfinkel, S. V. Fomin, and M. L. Tsetlin, pp. xi–xxv. Cambridge: MIT Press.

Greengard, P., and J. F. Kuo. 1970. On the mechanism of action of cyclic AMP. *Adv. Biochem. Psychopharmacol.* 3:287–306.

Griffin, D. R., ed. 1982. *Animal mind—Human mind.* Berlin: Springer-Verlag.

Grillner, S. 1975. Locomotion in vertebrates: Central mechanisms and reflex interaction. *Physiol. Rev.* 55:247–304.

———. 1977. On the neural control of movement—A comparison of basic rhythmic behaviors. In *Function and formation of neural systems,* ed. G. S. Stent, pp. 197–224. New York: Springer-Verlag.

Grillner, S., A. McClellan, K. Sigvardt, P. Wallen, and T. Williams. 1982. On the neural generation of "fictive locomotion" in a lower vertebrate nervous system *in vitro.* In *Brain stem control of spinal mechanisms,* ed. B. Sjölund and A. Björklund, pp. 273–95. Amsterdam: Elsevier.

Grumet, M., and G. M. Edelman. 1984. Heterotypic binding between neuronal membrane vesicles and glial cells is mediated by a specific neuron-glia cell adhesion molecule. *J. Cell Biol.* 98:1746–56.

Grumet, M., S. Hoffman, C.-M. Chuong, and G. M. Edelman. 1984. Polypeptide components and binding functions of neuron-glia cell adhesion molecules. *Proc. Natl. Acad. Sci. USA* 81:7989–93.

Grumet, M., S. Hoffman, K. L. Crossin, and G. M. Edelman. 1985. Cytotactin, an extracellular matrix protein of neural and non-neural tissues that mediates glia-neuron interaction. *Proc. Natl. Acad. Sci. USA* 82:8075–79.

Haas, H. L., and A. Konnerth. 1983. Histamine and noradrenaline decrease calcium-activated potassium conductance in hippocampal pyramidal cells. *Nature* 302:432–34.

Hall, W. C., and F. T. Ebner. 1970a. Parallels in the visual afferent projection of the thalamus in the hedgehog *(Parechinus hypomelas)* and the turtle *(Pseudemys scripta).* *Brain Behav. Evol.* 3:135–54.

———. 1970b. Thalamo-telencephalic projections in the turtle *(Pseudemys scripta).* *J. Comp. Neurol.* 140:101–22.

Halpern, M. 1976. The efferent connections of the olfactory bulb and accessory olfactory bulb in the snake *Thamnophis sirtalis* and *Thamnophis radix. J. Morphol.* 150:553–78.

Hamburger, V. 1963. Some aspects of the embryology of behavior. *Q. Rev. Biol.* 38:342–65.

———. 1968. Emergence of nervous coordination: Origins of integrated behavior. *Dev. Biol.* (Suppl.) 2:251–71.

———. 1970. Embryonic motility in vertebrates. In *The neurosciences: Second study program,* ed. F. O. Schmitt, pp. 141–51. New York: Rockefeller Univ. Press.

———. 1975. Cell death in the development of the lateral motor column of the chick embryo. *J. Comp. Neurol.* 160:535–46.

————. 1980. S. Ramón y Cajal, R. G. Harrison and the beginnings of neuroembryology. *Perspect. Biol. Med.* 23:600–16.

Harris, P. 1983. Infant cognition. In *Handbook of child psychology: Infancy and developmental psychobiology,* 4th ed., vol. 2, ed. P. Mussen and M. Haith, pp. 689–782. New York: Wiley.

Harrison, L. G. 1982. An overview of kinetic theory in developmental modeling. In *Developmental order,* ed. S. Subtelny and P. P. Green, pp. 3–33. New York: Alan R. Liss.

Harrison, R. G. 1935. On the origin and development of the nervous system studied by the methods of experimental embryology. *Proc. R. Soc. Lond. [Biol.]* 118:155–96.

Hatta, K., T. S. Okada, and M. Takeichi. 1985. A monoclonal antibody disrupting calcium-dependent cell-cell adhesion of brain tissues: Possible role of its target antigen in animal pattern formation. *Proc. Natl. Acad. Sci. USA* 82:2789–93.

Hawkins, R. D., T. W. Abrams, T. J. Carew, and E. R. Kandel. 1983. A cellular mechanism of classical conditioning in *Aplysia*—Activity-dependent amplification of pre-synaptic facilitation. *Science* 219:400–405.

Hayek, F. A. 1952. *The sensory order: An inquiry into the foundations of theoretical psychology.* Chicago: Univ. Chicago Press. (Midway Reprint, 1976.)

Head, H. 1920. *Studies in neurology.* Vol. 2. London: Hodder & Stoughton.

Hearst, E., and H. M. Jenkins. 1974. *Sign-tracking: The stimulus-reinforcer relation and directed action,* Psychonomic Monograph Series. Austin, Tex.: Psychonomic Society.

Hebb, D. O. 1949. *The organization of behavior: A neuropsychological theory.* New York: Wiley.

————. 1980. *Essay on mind.* Hillsdale, N.J.: Lawrence Erlbaum Associates.

————. 1982. Elaborations on Hebb cell assembly theory. In *Neuropsychology after Lashley,* ed. J. Orbach, pp. 483–96. Hillsdale, N.J.: Lawrence Erlbaum Associates.

Held, H. 1897a. Beiträge zur Structur der Nervenzellen und ihrer Fortsätze. Zweite Abhandlung. *Arch. Anat. Physiol., Anat. Abt.,* pp. 204–94.

————. 1897b. Beiträge zur Struktur der Nervenzellen und ihrer Fortsätze. Dritte Abhandlung. *Arch. Anat. Physiol., Anat. Abt.* (Suppl.), pp. 273–312.

Held, R. 1961. Exposure-history as a factor in maintaining stability of perception and coordination. *J. New Ment. Dis.* 132:26–32.

————. 1965. Plasticity in sensory motor systems. *Sci. Am.* 213(5):84–94.

Hemperly, J. J., G. M. Edelman, and B. A. Cunningham. 1986a. cDNA clones of the neural cell adhesion molecule (N-CAM) lacking a membrane-spanning region consistent with evidence for membrane attachment via a phosphatidylinositol intermediate. *Proc. Natl. Acad. Sci. USA* 83:9822–26.

Hemperly, J. J., B. A. Murray, G. M. Edelman, and B. A. Cunningham. 1986b. Sequence of a cDNA clone encoding the polysialic acid-rich and cytoplasmic domains of the neural cell adhesion molecule N-CAM. *Proc. Natl. Acad. Sci. USA* 83:3037–41.

Herrnstein, R. J. 1979. Acquisition, generalization, and discrimination of a natural concept. *J. Exp. Psychol. Animal Behav. Processes* 5:116–29.

————. 1982. Stimuli and the texture of experience. *Neurosci. Biobehav. Rev.* 6:105–17.

————. 1985. Riddles of natural categorization. *Philos. Trans. R. Soc. Lond. [Biol.]* 308: 129–44.

Herrnstein, R. J., and P. A. de Villiers. 1980. Fish as a natural category for people and pigeons. In *The psychology of learning and motivation,* vol. 14, ed. G. H. Bower, pp. 59–95. New York: Academic.

Herrnstein, R. J., and D. Loveland. 1964. Complex visual concept in the pigeon. *Science* 46:549–51.

Herrnstein, R. J., D. Loveland, and C. Cable. 1976. Natural concepts in pigeons. *J. Exp. Psychol. Animal Behav. Processes* 2:285–301.

Hinchliffe, J. R., and D. R. Johnson, eds. 1980. *The development of the vertebrate limb.* Oxford: Clarendon.

Hodgkin, A. L., and A. F. Huxley. 1952. A quantitative description of membrane current and its application to conduction and excitation in nerve. *J. Physiol. (Lond.)* 117:500–44.

Hoffman, S., and G. M. Edelman. 1983. Kinetics of homophilic binding by E and A forms of the neural cell adhesion molecule. *Proc. Natl. Acad. Sci. USA* 80:5762–66.

Hoffman, S., B. C. Sorkin, P. C. White, R. Brackenbury, R. Mailhammer, U. Rutishauser,

B. A. Cunningham, and G. M. Edelman. 1982. Chemical characterization of a neural cell adhesion molecule purified from embryonic brain membranes. *J. Biol. Chem.* 257:7720–29.

Hoffman, S., C.-M. Chuong, and G. M. Edelman. 1984. Evolutionary conservation of key structures and binding functions of neural cell adhesion molecules. *Proc. Natl. Acad. Sci. USA* 81:6881–85.

Hoffman, S., D. R. Friedlander, C.-M. Chuong, M. Grumet, and G. M. Edelman. 1986. Differential contributions of Ng-CAM and N-CAM to cell adhesion in different neural regions. *J. Cell. Biol.* 103:145–58.

Holtfreter, J. 1939. Gewebeaffinität, ein Mittel der embryonalen Formbildung. *Arch. Exp. Zellforsch.* 23:169–209.

———. 1948. Significance of the cell membrane in embryonic processes. *Ann. N.Y. Acad. Sci.* 49:709–60.

Horridge, G. A. 1968. *Interneurons: Their origins, action, specificity, growth, and plasticity.* London: Freeman.

Huang, L.-Y. M., N. Moran, and G. Ehrenstein. 1982. Batrachotoxin modifies the gating kinetics of sodium channels in internally perfused neuroblastoma cells. *Proc. Natl. Acad. Sci. USA* 79:2082–85.

Hubel, D. H., and T. N. Wiesel. 1970. The period of susceptibility to the physiological effects of unilateral eye closure in kittens. *J. Physiol. (Lond).* 206:419–36.

———. 1977. Functional architecture of macaque monkey visual cortex. *Proc. R. Soc. Lond. [Biol.]* 198:1–59.

Huganir, R. L., A. H. Delacour, P. Greengard, and G. P. Hess. 1986. Phosphorylation of the nicotinic acetylcholine receptor regulates its rate of desensitization. *Nature* 321: 774–76.

Hull, C. L. 1943. *Principles of behavior.* New York: Appleton-Century-Crofts.

———. 1952. *A behavior system.* New Haven: Yale Univ. Press.

Immelmann, K. 1984. The natural history of bird learning. In *The biology of learning,* ed. P. Marler and H. S. Terrace, pp. 271–88. New York: Springer-Verlag.

Ingram, V. M., M. P. Ogren, C. L. Chalot, J. M. Gasselo, and B. B. Owens. 1985. Diversity among Purkinje cells in the monkey cerebellum. *Proc. Natl. Acad. Sci. USA* 82:7131–35.

Isaacson, R. L., and K. H. Pribram, eds. 1975. *The hippocampus.* Vol. 2, *Neurophysiology and behavior.* New York: Plenum.

Ito, M. 1984. *The cerebellum and neural control.* New York: Raven.

Ito, M., M. Sakurai, and P. Tongroach. 1982. Climbing fiber-induced depression of both mossy fiber responsiveness and glutamate sensitivity of cerebellar Purkinje cells. *J. Physiol. (Lond.)* 324:113–34.

Jackson, J. H. 1931. *Selected writings of John Hughlings Jackson,* ed. J. Taylor. London: Hodder & Stoughton.

Jacobson, A. G. 1966. Inductive processes in embryonic development. *Science* 152:25–35.

James, W. 1950. *The principles of psychology.* New York: Dover (authorized edition based on the original publication by Harry Holt in 1890, two volumes).

Jeannerod, M. 1985. *The brain machine: The development of neurophysiological thought.* Cambridge, Mass.: Harvard Univ. Press.

Jenkins, H. M. 1979. Animal learning and behavior theory. In *The first century of experimental psychology,* ed. E. Hearst, pp. 177–228, Hillsdale, N.J.: Lawrence Erlbaum Associates.

———. 1984. The study of animal learning in the tradition of Pavlov and Thorndike. In *The biology of learning,* ed. P. Marler and H. S. Terrace, pp. 89–114. Berlin: Springer-Verlag.

Jerne, N. K. 1967. Antibodies and learning: Selection versus instruction. In *The neurosciences: A study program,* ed. G. C. Quarton, T. Melnechuk, and F. O. Schmitt, pp. 200–5. New York: Rockefeller Univ. Press.

John, E. R., Y. Tang, A. B. Brill, R. Young, and K. Ono. 1986. Double-labeled metabolic maps of memory. *Science* 233:1167–75.

Johnson, M., D. M. Ross, M. Myers, R. Rees, R. Bruge, E. Wakshall, and H. Burton. 1976. Synaptic vesicle cytochemistry changes when cultured sympathetic neurons develop cholinergic interactions. *Nature* 262:308–10.

Jones, E. G. 1975. Varieties and distribution of non-pyramidal cells in the somatic sensory cortex of the squirrel monkey. *J. Comp. Neurol.* 160:205–68.

———. 1981. Anatomy of cerebral cortex: Columnar input-output organization. In *The organization of the cerebral cortex*, ed. F. O. Schmitt, F. G. Worden, G. Adelman, and S. G. Dennis, pp. 199–236. Cambridge, Mass.: MIT Press.

Jones, E. G., H. Burton, and R. Porter. 1975. Commissural and cortico-cortical "columns" in the somatic sensory cortex of primates. *Science* 190:572–74.

Julesz, B. 1984. Toward an axiomatic theory of preattentive vision. In *Dynamic aspects of neocortical function*, ed. G. M. Edelman, W. E. Gall, and W. M. Cowan, pp. 585–612. New York: Wiley.

Jusczyk, P. W. 1981. The processing of speech and non-speech sounds by infants: Some implications. In *Development of perception*, vol. 1, ed. R. N. Aslin, J. R. Alberts and M. R. Petersen, pp. 192–215. New York: Academic.

Jusczyk, P. W., and R. M. Klein, eds. 1980. *The nature of thought: Essays in honor of D. O. Hebb.* Hillsdale, N.J.: Lawrence Erlbaum Associates.

Jusczyk, P. W., B. S. Rosner, J. E. Cutting, C. F. Foard, and L. B. Smith. 1977. Categorical perception of nonspeech sounds by 2-month-old infants. *Percept. Psychophys.* 21:50–54.

Jusczyk, P. W., D. B. Pisoni, A. Walley, and J. Murray. 1980. Discrimination of relative onset time of two-component tones by infants. *J. Acoust. Soc. Am.* 67:262–70.

Jusczyk, P. W., D. B. Pisoni, M. A. Reed, A. Fernald, and M. Myers. 1983. Infants' discrimination of the duration of a rapid spectrum change in nonspeech signals. *Science* 222:175–77.

Kaas, J. H., M. M. Merzenich, and H. P. Killackey. 1983. The reorganization of somatosensory cortex following peripheral-nerve damage in adult and developing mammals. *Annu. Rev. Neurosci.* 6:325–56.

Kamin, L. J. 1969. Selective attention and conditioning. In *Associative learning*, ed. N. J. Mackintosh and W. K. Horing, pp. 42–64. Halifax: Dalhousie Univ. Press.

Kandel, E. R. 1976. *Cellular basis of behavior.* San Francisco: Freeman.

———. 1981. Calcium and the control of synaptic strength by learning. *Nature* 293:697–700.

Kellman, P. J., and E. S. Spelke. 1983. Perception of partly occluded objects in infancy. *Cognit. Psychol.* 15:483–524.

Kelso, J. A. S., and B. Tuller. 1984. A dynamical basis for action systems. In *Handbook of cognitive neuroscience*, ed. M. S. Gazzaniga, pp. 321–56. New York: Plenum.

Koch, C., T. Poggio, and V. Torre. 1983. Nonlinear interactions in a dendritic tree: Localization, timing, and role in information processing. *Proc. Natl. Acad. Sci. USA* 80:2799–2802.

Kohonen, T. 1977. *Associative memory: A system-theoretical approach.* Berlin: Springer-Verlag.

Konishi, M. 1978. Auditory environment and vocal development in birds. In *Perception and experience*, ed. R. D. Walk and H. L. Pick, Jr., pp. 105–18. New York: Plenum.

———. 1984. A logical basis for single neuron study of learning in complex neural systems. In *The biology of learning*, ed. P. Marler and H. Terrace, pp. 311–24. Berlin: Springer-Verlag.

Korneliusen, H., and J. K. S. Jansen. 1976. Morphological aspects of polyneuronal innervation of skeletal muscle fibres in newborn rats. *J. Neurocytol.* 5:591–604.

Kosar, E., and P. J. Hand. 1981. First somatosensory cortical columns and associated neuronal clusters of nucleus ventralis posterolateralis of the cat: An anatomical demonstration. *J. Comp. Neurol.* 198:515–39.

Kramer, A. P., and G. S. Stent. 1985. Developmental arborization of sensory neurons in the leech *Haementeria ghilianii.* II. Experimentally induced variations in the branching pattern. *J. Neurosci.* 5:768–75.

Kramer, A. P., J. R. Goldman, and G. S. Stent. 1985. Developmental arborization of sensory neurons in the leech *Haementeria ghilianii.* I. Origin of natural variations in the branching pattern. *J. Neurosci.* 5:759–67.

Kubovy, M., and J. R. Pomerantz. 1981. *Perceptual organization.* Hillsdale, N.J.: Lawrence Erlbaum Associates.

Kuhl, P. K., and J. D. Miller. 1975. Speech perception in the chinchilla: Voice-voiceless distribution in alveolar plosive consonants. *Science* 190:69–72.

———. 1978. Speech perception by the chinchilla: Identification function for synthetic VOT stimuli. *J. Acoust. Soc. Am.* 63:905–17.

Kupfermann, I. 1979. Modulatory actions of neurotransmitters. *Annu. Rev. Neurosci.* 2:447–65.

Lamport, L. 1978. Time, clocks, and the ordering of events in a distributed system. *Commun. ACM* 21:558–65.

Landry, P., and M. Deschênes. 1981. Intracortical arborizations and receptive fields of identified ventrobasal thalamocortical afferents to the primary somatic sensory cortex in the cat. *J. Comp. Neurol.* 199:345–71.

Landry, P., J. Villemure, and M. Deschênes. 1982. Geometry and orientation of thalamocortical arborizations in the cat somatosensory cortex as revealed by computer reconstruction. *Brain Res.* 237:222–26.

Lashley, K. S. 1950. In search of the engram. *Symp. Soc. Exp. Biol.* 4:454–82.

Laskin, S. E., and W. A. Spencer. 1979. Cutaneous masking. II. Geometry of excitatory and inhibitory receptive fields of single units in somatosensory cortex of the cat. *J. Neurophysiol.* 42:1061–82.

Le Douarin, N. M. 1982. *The neural crest.* Cambridge, England: Cambridge Univ. Press.

Lee, K. J., and T. A. Woolsey. 1975. A proportional relationship between peripheral innervation density and cortical neuron number in the somatosensory system of the mouse. *Brain Res.* 99:349–53.

Lewontin, R. 1968. *Population biology and evolution.* Syracuse: Syracuse Univ. Press.

Leyton, A. S. F., and C. S. Sherrington. 1917. Observations on the excitable cortex of the chimpanzee, orangutan, and gorilla. *Q. J. Exp. Physiol.* 11:135–222.

Liberman, A. M., and M. Studdert-Kennedy. 1978. Phonetic perception. In *Handbook of sensory physiology,* vol. 8, *Perception,* ed. R. Held, H. W. Leibowitz, and H. L. Teuber, pp. 143–78. New York: Springer-Verlag.

Liberman, A. M., I. G. Mattingly, and M. T. Turvey. 1972. Language codes and memory codes. In *Coding processes in human memory,* ed. A. W. Melton and E. Martin, pp. 307–34. Washington, D.C.: Winston & Sons.

Liem, K. F. 1974. Evolutionary strategies and morphological innervations: Cichlid pharyngeal jaws. *Syst. Zool.* 22:425–41.

Lindner, J., F. G. Rathjen, and M. Schachner. 1983. Monoclonal and polyclonal antibodies modify cell-migration in early postnatal mouse cerebellum. *Nature* 305:427–30.

Llinás, R., I. Z. Steinberg, and K. Walton. 1976. Presynaptic calcium currents and their relation to synaptic transmission: Voltage clamp study in squid giant synapse and theoretical model for the calcium gate. *Proc. Natl. Acad. Sci. USA* 73:2918–22.

Locurto, C., H. S. Terrace, and J. Gibbons, eds. 1981. *Autoshaping and conditioning theory.* New York: Academic.

Lorente de Nó, R. 1938. Cerebral cortex: Architecture, intracortical connections, motor projections. In *Physiology of the nervous system,* ed. J. F. Fulton, pp. 291–339. New York: Oxford Univ. Press.

Lumsden, C. 1983. Neuronal group selection and the evolution of hominid cranial capacity. *J. Hum. Evol.* 12:169–84.

Lynch, G. S., and M. Baudry. 1984. The biochemistry of memory: A new and specific hypothesis. *Science* 224:1057–63.

Lynch, G. S., V. K. Gribkoff, and S. A. Deadwyler. 1976. Long-term potentiation is accompanied by a reduction in dendritic responsiveness to glutamic acid. *Nature* 263:151–53.

Lynch, G. S., R. Dunwiddie, and V. Gribkoff. 1977. Heterosynaptic depression: A postsynaptic correlate of long-term potentiation. *Nature* 266:737–39.

Lynch, G. S., S. Halpain, and M. Baudry. 1982. Effects of high-frequency synaptic stimulation on glutamate receptor binding studied with a modified *in vitro* hippocampal slice preparation. *Brain Res.* 244:101–11.

Lythgoe, J. N. 1979. *The ecology of vision.* Oxford: Clarendon.

Macagno, E. R., V. Lopresti, and C. Levinthal. 1973. Structure and development of neuronal connections in isogenic organisms: Variations and similarities in the optic system of *Daphnia magna. Proc. Natl. Acad. Sci. USA* 70:57–61.

MacArthur, R., and E. O. Wilson. 1967. *The theory of island biogeography.* Princeton: Princeton Univ. Press.

MacKay, D. M. 1970. Perception and brain function. In *The neurosciences: Second study program,* ed. F. O. Schmitt, pp. 303–16. New York: Rockefeller Univ. Press.

Mackintosh, N. J. 1983. *Conditioning and associative learning.* Oxford: Clarendon.

Macmillan, N. A., H. L. Kaplan, and C. D. Creelman. 1977. The psychophysics of categorical perception. *Psychol. Rev.* 84:452–71.

MacPhail, E. M. 1982. *Brain and intelligence in vertebrates.* Oxford: Clarendon.

Magleby, K. L., and J. E. Zengel. 1982. Quantitative description of stimulation-induced changes in transmitter release at the frog neuromuscular junction. *J. Gen. Physiol.* 80:613–38.

Marder, E. E., S. L. Hooper, and J. S. Eisen. 1987. Multiple neurotransmitters provide a mechanism for the production of multiple outputs from a single neuronal circuit. In *Synaptic function,* ed. G. M. Edelman, W. E. Gall, and W. M. Cowan, pp. 305–27. New York: Wiley.

Marler, P. 1982. Avian and primate communication: The problem of natural categories. *Neurosci. Biobehav. Rev.* 6:87–94.

———. 1984. Song learning: Innate species differences in the learning process. In *The biology of learning,* ed. P. Marler and H. S. Terrace, pp. 289–309. Berlin: Springer-Verlag.

Marler, P., and H. S. Terrace, eds. 1984. *The biology of learning.* Berlin: Springer-Verlag.

Marler, P., S. Zoloth, and R. Dooling. 1981. Innate programs for perceptual development: An ethological view. In *Developmental plasticity: Behavioral and biological aspects of variations in development,* ed. Eugene S. Gallin, pp. 135–72. New York: Academic.

Marr, D. 1969. A theory of cerebellar cortex. *J. Physiol. (Lond.)* 202:437–70.

———. 1982. *Vision: A computational investigation into the human representation and processing of visual information.* San Francisco: Freeman.

Mason, W. A. 1968. Early social deprivation in the non-human primates: Implications for human behavior. In *Environmental influences,* ed. D. C. Glass, pp. 70–100. New York: Rockefeller Univ. Press.

Masterton, R. B., M. E. Bitterman, C. B. G. Campbell, and N. Hotton, eds. 1976a. *Evolution of brain and behavior in vertebrates.* Hillsdale, N.J.: Lawrence Erlbaum Associates.

Masterton, R. B., W. Hodos, and H. Jerison. 1976b. *Evolution, brain and behavior: Persistent problems.* Hillsdale, N.J.: Lawrence Erlbaum Associates.

Matthews, P. C. 1982. Where does Sherrington's "muscular sense" originate? Muscles, joints, corollary discharges? *Annu. Rev. Neurosci.* 5:189–218.

Mattingly, I. G., and A. M. Liberman. 1987. Specialized perceiving systems for speech and other biologically significant sounds. In *Functions of the auditory system,* ed. G. M. Edelman, W. E. Gall, and W. M. Cowan. New York: Wiley (in press).

Maunsell, J. H. R., and D. C. Van Essen. 1983. The connections of the middle temporal visual area (MT) and their relationship to a cortical hierarchy in the macaque monkey. *J. Neurosci.* 3:2563–86.

Mayr, E. 1982. *The growth of biological thought: Diversity, evolution, and inheritance.* Cambridge: Harvard Univ. Press.

McCormmach, R. 1982. *Night thoughts of a classical physicist.* Cambridge: Harvard Univ. Press.

McGurk, H. 1972. Infant discrimination of orientation. *J. Exp. Child Psychol.* 14:151–64.

McGurk, H., and J. MacDonald. 1976. Hearing lips and seeing voices. *Nature* 264:746–48.

Merzenich, M. M., J. H. Kaas, J. T. Wall, R. J. Nelson, M. Sur, and D. J. Felleman. 1983a. Topographic reorganization of somatosensory cortical areas 3b and 1 in adult monkeys following restricted deafferentation. *Neuroscience* 8:33–55.

———. 1983b. Progression of change following median nerve section in the cortical representation of the hand in areas 3b and 1 in adult owl and squirrel monkeys. *Neuroscience* 10:639–65.

Merzenich, M. M., W. M. Jenkins, and J. C. Middlebrooks. 1984a. Observations and hypotheses on special organizational features of the central auditory nervous system. In *Dynamic aspects of neocortical function,* ed. G. M. Edelman, W. E. Gall, and W. M. Cowan, pp. 397–424. New York: Wiley.

Merzenich, M. M., R. J. Nelson, M. P. Stryker, M. Cynader, A. Schoppman, and J. M. Zook. 1984b. Somatosensory cortical map changes following digit amputation in adult monkeys. *J. Comp. Neurol.* 224:591–605.

Messer, A. 1980. Cerebellar granule cells in normal and neurological mutants of mice. *Adv. Cell. Neurobiol.* 1:179–85.

Messer, A., and D. M. Smith. 1977. *In vitro* behavior of granule cells from *staggerer* and *weaver* mutants of mice. *Brain Res.* 130:13–23.

Meyer, R. L. 1980. Mapping the normal and regenerating retino-tectal projection of goldfish with autoradiographic methods. *J. Comp. Neurol.* 189:273–89.

Middlebrooks, J. C., and J. M. Zook. 1983. Intrinsic organization of the cats' medial geniculate body identified by projections to binaural response—Specific bands in the primary auditory cortex. *J. Neurosci.* 3:203–24.

Miller, C. L., B. A. Younger, and P. A. Morse. 1982. The categorization of male and female voices in infancy. *Infant Behav. & Dev.* 5:144–59.

Mills, C. W. 1898. *The nature and development of animal intelligence.* London: T. Fisher Unwin.

Milner, B. 1985. Memory and the human brain. In *How we know: The inner frontiers of cognitive science*, Proceedings of Nobel Conference XX, ed. M. Shafto, pp. 31–59. San Francisco: Harper & Row.

Minsky, M., and S. Papert. 1969. *Perceptrons: An introduction to computational geometry.* Cambridge, England: MIT Press.

Mishkin, M. 1982. A memory system in the monkey. *Philos. Trans. R. Soc. Lond.* [*Biol.*] 298:85–95.

Mishkin, M., B. Malamut, J. Bachevalier. 1984. Memories and habits: Two neural systems. In *Neurobiology of learning and memory*, ed. G. S. Lynch, J. L. McGough, N. M. Weinberger, pp. 65–77. New York: Guilford.

Mobbs, C. V., and D. W. Pfaff. 1987. Estradiol-regulated neuronal plasticity. *Curr. Top. Membr. Trans.* 31 (in press).

Moonen, G., E. A. Neale, R. L. MacDonald, W. Gibbs, and P. G. Nelson. 1982. Cerebellar macroneurons in microexplant cell culture: Methodology, basic electrophysiology, and morphology after horseradish peroxidase injection. *Dev. Brain Res.* 5:59–73.

Morgan, C. L. 1896. *Habit and instinct.* London: Edward Arnold.

———. 1899. *Introduction to comparative psychology.* London: Walter Scott.

———. 1930. *The animal mind.* London: Edward Arnold.

Motter, B. C., M. A. Steinmetz, C. J. Duffy, and V. B. Mountcastle. 1987. The functional properties of parietal visual neurons: The mechanisms of directionality along a single axis. *J. Neurosci.* 7:154–76.

Mountcastle, V. B. 1978. An organizing principle for cerebral function: The unit module and the distributed system. In *The mindful brain: Cortical organization and the group-selective theory of higher brain function*, by G. M. Edelman and V. B. Mountcastle, pp. 7–50. Cambridge: MIT Press.

Mountcastle, V. B., J. C. Lynch, A. Georgopoulos, H. Sakata, and A. Acuna. 1975. Posterior parietal association cortex of the monkey: Command functions for operations within extra-personal space. *J. Neurophysiol.* 38:871–908.

Mountcastle, V. B., B. C. Motter, M. A. Steinmetz, and C. J. Duffy. 1984. Looking and seeing: The visual functions of the parietal lobe. In *Dynamic aspects of neocortical function*, ed. G. M. Edelman, W. E. Gall, and W. M. Cowan, pp. 159–93. New York: Wiley.

Murdock, B. B., Jr. 1979. Convolution and correlation in perception and memory. In *Perspectives in memory research*, ed. L.-G. Nilsson, pp. 105–19. Hillsdale, N.J.: Lawrence Erlbaum Associates.

Murray, B. A., J. J. Hemperly, W. J. Gallin, J. S. MacGregor, G. M. Edelman, and B. A. Cunningham. 1984. Isolation of cDNA clones for the chicken neural cell adhesion molecule (N-CAM). *Proc. Natl. Acad. Sci. USA* 81:5584–88.

Murray, B. A., J. J. Hemperly, E. A. Prediger, G. M. Edelman, and B. A. Cunningham. 1986a. Alternatively spliced mRNAs code for different polypeptide chains of the chicken neural cell adhesion molecule (N-CAM). *J. Cell Biol.* 102:189–93.

Murray, B. A., G. C. Owens, E. A. Prediger, K. L. Crossin, B. A. Cunningham, and G. M. Edelman. 1986b. Cell surface modulation of the neural cell adhesion molecule resulting from alternative mRNA splicing in a tissue-specific developmental sequence. *J. Cell Biol.* 103:1431–39.

Neale, E. A., G. Moonen, R. L. MacDonald, and P. G. Nelson. 1982. Cerebellar macroneurons in microexplant cell culture: Ultrastructural morphology. *Neuroscience* 7:1879–90.

Neisser, U. 1967. *Cognitive psychology.* New York: Appleton-Century-Crofts.

——. 1982. *Memory observed: Remembering in natural contexts.* San Francisco: Freeman.

Nguyen, C., M.-G. Mattei, J.-F. Mattei, M.-J. Santoni, C. Goridis, and B. R. Jordan. 1986. Localization of the human N-CAM gene to band q23 of chromosome 11: The third gene coding for a cell interaction molecule mapped to the distal portion of the long arm of chromosome 11. *J. Cell Biol.* 102:711–15.

Nieuwkoop, P. D., A. G. Johnen, and B. Albers. 1985. *The epigenetic nature of early chordate development.* Cambridge, England: Cambridge Univ. Press.

Nilsson, L.-G. 1979. *Perspectives on memory research: Essays in honor of Uppsala University's 500th anniversary.* Hillsdale, N.J.: Lawrence Erlbaum Associates.

Norman, D. A. 1969. *Memory and attention.* New York: Wiley.

——. 1981. Twelve issues for cognitive science. In *Perspectives on cognitive science,* ed. D. A. Norman, pp. 265–95. Hillsdale, N.J.: Lawrence Erlbaum Associates.

Northcutt, R. G. 1981. Evolution of the telencephalon in non-mammals. *Annu. Rev. Neurosci.* 4:301–50.

Nottebohm, F. 1980. Testosterone triggers growth of brain vocal control nuclei in adult female canaries. *Brain Res.* 189:429–36.

——. 1981a. A brain for all seasons: Cyclical anatomical changes in song control nuclei of the canary brain. *Science* 214:1368–70.

——. 1981b. Brain pathways for vocal learning in birds: A review of the first 10 years. In *Progress in psychobiology and physiological psychology,* ed. J. M. S. Sprague and A. N. E. Epstein, vol. 9, pp. 85–124. New York: Academic.

Oakley, D. A. 1979. Learning with food reward and shock avoidance in neodecorticate rats. *Exp. Neurol.* 63:627–42.

——. 1980. Improved instrumental learning in neodecorticate rats. *Physiol. Behav.* 24:357–66.

Obrink, B. 1986. Epithelial cell adhesion molecules. *Exp. Cell Res.* 163:1–21.

O'Keefe, J., and L. Nadel. 1978. *The hippocampus as a cognitive map.* Oxford: Clarendon.

Oldfield, R. C., and O. L. Zangwill. 1942a. Head's concept of the schema and its application in contemporary British psychology. I. Head's concept of the schema. *Br. J. Psychol.* 32:267–86.

——. 1942b. Head's concept of the schema and its application in contemporary British psychology. II. Critical analysis of Head's theory. *Br. J. Psychol.* 33:58–64.

——. 1942c. Head's concept of the schema and its application in contemporary British psychology. III. Bartletts' theory of memory. *Br. J. Psychol.* 33:111–29.

——. 1943. Head's concept of the schema and its application in contemporary British psychology. IV. Walter's theory of thinking. *Br. J. Psychol.* 33:143–49.

Orbach, J. 1982. *Neuropsychology after Lashley.* Hillsdale, N.J.: Lawrence Erlbaum Associates.

Osse, J. W. M. 1969. Functional morphology of the head of the perch *(Perca fluviatilis):* An electromyographic study. *J. Zool.* 19:289–392.

Owings, D. W., and S. C. Owings. 1979. Snake-directed behavior by black-tailed prairie dogs *(Cynomys indovicianus).* Z. *Tierpsychol.* 49:35–54.

Oxnard, C. E. 1968. The architecture of the shoulder in some mammals. *J. Morphol.* 126:249–90.

Palmer, L. A., A. C. Rosenquist, and R. J. Tusa. 1978. The retinotopic organization of lateral suprasylvian visual areas in the cat. *J. Comp. Neurol.* 177:237–56.

Pantin, C. F. A. 1968. *The relations between the sciences.* Cambridge, England: Cambridge Univ. Press.

Pasternak, J. F., and T. A. Woolsey. 1975. The number, size, and spatial distribution of neurons in lamina IV of the mouse SmI neocortex. *J. Comp. Neurol.* 160:291–306.

Patterson, P. H., and L. L. Y. Chun. 1974. Influence of non-neuronal cells on catecholamine and acetylcholine synthesis and accumulation in cultures of dissociated sympathetic neurons. *Proc. Natl. Acad. Sci. USA* 71:3607–10.

Peacock, J. H., D. F. Rush, and L. H. Mathers. 1979. Morphology of dissociated hippocampal cultures from fetal mice. *Brain Res.* 169:231–46.

Pearson, J. C., L. H. Finkel, and G. M. Edelman. 1987. Plasticity in the organization of adult cortical maps: A computer model based on neuronal group selection. *J. Neurosci.* (submitted).

Pearson, K. G., and C. S. Goodman. 1979. Correlation of variability in structure with variability in synaptic connections of an identified interneuron in locusts. *J. Comp. Neurol.* 184:141–65.

Pfaff, D. W., and C. V. Mobbs. 1987. Some concepts deriving from the neural circuit for a hormone-driven mammalian reproductive behavior. *Symp. Int. Union Physiol. Sci.* (in press).

Phillips, C. G., S. Zeki, and H. B. Barlow. 1984. Localization of function in the cerebral cortex—Past, present, and future. *Brain* 107:328–61.

Pierce, J. R. 1961. *Symbols, signals and noise: The nature and process of communication.* New York: Harper & Row.

Pitcher, G., ed. 1968. *Wittgenstein: The philosophical investigations.* London: Macmillan.

Pons, T., M. Sur, and J. H. Kaas. 1982. Axonal arborizations in area 3b of somatosensory cortex in the owl monkey, *Aotus trivirgatus. Anat. Rec.* 202:151A.

Poole, J., and D. Lander. 1971. The pigeon's concept of pigeon. *Psychonom. Sci.* 25:153–58.

Popper, K. R., and J. C. Eccles. 1981. *The self and its brain.* Berlin: Springer-Verlag.

Prestige, M. C. 1970. Differentiation, degeneration, and the role of the periphery: Quantitative considerations. *The neurosciences: 2nd study program,* ed. F. O. Schmitt, pp. 73–82. New York: Rockefeller Univ. Press.

Preyer, W. 1885. *Specielle Physiologie des Embryo: Untersuchungen über die Lebenserscheinungen vor der Geburt.* Leipzig: Grieben's Verlag.

Purves, D. 1980. Neuronal competition. *Nature* 287:585–86.

———. 1983. Modulation of neuronal competition by postsynaptic geometry in autonomic ganglia. *Trends Neurosci.* 6:10–16.

Purves, D., and J. W. Lichtman. 1983. Specific connections between nerve cells. *Annu. Rev. Physiol.* 45:553–65.

———. 1985. *Principles of neural development.* Sunderland, Mass.: Sinauer Associates.

Quine, W. V. 1969. Natural kinds. In *Ontological relativity and other essays,* pp. 114–38. New York: Columbia Univ. Press.

Raff, R. A., and T. C. Kaufman. 1983. *Embryos, genes and evolution.* New York: Macmillan.

Rakic, P. 1971a. Guidance of neurons migrating to the fetal monkey neocortex. *Brain Res.* 33:471–76.

———. 1971b. Neuron-glia relationship during granule cell migration in developing cerebellar cortex: A Golgi and electron microscopic study in macaque rhesus. *J. Comp. Neurol.* 141:283–312.

———. 1972a. Mode of cell migration to the superficial layers of fetal monkey neocortex. *J. Comp. Neurol.* 145:61–84.

———. 1972b. Extrinsic cytological determinants of basket and stellate cell dendritic pattern in the cerebellar molecular layer. *J. Comp. Neurol.* 146:335–54.

———. 1977. Prenatal development of the visual system in rhesus monkey. *Philos. Trans. R. Soc. Lond. [Biol.]* 278:245–60.

———. 1978. Neuronal migration and contact guidance in the primate telencephalon. *Postgrad. Med. J.* 54:25–37.

———. 1981a. Neuronal-glial interaction during brain development. *Trends Neurosci.* 4:184–87.

———. 1981b. Development of visual centers in the primate brain depends on binocular competition before birth. *Science* 214:928–31.

Rakic, P., and R. L. Sidman. 1973. Sequence of developmental abnormalities leading to granule cell deficit in cerebellar cortex of *weaver* mutant mice. *J. Comp. Neurol.* 152:103–32.

Ramón y Cajal, S. 1889–1904. *Textura del sistema nervioso del hombre y de los vertebrados.* 3 vols. Madrid: Moya.

———. 1904. *Histologie du système nerveux de l'homme et des vertébrés.* Translated by L. Azoulay. 2 vols. Paris: Maloine. Reprint. Madrid: Instituto Ramón y Cajal, 1952.

———. 1929. *Etude sur la neurogenèse de quelques vertébrés.* Translated by L. Guth as *Studies on vertebrate neurogenesis.* Springfield, Ill.: Charles C. Thomas, 1960.

———. 1937. *Recollections of my life.* Translated by E. Horne Craigie. Cambridge, Mass.: MIT Press.

Reed, E. S. 1981. Can mental representations cause behavior? *Behav. Brain Sci.* 4:635–36.

Reeke, G. N., Jr., and G. M. Edelman. 1984. Selective networks and recognition automata. *Ann. N.Y. Acad. Sci.* 426:181–201.

Rescorla, R. A. 1968. Probability of shock in the presence and absence of CS in fear conditioning. *J. Comp. Physiol. Psychol.* 66:1–5.

———. 1975. Pavlovian excitatory and inhibitory conditioning. In *Handbook of learning and cognitive processes,* vol. 2, ed. W. K. Estes, pp. 7–35. Hillsdale, N.J.: Lawrence Erlbaum Associates.

———. 1976. Stimulus generalization: Some predictions from a model of Pavlovian conditioning. *J. Exp. Psychol. Animal Behav. Processes* 2:88–96.

Rescorla, R. A., and J. C. Skucy. 1969. Effect of response-independent reinforcers during extinction. *J. Comp. Physiol. Psychol.* 67:381–89.

Rescorla, R. A., and A. R. Wagner. 1972. A theory of Pavlovian conditioning: Variations in the effectiveness of reinforcement and nonreinforcement. In *Classical conditioning II,* ed. A. Black and W. R. Prokasy, pp. 64–99. New York: Appleton-Century-Crofts.

Richardson, G. P., K. L. Crossin, C.-M. Chuong, and G. M. Edelman. 1987. Expression of cell adhesion molecules during embryonic induction. III. Development of otic placode. *Dev. Biol.* 119:217–230.

Rieger, F., M. Grumet, and G. M. Edelman. 1985. N-CAM at the vertebrate neuromuscular junction. *J. Cell Biol.* 101:285–93.

Rieger, F., J. K. Daniloff, M. Pincon-Raymond, K. L. Crossin, M. Grumet, and G. M. Edelman. 1986. Neuronal cell adhesion molecules and cytotactin are colocalized at the node of Ranvier. *J. Cell Biol.* 103:379–91.

Rockel, A. J., R. W. Hiorns, and T. P. S. Powell. 1980. The basic uniformity in structure of the neocortex. *Brain* 103:221–44.

Roland, P. E. 1978. Sensory feedback to the cerebral cortex during voluntary movement in man. *Behav. Brain Sci.* 1:129–71.

Romanes, G. J. 1884. *Mental evolution in animals.* New York: Appleton.

———. 1889. *Mental evolution in man.* New York: Appleton.

Rortblatt, H. L. 1982. The meaning of representation in animal memory. *Behav. Brain Sci.* 5:353–406.

Rosch, E. 1977. Human categorization. In *Studies in cross-cultural psychology,* ed. N. Warren, pp. 1–49. New York: Academic.

———. 1978. Principles of categorization. In *Cognition and categorization,* ed. E. Rosch and B. B. Lloyd, pp. 28–48. Hillsdale, N.J.: Lawrence Erlbaum Associates.

Rosch, E., and B. B. Lloyd. 1978. *Cognition and categorization.* Hillsdale, N.J.: Lawrence Erlbaum Associates.

Rosch, E., and C. Mervis. 1975. Family resemblances: Studies in the internal structure of categories. *Cognit. Psychol.* 7:573–605.

Rosch, E., C. Mervis, W. Gray, D. Johnson, and P. Boyes-Braem. 1976. Basic objects in natural categories. *Cognit. Psychol.* 8:382–439.

Rose, D., and V. G. Dobson. 1985. *Models of the visual cortex.* New York: Wiley.

Rose, J. E., and C. N. Woolsey. 1949. The relations of thalamic connections, cellular structure and evocable electrical activity in the auditory region of the cat. *J. Comp. Neurol.* 91:441–66.

Rothbard, J. B., R. Brackenbury, B. A. Cunningham, and G. M. Edelman. 1982. Differences in the carbohydrate structures of neural cell adhesion molecules from adult and embryonic chicken brains. *J. Biol. Chem.* 257:11064–69.

Rovainen, C. M. 1978. Müller cells, "Mauthner" cells and other identified reticulospinal neurons in the lamprey. In *Neurobiology of the Mauthner cell,* ed. D. F. Faber and H. Korn, pp. 245–69. New York: Raven.

Ryle, G. 1949. *The concept of mind.* London: Hutcheson.

Sahin, K. E. 1973. Response routing in Selcuk networks and Lashley's dilemma. *Int. J. Man Machine Stud.* 5:567–75.

Sarnat, H. B., and M. G. Netsky. 1981. *Evolution of the nervous system.* 2d ed. New York: Oxford Univ. Press.

Schmalhausen, I. I. 1949. *Factors of evolution: The theory of stabilizing selection.* Philadelphia: Blakiston.

Schmidt, J. T. 1982. The formation of retinotectal projections. *Trends Neurosci.* 46:111–15.

———. 1985. Factors involved in retinotopic map formation: Complementary roles for membrane recognition and activity-dependent synaptic stabilization. In *Molecular bases of neural development,* ed. G. M. Edelman, W. E. Gall, and W. M. Cowan, pp. 453–80. New York: Wiley.

Schmidt, J. T., C. M. Cicerone, and S. S. Easter, Jr. 1978. Expansion of the half retinal projection to the tectum in goldfish: An electrophysiological and anatomical study. *J. Comp. Neurol.* 177:257–78.

Schmitt, F., F. G. Worden, G. Adelman, and S. G. Dennis. 1981. *The organization of the cerebral cortex.* Cambridge, Mass.: MIT Press.

Schneider, G. E. 1969. Two visual systems. *Science* 163:895–902.

Scholes, J. 1979. Nerve fiber topography in the retinal projection to the tectum. *Nature* 278:620–24.

Schwartz, B., and E. Gamzu. 1977. Pavlovian control of operant behavior. In *Handbook of operant behavior,* ed. W. K. Honig and J. E. R. Staddon, pp. 53–97. Englewood Cliffs, N.J.: Prentice-Hall.

Scott, B. E., V. E. Engelbert, and K. C. Fisher. 1969. Morphological and electrophysiological characteristics of dissociated chick embryonic spinal ganglian cells in culture. *Exp. Neurol.* 23:230–48.

Scott, M. P., and P. H. O'Farrell. 1986. Spatial programming of gene expression in early *Drosophila* embryogenesis. *Annu. Rev. Cell Biol.* 2:49–80.

Sherrington, C. S. 1897. The central nervous system. In *A text book of physiology,* pt. 3, ed. M. Foster. London: Macmillan.

———. 1900. The muscular sense. In *Text book of physiology,* vol. 2, ed. E. A. Schafer, pp. 1002–25. Edinburgh: Pentland.

———. 1906. *The integrative action of the nervous system.* New Haven: Yale Univ. Press (2d ed. reprinted in 1947).

———. 1925. Remarks on some aspects of reflex inhibition. *Proc. R. Soc. Lond.* [*Biol.*] 97:519–45.

———. 1933. *The brain and its mechanism: The Rede lecture.* Cambridge, England: Cambridge Univ. Press.

———. 1941. *Man on his nature.* New York: Macmillan.

Shimbel, A. 1950. Contributions to the mathematical biophysics of the central nervous system with special reference to learning. *Bull. Math. Biophys.* 12:241–75.

Shinoda, Y., J. Yokota, and T. Futami. 1981. Divergent projection of individual corticospinal axons to motoneurons of multiple muscles in the monkey. *Neurosci. Lett.* 23:7–12.

———. 1982. Morphology of physiologically identified rubrospinal axons in the spinal cord. *Brain Res.* 242:321–25.

Shinoda, Y., T. Yamaguchi, and T. Futami. 1986. Multiple axon collaterals of single corticospinal axons in the cat spinal cord. *J. Neurophysiol.* 55:425–48.

Shirayoshi, Y., T. S. Okada, and M. Takeichi. 1983. The calcium-dependent cell-cell adhesion system regulates inner cell mass formation and cell surface polarization in early mouse development. *Cell* 35:631–38.

Shubin, N. H., and P. Alberch. 1986. A morphogenetic approach to the origin and basic organization of the tetrapod limb. In *Evolutionary biology,* vol. 20, ed. M. Hecht, pp. 319–82. New York: Plenum.

Sidman, R. L. 1974. Contact interaction among developing brain cells. In *The cell surface in development,* ed. A. Moscona, pp. 221–53. New York: Wiley.

Siegel, R., and W. Honig. 1970. Pigeon concept formation: Successive and simultaneous acquisition. *J. Exp. Anal. Behav.* 13:385–90.

Siegelbaum, S. A., J. S. Camardo, and E. R. Kandel. 1982. Serotonin and cyclic AMP close single K^+ channels in *Aplysia* sensory neurones. *Nature* 299:413–17.

Skinner, B. F. 1981. Selection by consequences. *Science* 215:501–4.

Slack, J. M. W. 1983. *From egg to embryo: Determinative events in early development.* Cambridge, England: Cambridge Univ. Press.

Smith, E. E., and D. L. Medin. 1981. *Categories and concepts.* Cambridge, Mass.: Harvard Univ. Press.

Smith, S. J., G. J. Augustine, and M. P. Charlton. 1985. Transmission at voltage clamped giant synapse of the squid: Evidence for cooperativity of presynaptic calcium action. *Proc. Natl. Acad. Sci. USA* 82:622–25.

Sober, E., ed. 1984. *Conceptual issues in evolutionary biology.* Cambridge, Mass.: MIT Press.

Spemann, H. 1924. Induction von Embryonalanlagen durch Implantation artfremder Organisatoren. *Arch. Mikrosk. Anat. Entwicklungsmech.* 100:599–638. English translation by V. Hamburger. Reprint. In *Foundations of experimental embryology,* ed. B. M. Willier and J. Oppenheimer, 2d ed., pp. 144–84. New York: Hafner Press, 1974.

———. 1938. *Embryonic development and induction.* New Haven: Yale Univ. Press.

Sperry, R. W. 1943a. Effect of 180° rotation of the retinal field on visuomotor coordination. *J. Exp. Zool.* 92:263–79.

———. 1943b. Visuomotor coordination in the newt *(Triturus viridescens)* after regeneration of the optic nerve. *J. Comp. Neurol.* 79:33–35.

———. 1945. The problem of central nervous system reorganization after nerve regeneration and muscle transposition: A critical review. *Q. Rev. Biol.* 20:311–69.

———. 1950. Neural basis of the optokinetic response produced by visual neural inversion. *J. Comp. Physiol. Psychol.* 45:482–89.

———. 1952. Neurology and the mind-brain problem. *Am. Sci.* 40:291–312.

———. 1963. Chemoaffinity in the orderly growth of nerve fiber patterns and connections. *Proc. Natl. Acad. Sci. USA* 50:703–10.

———. 1965. Embryogenesis of behavioral nerve nets. In *Organogenesis,* ed. R. L. DeHaan and H. Ursprung, pp. 161–71. New York: Rinehart and Winston.

———. 1969. A modified concept of consciousness. *Psychol. Rev.* 76:532–36.

———. 1970. An objective approach to subjective experience: Further explanation of a hypothesis. *Psychol. Rev.* 77:585–90.

Spitzer, N. C. 1985. The control of development of neuronal excitability. In *Molecular bases of neural development,* ed. G. M. Edelman, W. E. Gall, and W. M. Cowan, pp. 67–88. New York: Wiley.

Spitzer, J. L., and N. C. Spitzer. 1975. Time of origin of Rohon-Beard neurons in the spinal cord of *Xenopus laevis. Am. Zool.* 15:781.

Squire, L. A. 1982. The neuropsychology of human memory. *Annu. Rev. Neurosci.* 5:241–73.

———. 1986. Mechanisms of memory. *Science* 232:1612–19.

Squire, L. R., and N. Butters. 1984. *Neuropsychology of memory.* New York: Guilford.

Staddon, J. E. R. 1983. *Adaptive behavior and learning.* Cambridge, England: Cambridge Univ. Press.

Stanfield, B. B., and D. D. M. O'Leary. 1985. Fetal occipital cortical neurones transplanted to the rostral cortex can extend and maintain a pyramidal tract axon. *Nature* 313:135–37.

Stanfield, B. B., D. D. M. O'Leary, C. Fricks. 1982. Selective collateral elimination in early postnatal development restricts cortical distribution of rat pyramidal tract neurones. *Nature* 298:371–73.

Stebbins, G. L. 1968. Integration of development and evolutionary progress. In *Population biology and evolution,* ed. R. C. Lewontin, pp. 17–36. Syracuse: Syracuse Univ. Press.

———. (1982) *Darwin to DNA: Molecules to humanity.* San Francisco: Freeman.

Stein, R. B. 1982. What muscle variables does the nervous system control in limb movements? *Behav. Brain Sci.* 5:535–77.

Steinmetz, M. A., B. C. Motter, C. J. Duffy, and V. B. Mountcastle. 1987. The functional properties of parietal visual neurons: The radial organization of directionalities within the visual field. *J. Neurosci.* 7:177–91.

Stone, J. 1983. *Parallel processing in the visual system: The classification of retinal ganglion cells and its impact on the neurobiology of vision.* New York: Plenum.

Strauss, H. S. 1979. Abstraction of prototypical information by adults and 10-month-old infants. *J. Exp. Psychol. Hum. Percept.* 5:618–32.

Straznicky, C., R. M. Gaze, and M. J. Keating. 1981. The development of the retinotectal projections from compound eyes in *Xenopus*. *J. Embryol. Exp. Morphol.* 62:13–35.

Stryker, M. P., and W. A. Harris. 1986. Binocular impulse blockade prevents the formation of ocular dominance columns in cat visual cortex. *J. Neurosci.* 6:2117–33.

Sur, M., and S. M. Sherman. 1982. Retinogeniculate terminations in cats—Morphological differences between X-cell and Y-cell axons. *Science* 218:338–91.

Sur, M., M. M. Merzenich, and J. H. Kaas. 1980. Magnification, receptive field area, and "supercolumn" size in areas 3b and 1 of somatosensory cortex in owl monkeys. *J. Neurophysiol.* 44:295–311.

Szentágothai, J. 1975. The module-concept in cerebral cortex architecture. *Brain Res.* 95:475–96.

Taylor, I. J., ed. 1931. *Selected Writings of John Hughlings Jackson.* Vol. 1. London: Staples Press.

Terrace, H. S. 1983. Animal learning, ethology and biological constraints. In *The Biology of learning*, ed. P. Marler and H. S. Terrace, pp. 15–45. Berlin: Springer-Verlag.

Thiery, J.-P., J.-L. Duband, U. Rutishauser, and G. M. Edelman. 1982. Cell adhesion molecules in early chicken embryogenesis. *Proc. Natl. Acad. Sci. USA* 79:6737–41.

Thiery, J.-P., A. Delouvée, M. Grumet, and G. M. Edelman. 1985. Initial appearance and regional distribution of the neuron-glia cell adhesion molecule in the chick embryo. *J. Cell Biol.* 100:442–56.

Thompson, R. F. 1986. The neurobiology of learning and memory. *Science* 233:941–47.

Thompson, R. F., T. W. Berger, and J. Madden, IV. 1983. Cellular processes of learning and memory in the mammalian CNS. *Annu. Rev. Neurosci.* 6:447–91.

Thorndike, E. L. 1931. *Human learning.* New York: Century.

———. 1911. *Animal intelligence.* New York: Macmillan. Reprint. New York: Hafner, 1965.

Tinbergen, N. 1942. An objective study of the innate behavior of animals. *Biblio. Biotheoret.* 1:39–98.

———. 1951. *The study of instinct.* Oxford: Clarendon.

———. 1963. On aims and methods of ethology. *Z. Tierpsychol.* 20:410–33.

Treisman, A. 1979. The psychological reality of levels of processing. In *Levels of processing and human memory*, ed. L. S. Cermak and F. I. M. Craik, pp. 301–30. Hillsdale, N.J.: Lawrence Erlbaum Associates.

———. 1983. The role of attention in object perception. In *Physical and biological processing of images*, ed. O. J. Braddick and A. C. Sleigh, pp. 316–25. Berlin: Springer-Verlag.

Treisman, A., and G. Gelade. 1980. A feature-integration theory of attention. *Cognit. Psychol.* 12:97–136.

Tsukahara, N. 1981. Synaptic plasticity in the mammalian central nervous system. *Annu. Rev. Neurosci.* 4:351–79.

Turvey, M. T. 1977. Preliminaries to a theory of action with reference to vision. In *Perceiving, acting and knowing*, ed. R. Shaw and J. Bransford, pp. 211–66. Hillsdale, N.J.: Lawrence Erlbaum Associates.

Tusa, R. J., L. A. Palmer, and A. C. Rosenquist. 1981. Multiple cortical visual areas. In *Cortical sensory organization*, vol. 2, ed. C. N. Woolsey, pp. 1–32. Clifton, N.J.: Humana.

Ulinksi, P. S. 1980. Functional morphology of the vertebrate visual system: An essay on the evolution of complex systems. *Am. Zool.* 20:229–46.

———. 1986. Neurobiology of the therapsid-mammal transition. In *The ecology and biology of mammal-like reptiles*, ed. N. Hotton, III, P. D. MacLean, J. J. Roth, and E. C. Roth, pp. 149–71. Washington, D.C.: Smithsonian.

Ullman, S. 1979. *The interpretation of visual motion.* Cambridge, Mass.: MIT Press.

———. 1980. Against direct perception. *Behav. Brain Sci.* 3:373–415.

Underwood, G. U. 1978. *Strategies of information processing.* London: Academic.

Uttal, W. R. 1978. *The psychobiology of mind.* Hillsdale, N.J.: Lawrence Erlbaum Associates.

———. 1981. *A taxonomy of visual processes.* Hillsdale, N.J.: Lawrence Erlbaum Associates.

Van der Loos, H., and J. Dörfl. 1978. Does the skin tell the somatosensory cortex how to construct a map of the periphery? *Neurosci. Lett.* 7:23–30.

Van der Loos, H., and T. A. Woolsey. 1973. Somatosensory cortex: Structural alterations following early injury to sense organs. *Science* 179:395–98.

Van Essen, D.C. 1979. Visual areas of the mammalian cerebral cortex. *Annu. Rev. Neurosci.* 2:227–63.

———. 1982. Neuromuscular synapse elimination: Structural, functional and mechanistic aspects. In *Neuronal development,* ed. N. C. Spitzer, pp. 334–76. New York: Plenum.

———. 1985. Functional organization of primate visual cortex. In *Cerebral cortex,* vol. 3, ed. A. Peters and E. G. Jones, pp. 259–329. New York: Plenum.

Vernon, M. D. 1970. *A further study of visual perception.* Darien, Conn.: Hafner.

von Neumann, J. 1956. Probabilistic logic and the synthesis of reliable organisms from unreliable components. In *Automaton studies,* ed. C. Shannon and J. McCarthy, pp. 43–98. Princeton: Princeton Univ. Press.

Vrensen, G., and J. Nunes-Cardozo. 1981. Changes in size and shape of synaptic connections after visual training: An ultrastructural approach to synaptic plasticity. *Brain Res.* 218:79–97.

Wall, P. D. 1975. The somatosensory system. In *Handbook of psychobiology,* ed. M. S. Gazzaniga and C. Blakemore, pp. 373–92. New York: Academic.

Wall, P. D., and M. D. Eggers. 1971. Formation of new connexions in adult rat brains after partial deafferentation. *Nature* 232:542–44.

Walley, A. C., D. B. Pisoni, and R. N. Aslin. 1981. The role of early experience in the development of speech perception. In *Development of perception,* vol. 1, ed. R. N. Aslin, J. R. Alberts, and M. R. Petersen, pp. 219–55. New York: Academic.

Walshe, F. M. R. 1948. *Critical studies in neurology.* Edinburgh: E. & S. Livingstone.

Weiskrantz, L. 1978. *Functions of the septo-hippocampal system,* Ciba Foundation Symposium, n.s. 58. Amsterdam: Elsevier-North Holland.

Weiss, P. 1936. Selectivity controlling the central-peripheral relation in the nervous system. *Biol. Rev.* 11:494–531.

———. 1939. *Principles of development.* New York: Henry Holt.

———. 1941. Self-differentiation of the basic patterns of coordination. *Comp. Psychol. Monogr.* 174:1–96.

———. 1955. Nervous system (neurogenesis). In *The analysis of development,* ed. B. H. Willier, P. Weiss, and V. Hamburger, pp. 346–401. Philadelphia: Saunders.

Wertheimer, M. 1958. Principles of perceptual organization. In *Readings in perception,* ed. D. C. Beardslee and M. Wertheimer, pp. 115–35. Princeton: Van Nostrand. Originally published in 1923 in German in *Psychologische Forschung* 4:301–50.

Whiting, H. T. A., ed. 1984. *Human motor actions: Bernstein reassessed.* Amsterdam: Elsevier.

Wiesel, T. N. 1982. Postnatal development of the visual cortex and the influence of environment. *Nature* 299:583–91.

Wiesel, T. N., and D. H. Hubel. 1963a. Effects of visual deprivation on morphology and physiology of cells in the cat's lateral geniculate body. *J. Neurophysiol.* 26:978–93.

———. 1963b. Single cell responses in striate cortex of kittens deprived of vision in one eye. *J. Neurophysiol.* 26:1003–17.

———. 1965. Comparison of the effects of unilateral and bilateral eye closure on cortical unit responses in kittens. *J. Neurophysiol.* 28:1029–40.

Wigstrom, H., and B. Gustafsson. 1983. Heterosynaptic modulation of homosynaptic long-lasting potentiation in the hippocampal slice. *Acta Physiol. Scand.* 119:455–58.

Wigstrom, H., B. L. McNaughton, and C. A. Barnes. 1982. Long-term synaptic enhancement in hippocampus is not regulated by post-synaptic membrane potential. *Brain Res.* 233:195–99.

Winfield, D. A., R. N. L. Brooke, J. J. Sloper, and T. P. S. Powell. 1981. A combined Golgi-electron microscopic study of the synapses made by the proximal axon and recurrent collaterals of a pyramidal cell in the somatic sensory cortex of the monkey. *Neuroscience* 6:1217–30.

Winograd, S., and J. D. Cowan. 1963. *Reliable computation in the presence of noise.* Cambridge, Mass.: MIT Press.

Wittgenstein, L. 1953. *Philosophical investigations.* The english text of the 3d ed. New York: Macmillan.

Wolff, P. H., and R. Ferber. 1979. The development of behavior in human infants, premature and newborn. *Annu. Rev. Neurosci.* 2:291–307.

Woolsey, T. A., and J. R. Wann. 1976. Area 1 changes in mouse cortical barrels following vibrissal damage at different postnatal ages. *J. Comp. Neurol.* 170:53–66.

Woolsey, T. A., D. Durham, R. M. Harris, D. J. Sinions, and K. L. Valentino. 1981. Somatosensory development. In *Development of perception,* vol. 1, ed. R. N. Aslin, J. R. Roberts, and M. P. Petersen, pp. 259–92. New York: Academic.

Wright, S. 1932. The roles of mutation, inbreeding, crossbreeding and selection in evolution. *Proc. Sixth Int. Congr. Genet.* 1:356–66.

Young, J. Z. 1965. The organization of a memory system. *Proc. R. Soc. Lond.* [*Biol.*] 163:285–320.

———. 1973. Memory as a selective process. In *Australian Academy of Science Report: Symposium on Biological Memory,* pp. 25–45. Canberra: Australian Academy of Science.

———. 1975. Sources of discovery in neuroscience. In *The neurosciences: Paths of discovery,* ed. F. G. Worden, J. P. Swazey, and G. Adelman, pp. 15–46. Cambridge: MIT Press.

———. 1978. *Programs of the brain.* Oxford: Oxford Univ. Press.

Zeki, S. M. 1969. Representation of central visual fields in peristriate cortex of monkey. *Brain Res.* 14:271–91.

———. 1971. Cortical projections from two peristriate areas in the monkey. *Brain Res.* 34:19–35.

———. 1975. The functional organization of projections from striate to peristriate visual cortex in the rhesus monkey. *Cold Spring Harbor Symp. Quant. Biol.* 40:591–600.

———. 1978a. Functional specification of the cortex in the rhesus monkey. *Nature* 274:423–28.

———. 1978b. Uniformity and diversity of function in rhesus monkey prestriate visual cortex. *J. Physiol. (Lond.)* 277:273–90.

———. 1981. The mapping of visual functions in the cerebral cortex. In *Brain mechanisms of sensation: Third Taniguchi symposium on brain sciences,* ed. Y. Katsuki, R. Norgren, and M. Sato, pp. 105–28. New York: Wiley.

———. 1983. The distribution of wavelength and orientation selective cells in different areas of monkey visual cortex. *Proc. R. Soc. Lond.* [*Biol.*] 217:449–70.

ABBREVIATIONS AND
MATHEMATICAL SYMBOLS

ABBREVIATIONS

CAM	Cell adhesion molecule
CNS	Central nervous system
CS	Conditioned stimulus
L-CAM	Liver cell adhesion molecule
ld	Large domain polypeptide of N-CAM
M	Modifying substance
N-CAM	Neural cell adhesion molecule
Ng-CAM	Neuron-glia cell adhesion molecule
NGF	Nerve growth factor
PSP	Postsynaptic potential
ROC	Receptor-operated channel
SAM	Substrate adhesion molecule
sd	Small domain polypeptide of N-CAM
ssd	Small surface domain of N-CAM
US	Unconditioned stimulus
VSC	Voltage-sensitive channel

MATHEMATICAL SYMBOLS

Chapter 7

ξ_j	Presynaptic efficacy; amount of transmitter released by cell j for a given depolarization
η_{ij}	Postsynaptic efficacy; local depolarization produced at postsynaptic process of cell i for a given amount of transmitter released by cell j
t_L	Lag time between homosynaptic input and production of M
t_M	Time constant for persistence of modifying substance
t_D	Averaged conduction time delay for heterosynaptic effects
t_V	Time constant for persistence of voltage changes
K_f	Rate constant for "forward modification" from I to I^* in the postsynaptic rule
K_b	Rate constant for "back modification" from I^* to I state
K_{b2}	Rate constant for "back modification" from A^* to A state
$a(V)$	Voltage-dependent rate constant for I to A transition (rate decreases with depolarization)
$b(V)$	Voltage-dependent rate constant for A to I transition (rate increases with depolarization)
$a^*(V)$	Rate constant for I^* to A^* transition
$b^*(V)$	Rate constant for A^* to I^* transition

N	Total number of voltage-sensitive channels at a postsynaptic terminal
N^*	Total number of modified VSCs
N_k	Number of VSCs of ionic species k
N^*_k	Number of VSCs of ionic species k that are modified
$A(t)$	Number of channels in the Activated state at time t
$A^*(t)$	Number of channels in the modified Activated state at time t
$I(t)$	Number of channels in the Inactivated state at time t
$I^*(t)$	Number of channels in the modified Inactived state at time t
$M(t)$	Amount of modifying substance present at time t
g_k	Conductance of voltage-sensitive channel of ionic species k
g^*_k	Conductance of VSCs of ionic species k after modification
E_k	Reversal potential for ionic species k
I_L	Local synaptic current
$F_i(t)$	Facilitation at time t of neuron i
$D_i(t)$	Depression at time t of neuron i
$S_i(t)$	Activity of cell i at time t
κ	Proportionality constant between transmitter release and depression
ϵ	Proportionality constant between activity and facilitation
λ	Time constant for decay of facilitation
β	Time constant for decay of depression
N_{IJ}	Number of connections from group J to group I
S_I	Averaged activity of cells in group I
$\overline{S}_I$	S_I averaged over time

Chapter 10

$s_i(t)$	Activity or state of group i at time t $(0 \leq s < 1)$
c_{ij}	Connection strength of jth input to group i ($c_{ij} > 0$, excitatory; $c_{ij} < 0$, inhibitory)
l_{ij}	Identifying number of group connected to jth input of group i
θ_E	Excitatory input threshold; input j is ignored unless $s_j \geq \theta_E$
s_k	State of group defined by k, which ranges over all groups within a specified inhibitory neighborhood around group i
β	Inhibitory coefficient; plays same role for geometrically defined inhibitory connections as c_{ij} does for specific connections, but is same for all ik pairs in bands around each group in a given repertoire
θ_I	Inhibitory input threshold; input k is ignored unless $s_k \geq \theta_I$
N	Noise drawn from a normal distribution with specified mean and S.D.
ω	Persistence parameter, which defines decay rate for group activity $(\omega = e^{-1/\tau})$
τ	Characteristic time for decay of activity, s
θ_P	Positive firing threshold; the inputs to a group are ignored if their sum is positive but does not exceed θ_P
θ_N	Negative inhibitory threshold; the inputs to a group are ignored if their sum is negative but less than θ_N in magnitude $(\theta_N < 0)$
δ	A specified constant amplification factor
$\phi(c)$	A saturation factor to prevent $|c_{ij}|$ from becoming larger than 1 $[\phi(c) = 1 - 2c^2 + c^4]$
θ_{M_i}	Postsynaptic amplification threshold
θ_{M_j}	Presynaptic amplification threshold; the occurrence and sign of amplification depend on the choice of a rule that specifies what will happen in each of four cases according to whether s_i is greater or less than θ_{M_i} and s_j is greater or less than θ_{M_j}
R	Recognizer repertoire
R of R	Recognizer-of-recognizers repertoire
G	Virtual group
R_M	Recognizer-of-motion repertoire

CREDITS

Figure 1.1. A mnemon or single memory unit as proposed by J. Z. Young (1975). Permission granted by The Royal Society and by John Z. Young. Figure 2.4. Leaf patterns from Cerella's experiments (Cerella, 1977). Permission granted by the American Psychological Association and by John Cerella. Figure 2.5. Polymorphous rule for set membership after Dennis et al. (1973). Permission granted by Macmillan Journals Limited and by Ian Dennis. Figure 2.6. Anatomical variability (Pearson and Goodman, 1979; Macagno et al. 1973; Ramón y Cajal, 1904). Figure 2.6A. Permission granted by Alan R. Liss, Inc. Figure 2.6B. Permission granted by Eduardo R. Macagno. Figure 3.1. Dependency of two forms of recognition function on the number N of elements in a repertoire, calculated according to a simple model. From Schmitt and Worden, *The Neurosciences: 4th Study Program.* Permission granted by MIT Press. Figure 3.2. Two extreme cases of repertoires having unique (nondegenerate) and completely degenerate elements. From Schmitt and Worden, *The Neurosciences: 4th Study Program.* Permission granted by MIT Press. Figure 3.3. Comparison of theoretical and experimental recognition functions. From Schmitt et al. *The Organization of the Cerebral Cortex.* Permission granted by MIT Press. Figure 4.6. N-CAM at the motor end plate and changes in prevalence in muscle after denervation. In *Journal of Cell Biology,* volume 103, 1986, figure 2, p. 934. By copyright permission of The Rockefeller University Press. Figure 5.1. Schematic drawing of four radial glial cells and cohorts of associated migrating neurons. Permission granted by Elsevier Publications and Pasko Rakic. Figure 5.5. Temporal changes in somatosensory maps after lesions (Merzenich et al., 1983b). Permission granted by International Brain Research Organization. Figure 5.6. Receptive field changes in somatosensory cortex after a peripheral lesion (Merzenich et al., 1983b). Permission granted by International Brain Research Organization. Figure 5.7. A thalamic afferent to area 3b in the cat as revealed by horseradish peroxidase injection (from Landry and Deschênes, 1981). Permission granted by Alan R. Liss, Inc. Figure 5.8. Ocular dominance columns (Hubel and Wiesel, 1977). Permission granted by The Royal Society and by David H. Hubel. Figure 6.1. Visual network in *Pseudemys*, a typical challenge to evolutionary analysis (Ulinski, 1980). Permission granted by Milton Fingerman, Managing Editor of *American Zoologist.* Figure 6.2. The parcellation theory of Ebbesson (1980). Permission granted by Springer-Verlag and by Sven O. E. Ebbesson. Figure 8.1. Comparison of jaw muscle electromyographic activity and jaw movements of percoid and cichlid fish (Liem, 1974). Permission granted by Gary D. Schnell, Editor of *Systematic Zoology* and by K. F. Liem. Figure 8.2. As indicated by Bernstein (1967), circular movements made with the arm extended in various positions are accomplished by completely different innervational schemes for trajectories of the same type. Permission granted by Pergamon Press, Ltd. Figure 8.3. Gait patterns in running at different ages according to Bernstein (1967). Permission granted by Pergamon Press, Ltd. Figure 8.4. "Topology" according to Bernstein (1967). Permission granted by Pergamon Press, Ltd. Figure 9.1. Tree discrimination experiment by Herrnstein (1979). Permission granted by Matthew Wayner, Editor of *Neuroscience and Biobehavioral Review,* and by Richard J. Herrnstein. Figure 9.2. Examples of displays used by Kellman and Spelke (1983) to test perception of partly occluded objects by four month old infants. Permission granted by Academic Press and by Philip J. Kellman. Figure 10.2. Simplified construction plan for Darwin II. Permission granted by the New York Academy of Sciences. Figure 10.3. Responses of individual repertoires (R, R-of-R, and R_M). Permission granted by the New York Academy of Sciences. Figure 10.4. Response frequency histograms. Permission granted by the New York Academy of Sciences. Figure 10.6. Responses of individual R-of-R groups in an associative recall test. Permission granted by the New York Academy of Sciences.

INDEX

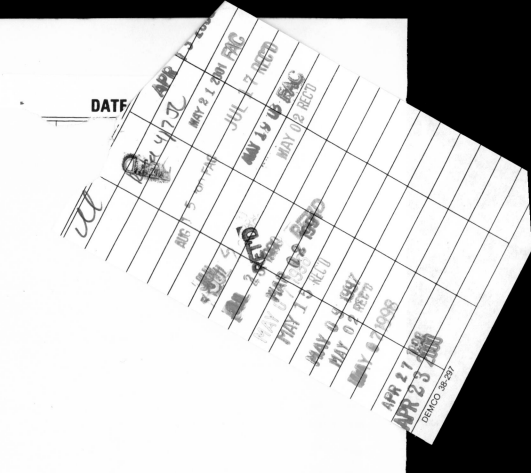